LITERATURE AND
RACIAL AMBIGUITY

Rodopi Perspectives on Modern Literature

27

Edited by
David Bevan

LITERATURE AND RACIAL AMBIGUITY

Edited by
Teresa Hubel
Neil Brooks

AMSTERDAM - NEW YORK, NY 2002

UNIVERSITY OF CHICHESTER

The paper on which this book is printed meets the requirements of
"ISO 9706:1994, Information and documentation - Paper for
documents - Requirements for permanence".

ISBN: 90-420-1428-8 (bound)
©Editions Rodopi B.V., Amsterdam - New York, NY 2002
Printed in The Netherlands

809.
3
LIT

To Brian and to Claire, David, and James

ACKNOWLEDGEMENTS

This book has been the first collaborative scholarship for both of us, and we have learned a good deal about the challenges and rewards of this kind of joint effort; we are grateful to one another for that. Many thanks to our colleagues on the faculty and staff in all the departments at Huron University College. Our ongoing discussions with them have helped us both to develop our ideas. We feel ourselves fortunate to have landed at this place among these fine people. And regarding our students we must say that, had they not constantly asked us to clarify our points and to defend our views, we could not have thought through the complications of racial ambiguity and arrived at the place where a book of essays was a possibility.

Among these students, we would like to mention one in particular, Luke Maynard, whose work on the last stages of this book was invaluable. He spent long hours proof-reading these essays and getting them ready for publication, and he did so in the cheerful, diligent, and resourceful way that is his manner in this world.

We would also like to take this opportunity to acknowledge David Bevan, the general editor of this series and our colleague, who provided much-needed expertise and advice throughout the course of this collection's creation.

Our gratitude extends as well and as always to our beloved spouses, Claire Brooks and Brian Patton. Not only did they provide the intellectual dialogue that makes them both such splendid spouses, but they also supported us through a difficult summer when we lost much-loved family members. Because our families are the foundation of our academic work, we feel it appropriate that we name those we lost: Teresa's grandmother, Bereen Stone Hubel, her stepfather, James Robert Hennessy, and Neil's father, David Brooks. We also want to thank our entire extended families for their support.

Neil also offers his sincere gratitude to Laurie, Cecily, Jeff, Cristy, Jen, Cory, jef, and Trish. Teresa wishes to gratefully acknowledge Wendy, Arja, David, Marilyn, Jim, Peter, Nandi, and, last but never least, Keshu and Molly.

Literature and Racial Ambiguity
edited by Teresa Hubel and Neil Brooks

CONTENTS

INTRODUCTION

It is a source of some frustration and some provocation that race is not inevitably apprehensible, that we cannot definitively determine that this physical feature means this and that one means that. (Though as editors of this collection of essays, we are indebted to such provocation and frustration, since these discomforts have incited the conundrums that gave rise to this book, which is about the ways that racial ambiguity gets worked out and played with in various pieces of literature in English.) And yet most societies in our world, in the present as well as the relatively recent past, have expended great rushes of energy trying to construct and institute definitive definitions of race. Laws have been conceived and sometimes brutally enforced to keep people in their racial places; entire academic disciplines have been devoted to proving that race is real and that it means something. In spite of the fluidity of racial realities, a fact that points to the sheer unreality of race on any biological level, race is nevertheless often discursively fixed, fixed, moreover, by the very ideologically-laden, people-driven formulations — government policies, unwritten social rules, hiring practices, capitalist enterprises, etc. — that create and re-create notions of race in the first place. That race is ultimately beyond such fixing is evident in those individuals and collectives that cannot be easily categorized. These are the people who have at some time or another and in various geographies been called `creole,' `mulatto,' `Burgher,' `mestizo,' `half-blood,' `half-caste', and the newly-popular `mixed race,' all of which terms (and many more besides) are meant to designate, contemptuously, appreciatively, or merely descriptively, those who are seen to exist in-between, and all of which terms appear in this book.

As a number of the contributors to this volume have theorized, it is precisely in this state of in-betweenness, specifically, in its propensity for fluctuation, that the potential for the subversion of established racial categories and the undermining of racist assumptions lies. But let's be clear about this: hybridity or mixed-racedness is no more an invariable site of radicality than is bisexuality or liminal class positioning. In fact, all three of these placements hold out the possibility of privilege and hence are sometimes routes to the conservation of a racist *status quo*. Many individuals who have been born into so-called mixed-race families and/or communities, for example, have `passed' into dominant racial communities and so have acquired the power and advantages associated with racial supremacism. Obviously, being `mixed' *can* work to confer the license to choose a privileged identity over an oppressed one as much as it can, on the other hand, guarantee oppression because of its link to those on the less powerful end of the racial spectrum, as in the case of a person whose features are thought to `betray' signs of a disenfranchised race or whose family genealogy is suspect and so cannot impart the authority that would secure an unambiguous connection to racial dominance. In-betweenness does not always trouble racist boundaries; it sometimes confirms them, and, consequently, it is not, in and of itself, a pathway to greater freedom for all members of a society or to the dismantling of racist systems.

To achieve these larger objectives, in-betweenness must be *made to mean* something radically destabilizing, just as skin colour has been made to mean so many things, and this is where works of literature come in handy. The literature studied here explores how toppling the stories of racial purity can be a liberating as well as an imprisoning act. The luxuriant language of literature, its often complex narrative and conceptual structures, and the densely-packed connotations available in its submerged layers seem to provide an appropriately creative setting for the interrogation of, or simply for ruminations on, prevailing discourses about race. Margaret Stetz's and Rita Treat's essays explore how artistic constructs such as Aestheticism and Modernism are not entirely separable from racial constructs, and they make the argument that authors Jessie Fauset and Mourning Dove re-write literary forms (and in Morning Dove's case anthropological ones) in ways that convey racial ambiguity as potentially both liberating and isolating.

Literature in English is full of stories of miscegenation and its consequences. And this is especially true in the English literatures that have emerged in the wake of the British Empire — the literatures of the Caribbean, Canada, Africa, New Zealand, the U.S., India, and Australia. For this political institution, this capitalist enterprise, put issues of race at the centre of its mission. Justified by a racist ideology in which whiteness and nonwhiteness were stretched along a vertical continuum, with whiteness accorded superiority and the whiteness of elite-class Englishmen deemed particularly above reproach, the British Empire was, among other things, a vast make-work project for Englishmen and their sons; all the best jobs were reserved for those whose whiteness and masculinity could never be questioned. But in order for them to procure and retain, generation after generation, a racial and gendered positioning beyond question, constant vigilance was required: the `facts' of race had to be established, expanded upon, and then reasserted time and again, and, through recourse to scientific and biblical authority, the naturalness and righteousness of racist positionings was repeatedly affirmed, even when, in many places, those men in power engaged in coercive sexual relationships that led to the existence of countless individuals whose very existence should have troubled those racist attitudes. Myriam Perregaux writes at length about the imperial vigour of this "myth of the purity of whiteness" in her essay on Kate Pullinger. So potent is this myth, she suggests, that it can erase the race of one's ancestors, leaving descendants, such as Audrey in Pullinger's *The Last Time I Saw Jane*, with the task of recovering their own family histories and refashioning their relationship to whiteness and the racial ascendancy it bequeaths. In Elizabeth DeLoughrey's essay on two memoirs by and about the Frisbies of the Pacific Islands, we see how Johnny Frisbie engages in a similar recovery and refashioning, this time of her memories of her white American father and of his carefully controlled self-representation. Knowing the immensely intricate contexts in which white fathers are constituted also leads us to a finer appreciation of what DeLoughrey aptly terms "the unevenness of travelling masculine whiteness."

Historically, then, one of the most notable features of the British Empire was this emphasis on race, an emphasis that shows itself in writing from the colonial period. Race was the subject for all sorts of texts — fiction, political policy, autobiography, academic papers, journalism, poetry, even personal correspondence. Given the prevalence of race as a topic in such amazingly diverse fields of human activity, it's not at all surprising that the postcolonial inheritors of the Empire should demonstrate in their literatures a pronounced interest and expertise in the workings of race. Most of the essay writers in this collection draw on this expertise through their focus on writing by authors who hail from these non-mainstream traditions of English literature. Hence, this book includes essays on literary works by people who are Sri Lankan, Asian Australian, African American, Jamaican, Scottish, Native North American, Canadian, Cook Islander, etc., though almost all of these national and regional categories are inhabited contentiously by both the authors themselves and the characters they create. These categories are, understandably, frequently the subject of interrogation by those who are not permitted to absorb them comfortably. It makes sense that, as scholars, we should turn to such people when we attempt to comprehend the contours of those fiercely protected and racially determined notions of nationality.

Because of the scorn and distrust leveled at them as well as the fascination they elicit from their more racially fixed fellows, these people reveal the constellation of processes that underpin beliefs in the reality of racial mixing. The inescapable outcome of an imperial binary of race that, first, proclaims the actual existence of race across immense collectives and, then, posits racial purities as real and valuable possibilities is the simultaneous construction of mixed-racedness as taint. Those who, for numerous political reasons, *not only* do not possess the power to define themselves but who are also regarded as the product of the sexual confounding of racial purities are shunted off to a nebulous middle between the binary ends, a place that gets characterized as contaminated because it's associated with the violation of some natural and cultural law prohibiting sex between races. This place is, significantly, tenanted by individuals — offspring of parents who each are believed to be racially pure — as well as by groups — communities, such as the Anglo-Indians of India, the Burghers of Sri Lanka, and the coloureds of apartheid-era South Africa and the antebellum U.S., that are distinguished by their histories of and tolerance for miscegenation.

The reason that representations of these communities and individuals are now, in this new century, extraordinarily important has much to do with political timing in the discipline of literary studies: for over twenty years critical analyses of race have considerably altered the way that we have interpreted literature. These analyses have opened up entire ideological systems to theoretical observation, systems that have remained unassailable for generations. (The only other discussion that could be said to have had an equal impact on our discipline would be feminist theorizations about gender.) But, though critical analyses of race were profoundly fruitful and continue to be so, they also proceed from a location firmly inside the ideologies they hope to disturb; they often accept, for instance, the imperialist notion of a biologically-forged racial divide. It is perfectly understandable why. Biological ramifications are not the only ones that matter when it comes to race. Since race is apprehended as a social, political, and cultural reality as much as it is experienced as a physical one, it's not enough to prove that race has no biological reality and then to proceed as if the whole apparatus of racism could be overturned with the discovery of that faulty assumption. Being "seen to exist" is a form of existence, as Kathryn Nicol's essay on Toni Morrison demonstrates. By operating on the premise that race is real and therefore can be charted, these critics were and are acknowledging this other experiential reality of race. Furthermore, there are fine and laudable results to be achieved from presuming the reality of race and assaulting racist epistemologies from the perspective of those damaged by them, one of which results is the maiming of those epistemologies, a maiming that, it is to be hoped, will contribute to the eventual overthrow of the systems that are supported by such unjust ways of thinking. Paul Allatson, Yvette Tan, and Jennifer Sparrow all deal with this issue of "self subalternization" as a political act. And, while their essays explore the limitations of that act, they all nevertheless acknowledge that racial pride among those discriminated against can itself be a formidable weapon against those who seek to define others as lesser humans or less than human.

But an unfortunate other consequence of this otherwise commendable strategy of accepting the biological premise of race is that those individuals and communities whose experiences of race are less classifiable are either made invisible by a social justice rhetoric that is founded on a belief in a racial divide that splits the racial haves from the have nots (in many cases today, particularly in the West, this split would separate the whites from all who are regarded as not white), or they are seen to be only the appendages of the racially powerful and consequently are regarded as the appropriate targets of another racism disguised as an anti-racism or as an anti-imperialism; that is, they are held in contempt not just by the dominant racial community but by the non-dominant ones too, who refuse to see them as anything but racially degraded and morally objectionable clingers on to power. Neluka Silva's essay examines this tendency in relation to Sinhalese and Tamil constructions of the Burghers of Sri Lanka and suggests that the enforcement of essential racial subjectivities has contributed to an ongoing civil war, while Jennifer Gibbs, taking a psychoanalytic tack, discusses how mixed race identity serves a seeming societal need to produce "scapegoats" to bear the corruption the dominant groups will not admit is their own. Clearly, the racial intricacy of the lives of mixed race persons and the difficulty of their choices, not to mention their oppression, cannot be recognized from a vantage point that is so cruel to them. Predicating a theory of racism on the acceptance of a racial divide also isn't an effective means of comprehending the circumstances of people who occupy the ever-shifting state of racial in-betweenness, because for such people no such divide can be said to exist; or perhaps it would be more accurate to say that how this divide is managed, incorporated, or dismissed as irrelevant cannot be seen by those who insist on the relentless reality of this divide.

This book, then, is meant to enter into these new discussions about race in our discipline, to explore how constructions of racial ambiguity in fiction can work to buttress conventions about race, question them, or even take a stab at disabling them. In the process of assembling and reviewing these essays, what has struck us, as editors, is how huge this topic is; we have here just barely begun to discuss its variations and implications, and we are forced into the predictable position of having to assert that there is indeed so much more to be done. But we have learned many things over the course of this past year or so, and we want to thank our contributors for their wonderfully thoughtful essays, which have helped us to intensify our understanding of this subject, far beyond what we might have accomplished on our own. With this newly formed knowledge at hand, we'd also like to offer some suggestions about future research and writing on racial ambiguity.

While reading the many submissions we initially received in order to select the essays that would finally appear, we noted with interest that few essays engaged in any sustained attempts to theorize how class works to alter race. We had imagined that this would be an obvious avenue for exploration, and we wondered if the sparseness of class critiques might be indicative of a larger blindness at work in North America certainly and in the university profession of literary studies generally. Although class is a subject as fraught with complications and ambiguities as race, it is surely the case that many, if not most, of us in this profession come from backgrounds that are though various, still middle class and we teach students who tend on the whole to share our class assumptions, placements, and perspectives. Considering the centrality of middle-classness in the great majority of capitalist nations, as well as the limitations in vision that that centrality inevitably imposes, along with the shrouding of that class's interests, a shrouding which keeps the middle-class so central to the social and economic fabric of our societies, it is, perhaps, only to be expected that we would find class an especially difficult category for analysis.

In our discipline, English, we are further hampered by a history of professing middle-class codes of thought, middle-class expressions of the English language, and a complex of values developed largely by middle-class thinkers, namely liberal humanism, and which functioned, at least partly, to ensure the political ascendancy of this class in the historical capitalization of the countries that made up the British Empire. We are tempted too to see a connection between these systemic shields that prevent us from seeing class functioning in the texts we study and an emphasis among the original submissions on "individualistic" responses, rather than communal ones, to racial categorizations. Teresa Zackodnik addresses many of these issues in her discussion of upward class mobility in Nella Larsen and Jesse Fauset.

And finally an admission: the majority of essays submitted dealt with American literature. We had put out a call for papers requesting essays about "literature from all parts of the world" and received more essays about Nella Larsen than we did about all of African literature. Some excellent essays were not included partly to keep the collection from being overwhelmingly "American." Many authors who wrote on non-American writers also employed a critical framework which cited almost exclusively American sources. So while we have sought in this collection to give "voice" to those who have been often denied expression, we must also concede that dominant voices still find ways of coming to the foreground even as we seek to explore the margins. As Michele Hunter urges, we need to constantly be aware that essays that take race as their subject, such as those gathered here, always run the risk of making "threatened whiteness" the primary object of our attention. Moreover, we can learn a lesson from Bella Adams's argument in her paper, that scholars who claim to be outside Orientalism are often simply reinscribing it in new, more covert, ways. Future works must further develop the self-understanding that scholars have of their own privileged and involved positions.

Our contributors come at the issue of racial ambiguity from a welcome variety of theoretical angles including post-structuralist, cultural materialist, psychoanalytical, and universalist. We are pleased too that they have chosen to communicate their arguments through a range of writing styles, since style itself implies a theoretical stance. But what all our selected essays have in common is an implicit call for a celebration of the lives of those who cannot be defined by traditional racial categorizations, yet they simultaneously warn of the dangers, both obvious and hidden, associated with disrupting established racial norms.

Ultimately, the continuity we find throughout this book is stated most directly by Peter Clandfield in the opening essay: "it is about the possibility, not the guarantee of hybridization as transcendence."

1.

"WHAT IS IN MY BLOOD?":
CONTEMPORARY BLACK SCOTTISHNESS
AND THE WORK OF JACKIE KAY

The work of the Scottish writer Jackie Kay (b. 1961) not only refutes simplistic definitions of race and racial attributes, but also challenges utopian idea(l)s about racial and cultural **hybridity** as a condition that, in itself, resolves problems arising from racial differences --that is, from dissimilarities, conflicts, and things in between. In her 1985 poem "So you think I'm a mule?," Kay, who is of mixed black-white (African-British) biological parentage, voices what sounds like an unequivocal rejection of white attempts to theorise about people of obviously complex racial ancestry:[1]

> If you Dare mutter mulatto
> hover around hybrid
> hobble on half-caste
> and intellectualize on the
> "Mixed race problem",
> I have to tell you:
> take your beady eyes offa my skin;
> don't concern yourself with
> the "dialectics of mixtures";
> don't pull that strange blood crap
> on me Great White Mother.
> Say I'm no mating of a she-ass and a stallion
> no half of this and half of that
> to put it plainly purely
> I am black   (lines 29-43)

This 66-line poem is given in full as an epigraph to Heidi Safia Mirza's Introduction to *Black British Feminism: A Reader* (Routledge, 1997), where it serves as a strong statement about the determination of black British women to set their own agendas. In the context of Kay's own evolving career, though, the poem's significance is much more ambiguous. While its speaker states emphatically that she is black and is "not mixed up" (line 50) about race, mixed-race voices in Kay's more recent works are less certain. Without being "mixed up" in the sense of being confused or incoherent, these works delineate complex emergent forms of racial and cultural identity that undermine fixed concepts not only of Britishness, blackness, or black Britishness but also of hybridity itself.

This essay will focus on three works: "The Adoption Papers" (1990-91), the sequence that lends its title to and forms the first half of Kay's first major volume of poems (1991*)*; *Bessie Smith* (1997), Kay's book on the legendary blues singer; and *Trumpet* (1998), Kay's Guardian Fiction Prize-winning first novel. Important to Kay's challenge to simplistic ideas about race and hybridity is the generic and thematic range of her writing. The poems of "The Adoption Papers" are laid out for multiple distinct voices, like a work of drama, and divided into ten chapters, like a novel; *Bessie Smith*, apparently a biography, incorporates elements of autobiography and of fiction; *Trumpet* features multiple points-of-view, emphasizing characters' distinctive voices with an intensity that evokes lyric poetry and juxtaposing them with a shrewdness that evokes drama. Furthermore, Kay's writings consistently and inventively underline the inextricability of racial issues from ones of gender, sexuality, class, and generation.[2] Her work demonstrates not only that Britishness and Scottishness are not synonymous with whiteness, and that British and Scottish identity have been irreversibly hybrid for much longer than is often acknowledged, but also that there is no definitive way to write about this hybridity. It follows that there is no one correct way to write about Kay's writing; accordingly, this essay reads the works I have mentioned in plural contexts: Kay's other writings; theoretical work on various kinds of hybridity and Britishness; recent British films concerning hybridity; and various brief critical commentaries on Kay's work.

(De)definitions: Kay and British hybridities

Kay's category-troubling qualities may help to explain the shortage of sustained critical attention to her writing. Her work has not been ignored altogether: at the end of an essay on the status of Britain's poet laureateship after the death of Ted Hughes, for example, Patrick Deane asks, "dare we hope that the Blair revolution will give us Jackie Kay as laureate? Or Carol Ann Duffy?" (506).[3] The choice of Andrew Motion as the actual successor to Hughes suggests that Kay and other black British writers still have a good deal to push against, not so much because of the characteristics of Motion's poetry or because he is another in an unbroken series of white male laureates (which of course he is) as because some of his scholarly work has associated him with residual imperialism. Motion's role as joint literary executor and sympathetic biographer to laureate manqué Philip Larkin links his public persona inevitably, if probably also misleadingly, to Larkin's narrow notions of Britishness, which included overt racism.[4]   The extent of Larkin's prejudices has been controversially indicated by Motion's biography (1993) and by the publication of Larkin's letters, but his attitudes were apparent as early as 1970 in his Introduction to *All What Jazz*, a collection of his writings about music, where he describes the harmonic innovations of Ornette Coleman and his peers as indications that "From using music to entertain the white man, the Negro had moved to hating him with it" (294). *Trumpet*, revolving around the life and music of a (fictional) mixed-race Scottish jazz musician of Larkin's own generation, serves as a rebuke both to Larkin's treatment of jazz as a fixed and finalized form, a one-way transaction between "Negro" performers and white audiences, and to the underlying assumption that there is a clear and stable distinction between "the Negro" and "the white man."

While critics who do acknowledge Kay's work usually judge it favourably, their discussions tend to be brief. Often highlighted is the vitality (see e.g. Niven 16) of Kay's readings of her own texts. This emphasis is in itself apt; voice, in more than one way, is a vital part of what Kay has done.[5] Poet and critic Sean O'Brien, *in The Deregulated Muse* (1998), a wide-ranging collection of his essays on contemporary British poetry, mentions Kay only as one of a group of black British poets (also including John Agard, Linton Kwesi Johnson, Grace Nichols, and Benjamin Zephaniah) whose theatricality and political commitment make "their live performances into acts of solidarity with audiences for whom the message is often a good deal more urgent than the medium" and who "tend to somewhat overshadow poets whose work depends on being read on the page, such as Fred D'Aguiar and David Dabydeen" (272). O'Brien's remarks suggest that Kay's performances may have obscured her **own** achievements on the page: one of the many hybrid features of her work is its combination--which is particularly striking, I will argue, in the final chapter of "The Adoption Papers"--of oral and textual effects. Her accomplishments as a live performer may have been crucial to her success, but they are not the only keys to her importance.

In one of the most detailed pieces on Kay, C. L. Innes notes that "Kay's distinctive Scots accent and idiom paradoxically identify her as British." Innes here points to the way in which Kay's performances embody a form of hybridity beyond the obvious one of her physical appearance as the biological "child of an unknown [white] British mother and Nigerian father" (335). Apparent on the pages of "The Adoption Papers," *Bessie Smith*, and *Trumpet* as well as in her performances, Kay's Scots voice functions both as a reminder that Scotland is a multi-racial territory despite its comparatively small share of Britain's non-white population and as a sign of the hybridity that is part of Britishness itself.[6] Sociologist and cultural theorist Paul Gilroy observes that "To be British is . . . to contract into a category of administrative convenience rather than an ethnic identity. It's an ambiguous word which often refuses its own obvious cultural referents . . . . The disjuncture between the two terms" British and English, he adds, "is a continual reminder not just of English dominance over Scots, Welsh and Irish people, but also that a British state can exist comfortably without the benefit of a unified British culture" (*Small Acts* 75). One illustration of the "British"-"English" disjuncture Gilroy refers to is provided--even embodied--by another leading analyst of British hybridities, Stuart Hall. Having arrived in England from Jamaica in 1951, Hall has been, through his teaching, writing, and administrative work, a crucial figure in British Cultural Studies. Yet in a 1992 interview, Hall explicitly refuses the nationality to which the location and the subject-matter of much of his work might seem to entitle (or condemn) him: "I'm not and never will be 'English'" ("Formation" 490).[7] Kay's combination of blackness and Scottishness exemplifies another form—comparable to but distinct from Hall's non-English and ambiguous nationality—of the resident hybridity that is changing Britain from within.[8]

The ambiguities of Kay's black Britishness and Scottishness are compounded and made potentially even more productive by the fact that the British state to which Gilroy refers has, since the election of a Labour government in 1997, begun devolving some of its power to Scotland. "Scottish Nationalist" would be a reductive label for Kay, but her work, through its ongoing interest in black and Scottish identities and in their intersections, participates in what (white) Scottish poet and critic Robert Crawford describes and celebrates (and helps to enact), in a 1997 essay, as the process of " **de**defining Scotland" (emphasis added):

> that complicating, enriching, and necessary work . . . which will ensure
> that no definition of 'Scottishness' becomes oppressively monolithic and
> that Scotland . . . remains imaginatively and intellectually freed-up--
> supplied with many visions of itself as well as many ways of looking at,
> engaging with, and being perceived by an increasingly interested world
> beyond. (95)

In his book *Identifying Poets* (1993), Crawford comments revealingly on the hybridity of the Scots language, as used in everyday life by many of the people of Glasgow and other lowland areas, "which frequently quotes, re-accents, and realigns elements of English vocabulary, mixing them in a rich impurity with alien elements (in the same way that some 'Black English' works)" (7). Kay's writing takes Crawford's celebration of "rich impurity" a logical step further by mixing Scots with varieties of "Black English."

In a more theoretical direction, another logical step further is one made both by Crawford and by Fred D'Aguiar. Crawford adds to the remarks just quoted by observing that "the use of [Scots] affects not only Scottish but English identity" and by quoting his Scottish colleague W. N. Herbert: "'Scots is a language . . . that criticises and, finally, extends English'" (*Identifying Poets* 7). In parallel fashion, D'Aguiar observes that "Dub poetry, poetry influenced by calypso, reggae, jazz and blues rhythm, creole language and Standard English articulating for the first time the black experience in Britain have all changed what it means to be British; deepened it in fact, making it more sophisticated, giving it a new lease of life" (70).[9] Kay's black Scottish writing, thus, represents what is potentially a very potent form of hybrid cultural vigour.

Crawford's, Herbert's and D'Aguiar's formulations bring me to the theoretical account of hybridity that seems most relevant to Kay's takes on black Britishness and black Scottishness. In *The Politics and Poetics of Transgression* (1986), Peter Stallybrass and Allon White, drawing on the work of Mikhail Bakhtin, define hybridization as the "inmixing of binary opposites, particularly of high and low, such that there is a heterodox merging of elements usually perceived as incompatible" (44). This process "produces new combinations and strange instabilities in a given semiotic system. It therefore generates the possibility of shifting *the very terms of the system itself*, by erasing and interrogating the relationships which constitute it" (58; original emphasis). Any given hybrid entity, thus, points to the possibilities and uncertainties of the future; as Hall's work insists, hybridity (whether racial, cultural, or both) is not a finalizable condition but an ever-evolving one (see e.g. "Formation" 502). In the case of contemporary Britain, then, the presence of racial hybridity redefines, or more precisely, opens for future redefinitions, the nature and possibilities both of "whiteness" and of "blackness." Coming to terms with such hybridity is therefore more than a matter of opposing racism and acknowledging that Britain has become a multicultural society.[10] It is also a matter of understanding that British culture will continue to evolve in unpredictable ways.

It is not only white Britons who must come to terms with "new combinations and strange instabilities"; Stallybrass and White's formulation helps to show why the dedefinition and reinvigoration of Britishness by Scottish and/or black cultural energies does not necessarily make life easy for the people carrying out this process. Gilroy explains in his 1993 book *The Black Atlantic* how "Striving to be both European and black requires some specific forms of double consciousness" and how, in situations where "these identities appear to be mutually exclusive, occupying the space between them or trying to demonstrate their continuity" is inherently stressful (1). If black culture has changed what it means to be British, this process has also changed what it means to be black in a Britain, or a world, where blackness itself is not necessarily a stable entity.

Gilroy has conducted an ongoing polemic against what he sees as a dangerous essentialism that has emerged in (or been sold to) black cultural formations in response to instabilities produced by insistent globalism and persistent racism. In his recent book *Against Race* (2000)[11] he exposes affinities, based on obsessions with racial purity, between certain kinds of black nationalism and European fascism (see e.g. 330) and argues that "An exemplary black physicality, mute and heroic, has been conscripted into service to build a militarized and nationalized version of planetary popular culture in which the world of sports counts for more than the supple, subtle public relationships improvised around the gestalt of song and dance" (274). Moreover, in what Gilroy calls this "swoosh-emblazoned age of Michael Jordan's planetary stardom" (*Against Race* 78), it appears that, as Kobena Mercer suggests, "hybridity" and other "keywords of postcolonial thinking" may have become "globalized as merely commonplace rather than critically interrogative" (Mercer 234). Perhaps the most widely-disseminated example in today's world of racially-hybrid vigour is Tiger Woods breaking records on both sides of the Atlantic and thereby helping to sell both swoosh-emblazoned products and the environment-menacing (Scottish) pastime of golf. "Although norms are not the same as trends," notes Mercer, "it could be said that the subversive potential once invested in notions of hybridity has been subject to pre-millennial downsizing" (235).[12] The claim I will develop in the rest of this piece, then, is that the blues- and jazz-influenced, socialist-feminist inflected British/Scottish blackness that Jackie Kay articulates through "The Adoption Papers," *Bessie Smith*, and *Trumpet* not only challenges Eurocentric forms of racism, but also represents an alternative to essentialist constructions of Black identity and, further, demonstrates that hybridity itself should not be conceived simply as a generic new global norm.

"The Adoption Papers"

Published by the Newcastle-based, poetry-specialized firm of Bloodaxe in 1991, "The Adoption Papers" is a revised version of the work broadcast by BBC Radio 3 in August 1990.[13] It follows the life of a woman who is born to a white Scottish mother and a black Nigerian father in Edinburgh in 1961, given up for adoption by her mother before her birth (the father having returned to Nigeria), and adopted and raised by a loving, left-wing white Glasgow couple. The sequence features not only the daughter's voice but also those of her biological and adoptive mothers, each voice being assigned its own typeface; from its outset, then, it goes beyond the implicit separatism of "So you think I'm a mule?" If the work's multiple voices, which often speak to one another's concerns, though they do not actually converse, evoke drama, its structure is distinctly novel-like. After an untitled one-page prologue which introduces the voice of each woman, the ten chapters are divided into three parts: the first (Chapters 1-5) is based on the daughter's birth and the adoption process in 1961-62 and also incorporates, in Chapters 2, 3, and 5, glimpses of the adult daughter's initial efforts to find the birth mother; the second part (Chapters 6-7), set in the daughter's later childhood (1967-71), concentrates on her anxieties about the way in which her adoptive mother is not her "real" mother and on her experiences of racism; the third part moves ahead to the 1980s and highlights the loneliness of both the birth mother and the adoptive mother, along with the daughter's efforts to contact the birth mother. Though these efforts give the work its strongest narrative thread, they, and it, are resolved in an ambiguous fashion that gives "The Adoption Papers" much of its force as a challenge to oversimplified accounts of multiracial Britain.

Each of the three women is characterized strongly: the adoptive mother is feisty and politically militant; the birth mother has a strong melancholic/poetic streak; the daughter combines these characteristics, both absorbing her adoptive parents' interest in political justice and, it would seem, inheriting her biological mother's interest in language. Critic Ian Gregson, though he identifies the biological mother inaccurately as black and as having "abandoned" her child (244), notes usefully that the work avoids "the too-easy definitiveness of obvious patterns of imagery and controlling metaphors" and that "by fully measuring the extent of the otherness it contains--the gaps between the women," it "finally evokes sympathy for each of them, and a sense of genuine, if precarious, identification" (244).[14] The three women never converse directly, but the structure of the work allows them to speak to, or echo, each other's concerns in ways that bear Gregson out. I will argue, though, that the end of the work defers full measurement of the gap between daughter and biological mother and only suggests the possibility of identification between them.

In *The Black Atlantic*, Gilroy describes his intellectual development as follows: "My search for resources with which to comprehend the doubleness and cultural intermixture that distinguish the experience of black Britons in contemporary Europe required me to seek inspiration from other sources [than British ones] and, in effect, to make an intellectual journey across the Atlantic" (4). Gilroy suggests not that the journey has led him to an essential source of authentic racial identity (in America, or Africa, or African America) but rather that the Atlantic serves to link black Britons to valuable cultural materials in other territories: the fluidity of the ocean itself matches the fluidity that characterizes racial and cultural identities in contemporary Britain. The middle part (Chapters 6-7) of "The Adoption Papers" finds the prepubescent daughter making her own trans-Atlantic journey. At the end of Chapter 6 she and her (white) best friend eschew Donny Osmond, David Cassidy, and Starsky and Hutch, the white American idols of their peers in the 1970s, in favour of Pearl Bailey and Bessie Smith (23). Moreover, the title of Chapter 7, "Black Bottom," incorporates a reference to the best-known set-piece of Bessie Smith's mentor Ma Rainey (see Kay Bessie Smith 26-43), and the last part of the chapter details the daughter's identification with activist and political detainee Angela Davis (26-27). This invigorating infusion of African-American culture into a Scottish life is reciprocated, as I will show, in Kay's book on Bessie Smith, where Scottish references and idioms make their way into an African-American biography.

Chapter 7 of "The Adoption Papers" also contains the work's most direct and sustained exposition of the challenges the daughter faces as a black-identified person in a white-dominated environment. Having begun with the adoptive mother worrying about over-emphasis on her daughter's colour and recalling that the adoption agency "told us they had no babies at first / [Until she] chanced it didn't matter what colour it was" (24), the chapter goes on to depict the daughter, through her own words, as she confronts a "wee shite" who calls her "Sambo" and "Dirty Darkie" (24).   The daughter's consequent encounters with a teacher who labels her a budding "juvenile delinquent" prove even more difficult for her and even more important to the work as a whole. The teacher goes on to voice even more simplistic judgements in an episode the daughter introduces as follows:

> We're practising for the school show
> I'm trying to do the Cha Cha and the Black Bottom
> but I can't get the steps right
> my right foot's left and my left foot's right.

The repetition of "right" at the end of two successive lines gracefully conveys the wrongness of the daughter's dancing.   It is the teacher's reaction to the daughter's difficulties that is truly crude:

> my teacher shouts from the bottom
> of the class Come on, show
>
> us what you can do I thought
> you people had it in your blood.
> My skin is hot as burning coal
> like that time she said Darkies are like coal
> in front of the whole class--my blood
> what does she mean? I thought
>
> she'd stopped all that after the last time

> my dad talked to her on parents' night
> the other kids are all right till she starts;
> my feet step out of time, my heart starts
> to miss beats like when I can't sleep at night--
> *What is in my blood?* The bell rings, it is time. (25; original italics)

The teacher's insensitivity causes problems with rhythm to spread from the daughter's feet throughout her body; over these three stanzas the poem itself, however, deftly uses repeated end-words to convey the persistence of the daughter's distress as she takes the teacher's crude synecdoche for heritage literally.

The chapter thus forms part of the work's deconstruction of racial essentialism—or, to adopt the more direct idiom of "So you think I'm a mule?," debunks "that strange blood crap." The question of blood is taken up again in Chapter 8, "Generations" (the first chapter of Part Three), where the adult daughter wonders about the physical details of her heritage in a long section whose line-breaks help to emphasize her feelings of incompleteness, and which articulates a much more nuanced sense than the teacher's of the ways in which blood, of both the actual and the synecdochal varieties, relates to racial and individual characteristics:

> I don't know what diseases
> come down my line;
> when dentist and doctors ask
> the old blood questions about family runnings
> I tell them: I have no nose or mouth or eyes
>   to match, no spitting image or dead cert,
> my face watches itself in the glass.
>
> I have my parents who are not of the same tree
> and you keep trying to make it matter,
> the blood, the tie, the passing down
> generations.
> We all have our contradictions,
> the ones with the mother's nose and father's eyes
> have them;
> the blood does not bind confusion,

> yet I confess to my contradiction
> I want to know my blood.
>
> I know my blood.
> It is dark ruby red and comes
> regular and I use Lillets.
> I know my blood when I cut my finger.
> I know what my blood looks like.
>
> It is the well, the womb, the fucking seed.
> Here I am far enough away to wonder--
> what were their faces like
> who were my grandmothers
> what were the days like
> passed in Scotland
> the land I come from
> the soil in my blood. (29)

The last section here reminds us that the daughter has Scottish as well as black/African blood (see note 11): she belongs to Glasgow, so to speak, and it belongs to her. More subtly, this passage links the daughter to the biological mother through the latter's obsession with earth and burial (see e.g. 18); thus it validates the biological mother's intuition, reported in the very next lines: "Put it this way: / I know she thinks of me often" (29). This linkage, in turn, reinforces the daughter's affirmation that she is Scottish as well as black.

Despite this textual connection between the daughter and the biological mother, the daughter's interest in getting to "know what [her] blood looks like" remains unfulfilled in the final chapter, "The Meeting Dream." The chapter begins with the daughter, who has contacted the biological mother's own mother and sister, remarking somewhat enigmatically, "*If I picture it like this it hurts less*" (original italics). It seems possible here that what hurts is an actual meeting that went badly, but the chapter as a whole suggests that it is, rather, the fact that the biological mother has been reluctant to have contact with the daughter at all. Even the daughter's "picture," which adds to the ambiguity by incorporating the voice, and special typeface, of the biological mother, depicts only tenuous connections between the two women--"We are not as we imagined" (32). The daughter's voice repeats "*If I picture it like this it hurts less*" before remarking that the biological mother "is too many imaginings to be flesh and blood" (33).

The final section of the chapter, and of the work, confirms that the daughter and biological mother have not in fact met; yet it also points tentatively beyond the exhaustion of imagination and/or representation evoked in the passage just quoted. "Her sister said she'd write me a letter," reads the first line of the section, which goes on to convey the daughter's anticipation of this promised textual contact:

> In the morning I'm awake with the birds
> waiting for the crash of the letter box
> then the soft thud of words on the matt.
> I lie there, duvet round my shoulders
> fantasising the colour of her paper
> whether she'll underline First Class
> or have a large circle over her 'i "s. (34)

Questions of bodily presence ("colour" and eyes) metamorphose into questions of textuality (stationery and handwriting—"i's"). The daughter still does not have eyes (see 29) through (or in) which to see her physical heritage, nor, yet, even "i's" through which to gain a more oblique impression of her biological mother's physical being. This striking substitution both calls into question the importance of physical characteristics and invites renewed attention to their roles in the text and in the construction of race more generally. The effect is an excellent example of one that, in O'Brien's words as quoted above, "depends on being read on the page"; not for nothing is the work called "The Adoption **Papers**" Moreover, the fact that an oral performance of these lines will to some extent feature a different emphasis--that is, one that evokes both eyes, and physical being, and i's, and textual being--makes "The Adoption Papers" two distinct texts in different media and augments its productive ambiguities.[15] The deferment of the meeting, and even of direct contact, between daughter and mother is not necessarily an indication that "The Adoption Papers" is ultimately pessimistic, though, since it helps the work to complicate assumptions that racial differences can be transcended quickly or easily.

This deferment of the meeting of differences almost inevitably evokes Derridean approaches to textual analysis, which can indeed help to show how passages like this one suggest a critique of the totalizing logic of representation in general by emphasizing the erasure of fixed terms and the indefinite deferral of final meaning. However, in this case it is important to consider Hall's critique of such approaches as they apply to representations of racial identity. Hall argues that Derrida

> has permitted his profound theoretical insights to be reappropriated
> into a celebration of formal "playfulness," which evacuates it of its
> political meaning. For if signification depends on the endless
> repositioning of its differential terms, meaning, in any specific instance,
> depends on the contingent and arbitrary stop – the necessary and
> temporary "break" in the infinite semiosis of language.
>
> ("Cultural Identity and Cinematic Representation" 216)

Hall has repeatedly made the point that awareness of the ways in which representations construct realities need not preclude the provisional, positional sense of identity and purpose that is necessary if cultural theorizing is to be more than an academic exercise (see e.g. "Postmodernism and Articulation" 145, "New Ethnicities" 446-47; see also Fiske 214). It would be disabling, so far as an effort to investigate specific relations between racial and textual ambiguity is concerned, to celebrate the formal subversiveness of a passage like the end of "The Adoption Papers" (or, indeed, to celebrate the sophisticated hybridities of the work as a whole) at the expense of its significance as a challenge to specific and current (mis)constructions of race and racial hybridity. The passage seems best read not as a definitive statement about the impossibility and/or the unrepresentability of real understanding between daughter and birth-mother or, by extension, between black and white Britons, but as a dramatization of some of the uncertainties generated by the racial hybridization of Britain in general and Scotland in particular. As I will show, comparable uncertainties--but, importantly, not identical ones--are integral to several of Kay's more recent works.

The subtleties of "The Adoption Papers" come into further relief when measured against the approach of Mike Leigh's film *Secrets & Lies* (1996), perhaps the most widely-known recent British cultural product to touch upon issues of adoption and racial mixing. The film begins with a situation strikingly similar to that of "The Adoption Papers": an adopted, mixed-race British woman takes steps to find her biological mother. In this case, however, the woman,

Hortense Cumberbatch (Marianne Jean-Baptiste), has black adoptive parents and is not aware that her biological mother is white--which makes the film's later events seem particularly contrived: Hortense quickly establishes a relationship with her biological mother through which she goes on inadvertently to bring about a cathartic crisis that clears up the "secrets and lies" that have debilitated the biological mother's family. The final shot has Hortense "enjoy[ing]" a sunny afternoon with her biological mother and (white) half-sister (see Leigh 103). While critic Bert Cardullo suggests that "the singularity of Leigh the director's unstable, aerial camera here causes us . . . to question the tidiness of Leigh the writer's feel-good ending" (485), the film has left behind not only Hortense's black adoptive family but also any feelings or detailed ideas she may have about the discoveries she has made. Coming to terms with unexpected kinds of racial hybridity thus seems for her to be a matter of taking her place in a society where whiteness is a relatively unproblematic norm--in other words, of assimilation. Reviewer Richard Porton, arguing that "Hortense is . . . nothing more than the catalyst who manages to unite the white protagonists" (54), suggests that the film partakes of the same reflexive celebration of traditional notions of Britishness that Gilroy and Hall have critiqued in white leftist theorists (see note 10). However, audiences and many critics have embraced *Secrets & Lies* wholeheartedly, and it remains prominently in circulation. While there appears, thus, to be a market for positive images of racially mixed families, the very popularity of Leigh's film creates a need for alternative perspectives on the implications of this form of hybridization.

Kay herself has written for television, and at least one of her poems, "Sabbath" (included in her third collection, 1998's *Off Colour*), has been the basis for a BBC-TV feature film, but it is hard to see how the paper-based effects of the final lines of "The Adoption Papers" could find a direct analogue in a moving-image medium. In arguing that the ambiguity-friendly textual strategies of "The Adoption Papers" provide a valuable counterweight to the cinematic utopianism of the conclusion of *Secrets & Lies* where the open-ended possibilities of racial mixing are concerned, I do not mean to suggest either that Leigh's film deserves none of its success or that films are intrinsically limited in the exploration of racial ambiguity by their emphasis on concrete visual images: other British films of the 1990s manage sharp takes on hybridity.[16] Still, the comparison indicates how literature, precisely because of its relative imprecison where physical facts are concerned, is especially suitable for evoking, and engaging audiences with, the ambiguities involved in racial mixing.

Bessie Smith and *Trumpet*

Bessie Smith (1997) amplifies the interest in the great blues singer that Kay expresses in "The Adoption Papers" (and sustains in her second collection, 1993's *Other Lovers*). The book fulfils many functions of a biography: it chronicles the key events and influences of Smith's life; it documents its sources with endnotes; and it takes a skeptical though sympathetic view of the popular account of Smith's death as resulting from the racism of segregated Mississippi hospitals (129-138). Kay celebrates Smith's defiance of boundaries, particularly ones of class and gender (see e.g. 65-66), and in the process, she herself moves well beyond conventional generic categories. The book itself is a hybrid, incorporating poems by Kay and others, fictional recreations of key events in Smith's life, and explicitly autobiographical material.

Kay's text begins by reproducing "The Red Graveyard," a poem from *Other Lovers* about Smith's haunting legacy (7-8). The first prose section then returns to the emphasis placed in "The Adoption Papers" on Smith as a figure with whom a black girl in Scotland in the 1960s could identify (9). The book revisits (and apparently confirms the factual basis of) specific autobiographical moments from the poem sequence, notably the childhood fondness for Smith and Pearl Bailey as role models (79; see also "Adoption Papers" 23) and the teacher's crude comments about music and rhythm being "in the blood" of people with black heritage (70-71). Kay invites the reader to see the affinity between these comments and American obsessions (as expressed through "one drop" laws) with racial purity (71). Yet this section of her text also suggests less sinister links between African-American and Scottish life: while she remarks, "I find it difficult to connect the history of the Charleston with my Scottish primary school" (70), in so doing she points to the fact that elements of Scottish consciousness **do** infiltrate her commentary on Smith's America. Throughout, Kay writes as someone who understands her own racial and cultural identity partly through the examples of African-Americans like Bessie Smith, but also as "a girl from Bishopbriggs near Glasgow" (17), someone whose cultural reference points and speech idiom are distinctively Scottish. For example, in one of the fictionalized passages, she likens the marriage of Ma and Pa Rainey, which reputedly camouflaged Ma's lesbianism (37), to that of a pair of Scottish cartoon characters: "*The names Ma and Pa are so asexual. It is never possible to imagine a wildly passionate relationship between a Ma and a Pa. (It is the same with the Broons.*

Ma and Pa Broon have heaps of kids but you can never imagine how they got them.) "
(38; original italics). Kay provides no gloss on the working-class Scots that
creates "Broon" from "Brown," nor does she explain the Broons themselves.
Thus, the reader who wants fully to understand the allusion must engage with
Scottish as well as African-American culture.[17]

In the final stages of *Bessie Smith*, Kay compares the singer's death to
those of other prematurely-lost black figures: "Martin Luther King, Malcolm X,
Billie Holiday, Bob Marley. Perhaps," she continues, "somebody is not truly
famous unless their death is also extraordinary, unusual, . . . terrifying to the
core of the human heart" (140). *Trumpet* takes up this comment on the excesses
of twentieth-century media culture by playing on myths created around the
death of its central character, Joss Moody. Kay acknowledges ("Conversation"
53) that the book was inspired by American jazz musician Billy Tipton, who was
discovered on his death to be biologically female. Kay borrows Tipton's story
for the mixed-race and proudly Scottish trumpeter Moody, whose death sets in
motion the events of the novel. These events are conveyed by multiple voices,
but mainly through Moody's (white) wife Millie, the only person who has
known his secret, and their adopted son, Colman, a thirty-something motorcycle
courier living in London.[18] Colman is not only mixed-race like his father, but
also mixed-up and pissed-off by the revelation of his father's "true" sex and the
fact of its having been hidden from him. "I'll write his fucking biography,"
Colman threatens; "I'll tell his whole story. I'll be his Judas" (62). Accordingly,
Colman collaborates with Sophie Stones, a freelance writer determined to do a
lucrative exposé of Moody's life. Colman's actions shape the novel, as Millie
tries to endure the media frenzy while dealing with powerful memories of her
life with her partner.

Kay suggests in an interview about *Trumpet* that "there's a sense in
which race within jazz is different, more fluid, less fixed" ("Conversation" 55).
Yet, while Joss has chosen and lived a life on his own terms, *Trumpet* celebrates
his success without making it represent a permanent transcendence of all forms
of racial (or gender) difference. If the combination of blackness and Scottishness
represents a potential source of rejuvenation for British culture, Colman's
difficulties show that hybrid racial and cultural heritage is not necessarily a
passport to success and happiness for individuals. Even Colman's name has a
complicated history: Millie reports that "Joss wanted a jazz or a blues name" but
that she preferred a Scottish one and mocked his suggestions--"Joss slapped me

across my face. 'That's enough,' he said. 'White people always laugh at black names'" (5). "After," Millie adds, "we compromised on Colman spelt the Irish way and not like Coleman Hawkins. That way we could get an Irish name and a jazz name rolled into one" (5-6).[19] Kay comments, in another recent interview, on the limited appeal of the "very macho, swearing, homeless, druggy writing" that has been prominently successful in recent Scottish fiction ("Scottish Music"), but through the foul-mouthed Colman she moves away, though not completely, from the autobiographical territory of "The Adoption Papers" and broadens her commentary on the complexities of late-20th-century Britain.

"The children of famous people aren't allowed to be talentless, ordinary fuckwits like me," complains Colman in his first section of the book (45). He goes on to comment repeatedly on the racism that he feels has further blighted his life: "practically every black guy my age that I saw on TV had just been arrested for something . . . . It's like we only had the one face to them . . . . I've been picked up by the police countless times, man, for doing fuck all . . . . But my old man, he didn't take my side about all this . . . . He thought I had it coming to me. He thought' I was a waster (162). While raising, through such passages, the persistence of racial stereotyping in Britain (see also Kay "Conversation" 59), *Trumpet* as a whole avoids suggesting that Colman's views are entirely objective. The funeral director who reveals Joss's real sex to Colman is struck not by Colman's race as such but by his "good looks" (113), but Colman himself looks into a mirror and feels "as if he can't actually see himself properly" (182); underlying his anger is ambivalence about his own personal worth.[20] Ambivalence also characterizes his attitude toward his father: he rebukes the prurience of Stones by telling her, "'Don't bother with this him/her bullshit. That's bollocks, man. Just say him'" (142). Thus he effectively defends his father's gender choice even in the middle of reacting angrily to it and even while he struggles with his own problems of identity.

Though dead, Joss himself twice speaks memorably in *Trumpet*. Near the centre of the book is an extended section that evokes his experience of playing, or being, jazz: "When he gets down, and he doesn't always get down deep enough, he loses his sex, his race, his memory," it begins (131). Intriguingly, the text mentions repeatedly that music is "in his blood" (131, 134) or "is his blood" (135). At first sight, these passages seem to lapse into the same kind of essentialist racial thinking exhibited by the teacher in Chapter 7 of "The Adoption Papers." But Joss is half-white and proud of his Scottish heritage, and these moments are much more akin to the long passage I have quoted from Chapter 8 of the poem sequence, where the daughter affirms that her mixed blood is fully Scottish. It is not necessarily black blood that has produced Joss's musicality, and in the words of his white Scottish drummer, his music is also "in the veins" (147) of his predominantly-white fans, which implies that jazz is more like a powerful (and on the whole therapeutic) drug than a biological inheritance.

The final part of the jazz section could seem to risk another kind of essentialism: "when he takes off he is the whole century galloping to its close. The wide moors. The big mouth. Scotland. Africa. Slavery. Freedom. He is a girl. A man. Everything, nothing . . . . Black, white" (136). These lines, celebratory as they are, could be held to reduce all differences unhelpfully to "everything" and thus also "nothing" and thereby to exemplify the kind of facile invocation of utopian hybridity that I am arguing Kay avoids. However, this section conveys a subjective impression of the sensations of jazz--its immediate effects on audiences--rather than an attempt at objective assessment of its long-term significance. It is about the possibility, rather than the guarantee, of hybridization as transcendence.

As *Trumpet* progresses, Colman does not, precisely, transcend his own situation, but he begins to get over his resentment of having to live up to his father's example of successful mixed/black masculinity. Stones discovers that Joss's white mother is still alive, and after meeting her (223-31) and obtaining a picture of his father as a young black girl (241, 254-55), Colman gains courage to stand up to the crass journalist. She has expressed a determination to "get right under [his] skin" (170), but after they drunkenly sleep together she reflects, "I've got him under my skin. Isn't that a jazz song? That could be the title. Yes!" (266). This passage might suggest her dawning sensitivity to black culture, though the vagueness of her knowledge of the song, along with the fact that its author, Cole Porter, was white (see note 19), suggests that she has yet to get very far "under the skin" of the subject of her book. Still, while Stones embodies a caricature of the frantic materialism of Thatcherized Britain (or England), the text suggests that even someone like her may not be irredeemably ignorant.[21]

Whatever the degree of consciousness-raising Stones undergoes, as *Trumpet* moves toward its conclusion Colman seems to be awakening to the positive potential of the Scottish part of his heritage, which he has previously discounted (see e.g. 190). He gains the courage to look at the letter his father has left him, in which Joss tells the (or a) story of his own father's arrival in Scotland at the turn of the century. The account may or may not be the "true" one, but the final stages of the book certainly document the historical extent to which blackness and Scottishness have been intermixed, and they link Colman's coming-of-age to his discovery of this historical fact. The letter implies that Colman is in some way now the custodian of Scotland's hybrid heritage: "you are my future" (277). However, its last words are enigmatic: "My father came off a boat right enough" (277). We do not learn details of Colman's response to the letter, nor do we find out for certain whether, or how, he will proceed with his collaboration with Stones. The book's final section, "Shares," is a single paragraph that evokes a reunion between Colman and Millie in the Scottish village where the family has a cottage: "He was walking towards her. He moved so like his father" (278). Here white parent and mixed child appear somewhat closer to contact and bonding than they do at the end of "The Adoption Papers": Colman, who has been bothered by the fact that he doesn't "even know which" of his biological parents "was black or where the black one came from" (58),[22] now seems both physically connected to his adoptive father and emotionally connected to his adoptive mother. Yet, as at the end of "The Adoption Papers" there is a deferral of anything suggesting definitive understanding between parent and child. In each work, Kay negotiates a path between facile optimism and disabling pessimism about prospects for inter-racial understanding in Scotland and Britain.

A Conclusion

Kay's most recent writing returns to the topics of "The Adoption Papers" and *Trumpet* in ways that continue her emphasis on the histories, the pitfalls, and the open-endedness of hybrid British identities. *Off Colour* includes "Christian Sanderson," for example, a grimly eloquent poem in the voice of a real 19th-century Scottish "mulatto" who was transported to Australia for theft (see also "Conversation" 58-59). "Pride," the last poem in the volume, has a persona who envisions her Ibo father's face in a train window and imagines a journey to the Nigeria of her heritage, only to be brought back, like the daughter in Chapter 8 of "The Adoption Papers," to her own face reflected in the glass: the poem thus both complements the earlier work's interest in biological ancestry and confirms its eschewal of easy celebrations of hybrid heritage. Moreover, "Big Milk," a story in *Granta* 63 (Fall, 1998), presents a further and startling take on the scenario of reunion with biological parents. Kay is by current self-identification a black writer (see "Conversation" 57), yet one "more Scottish than . . . African, in terms of culture" (see "Conversation" 60-61). Her work suggests why, as theorist Néstor García Canclini remarks, the most rewarding "object of study" for those interested in questions of race and culture "is not hybridity, but instead the process of hybridization" (43); she seems set to continue to supply wide-ranging and open-ended definitions of mixed British and Scottish blackness.

Peter Clandfield

NOTES

[1] As Paul Gilroy notes, races, and differences between them, "are imagined--socially and politically constructed" (*Small Acts* 20). In this essay I use the terms "race" and "racial" for lack of better alternatives and more or less according to the first construction of "race" given by the *Oxford Paperback Dictionary* (1988): "any of the great divisions of mankind with certain inherited physical characteristics in common." However, one of my assumptions is that the borders of these "great divisions" are impossible to locate. I use the term "black" in this essay in the awareness that in contemporary Britain it is widely used and understood to refer not only to people of African heritage but also to people of South Asian heritage; however, my emphasis falls on the former group.

[2] Kay's "language is Scots and English yet tied in with this is a complex notion of her blackness, her sexuality and her gender" (D'Aguiar 66).

[3] Deane's remarks seem rhetorical, at least as they apply to Kay: a November 1998 BBC report on laureateship oddsmaking shows Duffy fourth, at 8-1, and Kay not in the top 16.

[4] I should note that Motion's biography in no way advertises Larkin's kind of prejudice as a key to happiness. Larkin's racism isn't defensible, but it can be read as pathetic also.

[5] My own interest in Kay's work began with her appearance at Toronto's Harbourfront Poetry Festival in May 1993.

[6] On geographical distributions of ethnic minorities within Britain, see e.g. Skellington 45.

[7] The identity-label Hall unostentatiously adopts in this interview is that of "black West Indian, just like everybody else" (489). Here the adjectival phrase not only expresses Hall's modesty about his own status but also creates an interesting ambiguity: does "everybody else" refer to black West Indians in general or to black British West Indians? Or both? This interview also gives a fascinating account of the ambiguities of Hall's experience as a racially-mixed person in late-colonial Jamaica (484-89).

[8] As Historian Arthur Marwick observes, the postwar hybridization of Britain has some of its roots in "the notion of Britain's great imperial heritage which, as a concrete legacy, had left a

situation in which West Indians, Indians, Pakistanis and Africans were all full British subjects and entitled . . . to settle in Britain itself" (163).

[9] D'Aguiar's suggestion is in effect endorsed by critic Peter Childs's decision to conclude his "student-friendly critical survey" (back cover) of *The Twentieth Century in Poetry* (1999) with a section on black British poets. Childs mentions Kay, however, only in a list of "well-known poets with a Caribbean heritage" (203-04); in fact, Kay's biological father was Nigerian, and her heritage is Caribbean by Afro-diasporic association rather than by blood. This imprecision suggests that individual black British poets could be better-known despite their rising profile as a collective force.

[10] Innes reports that during the early postwar phase of black immigration to Britain, "Within British educational institutions, the term multicultural was really a code for two cultures, white and black, each perceived in fairly monolithic terms" (316). Gilroy and Hall have pointed out that the work of such pioneers of British cultural studies as Richard Hoggart and Raymond Williams invests, at times, in traditional notions of essential British or English ethnicity (see e.g. Stratton and Ang 382-83).

[11] The book's British version is less provocatively entitled *Between Camps*.

[12] On co-options and commodifications of hybridity, see also e.g. García Canclini 47-48.

[13] For a brief account of the radio version, see Niven.

[14] The biological mother is not explicitly identified by race, but I base the assumption that she is white on more than the details of Kay's own biography. In Chapter 7 the biological mother recalls her time with the Nigerian biological father: "Olubayo was the colour of peat / when we walked out heads turned / like horses, folk stood like trees / their eyes fixed on us" (26). Presumably, the cause of this effect is not Olubayo's colour alone, but its contrast to that of his companion. Certainly there is nothing to suggest that the biological mother is black. If she cannot be identified for certain as white, moreover, this ambiguity may be seen as adding to the provocative uncertainty that surrounds her.

[15] O'Brien is not the only critic to overlook Kay's textual inventiveness. In a provocative review of recent anthologies, Irish poet and critic Justin Quinn asserts that "there isn't really a plurality of poetic cultures in Britain and Ireland at the present time" and goes so far as to list Kay in a group of "formally conservative poets who come out of the central British tradition which Larkin exemplified so well" (Quinn section 1). It is true that formal adventurousness is not Kay's most obvious trait as a writer, but it is, *pace* Quinn, an important part of her mix.

[16] Isaac Julien's *Young Soul Rebels* (1991), a story of the adventures of two friends, one black, one mixed black and white, running a pirate radio station in London in 1977 (the year of Elizabeth II's Silver Jubilee) shares some of the utopianism of Leigh's film, since it ends with a sequence that suggests that musical pluralism will broadcast the way to a racially harmonious future. However, it also contains sequences which address the stresses of being of mixed race in the 1970s, notably one in which the mixed lead character, Chris, confronts another mixed man who has repudiated his hybrid heritage to hang with a group of white-supremacist skinheads.

The screenplay of *Young Soul Rebels*, along with detailed information on the difficult process of its making, is available in Julien and MacCabe's *Diary of Young Soul Rebel*. A shorter but notably incisive filmic take on the hybridities of contemporary Britain is Gurinder Chadha's *I'm British But...* (1990). This half-hour documentary, which the director introduces onscreen while wearing a sari and holding a leashed bulldog, features interviews with young adults of South Asian heritage living in various parts of Britain, such as a woman who states, in a broad Scots accent, that she prefers to think of herself as a Scottish Pakistani rather than as British. The subjects discuss hybrid forms of South-Asian-British popular culture and express diverging and sometimes clashing views on matters such as the desirability of nourishing their South Asian cultural roots and the persistence of racism. The film does not pretend to resolve the debates and ambiguities it exposes, but it illustrates hybridization as the kind of irreversible process of inmixing and generation of new combinations that Stallybrass and White theorize.

[17] Subversive takes on the Broons also feature in poems in *Off Colour*. "The Broons' Bairn's Black (a skipping rhyme)" (61), for example, offers an alternative conception of the Broons' sex life:

> Scotland is having a heart attack
> Scotland is having a heart attack
> Scotland is having a heart attack
> The Broons' Bairn's Black.

In addition to commenting implicitly on the conservatism of some forms of Scottish popular culture, these lines draw attention to the disjunction between racial designations and the physical characteristics they refer to: if the Broon's bairn were "black," its skin would presumably in fact be "broon." In short, there is more to Broon-ness than Scotland yet fully acknowledges.

[18] Kay says that "the form of [*Trumpet*] in a way equals jazz because you have your solo instruments with the different people who have all been affected by [Joss's] secret" ("Conversation" 56).

[19] Colman's name is even more evocative than Millie notes, since it both echoes the name of another great saxophonist, Larkin's nemesis Ornette Coleman, and points to the cultural intermixture between Scotland and Ireland. Moreover, Colman's nickname, Cole, links him to a great white jazz (or jazz-influenced) musician, Cole Porter.

[20] At least some of Colman's difficulties seem to arise from his habit of anticipating ill treatment: on his way to catch a train to meet Stones in Glasgow, he thinks angrily about the prospect of having to argue to claim his reserved seat from someone who will "treat . . . him as if he had no fucking right to a seat anyway," but no problem materializes (189). Suggested here is not that racism is entirely illusory but that its effects in contemporary Britain are often indirect and thus perhaps all the more difficult to deal with.

[21] For a more direct example of Kay's attacks on the iniquities of Thatcherism, see e.g. the poem "Death to Poll Tax" in *The Adoption Papers* (60). Kay's takes on class and politics, which I have mentioned only in passing, deserve detailed attention.

[22] This early passage, where Colman recalls how Joss invited him to "make up your own bloodline" (58), offers a small anthology of ways in which black people made their way to Scotland early in the twentieth century (58-59).

WORKS CITED

Cardullo, Bert. "Secrets and Lies." *Hudson Review* L, 3 (Autumn 1997). 477-86.

Childs, Peter. *The Twentieth Century in Poetry: A Critical Survey*. London: Routledge, 1999.

Crawford, Robert. "Dedefining Scotland." *Studying British Cultures: An Introduction*. Ed. Susan Bassnett. London: Routledge, 1997. 83-96.

---. *Identifying Poets*. Edinburgh: Edinburgh UP, 1993.

D'Aguiar, Fred. "'Have you been here long?' Black Poetry in Britain." *New British Poetries: The Scope of the Possible*. Ed. Robert Hampson and Peter Barry. Manchester: Manchester UP, 1993. 51-71.

Deane, Patrick. "British Poetry Since 1950: Recent Criticism, and the Laureateship." *Contemporary Literature* XL, 3 (1999). 491-506.

Fiske, John. "Opening the Hallway: Some Remarks on the Fertility of Stuart Hall's Contribution to Critical Theory." Morley and Chen 212-20.

García Canclini, Néstor. "The State of War and the State of Hybridization." Gilroy et al. 38-52.

Gilroy, Paul, Lawrence Grossberg, and Angela McRobbie, Eds. *Without Guarantees: In Honour of Stuart Hall*. London: Verso, 2000.

Gilroy, Paul. *Against Race: Imagining Political Culture Beyond the Color Line*. Cambridge, MA: Harvard UP, 2000.

---. *The Black Atlantic: Modernity and Double Consciousness*. London: Verso, 1993.

---. *Small Acts: Thoughts on the Politics of Black Cultures*. London: Serpent's Tail, 1993.

Gregson, Ian. *Contemporary Poetry and Postmodernism: Dialogue and Estrangement*. London: Macmillan, 1996.

Hall, Stuart. "The Formation of a Diasporic Intellectual." Interview with Kuan-Hsing Chen. 1992. Morley and Chen 484-503.

---. "Cultural Identity and Cinematic Representation." 1989. *Black British Cultural Studies: A Reader*. Ed. Houston A. Baker, Jr., Manthia Diawara, and Ruth H. Lindeborg. Chicago: U of Chicago P, 1996. 210-22.

---. "New Ethnicities." 1989. Morley and Chen 441-49.

---. "On Postmodernism and Articulation." Interview with Lawrence Grossberg. 1986. Morley and Chen 131-50.

I'm British But . . . . Dir. Gurinder Chadha. BFI Films/Channel Four Films. Great Britain, 1989.

Innes, C. L. "Accent and Identity: Women Poets of Many Parts." *Contemporary British Poetry: Essays in Theory and Criticism*. Ed. James Acheson and Romana Huk. Albany: SUNY Press, 1996. 315-41.

Julien, Isaac, and Colin MacCabe. *Diary of a Young Soul Rebel*. London: BFI, 1991.

Kay, Jackie. "Jackie Kay in Conversation." Interview with Maya Jaggi and Richard Dyer. *Wasafiri* 29 (Spring 1999). 53-61.

---. "Big Milk." *Granta* 63 (Autumn 1998). 99-109.

---. *Trumpet*. NY: Pantheon, 1998.

---. *Off Colour*. Newcastle: Bloodaxe, 1998.

---. *Bessie Smith*. Bath: Absolute Press, 1997.

---. *Other Lovers*. Newcastle: Bloodaxe, 1993.

---. *The Adoption Papers*. Newcastle: Bloodaxe, 1991.

---. "So you think I'm a mule?" 1985. *Black British Feminism: A Reader*. Ed. Heidi Safia Mirza. London: Routledge, 1997. 1-2.

Larkin, Philip. Introduction to *All What Jazz*. *Required Writing: Miscellaneous Pieces 1955-1982*. London: Faber, 1983. 285-98.

Leigh, Mike. *Secrets & Lies*. London: Faber, 1997.

Marwick, Arthur. *British Society Since 1945*. 3rd Ed. London: Penguin, 1996.

Mercer, Kobena. "A Sociography of Diaspora." Gilroy et al. 233-44.

Morley, David, and Kuan-Hsing Chen, Eds. *Stuart Hall: Critical Dialogues in Cultural Studies*. London: Routledge, 1996

Niven, Alastair. "Making Her Way." *Poetry Review* 80.4 (Winter 1990-91). 16-17.

O'Brien, Sean. *The Deregulated Muse*. Newcastle: Bloodaxe, 1998.

"Poetic Race for Royal Appointment." BBC News, November 8, 1998 . *BBC Online Network*. http://news.bbc.co.uk/hi/englishentertainment/newsid_ 208000/208527.stm. Accessed 3 August 2000.

Porton, Richard. Rev. of *Secrets & Lies*, dir. Mike Leigh. *Cineaste* XXII, 4 (January 1997). 51-52; 54.

Quinn, Justin. "Of Grids, Flux And The Patternless Expanse*.*" *Contemporary Poetry Review*. http://www.cprw.com/Quinn/grids.html. Accessed 30 September 2000.

Secrets & Lies. Dir. Mike Leigh. Perf. Brenda Blethyn, Marianne Jean-Baptiste. Channel Four Films/Thin Man Films. Great Britain, 1996.

Skellington, Richard, with Paulette Morris. *'Race' in Britain Today*. London: SAGE, 1992.

Stallybrass, Peter, and Allon White. *The Politics and Poetics of Transgression*. Ithaca: Cornell UP, 1986.

Stratton, Jon, and Ien Ang. "On the Impossibility of a Global Cultural Studies: British Cultural Studies in an International Frame." Morley and Chen 361-91.

Taylor, Helen. "Scottish Music." *New Times* 152, 9 October 1998. Online at http://www.democratic-left.org.uk/newtimes/articles/issue16/nt00162.html. Accessed 7 June 2000.

Young Soul Rebels. Dir. Isaac Julien. Perf. Valentine Nonyela, Mo Sesay. BFI Films/Channel Four Films/Sankofa. Great Britain, 1991.

2.

"EVERYONE WAS VAGUELY RELATED":
HYBRIDITY AND THE POLITICS OF RACE IN
SRI LANKAN LITERARY DISCOURSES IN ENGLISH

The preoccupation with race has dominated contemporary Sri Lankan identitarian discourses.[1] Racial consciousness is constructed *vis-à-vis* the binary of "purity" and "mixedness". In Sri Lanka, ambiguities of race are often effaced or suppressed in the national narratives, and historically mixed and hybrid communities come to connote impurity, pollution or dishonour to the nation. Thus the descendants of the Europeans, the Burghers, who were the result of miscegenation of the colonial past, are often positioned in terms of the "degenerate outsider", in opposition to the other so-called "ethnically pure" communities.

Unlike some erstwhile British colonies, part of the Sri Lankan nation's uniqueness can be attributed to its complex legacy of sustained colonial intervention.[2] Prolonged exposure to diverse political, socio-cultural and religious forces inevitably altered the ethnic, religious and social composition of the Island. A policy of Divide-and-Rule exacerbated the pre-colonial fractures among the ethnic groups while colonial rule set up "visible, rigid, and hierarchical distinctions between the coloniser and the colonised" and the physical and symbolic separation of the races maintained social distance and authority over subject peoples (Mohanty, 1991: 17). The racial and cultural boundaries were transmuted to a moral plane for the explicit and implicit regulation against intermixing and miscegenation.

Pre- and post-Independent nationalists operated according to binary oppositions constructed on the basis of ethnicity in order to define and demarcate a unique identity. By the end of the nineteenth century the resistance movement in India induced similar anti-colonial sentiments among the ethnic groups in Ceylon. The rise of ethnic-centred nationalisms was a defining characteristic of Ceylon even in the early years of anti-colonial resistance. Christianity, westernisation and British rule were placed along one continuum and it was felt that all three had to be rejected. One of the pioneers of the Sinhalese nationalist movement, Anagarika Dharmapala (1864-1933) started a process which has been termed "identity affirmation" – "a conscious process whereby an ethnic group is impelled to display its unity through visible symbols and overt symbolic actions or through the reiteration of grandiose ethnic myths" (Obeyesekere 1979: 303). Dharmapala's denigration of western ideology and valorisation of a "glorious" Sinhala past are recognisable strategies in the formulation of nationalist thought and sentiment. He designed specific "rules" for the Sinhala Buddhist lay person, which included a set of prescribed standards of conduct for women.

The emphasis on Sinhala Buddhism by the Sinhala nationalists was counteracted by an emergent Tamil identity. Tamil nationalism was expressed initially through religious and cultural revivals. Arumugam Navalar (1822-1879), a prominent figure within the Tamil nationalist movement, established a printing press which was employed to issue literature expounding Hindu doctrine and defending the people against the strictures of the missionaries. Navalar and other nationalists and scholars used their literary output in a similar way to the Sinhala nationalists. While agitating against the "alien" religious and cultural practices of the Imperialists, this propaganda also facilitated the rise of anti-Sinhala Buddhist sentiments. A distinct Tamil identity was increasingly mobilised for a political purpose and was reiterated in opposition to the emerging Sinhala identity. Those who were associated with the Imperialists became vilified.[3]

People In Between: The Burghers and the Middle Class in the Transformations within Sri Lanka 1790's - 1960's (Raheem *et al.*, 1989) provides evidence of the imaging of the Burghers by both the nationalists and the British colonial rulers as socially and racially inferior "half-castes". They cite, for example, a description of the Burghers in a letter written by Lord Torrington in May 1848:

> For all those who have been in the East admit that among the half-castes
> is to be found every vice that disgraces humanity and nowhere is this
> axiom more strikingly exemplified than in the male and female Burghers
> of Ceylon (Raheem *et al.*, 1989: 148).

Pejorative expressions like *karapotha* (literally meaning cockroach - alluding to the insect's physical appearance, a mixture of brown and white spots – a derogatory label for the tainted blood of the Burghers) were also a part of the vocabulary of indigenisation. Such terms of disparagement and ethnic stereotyping were harnessed during the socio-political transformation of 1956. With the Sinhala-Only Act of 1956, the rapid indigenisation and switch to the national language in educational, administrative and bureaucratic systems alienated the Burghers (whose first language was English), and the other minorities. The unfamiliarity with Sinhala precluded them from competing on a national level for jobs and denied them economic opportunities.

In the 1980s, with the rise of Tamil militancy and increasing socio-economic exigencies in Sri Lanka, the hegemonic nationalist forces have attempted to explain the country's problems through the alibi of westernisation. Since the Burghers are seen by the dominant communities as the repository of westernisation, the Burgher figure has continued to be positioned for the purposes of burlesque or derision in popular culture and discourse.

In this essay, I will explore the dominant representational modes employed towards this group, as a way of situating the Burghers in contemporary nationalist debates. Literary texts written by non-Burghers reveal how this character can be read as a device for concealing or circumventing the larger socio-economic problems within the nation-state. In this essay I explore two texts, Indu Dharmasena's play *It's All or Nothing* (1988) and Michael Ondaatje's *Running in the Family* (1982).[4]

It's All or Nothing has often been dismissed on the grounds that it is "popular entertainment". It foregrounds the politics of representation, for the dominant stereotypes attached to the Burgher woman are deployed in a denigratory rhetoric for comic purposes. Through the sub-plot of a Burgher woman's romance with a Sinhala character the historically-conditioned stereotypes assigned to this community emerge. Part of the chauvinism may be due to the insecurities of racial and cultural hybridity that surface in the popular discourses. Popular discourses are crucial in enabling the dissemination of ideas about authenticity, national identity and scapegoats. One could even argue that popular discourse works to secure the stability of the nation. While using the vehicle of burlesque, *It's All or Nothing* encapsulates some of the anxieties race epitomises for the majority communities.

Michael Ondaatje's *Running in the Family* sensitively captures the perplexities of constructing and negotiating identity within dominant nationalisms. The text works on two levels. Explorations into the indeterminacy of race, history and genre in the text challenge the "authoritative discourses" through the "hybridity" of its protagonists. Ondaatje forces an interrogation of the process of naming and foregrounds the slippage between constructs such as race and nationality. On another level, while debunking essentialist ethnic labels and stereotypes, he also grapples with the issue of racial ambiguity and the anxieties it engenders for the "hybrid" subject. His text is a recognition of the hierarchical racialisation of relationships, thereby eschewing a simplistic idealisation of mixedness.

The Burgherness of Brenda: Indu Dharmasena's *It's All or Nothing*

Indu Dharmasena, a Sinhalese, has been writing and producing plays for the English theatre in Sri Lanka since the early 1980s. In the sub-plot of *It's All or Nothing* Brenda, a Burgher woman, falls in love with Jagath, a wealthy, but "nerdish" Sinhalese man, who is terrified of his domineering mother. Jagath's two cousins, Priyan and Kumi (the hero and heroine of the play), conspire to bring Brenda to Colombo from Kandy (where Brenda lives) and marry her to Jagath without his mother's knowledge.

From her initial appearance on stage this character is deployed chiefly for comic effect. Brenda introduces herself to the family in the following way:

> Hello, hello, child. I was telling Kumi, I have heard so much about you that I feel I know you inside out. [...] Aiyo yes! My Jagath is very fond of you two. What for telling he says you are top class people (Dharmasena, 1988: 18).

Her effusiveness, conveyed through a breathless monologue, is intended as a radical departure from the conservative, "well-spoken" Sri Lankan middle-class woman that the English theatre audiences usually identify with. Her garish dress and accessories – bright pink dress, pink high-heeled shoes, pink handbag and plastic jewellery – feed into ideological assumptions held by the Sinhalese of a Burgher woman's unsophisticated manner and eagerness to attract the attention of men. The fact that she does not assume the demeanour of what is stereotypically "respectable behaviour", that is, speaking in a soft voice or acting shy and reticent, gives credibility to this perception.

One of her speeches to Jagath's cousins is useful in considering some of the central stereotypes associated with the Burgher woman: her "questionable" morals, linguistic features of what is called "Burgher English", and perceived lack of academic achievements.

> These cousins are all the same. Can't say a word without gettin' the back
> up. Right, now what do you want to know about me? I am a good
> Burgher girl from a middle-class family. I have my O-Levels but failed
> my A-Levels. What for the tellin', I worked for two years in the Middle
> East and saved up some money, which I have put in the bank. What else?
> (Dharmasena, 1988: 20).

On a linguistic level, the tendency to silence the final "g" in the v-ing form and expressions like "what for telling" are intended as a depiction of "Burgher English". This variety is denigrated as a pidginised derivative of Standard English and has traditionally been used for comic effect in Sri Lankan popular culture and writing. The humour feeds on audience snobbery, where "laughter is directed at what the audience perceives to be a register of English that is inferior to its own (the implied Standard), a comically distorted, 'ridiculous' (*mustee*) version of the 'normal' language" (Fernando, 1994: 139). This linguistic hierarchy works to reinforce the hierarchical opposition between the Sinhalese self and its other.[5]

Linked to the above perception is the belief that the Burgher displays no interest in educational pursuits. Brenda's admission that she "failed her A-Levels" reinforces the stereotype. Such a prejudice discounts the socio-political vicissitudes of the post-Independence State in which access to higher education (notably to the state universities) was attendant on the policies of Sinhala-only, policies which marginalised the minorities. Secondly, such intellectual snobbery may be read as a backlash against the colonial power structures that ensured that the Sinhalese and Tamil middle-classes were trained by Burgher schoolmasters (Raheem *et al.* 1989: 13). This stereotype erases the fact that the

Burgher women were among the Island's first educators and professionals. They were pioneer feminists advocating and procuring women's rights, and they "created an image for Burgher women based on intellectual activity, serious work and the courage to challenge orthodoxy and assert women's rights to equality in education" (Brohier, 1995: 51).

The most vituperative criticism levelled against the Burgher woman in this play as well as in the popular imagination in Sri Lanka impinges on morality and sexual relations. This issue is intricately linked to the perceived racial ambiguity of the Burghers. The racial affiliation with the West was posited as sexual permissiveness. The mantle of "immorality" fell most harshly on the Burgher woman, who was believed to exploit her sexuality for social gain. Kumari Jayawardena has made the point that the Buddhist clergy, for instance, defined the Burgher woman as the ultimate, immoral Other in the angel/devil paradigm, in sharp contrast to the "pure", "good" Sri Lankan wife/mother (1994: 118-119). In addition, the popular belief that the Burgher woman was intent on effacing her "Burgherness" by marrying into the ethnically "pure" communities reinforced the existing prejudices against them. If the most pronounced stereotyping of the Burgher is evident in the imaging of the Burgher woman, it is because women are the procreators. The control of female sexuality and of reproduction becomes a key material and ideological issue in the transaction of the nation. The purity and chastity of women have to be ensured so that the group is not polluted from outside (Jayawardena, 1994: 54). Female sexuality is often the grounds on which ideological debates about nationalism are waged.

In the context of the play, Brenda's experience of working in the Middle East today is intended as a measure of this sexual "liberality". However, the actual movement of Sri Lankan (mostly Sinhalese) women who are seeking employment to the Middle East can be conveniently justified and/or ignored by a middle-class audience on the grounds that it is primarily women from the lower classes who seek work abroad. Within the denigratory rhetoric directed against the underclass woman, leaving home for employment purposes signifies moral laxity. *It's All or Nothing* illustrates how popular culture becomes an effective conduit through which the legacies of female morality are re-articulated.[6]

The resurgence of racial prejudice, at a larger level amongst the competing Sinhala and Tamil nationalist forces and in the more "liberal" segments of the population, is reflected in the play in the reaction of Jagath's cousins to Brenda's ethnic background.

> Priyan: ... And Kumi, I didn't know she was ...
> Kumi: I know, I didn't realise it myself until I met her (Dharmasena, 1988: 19).

From their reluctance and doubt and inability even to articulate the word Burgher an audience can infer that, had they been previously aware of Brenda's ethnic background, they may not have been so enthusiastic to help Jagath. This brief exchange is an index of the way in which ethnicity impinges upon social and personal relationships, where within the pervasive arena of ethnic conflict, identity politics hinge on questions of race, and social groups are defined by, and contingent upon, these terms of reference. Whether it is "pure Sinhalese, Tamil or Muslim", these categories are unequivocally fixed. Within this perspective, the Burghers' light complexion, language (English) and religion (Christianity) can still be utilised to symbolise the continuing vestiges of oppression. In *It's All or Nothing* Brenda's love for Jagath is coded in terms of an anxiety over miscegenation. This anxiety is detailed in Frantz Fanon's interrogation of the dynamics motivating the Black woman's desire to capture "whiteness" through relationships with a white man in *Black Skin, White Masks*. He argues that the black person's sense of "inferiority" instituted by colonialism is "transformed" through sexual and/or marital relations with a European. Cross-racial relationships are governed by the colonial imperative of "whiten[ing] the race, sav[ing] the race" (Fanon, 1986: 47).

In the post-Independence terrain when the hierarchies are reversed and "white" is no longer held to be "good" and "black" no longer evil, and marrying a European, or a European-looking man, is neither socially nor politically advantageous for the Sinhalese or Tamils, it is the "racially-pure" man of the hegemonic social formation who becomes the desired partner. This inversion of Fanon's theoretical stance explains the dominant Sinhala and Tamil construction of the Burghers' desire to intermarry. The dominant assumption is that the Burgher woman needs to "salvage" her ethnicity after colonialism or, figuratively "darken" herself by marrying into the "pure races". This anxiety about race is then justified by making the Burgher woman culpable for cultural bastardisation/moral degeneration. What is most blatant about the stereotyping of the Burgher is that when the emphasis of national identity is placed on racial authenticity, hybridity is disavowed and stigmatised. However, a quotation from Michael Ondaatje's *Running in the Family* foregrounds the "hybrid" lineage of the Sri Lankan people and renders notions of ethnic-based nationalism nonsensical:

> Everyone was vaguely related and had Sinhalese, Tamil, Dutch, British and Burgher blood in them going back many generations. [...] Emil Daniels summed up the situation for most of them when he was asked by one of the British governors what his nationality was – God alone knows your Excellency (Ondaatje, 1982: 41).

This passage prefaces my discussion of Michael Ondaatje's text *Running in the Family*. While *It's All or Nothing* unveils the dominant prejudices of the "ethnically-pure" groups, *Running in the Family* contests the stereotypes of the Burgher.

Anxieties and Ambiguities of Race: Michael Ondaatje's *Running in the Family*

Michael Ondaatje's *Running in the Family*, which charts two journeys made by the writer to Sri Lanka, is often classified for the purposes of convenience as a "travel memoir" (Russell, 1992: 23).[7] However, the text defies any attempt at easy categorisation. In keeping with its subject matter, it is "hybrid" in form, interweaving photographs, poems, conversations, personal memories and excerpts from socio-historical documents. "Numerous modes of discourse are juxtaposed within the dominant pattern of a discontinuous narrative" to reflect the "arbitrariness of generic classification" (Thieme, 1991: 41) and the inadequacy of a "fixed" narrative for a subject as complex as the retrieval of personal history.

The intertextual and eclectic character of *Running in the Family* goes beyond alluding to and reflecting Ondaatje's *personal* claim to a multi-cultural inheritance; it also bears testimony to the multi-cultural topography of Sri Lanka as a whole, which, in the present nationalist climate, has several ramifications. His preoccupation with cartography and topography in the text makes a comment about the arbitrariness of geographical or ethnic boundaries, and Ondaatje displays a self-consciousness regarding the impossibility of realising his desire to "fix" and define those abstract concepts such as "lineage" and "history". Family vignettes in *Running in the Family* function as a microcosm for the world of the upper-class Burgher. They enact the traumas of finding hitherto-accepted realities and identity destabilised in the transitional era of decolonisation.

The representation of the lifestyle of this minority sets out the socio-political backdrop for understanding the emergent stereotyping of the Burgher. Central to the development and understanding of these stereotypes are the ways in which hybridity and mimicry have been inscribed in the construction of a Burgher identity in the dominant nationalist discourses.

Ceylon, Ondaatje's homeland, is imaged through the trope of marriage, reinscribing the "sexualisation" of foreign territories in colonialist discourses.[8] Territorial expansion was accompanied by a "pervasive" preoccupation with sex. Ronald Hyam has identified the ample opportunities for sexual indulgence throughout the Empire in the nineteenth century. In Hyam's account, Empire was not only a matter of Christianity and commerce but "an unrivalled field for the maximisation of sexual opportunity, copulation and concubinage" (1990: 2, 211).[9] Ondaatje repeats the sexual metaphor of imperialist discourses. He establishes his own ancestry and inscribes the historical circumstances that have shaped the diverse character of the modern Sri Lankan nation-state:

> [Ceylon was] the *wife* of many marriages, *courted* by invaders who stepped ashore and claimed everything with the power of their sword or bible or language (Ondaatje, 1982: 64, my emphases).

In *Running in the Family* Ondaatje encodes the *raison d'être* of the fatalistic attraction of races, through his particular use of words like "courted" and "wife". These words deliberately locate the Island as a mystical paradise that is conducive to romantic liaisons. However, this "exotic" ambience enshrouds the more inimical aspects behind the ideological project of the "civilising" mission. A seemingly innocent comment like "Ceylon falls on a map and its outline is the shape of a tear" can be read as a symbolic enactment of the complexities of the interrelations between the coloniser and the colonial subject (Ondaatje, 1982: 147). John Russell foregrounds the European mixedness of Ondaatje's people when he says that they had "come from European stock, intent on setting up domiciles in Ceylon. Thus [they] were partial to intermixing of bloodlines with the natives", an instance of the fortunes and misfortunes of the sexual economy of Empire.

The interrelations between coloniser and colonised manifest themselves not just in physical terms, but also at a psychological level. The anxieties of racial ambiguity are conspicuous in the incidents which involve Mervyn Ondaatje, the writer's father. Although he is a product of a cross-cultural union, the writer notes that "My father always claimed to be a Ceylon Tamil, though that was probably more valid about three centuries earlier" (Ondaatje, 1982: 41). Constituted and defined by Dutch, Tamil and English, while straddling these multiple cultures Mervyn also represents the trauma of racial mixedness. This trauma is all-the-more acute since he is placed in a historical moment of chaos, in the aftermath of colonialism. It is a moment when the colonial hierarchies are no longer normative. Yet since the nation-state is in the wake of establishing itself, categories such as race and nationality hold stronger than ever.

From Ondaatje's narrative, then, it appears that Mervyn is situated in a liminal space, what constitutes for Homi Bhabha, the elliptical *in-between* (1994a: 60). The operative dynamics in his character can be read against Bhabha's conceptualisation of hybridity. Bhabha argues that the "structure of identification . . . occurs precisely in the 'elliptical in-between'", where the repetition and reproduction of the influences of colonialism emerges as a mutation or hybrid.[10] Hybridity is valorised as a condition where cultural differences "contingently" and "conflictually" touch, where differences of culture can no longer be identified as "objects of epistemological or moral contemplation" (Bhabha, 1994a: 114). The presence of hybridity offers certain advantages in negotiating the collusion of language and race in a world of disparate peoples who are the result of colonial miscegenation, and it incorporates the potential to destabilise the essentialist nationalist claim to a "pure" race. "The paranoid threat from the hybrid is finally uncontainable because it breaks down the duality of self/other, insider/outsider" and embodies the potential to challenge and change the terms of authoritative discourses, either those which have remained as a legacy of colonialism or which persist in the form of neo-colonialism (Bhabha, 1994: 111-116).[11]

A close reading of his student days at Cambridge is a useful starting point for decoding the complexities of Mervyn's condition. Unlike his father, he assimilates himself into English culture with ease. It can be assumed that his light complexion (signifiying his European ancestry) contributes to making this process easier:

> It was two and a half years later, after several modest letters about his
> successful academic career, that his parents discovered he had not even
> passed the entrance exam and was living off their money in England. He
> had rented extravagant rooms in Cambridge and simply eliminated the
> academic element of university, making close friends among the
> students, reading contemporary novels, boating and making a name for
> himself as someone who knew exactly what was valuable and interesting
> in the Cambridge circles of the 1920s (Ondaatje, 1982: 31-32).

This passage inscribes the terms of reference that enable Mervyn to situate himself within the space of the "English" aristocracy. It can be argued that he is entitled to this lifestyle, since he is the product of the colonial legacy. He acquires a level of sophistication that allows him access to the "privileged" Imperial domain of the Armed Forces. He commands a limited degree of autonomy over his Ceylonese subordinates. Indeed, Mervyn typifies, as Carl Muller notes, the "fair skinned relics of colonial trespass, eminently usable by the British . . . and although there was something vaguely off-white about them, . . . [they] were rooted in the West" (1994: 11). Yet this position of authority is illusory. His exploits while serving as an officer in British Uniform in the Ceylon Light Infantry problematise the valorisation of hybridity. Although he has access to the coloniser's world, and does "disrupt" colonial authority at a personal level, for Mervyn the experience of hybridity is traumatic since he is gripped by the need to protect the Empire.[12]

Even after Independence he is fixated by a need to *protect* (Ondaatje, 1982: 194). He displays the overarching anxiety of trying to work within a context in which the fundamental features of his world (generated by colonialism) are no longer valid. This condition derives from the psychological dilemma wherein he is unable to shape for himself an alternative world in which the oppositions set up by the coloniser, of us/them, no longer operate. Mervyn's anxiety corresponds to Shelagh Gunawardene's comment that, "The mere proclaiming of political independence in 1948 did not bring about a clear articulation of national identity" (1994: 86).

This angst is exacerbated by the hierarchical nature of ethnic relations, which encroach on the workings of personal relationships. In the text, the racial snobbery of Ondaatje's family contests the dominant stereotypes about the Burghers. Ondaatje's positive stance towards the Burgher is crucial not only for destabilising the stereotypes, but also for demystifying the underpinnings of race in nationalist discourse. The upper-class Burghers emerge as an educated minority who are in the forefront of the Island's political life. The popular myth about the "half-breeds" who are intent on effacing and "salvaging" their ethnic identity by marrying into the Sinhalese and Tamil communities is debunked in Lalla's (Mervyn's mother-in-law) snobbery towards her son-in-law's ethnic origin. The episode of Lalla's dismissal of the news of her daughter's engagement to a Tamil man does not merely have comic value in the text. The ramifications of denigrating Mervyn's race not only undermine the relationship between Mervyn and Lalla but have long-term implications for the state of his marriage. The rivalry is first established when Lalla discovers that her prospective son-in-law is not a Burgher. Lalla, who is familiar with his family background, knows that he is Tamil:

> When my mother eventually announced her engagement to my father, Lalla turned to friends and said, 'What do you *think*, darling, she's going to marry an Ondaatje . . . she's going to marry a *Tamil!*' (Ondaatje, 1982: 118).

She then laughs for the duration of the wedding ceremony marking the "beginning of a war" between mother-in-law and son-in-law (Ondaatje, 1982: 119). They proceed to provoke each other in the most outlandish and comic ways. Such incidents, albeit comic, render claims of racial "superiority" facile, because they are based on specious abstractions which obviate the possibilities of forging more meaningful issues in personal relationships. This episode offers useful insights for envisioning a more moderate Sri Lankan nation. It underscores the need to cast aside arbitrary classifications such as race at the level of domestic and personal relations, as well as the macro, political level.

Chauvinistic constructions of the Burgher woman as sexually promiscuous are also dispelled through the depiction of Lalla, Ondaatje's grandmother. The overriding impression of Lalla is not that she is "sexually promiscuous" but rather non-conformist. Her narrative enlists the elements of humour and fantasy. In narrating the episode of a man squeezing her false breast in a bus and being deluded into believing it is the "real thing", Ondaatje illustrates the sexual codification of the incident by the onlookers. Lalla, though, on discovering that he had been "ardently fondling the sponge beneath her gown", reacts with unmitigated mirth (Ondaatje, 1982: 43). The narrator's tone clearly endorses her reaction, thereby undermining the sense of moral outrage awakened in the passengers. Significantly, the stranger's advances do not provide any sexual gratification for Lalla; on the contrary, her delight comes from the way the episode misleads both the passengers and the perpetrator.

Her social excesses after her husband's death are similarly recounted with a degree of familial pride and register a positive shift within the paradigm of nationalist morality. Lalla's character, therefore, transforms the negative stereotype of the Burgher women into an enabling device that unsettles and challenges the dominant assumptions. Her easy rapport with the fishermen and workers in the marketplace exemplifies her defiance of social dictates. In fraternising with men, Lalla undermines sexual licentiousness by her capacity to traverse class and race boundaries. However, within a particular religio-cultural code and vigorous nationalist context, this behaviour is construed as atypical. Partha Chatterjee's comment about the construction of women can be applied to the way in which Lalla's behaviour is construed in his text.

> Women identified as westernised would invite the ascription of all that the 'normal' woman (mother/sister/daughter) is not, brazen, avaricious, irreligious, sexually promiscuous and this is not only from males but also from women who see themselves as conforming to the legitimate norm which is precisely an indication of the hegemonic status of the ideological construct (1993: 131).

Lalla, who flouts the orthodoxies of modesty, "invites" the label of "abnormality". She is placed as a marginal figure, and this ascription reinforces the dominant stereotype of the Burgher woman.

In documenting and reclaiming his family history, Ondaatje's text is a microcosmic portrait of the Burgher community whose lineage blurs the distinctions of race and history. The graphic representation of racial mixing in the text celebrates the diverse composition of the Sri Lankan nation. Throughout the text Ondaatje endeavours to present an alternative version of history. As Thieme suggests, "[the text] resists unitary classification, closure and essentialist

definitions of personality and the past, and suggest[s] that both individual and
national identities are formed through a series of random, and frequently bizarre,
accretions" (1991: 41). The juxtaposition of the bizarre accretions (often manifest
through the theatrical mode) with the more rational political events is an index of
the way in which such ideological constructs are fashioned.

Although *Running in the Family* was written in 1982, a year before the
ethnic crisis erupted, the text is valuable as a springboard to interrogate and
deconstruct hegemonic myths of a pure national identity in Sri Lanka, an identity
that entails the erasure of division and diversity. Ondaatje makes a plea for the
recognition of multiple identities by problematising racial divisions. His position
as a writer living in Canada, away from the intensities of political violence and
racial prejudice, raises the question of agency. As an outsider he approaches
contemporary politics and the issue of ethnic hostilities with a self-consciousness
and uncertainty that is productive. He does not offer solutions or make any
claims about the tenuous politics of the Island. His agenda is primarily to
rehabilitate his own past and restore the umbilical chord that was severed by his
migration to Canada. In doing so he locates his family portraits within the spatio-
temporal relations of the pre- and post-Independence nation. The ambivalences
and ambiguities within his familial domain unveil parallel complexities within
national "genealogies".

I want to conclude this essay by alluding to a poem by a Burgher poet,
Jean Arasanayagam, whose work has been instrumental in unveiling the politics
of race and nation. In the poem "Mother-in-law" she cogently depicts a historical
situation that was common among certain upper class families in Sri Lanka.
Below, is a granddaughter's reaction to a Tamil mother-in-law's description of
how a *Sinhala* wet nurse fed her:

> 'Achchi you have *Sinhala* blood,
> You drank milk of a *Sinhala* woman'
> 'Who told you that? A *Sinhala* nona
> Gave me milk. They were all
> Respectable *Sinhala* nonas.' (Arasanayagam, 1991: 97, my emphases) [13]

The irony here is unmistakable. The older woman fails to grasp her
granddaughter's persistent questioning and the horror of being suckled by a
Sinhalese woman. She misunderstands the irony and retaliates by invoking class

rather than racial contours. Later on in the poem, the older woman goes on to display a fierce pride in her son's marriage to an English woman, but she cannot reconcile herself to her Burgher daughter-in-law. Through the controlled tone this situation metonymically captures patriarchal anxieties, which often coincides with the anxieties of the nation. It is, on one level, evidence of the close alliance between the races where the "milk" of one race, literally and metaphorically, nourishes the other. Hers is also the voice of the post-colonial nation, continually exposing and concealing the fractures and fissures that lie within a facade of coherence, and bringing to crisis the Sri Lankan nation's claims to ethnic, religious and linguistic "authenticity". Thus, as Ondaatje keeps reminding his reader, it is not simply the presence of the Burghers that transmogrifies the ethnic character of the peoples of Sri Lanka.

The ethnic "in-between" space that the Burgher inhabits inscribes the ambivalence of the Sri Lankan nation as a whole, its pluralism in race, religion and culture in the aftermath of decolonisation, combined with its the search for an "essential" cultural identity. The price that the nation has paid for reinforcing an "essential" identity is an ongoing separatist war. Although the political stereotypes of nationalist rhetoric are often represented and reinforced in popular culture, the fragility of such constructions can be evinced from their subtexts, and when they conflict with the "real situations". Sri Lanka as a nation straddles the contradiction of, on the one hand, the overplay of racial purity denigrating hybridity and westernisation, while, on the other hand, contending with the daily reminders of the presence of mixedness and the influences of westernisation on its culture and race. However, such contradictions may ultimately be enabling, for it is within them that the potential for challenging both racist and sexist ideologies may operate.

Neluka Silva

NOTES

[1] Qadri Ismail has made a useful point, noting the interchangeability of the terms "racial" and "ethnic" in Sri Lankan discourses. He states that "this is not to negate the substantive

distinction between the two, . . . but since they inhabit the same continuum, in both chronological and imaginary terms, they are occasionally inflated" (1995: 60).

2 Ceylon was successively colonised by three European powers from 1505 to 1948, the Portuguese in 1505, the Dutch in 1658 and finally the British from 1796 to 1948.

3 During the height of colonialism, the Burghers' access to education, a westernised lifestyle and European languages secured for them a privileged space among the colonialists, especially the British. Thus they, along with the British, became the targets of the pre-Independence nationalists. In 1892, Anagarika Dharmapala identified the Burghers as the "hybrids and bastards of Sinhalese, who have become traitors to the country honoured with Christian names, given ranks and made leaders of society" (Raheem *et al.*, 1989: 10). Although after Independence the Burghers' position of privilege was divested from them, they have continued to inhabit a denigrated position in the popular imagination for their racial composition and putative immorality.

4 I am grateful to Shirley Chew of the University of Leeds, UK, and to Susan Spearey for their advice and discussions during the analysis of Ondaatje's *Running in the Family*.

5 It is ironic that these linguistic forms, denigrated as a mark of linguistic "inferiority" are, in effect the contrary. They reveal traces or remnants of the Burghers' empowered position in pre-Independence Ceylon, because the Burghers' pronunciation of the v-ing is a close approximation of the British colonisers who were stationed in the Indian subcontinent.

6 I use the term popular culture somewhat cautiously, recognising its ambiguity and fluidity, and changes in meaning according to spatio-temporal configurations. Here I use it to mean mass appeal, the consumers of popular culture represent a range of class and ethnic backgrounds. It falls outside "traditional literature" and "high-brow" literature.

7 Ondaatje, poet and novelist of Tamil and Burgher ancestry, was born in Sri Lanka and left the Island at the age of eleven.

8 See De Quincey's portrayal of the Island of Ceylon, in which the sexual undertones are striking: "She combines the luxury of the tropics with the sterner gifts of her own climate. She is hot; she is cold. She is civilised; she is barbarous. . . . She has all the climates; she is the 'Pandora of Island', all-gifted, and ready, if approached properly, to give everything. Ceylon will but too deeply fulfil the functions of a paradise. Too subtly she will lay fascinations upon man" (1889-90: 429, 430, 434, 435).

9 See Robert Young (1995), especially the chapter "Sex and Inequality – the Cultural Construction of Race" for an elaboration of the linkages between sexuality and race during Imperialism.

10 Hybridity, according to Bhabha, represents that "ambivalent 'turn' of the discriminated subject into the terrifying, exorbitant object of paranoid classification – a disturbing questioning of the images and presences of authority" (1994: 113).

11 While recognising the relevance of Bhabha's metaphors in engaging with the issue of ethnicity, one must be alert to and register his tendency to homogenise without mapping specificities within the cultural terrains he speaks of.

12 See the episode of his last train ride on the Colombo-Trincomalee train, where he believes that the train is mined with bombs and is convinced that he is saving the sleeping British officers on the train, and Colombo (Ondaatje, 1982: 152-155)

13 *Nona*, the Sinhala term for lady, is a classed term also referring to the mistress of the house.

WORKS CITED

Arasanayagam, Jean. "Mother-in-Law". *Reddened Water Flows Clear*. London & Boston: Forest Books, 1991. 94-98.

Bhabha, Homi. *The Location of Culture*. London: Routledge, 1994.

Brohier, Deloraine. *Dr. Alice de Boer and Some Pioneer Burgher Women Doctors* . Colombo: Social Scientists' Association, 1995.

Chatterjee, Partha. *The Nation and Its Fragments*. New Jersey: Princeton U P, 1993.

De Quincey, Thomas. *The Collected Writings of Thomas de Quincey* , *14 Vols,* Ed. D. Masson. Edinburgh: Adam and Charles Black, 1889-90. Vol 7.

Dharmasena, Indu. *It's All or Nothing*. 1988 (manuscript).

Fanon, Frantz. *Black Skin, White Masks*. trans. C. L. Markmann. London: Pluto, 1986.

Fernando, Nihal. "Representing the Burghers: A Review of *The Jam Fruit Tree* by Carl Muller". *The Sri Lanka Journal of the Humanities* , 20, 1994. 133-140.

Gunawardene, Shelagh. "Stage and Set: A Theatrical Odyssey of Our Time". *Navasilu: Journal of the English Association of Sri Lanka and the Association for Commonwealth Literature and Language Studies,* 11&12, 1994. 86-98.

Hyam, Ronald. *Empire and Sexuality: The British Experience* . Manchester and New York: Manchester U P, 1990.

Ismail, Qadri. "Unmooring Identity: The Antinomies of Elite Muslim Self-Representation in Modern Sri Lanka". *Unmaking the Nation*. Eds. Qadri Ismail and Pradeep Jeganathan. Colombo: Social Scientists Association, 1995. 55-105.

Jayawardena, Kumari. "Religious and Cultural Identity and the Construction of Sinhala Buddhist Womanhood". *Nivedini*, 2(1), 1994. 111-139.

Mohanty, Chandra Talpade, Anne Russo and Lourdes Tourre (Eds.). Introduction in *Third World Feminism and the Politics of Struggle* , Bloomingdale: Indiana University Press, 1-47.

Muller, Carl. *Yakada Yaka*. New Delhi: Penguin,1994.

Obeyesekere, Gananath. "The Vicissitudes of the Sinhala-Buddhist Identity Through Time and Change." *Collective Identities, Nationalisms and Protest in Modern Sri Lanka* . Ed. Michael Roberts. Colombo: Marga Institute, 1979. 279-303.

Ondaatje, Michael. *Running in the Family*. London: Picador, 1982.

Raheem Ismeth, Micheal Roberts and Percy Colin-Thome. *People InBetween: The Burghers and the Middle Class in the Transformations Within Sri Lanka 1790's - 1960's* . Ratmalana: Sarvodaya Press, 1989.

Russell, John. "Travel Memoir as Non-fiction Novel: Michael Ondaatje's *Running in the Family*". *Ariel,* 22(2), 1992. 23-40.

Thieme, John. "Historical Relations: Modes of Discourse in Michael Ondaatje's *Running in the Family*". Eds. Coral Ann Howells and Lynette Hunter, *Narrative Strategies in Canadian Literature: Feminism and Post-Colonialism* . Philadelphia: Open U P, 1991. 40-48.

Young, Robert J. C. *Colonial Desire: Hybridity in Theory, Culture and Race* . London and New York: Routledge, 1995.

3.

PASSING TRANSGRESSIONS AND AUTHENTIC IDENTITY
IN JESSIE FAUSET'S *PLUM BUN* AND NELLA LARSEN'S *PASSING*

Writing on African American drama, Sandra Richards notes that "thanks to feminism, we have apparently come to understand that gender is performative. However, race – or, more properly stated, visible difference in skin color – remains tied to a metaphysics of substance" (47). Currently, race theory speaks of race as power-effect, a metaphor or construct naturalized or grounded through appeals to the body and bodily differences. Just as black British cultural studies theorists like Stuart Hall, Paul Gilroy, and Kobena Mercer call for "de-essentializing" blackness, several African American critics and theorists likewise maintain that "blackness must now be defined as a mediated, socially constructed, and gendered practice" (Wall, "Response" 188).[1] Yet there remains a certain resistance to conceiving of race as performative, as an accretion of behaviors and stylizations on the body's surface that, to quote Judith Butler theorizing gender as performative, produces "the effect of an internal core or substance . . . . or identity" (*GT* 136). That resistance arises from contested and politicized notions of identity in which people are deeply invested. African American performance artist Adrian Piper, in an essay relating her personal experiences of being repeatedly taken for white, maintains that being black in America is "a social condition, more than an identity. . . . Racial classification in this country functions to restrict the distribution of goods, entitlements and status as narrowly as possible, to those whose power is already entrenched" (232). However, while Piper argues that racial categories are too "rigid and oversimplified to fit anyone accurately" (246), she also acknowledges the importance of what Karla Holloway calls "privately authored" identities that invoke race as grounding and binding African American communities together while driving a variety of politics.[2] African Americans, Piper observes, have taken a "social condition" of rupture and dispossession and made of it "privately authored" identities of self- and communal-affirmation, yet this is also an identity politics that can disavow what are perceived to be diminutions and dilutions of "blackness":

> [F]or others, it is the mere idea of blackness as an essentialized source of self-worth and self-affirmation that forecloses the acknowledgement of mixed ancestry. . . . Having struggled so long and hard to carve a sense of wholeness and value for ourselves out of our ancient connections with Africa after having been actively denied any in America, many of us are extremely resistant to once again casting ourselves into the same chaos of ethnic and psychological ambiguity our diaspora to this country originally inflicted on us. (234)

Piper speaks here of acknowledging biracial and mixed ancestry, but I also read her insights as applicable to the idea of race as a performative and the possible limits to conceiving of it as such. While identity as performance may be rooted in communal and cultural traditions that inform that performance, it may also be perceived by some to be a profoundly rootless instability that does not adequately address the lived experience or serve the interests of a good many people.[3] Its very chaotic ambiguity, to borrow Piper's phrasing, may be liberating for some and lacking in historical and material specificity for others, thereby proving its very failing. I would contend, then, that a politics of identity rooted in the affirmation of African American "community" and shared historical experiences motivates the continued unease with reading racial passing as anything more than an individual's attempt to better his or her material position. Rather than reading narratives of passing as making a political intervention in conceptions of race at a time when racial difference was obsessively policed and violently asserted, critics have continued to regard them as limited in subversive potential and impotent in political strategy.[4] Whether guarded on one side of the color line or the other, "blackness" continues to go carefully policed in American culture and elsewhere in the West, as Stuart Hall argues: "[A]s always happens when we naturalize historical categories, we fix that signifier ['black'] outside of history, outside of change, outside of political intervention. . . . We are tempted to display that signifier as a device which can purify the impure, bring the straying brothers and sisters . . . into line, and police the boundaries – which are of course political, symbolic, and positional boundaries – as if they were genetic" (30).

This kind of border patrol and identity politics has made for one rather longstanding reception of passing narratives as advocating a rejection of "blackness" for the social access and economic security gained by passing for white, and of passing itself as a "dishonorable" act that indicates the character's lack of "integrity" or loyalty to their "race" (Wall, "Passing" 109). [5] In fact, passing narratives have been largely understood to be assimilationist in nature and intent: "The narrative trajectories of classic passing texts . . . . depend . . . upon the association of blackness with self-denial and suffering, and of whiteness with selfishness and material comfort. The combination of these points – passing as betrayal, blackness as self-denial, whiteness as comfort – has the effect of advocating black accommodationism, since the texts repeatedly punish at least this particular form of upward mobility" (Smith 44). We have, then, a rather stark set of available readings firmly established when it comes to narratives of passing, to which recent criticism has added the post-struturalist contention that these narratives expose identity itself as a fiction. [6] While I will argue that Jessie Fauset's *Plum Bun* (1928) and Nella Larsen's *Passing* (1929) offer political critiques of race as it circulated and was inter-implicated with gender, class and sexuality during the jazz age, I maintain that forwarding a constructionist view of identity is not the thrust of their politics. Certainly, given a current favor for anti-essentialist views of identity in literary and cultural studies, it would seem that their narratives are most radical when representing identity as performative and unfixed, but that kind of retrospective reading risks eliding central elements of passing as Fauset and Larsen work with it. Rather than enacting an either/or of communal versus individualist politics and practice, of identity as fixed or fluid and understood through essentialist or constructionist paradigms, I would argue that Fauset's and Larsen's novels instead expose the tensions, ambiguities and interactions of such oppositions as they compete in a debate over black identity. Contrary to the current critical vogue, then, I will explore the ways in which Fauset and Larsen use the very stabilizing grounds of identitarian categories – race, gender, class, sexuality – to configure identity as potentially dangerously fluid yet nevertheless circumscribed within policed borders that are consistently and at times violently reasserted.

Fauset is often regarded as a mere "midwife" of the Harlem Renaissance even though she was a central player in that movement as literary editor of *The Crisis,* and Larsen has only recently been "recovered." [7] Despite increased critical attention to their work, they have yet to be seen as deeply engaged in interrogating both notions of race circulating in the wider culture and debates over "blackness" and its representations within the Harlem or New Negro Renaissance. Through the ambiguous racial identity of the mulatta [8] and the ambivalence of passing itself, Fauset's and Larsen's narratives move between and play on two competing discourses of black identity in the 1920s: an essentialist discourse of "authentic" blackness believed to be embodied in "the folk," the southern, rural, poor African American; and an emerging constructionist discourse refuting notions of essential racial difference, usually identified as a "Talented Tenth" politics and associated with the "bourgeoisie," the Northern, urban, middle-class African American. [9] For some time Harlem Renaissance politics have been understood as split along these class lines; however, recent studies like J. Martin Favor's *Authentic Blackness* argue that even W.E.B. DuBois "advocate[d] a wide range of black representations and acknowledge[d] a broad spectrum of black experience," yet also placed "the folk at the center of the discussion of black identity" (12). [10]

While this promotion of "the folk" as embodying authentic blackness held ascendancy, it did not go uncontested not the least because it could be used to fuel, rather than counter, what Carla Kaplan calls the "taxonomic fever" of the early twentieth century: "At every turn, this mania was underwritten by hysterical devotion to notions of 'loyalty,' 'pride,' and 'group sense' and racial identity was implicitly understood as an ethics, an obligation to choose one's type, remain constant to it. . . . [E]ven radical black artists and intellectuals could be said to have contributed to this taxonomizing structure of feeling" (152-53). [11] The outcome of such taxonomic fever was "a profound cultural tension between . . . an impulse to stabilize and fix identity and . . . the beginning of our own social constructionist arguments for its destabilization. To make matters even more complicated, celebratory, even if strategic, uses of identity constructions are as likely to inhabit social constructionist terrain as they are to be found among essentialists" (Kaplan 153). We must, then, consider Fauset and Larsen's passing narratives in their historical context, one in which questions of "authentic" blackness were at the center of New Negro identity politics, while anxieties about miscegenation and race hygiene were fuelling racial segregation and an obsession with discerning racial difference in American culture at large. Fauset's and Larsen's intervention in this debate over racial difference and black identity was to explore the cultural tension Kaplan speaks of through the mulatta figure who passes for white. The mulatta has been read almost exclusively as a mediator between white and black, facilitating the exploration of the relationship between the races, [12] but Fauset and Larsen make her a much more challenging figure. Far from simply facilitating a rather benign exploration of racial difference and relations across the color line, Fauset and Larsen's mulattas threaten to call their era's conception of race into crisis.

The mulatta is a key figure through which to consider the fixing of identity and its transgressions. In *American Anatomies*, Robyn Wiegman contends that race in America is dependent upon the differential relationship of black to white in a "politics of visibility." "[T]he 'logic' of race in United States culture anchors whiteness in the visible epistemology of black skin," maintains Wiegman, "contributing above all to the recurrent and discursively, if not always materially, violent equation between the idea of 'race' and the 'black' body" (21). However, I would argue the mulatta is called to function in the production of race quite differently than the black body Wiegman speaks of. A body legally designated black, the mulatta frequently does not "tell" in this American politics of visibility. However, she is nevertheless invested with the ability to mark the bounds of blackness and whiteness, ultimately asserting the power of race even as she is figured forth as the greatest threat to it – the illegibility of race in certain "unreadable" bodies. As a corporeal racial borderland, the mulatta comes to anchor the meaning of whiteness and blackness even while she threatens to undo notions of racial difference, thereby marking most clearly what Robert Young calls the dialectics of race: "[H]ybridity. . .maps out [racial theory's] most anxious, vulnerable site. . . . The idea of race here shows itself to be profoundly dialectical: it only works when defined against potential inter-mixture, which also threatens to undo its calculations altogether" (19).

However much the mulatta might prove the anxious and vulnerable site of racial categorization in America, that anxiety has not been limited to one side of the color line. Throughout the term's history, "mulatta" has signalled a failure to naturalize what Haryette Mullen calls a "genetically illogical racial system" that reduces "racial identity to a white/non-white binary" (73-4). Yet if the mulatta has been identified as black and assigned to the other side of the color line so that whiteness may "remain" ostensibly pure, she has also been labelled illegitimate by African Americans. "Yella," "high yella," "all that yellow gone to waste" – the biracial individual has been reminded she is "not black enough" by African Americans. The mulatto's racial identity, then, has been constructed by white Americans as decidedly "blacker" than either biology would indicate or some African Americans have wanted to accept. She has been overdetermined in American culture from both sides of the color line, but that over-determination holds in tension both the repeated reassertion of racial difference and the possibility of its subversion. As such, she is a figure who not only forms the corporeal bound or limit of whiteness and blackness, but one who also "haunt[s] those boundaries as the persistent possibility of their disruption and rearticulation" (Butler, *Bodies* 8). In and through the mulatta, essentialist notions of absolute racial difference are asserted, even as their impossibility is given a "bodily" proof that exposes race as construct. The mulatta's racial overdetermination, in turn, becomes imbricated with the overdetermination of both her gender and sexuality in ways that have often gone misrecognized. Considering passing narratives within his larger study of black masculinity, *Are We Not Men?*, Philip Brian Harper reads the literary conventions of "tragic mulatta" narratives as the highly feminized precursor to the passing novel. Citing conventions like the tragic mulatta's routine position as "the suffering victim of tragic circumstances" and as "the source of moral degradation . . . [resulting from her] failure to be chaste" and her ability to seduce any white man, Harper argues that the mulatta's "illicit sexuality" signals her "fundamental femininity" (104-08). This fundamental femininity then engenders "the conceptual limits that govern the novel of racial 'passing'" for Harper, its "inevitable" tendency "to support a conservative gender politics . . . . with the effect that 'passing' itself appears as a profoundly feminine undertaking" (112-16). Yet Harper fails to consider in his troubling analysis that gender and femininity are articulated in racialized forms: however "feminized" Harper might argue the mulatta is, her dangerously illicit sexuality has positioned her outside dominant constructions of womanhood rather than signalled her "fundamental femininity." If, as Ann duCille argues, black women became the jazz age's erotic icons – "sex . . . was precisely what hot-blooded African women were assumed to have always in mind and body" (73) – mulattas were even further sexualized, said to "prey upon . . . [the men of] the pure-blood race" as "the chief sinners" amongst African Americans (Reuter 94, 163).[13] Far from "feminine" in any dominant sense within a wider American culture that continued to value woman as sexually pure moral agent, the mulatta was excluded from a gender identity she would instead define and police. Ostensibly marking the limits of both white womanhood's propriety and exotic black female sexuality with her extremely illicit and "salacious" behavior, the mulatta takes on a triple border duty defining the margins of womanhood, race, and acceptable sexuality.

Valerie Smith's reading of passing narratives as gendered takes us in a different direction from Harper's, for rather than arguing that the mulatta makes the genre itself feminized, Smith argues that the trajectories of these narratives differ according to the gender of their protagonists:

> Passing male characters can either be re-educated and returned to the bosom of home and community to uplift the race, or they can remain in the white world and be constructed with some measure of condescension, ambivalence, or even approval. . . . Passing women characters, on the other hand, are either re-educated and returned to the bosom of home and community, or they receive some extreme form of punishment such as death or the sacrifice of a loved one. (45)

In some passing narratives this punishment of the biracial female who chooses to pass for white may serve, as Smith observes, to "restrain the options and behavior of black women" (45), but I would argue that in Larsen's and Fauset's novels "punishment" is used to mount a critique of those very restrictions. In both *Plum Bun* and *Passing*, femininity or womanhood is interrogated rather than naively or conservatively inscribed as Harper would argue. Even as a young girl, *Plum Bun*'s Angela Murray actively pursues dominant definitions and attributes of femininity. Though she has approached very few tasks in her life with diligence, Angela applies herself to studying French in which she sees "an element of fine ladyism" (37). [14] Overall, Angela desires a largely passive life in which her chief occupations will be exerting a "womanly" influence: "Power, greatness, authority, these were fitting and proper for men; but there were sweeter, more beautiful gifts for women, and power of a certain kind too. . . . [in] sympathy and magnetism. To accomplish this she must have money and influence . . . she would need even protection; perhaps it would be better to marry . . . a white man" (88). However, embedded in Angela's traditionally feminine aim to marry and exert a "sweet" and "beautiful" influence upon family, friends, and acquaintances are her decidedly unladylike aims for power, money, and independence: "[I]t would be . . . great fun to capture power and protection in addition to the freedom and independence which she had so long coveted" (88-89). Fauset effectively casts Angela's "unwomanly" desires for power and freedom as driving her decision to pass; Angela realizes that in American society "men had a better time of it than women, coloured men than coloured women, white men than white women" (88), and she determines to better her position in a hierarchy that has blocked her access to further artistic training and will limit her social, political and economic freedoms. Paradoxically, however, the protection Angela seeks as a route to some form of power also necessitates a very "womanly" dependence that would effectively limit the freedom she desires.

Even as Fauset seems to suggest that passing for a white woman will be Angela's ticket out, she exposes the ways in which the very attributes of femininity necessary for Angela's successful pass will ultimately restrict her. While passing for white, Angela tries to barter for marriage and security with Roger Fielding, but Roger knows too well his value as an eligible bachelor and his parents' expectation that he marry within "his station." Even though Angela realizes, despite denying it, that becoming Roger's lover will cost her the security and upward mobility she has been seeking, she nevertheless agrees to a lifestyle she sees as "promiscuous." Angela's passing – her performance of conventional femininity and its "virtues" – is represented as most successful, however, when she agrees to Roger's proposition; significantly, Fauset describes Angela as conspicuously "los[ing] . . . her colour" when she decides to become sexually involved with Roger (179). An independent young woman who leaves home, family and friends to pass for white in a strange new city, Angela takes on a ladylike passivity soon after her first sexual encounter with Roger: "Without him life meant nothing; with him it was everything . . . . Now for the first time she felt possessive; she found herself deeply interested in Roger's welfare . . . . [H]is wishes, his pleasure were the end and aim of her existence; she told herself . . . that the sole excuse for being a woman was to be just that, – a woman. Forgotten were her ideals about her Art; her ambition" (203-4). Fauset's tone is unmistakably ironic, with its melodrama and excessive romanticizing of what is effectively Angela's entrapment. [15] In fact, Fauset parodies both the notion of the African American woman as lascivious and the white woman as virtuous through Angela's passing, making her never more believable as a white woman than when in the midst of her illicit affair with Roger. Heightening our awareness of their inter-implication, Fauset offers her most severe and incisive critique of gender and racial hierarchies in Angela's experiences passing for white. Angela is effectively a "fallen" woman with the most "ladylike" of devotions and motives, at her most "unwomanly" when self-reliant, independent, yet also virtuous. Angela's "punishment" appears to come when Roger ends their affair and she realizes she has given up everything; however, as I will go on to argue, Fauset makes her a more dangerous and threatening figure in the end rather than returning her to that "safe" position in home and community that Smith outlines.

Although Fauset parodies racialized gender identities through her African American character's performance of white womanhood, she does not treat issues of class in as much depth as Larsen does in *Passing*. In her reading of the novel, Lauren Berlant has argued that "Passing for nonblack allows these women [Irene Redfield and Clare Kendry] to wear their gender according to a particular class style" (111). There are, however, significant differences between Irene's passing and Clare's, differences that go beyond the fact that Irene occasionally passes for convenience, while Clare has "passed over" into the white race. While Irene carefully regulates her life, her behavior, and her appearance in order to solidify her position in the black bourgeoisie – an act of passing which, like Angela's, also entails her performance of bourgeois femininity – Clare stages a much more "daring" and "having" performance in which she refuses to keep in her place as either white or black. To note that Irene's passing is not limited to her occasional masquerades as a white woman is hardly a new reading of the text. [16] Larsen works to undermine the racialization of gender and class identities by representing Irene as mastering and ultimately parodying bourgeois standards of womanhood. Predictably, Irene takes a certain pride in her skilful domesticity – "Pouring tea properly and nicely was an occupation that required a kind of well-balanced attention" – extending those skills from the tea-table throughout the house in the pursuit of a well-appointed home, a home Larsen significantly describes as "furnished with a sparingness that was almost *chaste*" (218, 219, my emphasis). [17] Irene is a consummate hostess, arranging "successful" parties as carefully as she arranges a home life for her family. As the curator of domestic matters and her family's morality, Irene "wanted only to be tranquil. Only, unmolested, to be allowed to direct for their own best good the lives of her sons and her husband" (235).

It is Irene's carefully constructed and maintained gender identity that Clare Kendry threatens to disrupt with her insistent presence in Irene's life. Passing for white and married to wealthy John Bellew for 12 years, Clare repeatedly disturbs Irene who finds her "peculiar, caressing smile just a shade too provocative" (149). Clare is said to behave in "a having way," at the expense of anything and anyone: "'Can't you realize that I'm not like you a bit? Why, to get the things I want badly enough, I'd do anything, hurt anybody, throw anything away'" (153, 210). Irene recognizes that Clare's challenge to inhibiting prescriptions of propriety threatens the stability of her own carefully constructed bourgeois gender identity, as much as Clare seems to threaten the stability of Irene's marriage itself. If Clare turns her provocative smile upon a waiter rather than reserving it for her husband, if she can confess to Irene a lack of "racial ethics" or duty to a "group sense" – "'It's just that I haven't any proper morals or sense of duty, as you have, that makes me act as I do'"– but still retain her social position, Irene is forced to acknowledge that no amount of prudery will secure her place in the bourgeoisie (210).

While Irene fiercely claims an allegiance to "her race" – that loyalty and race pride that Kaplan identifies as a "fixing" essentialism – like other members of the black bourgeoisie she nevertheless distinguishes herself from the "disagreeably damp and sticky crowds" of working-class blacks that threaten to "damage . . . her appearance" (147), and she employs dark-skinned maids to further secure the class divide underscored by colorism. Irene, a consummate "race woman," denies she passes for white "except for the sake of convenience" (227), but the most obvious example of Irene's adoption of a class-inflected colorism is the nature of her participation in racial uplift. Irene, by selling tickets for the Negro Welfare League dance to whites who attend to "get material to turn into shekels . . . . to gaze on those great and near great while they gaze on the Negroes" (197), sells blackness as spectacle. And in participating in a primitivist commodification of "the race," Irene must distinguish herself as somewhat apart from it, for she would be mortified to be seen as a spectacle herself. Both Irene and her husband Brian undertake what they call racial uplift primarily to further distinguish themselves as members of the middle class and to further distance themselves from working-class blacks in Harlem: "'Uplifting the brother's no easy job. . . . Lord! how I hate sick people, and their stupid, meddling, families, and smelly, dirty rooms, and climbing filthy steps in dark hallways'" (186). By characterizing Brian as indulging in classist stereotypes of the "ignorant" and "dirty" masses just as Irene does, Larsen indicts the elitist notion of uplift that, in the name of elevating the image of African Americans as a whole, often attempted instead to raise the image of bourgeois blacks by arguing for their similarity to middle-class whites and their difference from the urban working classes and poor. Brian would rather live in Brazil, a country less racist than America but also one in which, as Carl Degler notes wealth and color were co-determinants of social acceptance and position, so that a middle-class income and position could "whiten someone of African descent" like Brian (102). Yet, Larsen ironizes Brian's desire to escape Harlem for Brazil; he seems unaware that by the end of the 1920s Brazil had come to virtually deny blacks entry into the country through a series of visa denials to applicants of African descent (Little 182, note 2).

Brian also fails to recognize that his bourgeois elitism and distaste for his work, which brings him into the homes of Harlem's working class, amount to an act of passing of sorts, but Larsen represents Irene as all too aware of what it takes to maintain her identity. Far from criticizing whites who visit Harlem in such numbers that "pretty soon the coloured people won't be allowed in at all, or will have to sit in Jim Crowed sections" (198), Irene actively cultivates the shared society and attention of Manhattan's elite, like " *the* Hugh Wentworth." Irene flatters the "too sincere" Hugh as though he was the one exception to the "purely predatory" or merely "curious" white men who frequented Harlem (207). Moreover, concerned that the whiteness she has adopted remain secure, Irene views passing with disdain in order to deny both the passing she enacts and the danger she is well aware accompanies all forms of it: "'Tell me, honestly, haven't you ever thought of "passing"?' Irene answered promptly: 'No. Why should I?' And so disdainful was her voice and manner that Clare's face flushed" (160). Irene is obsessed with securing both herself and others to the place in which they belong and is frightened by Clare because she can neither place her nor be certain that Clare will keep to her place; consequently, Irene desperately tries to keep Clare at a distance: "Actually they were strangers. Strangers in their ways and means of living. Strangers in their desires and ambitions. Strangers even in their racial consciousness. Between them the barrier was just as high, just as broad, and just as firm as if in Clare did not run that strain of black blood" (192). Even though Irene must deny affinity with Clare and her actions in order to deny her own passing, she is unable to "fix" Clare despite warning her that returning to Harlem "isn't safe." Clare refuses to occupy a marginal position, nor does she seem to be willing to continue to choose one racial identity at the expense of the other. Clare comes to threaten both Irene's security and the "purity" of whiteness because she views identity as performable and therefore fluid, rather than a fixed essence.

To this point, it would appear that Fauset and Larsen are focused primarily on the imbrications of gender, race and class as "fixers" of identity that the passing mulatta can render performable and thereby destabilize. But,

as Kaplan points out in her brief reading of *Passing*, "though Clare is a master of performativity, she turns out to be a fervent . . . essentialist," making her a figure "whose racial identity is profoundly torn between essentialism and constructionism" (162, 164).   In fact, driving Clare's daring and "having" decision to pass between white and black and making her passing all the more threatening is her reawakened desire to somehow become black again through association: "'You don't know, you can't realize how I want to see Negroes, to be with them again, to talk with them, to hear them laugh" (200). Through her repeated trips uptown to Harlem, Clare hopes to recover that "black" something "not definite or tangible" that passing for white has cost her (206). Clare's desire to recover her essential "blackness" and the conversation between Brian, Irene and Hugh Wentworth at the Negro Welfare League dance foreground various notions of race popular during the early twentieth century.
  In this conversation, Brian espouses a belief that race is mystical to a certain extent, that passers are almost always drawn back to "the race" for some inexplicable reason: "'If I knew that, I'd know what race is'" (185). Irene also expresses a similar view, telling Hugh that African Americans can always determine an individual's race, if "not by looking," then by some almost sixth sense: "'I'm afraid I can't explain. Not clearly. There are ways. But they're not definite or tangible'" (206). Whites, on the other hand, cling to the belief that an individual's appearance will always betray his or her race, a notion which Larsen and her African American characters mock and play on. At the novel's outset, Irene fears that she has been found out while passing for white at the Drayton Hotel in Chicago, but she quickly dismisses the possibility because whites can never "tell": "White people were so stupid about such things for all that they usually asserted that they were able to tell; and by the most ridiculous means, finger-nails, palms of hands, shapes of ears, teeth, and other equally silly rot" (150). However much Brian and Irene believe race cannot be determined by relying on the body as decipherable text or repository of racial difference, they nonetheless insist that blacks can recognize some black "essence" in an individual passing for white, while whites cannot: "'We know, always have. They don't. Not quite. It has, you will admit, its humorous side, and, sometimes, its conveniences'" (185). Irene, Brian and whites like Hugh Wentworth seem equally unwilling to view race as a performative and prefer instead to believe that there is a "trick" by which they can somehow detect an individual's race or who is passing for what. Indeed, Hugh is convinced that if he were to spend some time with Clare he would know with certainty whether she is as white as she seems.

While they saw constructionism as one view of identity alongside essentialism, Fauset and Larsen were also highly aware of the limits of conceiving identity as performative within a racist society. Passing for white may be figured by Fauset and Larsen as a strategy for redressing an imbalance of power in America, but the passer must necessarily access and thereby reinscribe that power imbalance to a certain degree in order to pass successfully. Moreover, this is an act that is limited in scope by the fact that only the fair-skinned can possibly pass for white. Fauset and Larsen dramatize an individual act that few African Americans can choose to perform as potentially subversive of constructions that structure an entire society around difference. In passing for white, Fauset's and Larsen's heroines are simultaneously complicit with the racial, class, and gender hierarchies they also subvert, and these writers appear to be quite interested in attending to the costs exacted in order to keep the color line firmly in place. Fauset's *Plum Bun* treats passing with just such ambivalence; while Fauset foregrounds the subversive potential in Angela's decision to pass for both white and black, she seems more critical of Angela's mother's acts of passing[18]. Mattie Murray, quick to proclaim a certain racial solidarity by being the "first to announce that she liked to sit in the balcony or gallery" (115), occasionally passes for convenience, but Fauset is careful to point out that this is a convenience in which the majority of African Americans cannot partake: "Much of this pleasure, harmless and charming though it was, would have been impossible with a dark skin" (16). Mattie repeatedly reassures herself that her brief acts of passing violate no "genuine principle" (19, 32); but her passing ultimately brings about her husband's death by pneumonia, contracted on a bitter winter day while waiting outside a whites-only hospital to which Mattie has been rushed after fainting while passing for white. Even though she writes the passer's body as an illegible and malleable text through which both whiteness and blackness can be staged, Fauset confronts the limits of particular bodies as they are blocked by a color line that exacts very high costs. Angela's passing hurts no-one materially but herself, yet her mother's passing arguably exacts her father's life, thereby raising the question of whether a constructionist view of identity (Angela's passing as performative) risks more than an essentialist view (Mattie's passing as an intermittent dalliance from her "authentic" identity). A performative notion of race might appear to radically undo the logic of racial difference operative in Fauset's time, but can it speak to the material conditions that secure the color line? Fauset seems both critical of passing and interested in its subversive potential and limits in *Plum Bun*, as she interrogates the various possibilities opened up by the epistemological paradigms undergirding it.

Ultimately, however, Larsen's and Fauset's novels differ from most narratives of passing by moving beyond a representation of passing as an act in which the goal is to be mistaken for white. Rather, their novels hold in tension a "residual essentialism" with their challenge to a conventional understanding of passing as an act of suppressing a "prepassing" identity in order to perform as the racial "other.",[19]   Using the mulatta's "genealogy" to hold in tension essentialist and constructionist understandings of passing and race, Fauset and Larsen remind us that the mulatta is no more authentically "black" before passing than she comes to be "white" in and through the pass. In an era that understood race as a white/non-white binary, to refuse to stabilize the mulatta's racial identity as either black before or white after the pass is to challenge conceptions of race at their core. What their readers might miss when it comes to this critical understanding of the mulatta, Fauset and Larsen choose to dramatize in Angela's and Clare's determination to pass for both black and white, to move between and within both cultures and communities. Significantly, Angela realizes that race is asymmetrically inflected with power in the novel's opening section where her experiences teach her not only that whiteness is a "badge of power," but also that for some Americans racial identity is malleable rather than stable: "[T]hey had power and the badge of that power was whiteness. . . . She possessed the badge, and unless there was someone *to tell* she could possess the power for which it stood" (73-4, my emphasis). Angela also realizes that race is predicated on a belief in the body as a repository of racial "traits" and is thereby rooted in a politics of visibility, and she chooses to play race against itself by "telling" only her whiteness: "'I am both white and Negro and look white. Why shouldn't I declare for the one that will bring me the greatest happiness, prosperity and respect?'" (80). Fauset seems to argue for a view of race as neither a self-contained polarization of white and non-white, nor a stable, reliable text written on the body, yet she also inscribes a rather essentialist view of race in certain scenes. Depicting Angela dressing for her first date with Roger – a man she quickly discovers is a racist, making the credibility of her performance all the more necessary and potentially subversive – Fauset invokes the racialization of gender identities as well as beliefs in the body as an index of "racial character": "There was never very much colour in her cheeks, but her skin was *warm and white*, there was *vitality beneath her pallor*; her hair was *warm*, too, . . . there were little tendrils and wisps and curls in front and about the temples which *no amount of coaxing could subdue*. . . . Her dress was flame-colour. . . . The neck was high in back and *girlishly modest* in front" (122, my emphasis). Fauset plays on the idea of race read in the body by invoking the notion that blackness – a warm vitality lurking beneath fair skin and in hair that cannot be completely straightened – cannot be "subdued" and will betray the passer even if only in very subtle ways, and by representing Angela's whiteness as a "pallor" finding expression in a high-necked and "girlishly modest" dress.

Angela neither "becomes" white nor "remains" black; rather, Fauset holds suspends these within the mulatta figure. Angela's performance comprises both identities, and while Roger and the novel's other white characters do "mistake" Angela for white, there is evidently a certain blackness to her performance of whiteness that an African American teacher seems to notice at a party given by Angela's bohemian friends: "The young woman [was] perfectly at ease in her deep chair . . . with a slightly detached, amused objectivity . . . which she had for everyone in the room including Angela at whom she had glanced once rather sharply" (115). Amy Robinson's argument that passing is "a triangular theater of identity" enables us to read this scene as yet another instance of Fauset's play on "New Negro" identity politics (716). "In response to the threat of the pass," contends Robinson, "members of the in-group resubstantiate the ground of identity endangered by the passer" (721). Suggesting it takes one to know one, Fauset's scene positions the "detached and amused" black schoolteacher as what Robinson calls the "in-group clairvoyant," who along with the passer and her white "dupes" form a triangle that "poses the question of the passer's 'real' identity as a function of the lens through which it is viewed. Resituating the question of knowing and telling in the terms of two competing discourses of recognition, the pass emerges as a discursive encounter between two epistemological paradigms" (723-34). We could say that while the clairvoyant reads race through an essentialist lens – the passer's real identity is knowable, the dupe sees only the performance – the passer is taken to be the white woman she passes for. Rather than configuring Angela's "real" identity as ultimately detectable by an insider, then, this scene and those conversations in *Passing* where race and its detectability are discussed work to play essentialism and constructionism against one another in ways that Fauset and Larsen work to keep open.

Critics have argued, however, that the ending of *Plum Bun* marks it as a conventional novel of passing because eventually "the passer learns that, regardless of the motivations for passing, such a choice has overwhelming costs" (Little 173).[20] However, Fauset in fact violates the convention of returning the repentant passer to the black community and disappoints the expectations raised by this section's title, "Home Again," by making Angela most at home when on the move between Harlem and Greenwich Village, between black and white, and between America and Europe. Fauset "redeems" Angela's transgression against her family ties and "race loyalty," conventional consequences of choosing to pass for white, in a sentimentalized fashion that paradoxically moves her further from that return to "home" inscribed in narratives of passing. Angela comes to see her life passing for white as "pale" and, coupled with the melodrama of her love for Anthony Cross (who is engaged to her sister Virginia), is represented as fittingly "punished" for her transgressions. Angela contemplates death "more than once" as an escape, but her "blackness" is credited with her determination to "set up a dogged fight. . . . She thought then of black people . . . and of all the odds against living which a cruel, relentless fate had called on them to endure. And she saw them as a people powerfully, almost overwhelmingly endowed with the essence of life" (309). In romantic racialist rhetoric, Fauset represents Angela as saved from death by a black "essence of life" and a willingness to endure all cruelty from which she gains a "newly developed sympathy and under-standing" that makes her think of others in an ideally selfless manner. Angela is certainly "re-educated," but rather than returning home to her black family and community, she decides to live "a double life, move among two sets of acquaintances. . . . when it seemed best to be coloured she would be coloured; when it was best to be white she would be that" (252-53). Fauset represents Angela's life within and passing between white and black as both a performance and the "natural" consequence of her being neither white nor black but both. Yet while Angela's biraciality places her within both races, she also realizes that much of her life will be a performance of both the identity she chooses to adopt in different circumstances and that determined for her by others: "'I can't placard myself, and I suppose there will be lots of times when in spite of myself I'll be "passing"'" (373). Even in what appears to be a conventional ending, Fauset holds in tension the notion that identity is constructed and therefore performable and that it is essential, that identity categories can be subverted and played upon at will and that they determine our identities. In the end, Angela's racial identity is represented as so ambivalent that it is difficult to determine what is performance and what is "genuine," what is constructed and what is "natural."

Like Angela Murray, Clare Kendry tests boundaries that she can at times subvert but that are also reasserted in decidedly more forceful ways than Fauset depicts. Clare could be said to pass between white and black so successfully that she renders herself racially ambiguous: her white husband jokingly teases that Clare's complexion is "gettin' darker and darker" and that one day he might "find she's turned into a nigger" (171), but he never suspects she has gone the other way; and neither Irene's African American nor her white friends seem able to tell if Clare is as white as she seems, or if she is black. As Irene so accurately perceives, Clare is "some creature utterly strange and apart" (172). Clare's excessive performance spills over limits in ways Irene finds threatening, but the excesses of Clare's performance also signal Larsen's revision of the narrative of passing. Larsen invokes the fear of detection that drives passing narratives in order to play on it, and Clare, it seems, is in on the game. Irene repeatedly discourages Clare from coming to Harlem under the pretext of concern for her "safety." And while Irene is clearly more concerned with her own safety than Clare's, Clare, conversely, is so unconcerned that she seems to take a certain delight in placing herself in situations of potential jeopardy, "stepping always on the edge of danger. Always aware, but not drawing back or turning aside" (143). [21] Rather than dressing "inconspicuously" to avoid attracting attention, however, she chooses to "flaunt" herself:

> Clare, exquisite, golden, fragrant, flaunting, in a stately gown of shining black taffeta, whose long, full skirt lay in graceful folds about her slim golden feet; her glistening hair drawn smoothly back into a small twist at the nape of her neck; her eyes sparking like jewels. Irene. . . . regretted that she hadn't counselled Clare to wear something ordinary and inconspicuous. What on earth would Brian think of deliberate courting of attention? (203)

Clare draws attention to herself and to the excesses of her performance, rousing suspicion that she may be "acting" and eventually attracting the speculation that there is something in her that must be "found out" (205).

Clare's flaunting display not only runs the risk of exposing her passing, but also works to expose and transgress the very limits of the identities she performs. While transgressing limits eventually jeopardizes Clare's ability to continue her performance, reading her passing through Homi Bhabha configures its power as lying in those self-jeopardizing moments, in their *"performative deformative* structure that does not simply . . . transpose values 'cross-culturally' . . . [but] introduce[s] another locus of inscription and intervention, another hybrid, 'inappropriate' enunciative site" (241-42). Clare's skin color becomes neither a mark of inclusion nor victimage, but "an ivory mask" (157) with which she accesses and challenges notions of identity as embodied and fixed in the body. Clare's skin is both "ivory" and "gettin' darker and darker"; rather than concealing a mastery of whiteness, Clare's "ivory face was what it always was . . . . *a little masked* " (220, my emphasis). Clare uses her body and that body's acts – the supposed indices of her identity – as masks that both conceal and display, are both ivory and dark. Following Judith Butler's contention that "gender is always a doing. . . . performatively constituted by the very 'expressions' that are said to be its results" (*GT* 24-5), Clare's performance of both whiteness or blackness refuses a conformity to those identities and, therefore, an affirmation of their stability and a contribution to their regulation. Whiteness and blackness do not pre-exist in some "original" state that Clare re-presents. Rather, we might translate Butler's notion of "gender trouble" to a racialized context and argue that Clare transforms whiteness and blackness to include something other that renders them impure and unstable.

Just as we can argue that Clare unsettles received understandings of race as natural and fixed by passing within and between blackness and whiteness, she can also be read as unsettling sexuality as a valence of identity. Clare lives as heterosexual with her white husband, yet she also flirts with homosexuality in a number of "encounters" with Irene that Deborah McDowell was the first to argue form a homosexual subtext to Larsen's novel. [22] However, reading Clare's sexuality as homosexual passing for heterosexual, as McDowell's reading suggests, elides the possibility that Clare is in fact "passing" between these sexualities, neither of which is more "authentic" than the other, more "true" to who Clare is. Clare does "caress" Irene with her smile, her touch, and her kiss in flirtations that clearly appeal to Irene, who is repeatedly struck by how "lovely" Clare is. With Irene, our gaze lingers on Clare in what are decidedly sensual descriptions:

> [T]hat pale gold hair, which, unsheared still, was drawn loosely back from
> a broad brow . . . . Her lips, painted a brilliant geranium-red, were sweet

and sensitive and a little obstinate. A tempting mouth. The . . . ivory skin
had a peculiar soft lustre.   And the eyes were magnificent! dark,
sometimes absolutely black, always luminous, and set in long, black
lashes. Arresting eyes, slow and mesmeric. . . . mysterious and concealing.
. . . [T]here was about them something exotic. (161)

However, Larsen is careful to point out Clare's flirtatious behavior with men as
well; Clare turns "provocative" smiles and her "husky voice" on waiters, her
husband, and the husbands of other women as well (220-21). Martha J. Cutter
has also noted that "Clare insists on being an object of attraction to *both* sexes"
(90) and that she consistently incites interest to successfully further her own
aims. This act of passing for and between heterosexual and homosexual is yet
another instance of the subversive disruption Clare's performance presents, for
it challenges our notions of sexuality as fixed rather than another performative
identity.

Still, even as we can read their narratives through theories of identity
as performative, Fauset and Larsen do not deny or ignore that such
transgression carries with it punishments. Valerie Smith speculates that she
finds "discussions of the performativity of race and gender . . . of limited
usefulness precisely because . . . I resist the evacuation of historical experience
from the construction of raced and gendered bodies" (51). However, texts like
Fauset's and Larsen's enable readings of race as performative, even as they
work throughout to inscribe the historical experience of African American
women in their explorations of identity politics. [23] Nor do Fauset and Larsen
ignore what has been, historically, the outcome of transgressing the color line in
America. However much Angela might continue to pass at her will, she is
nevertheless banished from American society with Fauset's decision to relocate
her to Paris where she may appear to be far less threatening. But that removal
also acknowledges the realities of racism in America at a time when African
Americans were being lynched on the mere suspicion that they had stepped out
of place. Fauset suggests that, while seeing identity as construct and radically
unfixed has political potential, the potential of passing for both black and white
in America is severely limited and imminently dangerous. Clare's punishment
is far more extreme – she falls to her death from a sixth floor window. While
Larsen leaves the cause of Clare's death ambiguous, inviting readers to imagine
that her husband or Irene may have pushed her or that Clare jumped, she
clearly underscores the fact that Irene's and John Bellew's identities are re-

secured with Clare's death. In their endings, then, Fauset's and Larsen's novels acknowledge the very real material effects of passing on the lives of their characters. It is, then, in their use of the passing mulatta to challenge notions of essential racial difference and to dramatize the limits and potentials of identity politics in their time that Fauset and Larsen are not only at their most political but also their most relevant to the continuing debates over "blackness." By carefully attending to the complex imbrications of gender, race, class and sexuality, they suggest that choosing either authentic or performable blackness (and whiteness) will not sufficiently address the investments in and resulting contests over this identity, nor will doing so adequately attend to the highly varied material conditions impinging upon it at particular moments and in specific locations.

Teresa Zackodnik

NOTES

[1] See also the contributions to Henry Louis Gates, Jr (ed), *"Race," Writing, and Difference* (Chicago: U of Chicago P, 1986); Mae Henderson (ed), *Borders, Boundaries, and Frames: Cultural Criticism and Cultural Studies* (New York: Routledge, 1995); Gina Dent (ed), *Black Popular Culture,* and Michael Awkward, *Negotiating Difference: Race, Gender, and the Politics of Positionality* (Chicago: U of Chicago P, 1995).

[2] In *Codes of Conduct,* Holloway maintains that "[i]n American culture, and in the imaginative representations of that culture in literature, our compromised environments valorize publicly constructed racial and sexual identities, but they do not support privately authored identities that may be at odds with public representations" (60).

[3] For an example of stylizations that can reach back to tradition as well as address current political concerns as they stake an identification, see Kobena Mercer's "Black Hair/Style Politics," *Out There: Marginalization and Contemporary Cultures,* ed. Russell Ferguson, et al (Cambridge: MIT P, 1990), 247-64.

[4] See Philip Brian Harper, "Passing for What? Racial Masquerade and the Demands of Upward Mobility," *Callaloo* 21.2(1998): 381-97; and Amy Robinson, "Forms of Appearance of Value: Homer Plessy and the Politics of Privacy," *Performance and Cultural Politics,* ed. Elin Diamond (London: Routledge, 1996), 239-61.

[5] In "Passing for What? Aspects of Identity in Nella Larsen's Novels," Cheryl Wall distinguishes between Helga Crane of *Quicksand* and Clare Kendry of *Passing.* "Helga is an admirable character

because she recognizes early on that 'passing' is not worth the price. Her integrity earns her no victory; her rebellion is as ineffectual as the dishonorable Clare's" (109). Haryette Mullen echoes Wall's contention in her characterization of African American authored passing narratives as a whole (see especially p. 73).

6 See, for example, the essays collected in Elaine K. Ginsberg (ed), *Passing and the Fictions of Identity* (Durham: Duke UP, 1996) for readings that contend passing narratives render the notion of stable or fixed identity and identity categories like race, gender and sexuality a fiction.

7 In her introduction to *The Sleeper Wakes: Harlem Renaissance Stories By Women*, Marcy Knopf notes that DuBois and Fauset "together . . . published the literature of the 'Talented Tenth.' In fact, Fauset was most responsible for this, although DuBois received most of the credit" (xxi).

8 Throughout, I use the term "mulatta" to indicate an American literary figure in use through the 19th to the early 20th centuries in both passing or "tragic mulatta" narratives that explore, to varying degrees, American preoccupations with race and the "threat" of miscegenation.

9 Talented Tenth uplift is regarded as stressing differentiation within African American communities through an attention to class in order to counter homogenizing notions of "blackness." As Alain Locke, who first coined the term "New Negro," would put it, "if it ever was warrantable to regard and treat the Negro *en masse* it is becoming less possible, more unjust and more ridiculous" (6). Even though white Americans found the existence of a black middle class unbelievable, Talented Tenth racial uplift argued that it was this segment of "the race" that could best prove its equality with whites and lift the poor and working-class African American along with it. This kind of disbelief in the existence of a black middle class is evident in Fauset's own publishing career. In 1931 the Frederick A. Stokes Company, having published *Plum Bun* in 1929, expressed reluctance to publish *The Chinaberry Tree*. Fauset's correspondence reveals that the readers at Stokes were uneasy with the novel because it focused on black middle-class characters, and "declare[d] plainly that there ain't no such colored people as these who speak decent English, are self-supporting and have a few ideals" (Fauset qtd in Sylvander 74). While the Talented Tenth could be said to have understood the imbrications of race and class as constructs that bore little relation to African American lived experience, they have been criticized for endorsing white bourgeois norms and regarding the behavior of the black urban working class as impeding their work for social change. See Hazel Carby's "Policing the Black Woman's Body in an Urban Context," *Critical Inquiry* 18(1992): 738-55 for an examination of how black female migrants were policed and pathologized by such a politics.

10 Favor renders this stark opposition more complex by noting that not only DuBois, but also intellectuals like Alain Locke and Arthur Schomburg saw "the rural folk, who [were] in the process of becoming urban proletariat, [as] the basis of African American experience. . . .[F]olk experience [was regarded as] form[ing] the core of the New Negro's identity" (12).

11 Indeed, blood as an image of race loyalty figured prominently in Marcus Garvey's popular "back to Africa" movement of the 1920s. Garvey's Universal Negro Improvement Association agitated for a halt to miscegenation; required its officers to prove that they were "pure African" and forbade them to marry whites; and routinely castigated the NAACP and its "near-white" African American members like DuBois and Walter White for being a "bastard aristocracy" (qtd in Williamson 160). DuBois also invoked "blood" though his politics differed substantially from Garvey's. In "The Conservation of Races," DuBois argued for racial difference: "[Y]et

there are differences – subtle, delicate and elusive, though they may be – . . . which have
generally followed the natural cleavage of common blood, descent and physical peculiarities, . .
divid[ing] human beings into races" (816-17).

[12] For example, see Hazel Carby, *Reconstructing Womanhood: The Emergence of the Afro-American
Woman Novelist* (Oxford: Oxford UP, 1987), and "'On the Threshold of Woman's Era':
Lynching, Empire, and Sexuality in Black Feminist Theory," in *"Race," Writing, and Difference*;
Barbara Christian, *Black Women Novelists: The Development of a Tradition 1892-1976* (Westport:
Greenwood, 1980); and Hortense Spillers, "Notes on an Alternative Model – Neither/Nor," *The
Difference Within: Feminism and Critical Theory,* eds. Elizabeth Meese and Alice Parker
(Philadelphia: John Benjamins, 1989), pp 165-187.

[13] Joel Williamson notes that "light mulattoes in Harlem were also . . . associated with
pandering to salacious if not criminal tastes," a stereotype he speculates was, in part, the result
of a policy on the part of cabaret owners to hire only fair-skinned African American women for
their chorus lines (117).

[14.] Jessie Fauset, *Plum Bun; A Novel Without a Moral* , ed. Deborah E. McDowell (Boston: Beacon P.
1990). All subsequent references will be to this edition.

[15] Several critics have noted that Fauset uses the conventions of the fairy-tale, romance, and novel of
manners for purposes contrary to their traditional functions. However, this is a largely unexplored
dimension of her work that time and space do not permit me to develop fully here, but a dimension
that is certainly worthy of further study. I would argue that just as   Angela passes to gain the
protection and privilege denied her as a black woman, Fauset's text passes as a combination of
fairy-tale, romance, and novel of manners in order to gain her a publisher and audience. More
importantly, I would say that Fauset's novel passes to gain a hearing for her political
contentions about the identity politics that were so central to the Harlem Renaissance. See:
Deborah McDowell, "The Neglected Dimension of Jessie Redmon Fauset," *Conjuring: Black Women,
Fiction, and Literary Tradition* , Marjorie Pryse and Hortense Spillers (eds) (Bloomington: Indiana UP,
1985), 86-104; and her introduction to the Beacon Press edition of *Plum Bun*, "Regulating Midwives";
Gabrielle Foreman, "'Looking Back from Zora, or Talking Out Both Sides My Mouth for Those Who
Have Two Ears," *Black American Literature Forum* 24 (1990): 649-666; Ann duCille, *The Coupling
Convention*, Ch. 5; and Jacquelyn McLendon, *The Politics of Color in the Fiction of Jessie Fauset and Nella
Larsen* (Charlottesville: UP of Virginia, 1995), pp 30-49.

[16] Since the work of Mary Mabel Youmans, virtually every critic working with the novel has
made this argument. See Youmans' "Nella Larsen's *Passing*: A Study in Irony," *CLA Journal*
18(1974): 235-41.

[17.] Nella Larsen, *Passing, American Women Writers Series,* ed. Deborah E. McDowell (New Brunswick:
Rutgers UP, 1994). All subsequent references will be to this edition.

[18] For an alternative interpretation of Mattie Murray's passing see Margaret Stetz's essay on
page 256 of this volume.

[19] I borrow the phrases "residual essentialism" and "prepassing identity" from Amy Robinson's
article "Passing and Communities of Common Interest."

[20.] See also Cheryl A. Wall, "Poets and Versifiers, Singers and Signifiers: Women of the Harlem
Renaissance," *Women, the Arts, and the 1920s in Paris and New York* (New Brunswick, N.J.: Transaction,

1982); and Valerie Smith, "Reading the Intersection of Race and Gender in Narratives of Passing."

[21] Jennifer DeVere Brody also reads Clare as inviting detection: "Clare has never been afraid of being 'found out' – that is Irene's fear. Indeed, Clare might have looked forward to the moment when Bellew would realize that he had been duped by his wife . . . . a triumphant trickster" (1064).

[22] See her introduction to the *American Women Writers Series* edition. A somewhat different version, entitled "'That nameless . . . shameless impulse': Sexuality in Nella Larsen's *Quicksand* and *Passing*," appears in *Black Feminist Criticism and Critical Theory* , eds. Joe Weixlmann and Houston A. Baker, Jr. (Greenwood: Penkevill, 1988), 139-167. Judith Butler, in a chapter of her recent book *Bodies that Matter: On the Discursive Limits of Sex* entitled "Passing, Queering: Nella Larsen's Psychoanalytic Challenge," also attends to the homosexual subtext of the novel but does not explore the possibility that Clare may be passing between sexualities. Similarly, Blackmore argues for a reading of Brian as closeted, and of Irene's desire for Clare as a sexual longing she cannot bring herself to acknowledge, yet does not explore this possibility of passing for and between hetero- and homosexual.

[23] Fauset characterizes the Murrays as part of the black middle class, and attends to the ways in which their class position still cannot afford Angela the access to further education and artistic training that she desires during a period in which segregation limited educational and employment opportunities for African Americans. Larsen positions Clare as the working-class outsider in her largely middle-class circle of schoolgirl friends, and traces her passing back to her desire to have the kind of security and acceptance she lacked then.

WORKS CITED

Berlant, Lauren. "National Brands/National Body: *Imitation of Life*." *Comparative American Identities: Race, Sex, and Nationality in the Modern Text* . Ed. Hortense Spillers. New York: Routledge, 1991. 110-40.

Bhabha, Homi K. "Conclusion: 'Race," Time and the Revision of Modernity." *The Location of Culture*. New York: Routledge, 1994. 236-56.

Brody, Jennifer DeVere. "Clare Kendry's `True' Colors: Race and Class Conflict in Nella Larsen's *Passing*." *Callaloo* 15.4(1992): 1053-65.

Butler, Judith. *Bodies that Matter: On the Discursive Limits of Sex* . New York: Routledge, 1993.

---. *Gender Trouble: Feminism and the Subversion of Identity* . New York: Routledge, 1990.

Cutter, Martha J. "Sliding Significations: Passing as a Narrative and Textual Strategy in Nella Larsen's Fiction." *Passing and the Fictions of Identity* . Ed. Elaine K. Ginsberg. Durham: Duke UP, 1996. 75-100.

Degler, Carl N. *Neither Black Nor White: Slavery and Race Relations in Brazil and the US* . New York: Macmillan, 1971.

duCille, Ann. *The Coupling Convention: Sex, Text,and Tradition in Black Women's Fiction* . Oxford and New York: Oxford UP, 1993.

Fauset, Jessie Redmon. *Plum Bun; A Novel Without a Moral*. 1928. *Black Women Writers Series*. Ed. Deborah E. McDowell. Boston: Beacon P, 1990.

Favor, J. Martin. *Authentic Blackness: The Folk in the New Negro Renaissance* . Durham: Duke UP, 1999.

Hall, Stuart. "What is this 'Black' in Black Popular Culture?" *Black Popular Culture: A Project by Michele Wallace*. Ed. Gina Dent. Seattle: Bay P, 1992. 21-33.

Harper, Philip Brian. *Are We Not Men? Masculine Anxiety and the Problem of African-American Identity*. Oxford and New York: Oxford UP, 1996.

Holloway, Karla F.C. *Codes of Conduct: Race, Ethics and the Color of Our Character* . New Brunswick: Rutgers UP, 1995.

Kaplan, Carla. "Undesirable Desire: Citizenship and Romance in Modern American Fiction." *Modern Fiction Studies* 43.1(1997): 144-69.

Larsen, Nella. *Passing*. 1929. *Quicksand and Passing. American Women Writers Series*. Ed. Deborah E. McDowell. New Brunswick: Rutgers UP, 1994.

Little, Jonathan. "Nella Larsen's *Passing*: Irony and the Critics." *African American Review* 26(1992): 173-82.

Lott, Eric. *Love and Theft: Blackface Minstrelsy and the American Working Class* . Oxford and New York: Oxford UP, 1994.

Mullen, Haryette. "Optic White: Blackness and the Production of Whiteness." *Diacritics* 24.2-3 (1994): 71-89.

Piper, Adrian. "Passing for White, Passing for Black." *New Feminist Criticism: Art, Identity, Action*. Eds. Joanna Frueh, et al. New York: Harper Collins, 1994. 216-47.

Reuter, Edward B. *The Mulatto in the United States* . 1918. The Basic Afro-American Reprint Library, 1970.

Richards, Sandra L. "Caught in the Act of Social Definition: *On the Road* with Anna Deavere Smith." *Acting Out: Feminist Performances*. Eds. Lynda Hart and Peggy Phelan. Ann Arbor: U of Michigan P, 1993. 35-53.

Robinson, Amy. "It Takes One to Know One: Passing and Communities of Common Interest."
        Critical Inquiry 20(1994): 715-36.

Smith, Valerie. "Reading the Intersection of Race and Gender in Narratives of Passing."
        diacritics 24(1994): 43-57.

Wall, Cheryl A. Response to "Performing Blackness: Re/Placing Afro-American Poetry."
        Kimberly W. Benston. *Afro-American Literary Study in The 1990s*. Eds. Houston A.
        Baker, Jr. and Patricia Redmond. Chicago: U of Chicago P, 1989. 185-90.

---. "Passing for What? Aspects of Identity in Nella Larsen's Novels." *Black American Literature
        Forum* 20(1986): 97-111.

Williamson, Joel. *New People: Miscegenation and Mulattoes in the United States* . New York: Free
        P, 1980.

Young, Robert J.C. *Colonial Desire: Hybridity in Theory, Culture and Race* . London and New York:
        Routledge, 1995.

4.

WHITENESS AS UNSTABLE CONSTRUCTION :
KATE PULLINGER'S *THE LAST TIME I SAW JANE*

'Maybe it is this thing about whiteness,' she said,
'the social construct of whiteness, of white femininity'.
(Pullinger 246)

Making whiteness visible and de-normalising it in an anti-racist perspective is no longer a new phenomenon. Emerging from different fields such as feminist theory, sociology and psychology, numerous books and articles have been written on the topic. The pace has accelerated lately and today a danger seems to be writing too much (because that literature runs the risk of re-inscribing whiteness in the centre of inquiry) rather than not enough about what has sometimes (and ironically) been labelled white studies.

However, one field which has so far been mostly ignored in thinking about whiteness is the literary field. Indeed, with the notable exception of Toni Morrison's essay *Playing in the Dark*, published in 1992, not much has been written about the relation between literature and whiteness, or whiteness in literature. This is a rather strange state of affairs because, as Morrison demonstrates in her essay, the opposition between whiteness and blackness is constitutive of American canonical literature and works as the unacknowledged referent from which Americaness is defined. Moreover, numerous works of fiction, in and beyond the American context, are today addressing the issue of whiteness, even if critical responses are lacking.

This concern with whiteness is especially visible in the case of emergent literatures that are intertwined with the history of the British Empire and its aftermath and which are often engaged in destabilising the arbitrary link between whiteness and the universal. The novel *The Last Time I Saw Jane* belongs to that category of fiction. In this novel, Kate Pullinger explores 'this thing about whiteness' and presents a complex vision of the meanings and contradictions inherent in de-normalising white identities. She does so by discussing the concept of racial purity and by exposing the way it is historically situated and constructed. Tracing the process that brings Audrey, the main character of the novel, to articulate an understanding of, on the one hand, whiteness as a racial identity and, on the other hand, her shifting location as a white woman in the axes of power will be the focus of my analysis. An incursion into theoretical territory will frame my discussion. In addition to racial purity, I will develop here an account of the relational dimension of white identities. Thinking whiteness in those terms will lead me, finally, to conclude that whiteness should be analysed as a performative category, and not as an ontological one.

Whiteness and the myth of racial purity

The 19th century saw the systematic theorising of racial purity from a "scientific" perspective, though such preoccupation had emerged even before that time. Looking for the genealogy of the white race and of European languages, European scientists traced it to the Aryans or Caucasians, the ancient inhabitants of what is today North West India and Pakistan. According to this theory, the Aryans came to Europe through the Caucasus mountains. In *White* Richard Dyer notes that "the Caucasian variant both stressed the Caucasus mountains themselves as a determinant factor on white racial formation and enabled the Aryan myth to be severed, most notably at the hands of Nazism, from its Asian associations" (21). In other words, the Caucasus mountains served as a regenerative metaphor for establishing the purity of white people who were, according to the agenda pursued by the scientists engaged in the research, the purest expression of the human race. Richard Dyer adds that

> the Aryan/Caucasian myth established a link between Europeans and a
> venerable culture known to pre-date Europe's oldest civilisation, ancient
> Greece. . . . The myth's function was to provide a white (that is European-
> like) origin for ancient Greece society. Before the early 19th century, it was
> widely accepted that Greece had been conquered by the Egyptians and
> Phoenicians, from whom the characteristics of ancient Greek culture
> derived. However, . . . in an age of imperialism, such an idea was
> intolerable. Greece was seen as the cradle of Europe, but something had
> given birth to Greece, and that had to be compatible with the European

sense of self and could not therefore be located in Africa. (21)

As Dyer suggests, the deployment of the concept of white racial purity cannot be isolated from its inscription in the western imperialist project, which constructed non-white human beings as degenerative in order to justify their conquest and subjection by European powers.

Such a process of inscription does not imply, however, that the boundaries between self and other, between those who are white and those who are not, were—or still are—static and unproblematic. On the contrary, belonging to the category white, because of its derivation from European imperialism, does not, in fact, depend on phenotypic characteristics, but on relations of power. This is in keeping with the idea that race is not a biological category, but a historical, cultural and ideological one. Thus, for instance, the Irish have not always been included in the category, and had to "earn" their whiteness, or, to paraphrase Noel Ignatiev, to "become white," in the United States in the 19th century. In addition, the category is not homogenous, and some groups, in particular northern Europeans, have, historically and ideologically, been seen as more white—more purely white, one could say—than others, such as southern Europeans.

The myth of racial purity takes particular significance in relation to the construction of white femininity. Examining white femininity in terms of the more general problematic of embodiment, Dyer writes that "all concepts of race are always concepts of the body and also of heterosexuality. Race is a means of categorising different types of human bodies which reproduce themselves" (20). This view is shared by Judith Butler, who asks in "Passing, Queering: Nella Larsen's Psychoanalytic Challenge":

> What would it mean . . . to consider the assumption of sexual positions, the disjunctive ordering of the human as 'masculine' or 'feminine' as taking place not only through a heterosexualizing symbolic with its taboo on homosexuality, but through a complex set of racial injunctions which operate in part through the taboo of miscegenation. Further, how might we understand homosexuality and miscegenation to converge at and as the constitutive outside of a normative heterosexuality that is at once the regulation of racially pure reproduction? (167)

As suggested here, sexual and racial oppressions cannot be understood as part of two separate systems, but must be analysed together as two axes of the same mechanism used by the dominant, heterosexual perspective to define otherness and deviance.

Because of the link between the sexual and the racial, men and women do not experience the "problem of whiteness and sexuality" (Dyer 27) in the same way. As Dyer suggests, "the relation of white men and white women to sexuality is of a piece with Christian iconography and other aspects of white gender roles" (27). According to these roles, white men are the active agents of sexuality who must struggle against their sexual desires because unbridled sexuality is often associated, in the white mind, with black people who are imagined as sexually promiscuous. Thus, sexual drives "are typically characterised as dark" (28) and as a consequence, "dark desires are part of the story of whiteness, . . . as what the whiteness of whiteness has to struggle against" (28).

By contrast with both white men and black people, white women are constructed as pure and innocent. As a result, white women are put in a paradoxical location: they are supposed to be pure, not connected to the body and its desires, but, at the same time, they are the "literal bearers of children" (29). It follows that if whiteness maintains itself at the apex of racial hierarchy because of its assumed universality and invisibility and because the relation of whiteness to the body is one that "aspires to [a state of] *dis*-embodiment" (39), that state "is not entirely available to white women, since femininity itself is characterized by embodiedness. By virtue of gender, white women are also closer to nature, also embodied and therefore less 'dead,' and less deadly empowered, than men" (Davy 196). White women, then, can never be as "white" as white men, simply because of their gender. Thus, the relationship that white women entertain with whiteness is complex because of their unstable position in the axes of power: situated at the crossroad of race and gender, white women are both privileged and discriminated against.

This analysis suggests that the problematics of race and gender are inescapably entwined: simple binaries have to be replaced by more complex patterns in order to analyse domination. Consequently, the concept of whiteness becomes multiple and, at times, paradoxical.

Identity as a relational process

Complexifying binaries is Susan Stanford Friedman's aim in "Beyond White and Other: Relationality and Narratives of Race in Feminist Discourse." In this article, Friedman argues that thinking about identity in terms of binary opposition between self and other "create[s] dead ends" (7). Binaries "must be supplemented by . . . relational narratives in which the agonistic struggle between victim and victimizer is significantly complicated" (7). As we saw above, such a proposition has a particular resonance in the case of white women.

According to Friedman, the main problem with binary narratives that divide the world between self and other is that they "are too blunt an instrument to capture the liminality of contradictory subject positions or the fluid, nomadic, and migratory subjectivities of . . . the 'new geography of identity'" (7). Friedman is arguing here that binary thinking cannot account for a postmodern subjectivity, a subjectivity in which "identity is neither continuous nor continuously interrupted but constantly framed between the simultaneous vectors of similarity, continuity and difference" (Hall qtd in Frankenberg and Mani 295). Such a pattern disrupts the workings of power because it means that one can be, simultaneously, self and other, depending on one's position in the axes of power and representation. The fluidity of this model of subjectivity, based on an understanding of the relational nature of identity, presents a challenging framework from which to think whiteness: by looking simultaneously at the different axes that cross and shape one's identity, such as, for instance, the axes of gender and ethnicity, it appears that one's white identity, in relation to power dynamics, is not fixed; as we have seen previously in relation to white women, one can be at the same time discriminated against and privileged, depending on the axis of power envisaged. This disrupts simple narratives of oppression and privilege embedded in binary thinking. Furthermore, that fluid conceptualisation of identity has very real and concrete consequences. One of which is that if "I" can be, at any time, the other, the way "I" behave towards others will be mirrored by the way others behave towards "me" in my positionality as other in respect to them. In other words, if "Je est un Autre" (Todorov 11), the relationship that "I" built towards others is, in some sense, a reflection of the relationship "I" entertain with "myself".

Moving beyond binaries, Friedman identifies a set of practices that emerged in the 1980's, practices that suggest a new direction for thinking about the relation between self and other: scripts of relational positionality. Connected to discussions about standpoint in the production of knowledge as well as influenced by psychoanalysis, poststructuralism and postcolonial theories, "these scripts regard identity as situationally constructed and defined and at the crossroads of different systems of alterity and stratification" (17). By advocating the "nonunitary, indeterminate, nomadic, and hybrid nature of a linguistically constructed identity" (17), these scripts reject the concept of fixity on which, according to Homi Bhabha, "the ideological construction of otherness" (quoted in Friedman 17) depends. Thus, "scripts of relational positionality construct a multiplicity of fluid identities defined and acting situationally" (Friedman 17) and propose "permeable boundaries between races and ethnicities" (18) that can be crossed flexibly. However, they do not suggest the erasure of differences. On the contrary, "the analysis of structural power relations and systems of domination" (18) remains in the foreground of any examination of identity linked to relational positionality.

Those scripts complicate the link between self and other, and, through thinking in relational terms, show that the concepts of self and other are themselves fluid, thus not locking them in an antagonistic relationship. Here, the concept of *différance* as coined by Jacques Derrida offers an interesting comparison. Instead of positing, as structuralists do, that "meaning is produced . . . through binary oppositions" (Moi 105), Derrida believes that it is "the interplay between presence and absence that produces meaning" (106). That interplay "is posited as one of *deferral*: meaning is never truly present, but is only constructed through the potentially endless process of referring to other, absent signifiers" (106). By means of the concept of *différance*, Derrida shows that meanings are not the result of binary oppositions but that their construction is entangled in the whole web of the linguistic system, thus being connected not to only one other meaning, but to all others.

A parallel can be made between the construction of meanings according to Derrida and relational positionality. In both cases, it is the place of the subject—or the word—its positionality in the system, that determines its meaning or identity. Identity is "fundamentally relational" (Martin and Mohanty qtd in Friedman 20). This accounts for the fact that "victims can also be victimizers; agents of change can also be complicitous, depending on the particular axis of power one considers" (Friedman 18) and that "no single system of domination determines the totality of experience" (19). As long as the users of those scripts of positional relationality do not "obscure important power differentials between individuals and peoples" (39)—a danger that Friedman links to the highly abstract theories of poststructuralism—and ground them "in some patch of terra firma from which to advocate change and exercise agency" (39), those scripts remain a powerful way of moving beyond the binaries of same and other.

The Last Time I Saw Jane

The story of *The Last Time I Saw Jane* revolves around issues such as memory, history and the difficulty of connecting with others. Audrey, the main character, is a white Canadian journalist established in London. The racial diversity she finds in the ex-metropolis clashes with the supposed homogeneity of her native British Columbia. At the beginning of the book Audrey meets Shereen, an Indian lawyer, who becomes her friend, and Jack, an African American TV producer, with whom she starts an affair. After a few months, Jack leaves her to be with Shereen. Nonetheless, Audrey and Jack remain lovers. The trio they form reminds Audrey of a prior triangle she was part of, when still in Canada, formed by her best friend, Jane and by their English teacher, David, with whom Jane had an affair. Later, once at university, Audrey also became David's lover. This first layer of memories, to which Audrey is drawn because of her present situation, is supplemented by another, more ancient one. This second layer stems from Audrey's interest in an historical figure, James Douglas, who left Scotland in 1819, aged 16, to become an agent of Empire in Canada. Douglas's own story, which takes more and more importance in the narrative as the novel unfolds, shows that the concept of racial purity cannot be sustained, but that it is, nonetheless, a carefully elaborated myth. This journey into a double past enables Audrey to articulate her present situation of (un)belonging, to connect with Shereen, and to understand the difference whiteness makes. As Audrey writes about James Douglas, "it comes full circle to me. I feel I'm implicated in all this . . . through whatever it was that brought me to London, to this place" (219).

The novel moves back and forth from the present to the past, interrogating whiteness and showing the relevance of the past in the construction of whiteness as hegemonic and pure, especially in relation to the logic of Empire. The complex sequences of temporal crossings on which the narrative is constructed mirror Audrey's journeys into the past and back. Those journeys enable Audrey to realise that she is white and to ponder the implications of that discovery as well as its consequences.

The Present: a Product of Empire

At the beginning of the novel, Audrey is not aware of her whiteness as such. Or rather, even though she has some kind of superficial knowledge that whiteness is a construct, she does not see herself as implicated in the issue and does not grasp the political ramifications of the domineering status of whiteness in Britain. Even though she writes articles on racial issues and has an affair with a black man, she does not interrogate her own position in the dynamics of power. However, about halfway through the novel, Audrey starts asking herself questions about her past and her origins. She wonders, while looking at her mother's family tree, which shows her English ancestry, "what does it mean to be a product of that Empire, of this migration?" (81) Adjacent to that question lies an interrogation of her own responsibility in the power dynamics inherited from the Empire, because of her whiteness. Yet, that crucial query is only articulated at the very end of the novel, after Audrey's journey into the past has been completed. Until then, she chooses to ignore that variable of her experience. She also chooses not to think of her relationship to Jack, in which she appears to be rather passive, in power terms. As a result, the difference colour makes in a white supremacist society like Britain seems to be ignored by both partners:

> They didn't talk about her whiteness, his blackness. If Jack had thoughts on the subject — whether that might be the tender luminosity of the skin beneath her breasts or the politics of jungle fever, sleeping with the white devil — he did not mention it. And Audrey kept mum too, but it was around them, the immutable fact of the colour of their skin. It does not really exist, Audrey told herself, race is a concept somebody invented to keep us apart. If whiteness is a construct, blackness is too. She didn't worry about the contradictions inherent in what she was thinking, it was easy to block it all out with a kiss. It wasn't a problem. There was no problem. She liked it that way. (91)

The issue of race is present in the background, but it is not articulated explicitly by either member of the couple. Audrey does not see it as relevant to the affair, as if the social context in which it evolves does not have any influence on the relationship. Interestingly, though, the narrator indicates that even though both whiteness and blackness are constructs, the power attached to each of them is vastly different. Thus, it is not enough to uncover whiteness for the construct it is; this must be followed by a deconstruction of the very system of which it is a part. When Jack leaves her to be with Shereen, "Audrey suspect[s] that her other friends would be more approving of the new racial combination, preferring Shereen the Indian with Jack the African-American to Jack the black American with Audrey the white Canadian, but Audrey couldn't see where the cultural advantage might lie" (167). Here as in the earlier quotation, Audrey still cannot figure out the system of which each of those different combinations is part. Because she is not aware of that system – or rather does not want to see it – she can pretend there is nothing that makes her relationship to Jack special. However, in a society such as Britain, the very fact of their racial difference constitutes a statement. Audrey ignores it because it would mean recognising her own colour – whiteness – and realising that even though "race is a concept" (91), it does really exist, in the sense that it has very real consequences in the society she lives in.

This voluntary blindness about her colour is the reason why Audrey, as a journalist, writes articles about others, that is black people, but rarely about white ones and erects solid boundaries between the two. She doesn't recognise herself in the equation. Hence, when she needs to interview people for an article on inter-racial relationships, she thinks about Shereen, who is still only an acquaintance at this stage. The first reluctant impulse over, Shereen agrees to talk to her. The next time they meet, Shereen is curious to know why Audrey writes on racial issues:

> 'Why do you write about race so often?'
> 'Race?' Audrey repeated as though unfamiliar with the word. She blushed. 'Colour?' she said, although she didn't like the sound of that either. 'I do not know. You thought that? I'm embarrassed. I've never been asked that before.'
> 'Haven't you?' said Shereen. 'I do not object, I'm just curious.'
> 'That's okay.' Audrey felt unable to answer. 'I do not know.' Her brain was empty. 'Those things interest me. It's that intersection of cultures that London provides . . . The magazines love it, it's easy to sell, "Inter-racial love", "Inter-racial sex", "Inter-racial parenting". For white

readers it's like going on a cultural safari, is not it? An experimental tour.
Editors especially like anything they think is exotic or strange. There are
not enough black journalists? It's easy to sell. I think I write responsibly.
It's – I do not know.' . . .

Later Audrey felt a little drunk. She lit a cigarette and returned
to Shereen's original question. 'White people who are interested in racial
politics are regarded as weird, voyeurs, cultural interlopers. Aren't they?'
'By whom?'
'Black people. White people . . .'
'I wouldn't know,' Shereen interrupted. 'I'm not an
expert.' (21-22)

Audrey's lack of awareness of the racial dimension of her life and of the articles
she writes is disrupted by Shereen's question. Feeling threatened by Shereen's
comments, Audrey wants to answer. But her motivations prove "difficult to
explain" (21), both to Shereen and to herself because the concepts needed to
answer are not available to her—yet. Shereen's question will become one thread
sustaining the whole narrative because it will make Audrey name precisely
what she is doing and recognise her own involvement in racial problematics. At
this stage, though, Audrey needs to put Shereen at the place of the other in
order to engage with the issue. She does so by establishing a binary opposition
between herself and black people, thus invoking a categorical distinctness
between white and black people. In addition, Audrey tries to turn Shereen into a
representative for all black people. However, Shreeen refuses to be placed in
that role by answering that she is "not an expert" to Audrey's question. This
refusal, along with Shereen's question, will enable Audrey to look for answers
herself, by deconstructing the imperial history and her own history inside it.

But if, as it seems so far, Audrey's own ethnicity, her whiteness, is not
something she is conscious about, or thinks about, why does she arrive at an
attempt to articulate its effects by the end of the novel? What makes it possible
for her to suspect that there is something (of which she has only an intimation at
this stage) to question? Why does she sense that the system of which she is a
part, and in which whiteness is not questioned because of its normative status, is
indeed a system that can be deconstructed?

I would suggest that it is her experience of migration that gives her the
means for such an insight. As we have already seen, Audrey is Canadian. Thus,

her experience of London is one of dislocation, even though she feels somehow at home there. As she says, in London she "found something that belonged to her, something that made her feel she belonged" (158). One reason for that feeling is that London offers a diversity unknown — or rather unacknowledged — in British Columbia. Audrey recalls that

> when she was a teenager . . . [she] used to think that everyone was basically the same. She thought the people around her all came from white Anglo-Saxon stock, or maybe German at a pinch. There were always Chinese kids in her school, even in the interior, Japanese, people from the Asian sub-continent, and of course native people, particularly on the coast. But they — who? her family? her teachers? — thought of BC as a white place, a white British place somehow. Her parents' friends were all white, and that seemed ordinary. (126-127)

Raised in an ethos in which difference does not exist because it is not recognised, London comes as a shock to Audrey:

> when Audrey first came to London she was amazed by how black the city could be. This was something she had not considered when she thought of London, dreamy at seventeen. But it pleased her: she came from a place where on the surface everyone seemed pretty much the same and she craved difference, she craved change. (157)

The juxtaposition of the two quotations shows that Audrey can see difference only when she is prepared to do so. Indeed, British Columbia is not an homogenous place, but, conditioned to see it this way, Audrey cannot envisage another perspective from which to look differently at her surroundings. However, in London she can because she is, in many ways, an outsider. This leads her to engage in a process of defamiliarisation of British Columbia that will allow her to interrogate the system it enacts. It will also allow her to explore the diversity and heterogeneity she herself is made of, rather than containing herself in an identity inherited from the age of Empire.

Experimenting London as a foreigner also allows Audrey the freedom to look at history and to interrogate the norm. For her, London is "a city with a history, not like where she came from" (82). This is the way Audrey has learned to think about her place of birth. London has history, because it represents

Britain and the Empire it used to be, but British Columbia cannot be written into history until colonised, because recognising it to be part of a history before colonialism would disturb the narrative of imperialism as civilisation. That narrative posits that history is the mark, and correlative, of civilisation. However, in her new surroundings, Audrey will be able to look at Canada in a different light and to uncover an alternative history to the one conveyed by the logic of Empire. She will understand that official history is one way of making sense of events, but that other versions, other names, can be applied to the past. Plunging into that alternative history, she will realise how she herself is part of it, because of the continuity between past and present, both diachronically and synchronically.

During Shereen and Audrey conversation I referred to earlier, the issue of migration is addressed by Audrey:

> Audrey . . . ploughed ahead, 'I'm interested in . . . difference.
> The English invented foreigners, it's a national obsession. And yet, we're
> expected to stay in our own corners, are not we?'
>   Shereen gave a polite nod and Audrey let the conversation veer
> away to other things. (22)

The quotation shows Audrey thinking about the consequences of her status and linking the trajectories of herself and Shereen, and also, by implication, Jack. The three of them are foreigners in England — none of them was born there — and the three of them are also products of the same Empire, albeit from different corners of it. Audrey wants to share with Shereen the commonality of their history and experience. However, as when she was thinking about the construction of whiteness and blackness, Audrey does not want to see that the very fact of her whiteness means that her experience of migration, and her history, cannot be superficially paralleled to those of Shereen or Jack. Audrey fails to see the difference whiteness makes in relation to Empire and migration. She refuses to acknowledge that, as Salman Rushdie wrote, "Britain is now two different worlds, and the one you inhabit is determined by the colour of your skin. [As a result] white and black perceptions of everyday life have moved so far apart as to be incompatible" (134) because of the racism of English society.

The Past: History as a Memory

The past that Audrey excavates, and in the process revisits, is not monolithic. On the contrary, it is composed of several layers, all of them ramifying into the present. Jane and David are parts of the first layer. Audrey uses those characters and her memories of that time as a passage between the present and the second layer, that is the nineteenth century, the historical period James Douglas and his half-Cree wife, Amelia, inhabit. Furthermore, a third layer is added with the inclusion of the dynamics of Empire implicit in the story of James's father, John, a white Glasgow merchant, and James's mother, Martha Ann, the daughter of a freed slave. The last two last layers of the past focus on an interrogation of the concept of racial purity, especially in relation to James Douglas. The questions raised in the past are echoed in the issues developed by the contemporary character of Shula Cronin, a social anthropology professor at Toronto University who hires Audrey to do research for her.

The official story of James Douglas, a real historical figure, nicknamed the "father of British Columbia" because he was appointed the first Governor of the mainland colony of British Columbia, obscures his origins. As Audrey recalls,

> there was a mystery about Douglas's origins. . . . The early biographers and historians claimed he was born in Scotland; Douglas's youngest daughter, Martha, who lived well into the twentieth century, had been interviewed and she herself said her father came from Lanarkshire. But later writers cast doubt on this claim. In Hudson's Bay Company journals James was often referred to as 'the Scotch West Indian', and they picked up on this and began to look for clues. However, the truth was very obscure. Apparently Douglas had seen to that. (188)

For the narrative of Empire and its correlation of whiteness as civilisation to be sustained, Douglas had no choice but to erase voluntarily his origins. In order to underline the importance of that "unauthorised" story, the account of James's origins is isolated in *The Last Time I Saw Jane*. It forms a separate part, called "Between". This textual arrangement suggests that it is easy to ignore some aspects of the past, and thus to settle for fragmented stories that perpetuate certain ideologies and, in this particular case, the myth of the purity of whiteness.

The story of James's father, John Douglas, is actually very different from the one James's daughter told to interviewers. John, a merchant from Scotland, holds sugar interests in the Caribbean. On his first trip to Demerara in 1799, he meets Martha Ann Ritchie, a young woman from Barbados, whose mother is a freed slave and her father the mother's previous "owner". Martha Ann becomes John's housekeeper—"housekeeper, mistress, mistress, housekeeper – the words were interchangeable, in Demerara they amounted to the same" (206)—and they have two sons together, Alexander and James. Whereas Martha Ann remains in the Caribbean, John makes frequent journeys back and forth, from Scotland to Demerara. It inevitably follows that "during one of his spells at home in Glasgow, [he meets] Jessie Hamilton at a Green Cloth Club evening party. Jessie Hamilton's *décolletage* was very white. . . . This Glasgow woman would make a good wife" (213). Thus, John Douglas effectively lives two lives:

> John Douglas told Jessie Hamilton nothing about the other woman, his other family in fact, across the Sargasso Sea. And he did not mention his new domestic arrangements to Martha Ann either, although once he made plans for the boys to go [to England], she understood. There was never any communication between the two women, but they knew of each other, they dreamt of each other, they saw themselves reflected in those dreams. North. South. Old. New. Empire and colony. (213-214)

The journey from South to North works as a regenerative metaphor: the two children, separated from their mother to be educated in England, are reborn, made symbolically white in the process of shedding their place of birth and their mother. This way they can be incorporated into the ideological construction of white racial purity. Richard Dyer echoes this point in *White* when he discusses the work of critic Cleo McNelly:

> She suggests that imperialism (and anthropology) are represented in the motif of the journey, which is posited on a notion of '*here* and *there*, home and abroad', which in turn reproduces two figures, 'the white woman at home and her polar opposite, the black woman abroad'. The geographical structure of imperial narrative confirms the binarism discussed above, the white woman as the locus of true whiteness, white men in struggle, yearning for home and whiteness, facing the dangers

and allures of blackness. (36)

The crux of the colonial encounter revolves around sexual transactions between the imperial male subject and his colonial female other, and their rules. Those tacit rules state that black women can be sexually used but that they should never be officially acknowledged, for the symbolic ascriptions of their very colour are a threat to the purity of whiteness and the ideological system it stands for. Only women with a white "décolletage" can perform the role of wives, since their whiteness — and the construction of white femininity as pure and gentle that follows — means the perpetuation of the myth. However, James's story illustrates the vacuity of the concept. Indeed, although the myth has been carefully elaborated in order to sustain the privileges attached to whiteness, whatever historical moment one returns to, there will always be a prior moment, which shows that cultural and racial cross-fertilisation has always existed and that original purity can never be attained. Derrida among others has argued this point in relation to literature, stating that origins do not exist, that deferral is always possible. This radically undermines the myth of white purity, which can only be deployed by negating the endless deferral of meanings.

James Douglas's efforts to hide his origins are to be understood as "myth making" or "ideology sustaining" in progress. This is why, as Audrey recalls, "most biographical portraits of James and Amelia obscured and bleached-out their origins, made them both white and British, good colonial rulers, their Caribbean and Cree mothers erased. Sir James Douglas ensured that things turned out the way London demanded; he secured his place in official history" (247). Interestingly, though, James himself will not follow the rules of Empire beyond rewriting his own past. Indeed, confronted by the example of his father and his father-in-law (William Connolly, who repudiates his Cree wife, Suzanne Pas De Nom, in order to marry a white cousin), James decides to break the implicit rules and to stand by his half-Cree wife, Amelia, marrying her twice, "in the custom of the land and then in the custom of the colony" (122). In doing so publicly and officially, James signifies that from that temporal moment on, ignorance and deception can no longer govern official historical narratives. In some sense, standing by Amelia is a way of reclaiming his own identity, and his mother. In fact, he has understood that what Connolly has done is to repudiate

the very thing upon which [Amelia and himself] were building their lives, mixed blood, the very thing that ran through their veins. In the populated east, people approved of Connolly's actions, they thought he had done the right thing in leaving the Cree woman and marrying one of his own kind. One of their own kind was the very thing that Amelia and James could never be. (103)

Or rather, they could never be one of their own kind in the colonial society in which they live and which abides by the myth of purity. It can be argued, however, that since racial purity does not exist, this couple is a representative of the whole of humankind. James in fact enacts a contradiction between the desire to be part of the narrative of Empire and the profound understanding of the hybrid condition of humanity.

Even though James's and Amelia's marriage seems to make obsolete any further suggestion of racial purity, the power of the ideology of whiteness, which sustained the enterprise of Empire, outlives them. In relation to this, the character of Shula Cronin provides a synchronic link between the past and the present by connecting the history of Canada—of which James Douglas is an agent—with the contemporary movement of Québecois nationalism. When Audrey goes to visit her in Toronto, she says,

> Those nationalists – at their most extreme – believe in racial purity. They think the Québecois are a race. They do – believe me. I am going to write a book that shows how those people, that race, from Samuel de Champlain onwards are descended from mixed blood – the blood of the English as well as the French, the Algonquin, Huron, Iroquois, Mohawk . . . the blood of the French empire – West Indian, Vietnamese, Haitian . . . and that their notion of racial purity is as backward and ill-informed as that of the Ku Klux Klan. . . . Certain things need to be said – it's not their land, how can it be, if it belongs to anyone it belongs to the indigenous people. That's true of the whole of Canada. Same goes for the water, the right to sell hydro-power to the Americans. It's all a lie. Modernity is too mixed up – no one is pure. Purity is a disguise. (118-119)

This paragraph suggests that believing in racial purity, and especially in the racial purity of whiteness, summons a chain of connotations that can only be sustained through the elaboration of rigid borders that exclude some and 'otherise' them through the construction of binaries. Shula Cronin's work aims at destabilising that chain by showing the fluidity and complexity of identity so that the category of the other is continually displaced and, as whiteness becomes visible in the process, at interrogating the imperial ideological system that still governs the logic of the chain. Shula's project disavows the fallacious link between history and civilisation and conjures up the possibility of breaking free from the narrative of official history and the values it conveys, such as the one of origins. Ultimately, Shula's work goes against the idea of forgetting. She wants to remember the past—although not in its official translation—in order to fight ideas that claim to have their roots in the past, such as the notion of racial purity, but that are, in fact, fictions. It is why she says to Audrey, whose father is related to James Douglas, that "our family histories often have relevance to our futures" (120). Audrey will emerge changed from her confrontation with the past because it will make her directly address her whiteness and its consequences. Thus, she will be able to re-create herself through both her personal story and the larger history.

The Present: The (Im)Possibility of Connecting

Towards the end of the novel, Audrey writes a letter to Shula, telling her about the significance of James's story as she understands it:

> It's nine o'clock in the evening, end of the twentieth century. When I think about them now it feels to me as though James and Amelia provided a direct physical link between Britain and its colonies. It's as though these two people were bridges from the past into the future, James descended from both slaver and slave, Amelia from conquered and conqueror, their bodies spanning the abyss. They were it, it was them, they were Empire at its most emblematic and contradictory. They were the conduits over which Europeans could walk into the new world, they provided the passage, they made it easy. (219)

This passage suggests that the complexity of James's and Amelia's identities, constructed at the intersection of power structures (representing as they do both the oppressor and the oppressed), symbolises the very structure of Empire, its constitutive alterity. However, as we have seen, colonisation could only deploy itself through the paradoxical negation of these identities in the name of racial purity (which takes meaning only in contrast with its opposite, impurity). Thus, the myth demands the erasure of the very conditions of its possibility for the imperial historical narrative to be established.

At this point, Audrey understands the significance not only of James and Amelia story, but also of recovering the hybridity they stand for. Furthermore, it seems that the purpose of Audrey's own itinerary is to bring her to recognise the importance of connecting with others without erasing differences, and to an awareness of the distinct positions people occupy in the interplay of power, herself included. The chain goes from James and Amelia to Jane, who is both a gateway to the past and to the present, to Shereen, whose influential presence pervades the last pages of the book. Those pages show the provisional conclusions at which Audrey has arrived in relation to whiteness as well as the consequences of such an awareness.

This last scene starts as a confrontation between Shereen and Audrey over Jack but evolves into a connecting experience between the two women. I would suggest that it is because Audrey has been able to make sense of her memories, both recent and more ancient, as the deconstruction of one particular aspect of whiteness — racial purity — implies, that she can start talking. She can now recognise and articulate the role whiteness is playing in her life. She can name it, thus making it visible, and can start interrogating it. Audrey's conceptualisation of her experience leads her to see the position her colour ascribes to her in the axes of power: "she had been kept separate from Jack, from Shereen, they were different, they each had something she did not, she had something they didn't" (247). Thus, as she failed to do at the beginning of the novel, Audrey now understands the complexity and particularity of her own as well as her friends' experiences, but she also understands that they are all linked to a larger logic, that is the racial dynamics that inform English society.

Furthermore, Audrey grasps now that the social constructions of whiteness and blackness do not hold the same ideological powers. Consequently, she can look at her relation to Jack in a new light: "Maybe it is this thing about whiteness . . . the social construct of whiteness, white femininity. And black masculinity" (246). By saying this, Audrey enters a new dimension of the dynamics of power, at the intersection of gender and racial axes. However, these complex connections between gender and colour, which I touched upon earlier on, are not pursued in the novel in which the main interest of Audrey's relationship with Jack is the impulse it gives her to look at whiteness. She does so first by contrasting her whiteness to his blackness, the same way she otherised Shereen. It is only after she has done so that she can think about whiteness as a specific domain of inquiry in itself.

In *The Last Time I Saw Jane* Audrey exemplifies the importance of destabilising whiteness so that it becomes a specific racial identity rather than the universal referent. However, the threads that make her very being question the pertinence of thinking race (and whiteness) in those terms. Indeed, what Audrey believes to be "reality's betrayal of fantasy" (247), that is the destruction of the illusion of sameness that enforced her whole vision of reality until her migration to London, might in fact reveal a final twist. In fact, the ultimate question that the novel addresses has to do with perceptions of sameness and difference in relation to racial divisions and the relevance of racial boundaries. Throughout the book Audrey is described as white, both in her own and in other people's eyes. However, she is a descendant of James and Amelia Douglas, both of mixed blood origins. In that context, what does it mean to say that Audrey is white? First, it demonstrates that whiteness is an ideology and works symbolically in white supremacist societies. As Shula Cronin argues, "notions of racial purity are a nonsense in a land with a history such as ours" (69), but they are used to erect systems of domination and exclusion by naturalising notions such as purity. This re-conceptualisation of Audrey's identity, by opening a space for questioning purity, also challenges reifying notions about the meaning of racial divisions. In conjunction with Friedman's argument, Pullinger suggests that identity is a relational process and that racial boundaries are not fixed, but permeable because they depend on relations of power, and not on ontological characteristics.

Thus, the very instability of the concept of whiteness becomes explicit, and the performative dimension of white identities emerges. Thinking identity in this way asks for a separation between being white and acting white, between the ontological and the phenomenological. Vron Ware summarises this position when she rejects essentialised notions of whiteness and argues that "whiteness is ultimately about learned behaviour and social consciousness [and that] seeing a distinction between the idea of 'white' as a visible 'racial' type and as a way of thinking and acting in the world is an important step towards exposing the emptiness of the category" (144). Refusing to act white becomes a possibility open to every individual. However, whiteness cannot be understood as simply an individual issue that can be resolved individually. The political disruption of whiteness as performative suggested here must be addressed by both individuals and the larger community to become effective because it seeks to challenge structural relations. Thinking whiteness, in this sense, is a destabilising practice in societies in which power operates at the intersections of race, gender, and class.

By foregrounding the performative dimension of whiteness, *The Last Time I Saw Jane* asks its readers to do exactly what Ware suggests. It appears, as a result, that even though apprehending whiteness in its particularity and dislodging it from its dominant position are two crucial practices of destabilisation, it remains that the category itself is a fiction, albeit a very powerful one. Whiteness deconstructed through those practices could become, once stripped from its oppressive symbolic ascriptions, a non racial signifier, a hue among others.

Myriam Perregaux

NOTES

I am grateful to Alexandra Chasin in Geneva and Louise Staunton in Dublin for their stimulating comments and suggestions.

WORKS CITED

Butler, Judith. "Passing, Queering: Nelly Larsen's Psychoanalytic Challenge". *Bodies That Matter*. New York and London: Routledge, 1993. 167-185.

Davy, Kate. "Outing Whiteness: A Feminist/Lesbian Project". *Theatre Journal* 47 (1995): 189-205.

Dyer, Richard. *White*. London and New York: Routledge, 1997.

Frankenberg, Ruth and Mani, Lata. 1993. "Crosscurrents, Crosstalk: Race, 'Postcoloniality' and the Politics of Location". *Cultural Studies* 7.2 (1993): 292-310.

Friedman, Susan Standford. "Beyond White and Other: Relationality and Narratives of Race in Feminist Discourse". *Signs* 21.1 (Autumn 1995): 1-49.

Ignatiev, Noel. *How the Irish Became White*. New York and London: Routledge, 1995.

Moi, Toril. *Sexual/Textual Politics: Feminist Literary Theory*. London and New York: Routledge, 1995.

Morrison, Toni. *Playing in the Dark. Whiteness and the Literary Imagination*. London: Picador, 1992.

Pullinger, Kate. *The Last Time I Saw Jane*. London: Phoenix, 1996.

Rushdie, Salman. "The New Empire Within Britain". *Imaginary Homelands*. London: Granta Books, 1989. 129-138.

Todorov, Tzvetan. *La Conquête de l'Amérique. La question de l'autre*. Paris: Seuil, 1982.

Ware, Vron. "Defining Forces: 'race', Gender and Memories of Empire". *The Post-colonial Question. Common Skies, Divided Horizons*. Eds. Iain Chambers and Lidia Curti. London and New York: Routledge, 1996. 142-156.

5.

BECOMING CHINESE:
RACIAL AMBIGUITY IN
AMY TAN'S *THE JOY LUCK CLUB*

One of the main issues in *The Joy Luck Club* is racial identity. The way in which Amy Tan's novel represents 'Chineseness' typically generates two related responses from mainstream critics. A consideration of mainstream criticism is necessary because it is often unambiguous in its appraisal, complimenting and/or condemning *The Joy Luck Club* for Orientalizing 'things Chinese'.[1] It is the task of this discussion to problematize debate about racial identity in mainstream criticism via a reading of Tan's novel. The first response from mainstream critics is 'old' Orientalist and is often uncritically committed to this racist ideology. The second response is 'new' Orientalist and comprises two groups, both of which adopt a critical stance regarding the racism of 'old' Orientalism.[2] On the one hand, there are the benevolent intellectuals who approach Tan's novel "with enthusiastic purchases as well as a pleasurable mixture of respect and voyeurism, admiration and condescension, humility and self-congratulation." (Wong 185) They believe that literature by the 'racial other' is "good [and] . . . necessarily right." (Spivak, *Outside in the Teaching Machine*, 188-89) *The Joy Luck Club* thus understood is assumed to deliver reliable information not only about 'things Chinese' but also about "'the really important things in life--Roots, Culture, Tradition, History, War, Human Evil.'" (Wong 200) On the other hand, there are the "'China specialists'" who authoritatively announce that "'this is Chinese' and 'this is not Chinese'" (Chow, "Violence," 89). With respect to *The Joy Luck Club*, China specialists proclaim that it misrepresents China, particularly Chinese myths. More specifically, Chinese myths are faked according to the logic of white racism, western capitalism and first world feminism.[3]

Benevolent intellectuals and China specialists, although offering seemingly opposite responses to *The Joy Luck Club*, imagine the possibility of a non-Orientalist viewpoint.   In other words, Orientalism is understood as having an inside and an outside, with both benevolent intellectuals and China specialists claiming exteriority in order to accomplish ideology critique. Ideology critique exposes Orientalism as mistaken without apparently succumbing to the same ideological misdemeanours of that which it criticizes. That ideology critique seems able to designate 'Chineseness' reliably by disengaging benevolent intellectuals and Chinese specialists from Orientalist ideology is undoubtedly useful. Indeed, their negative critique of Orientalism, coupled with their ability to offer a positive solution to the problems engendered by this ideology, empowers both groups as regards the project of "putting some sort of platform against the white majority" (Spivak, "Neocolonialism," 227).   However, benevolent intellectuals and China specialists overlook the fact that "we are never so much 'in' ideology when we think ourselves 'outside' it" (Warminski 10).   In short, ideology critique is ideological, leaving both groups in Orientalism.   Following this logic, Orientalist ideology is ineradicable, an insight that is also promoted by Edward Said: "the Orient was not (and is not) a free subject of thought or action." (3) *The Joy Luck Club* concedes the persistence of this racist ideology as well. There are no shortage of stereotypical representations of 'the Chinese' and 'the Chinese American' in *The Joy Luck Club*. The fact that these stereotypes feature in Tan's novel suggests that it barely problematizes and, worse, openly promotes Orientalism. Although it is possible to imagine *The Joy Luck Club* in terms compatible with Orientalist ideology, as Sau-ling Cynthia Wong has powerfully argued, it is also worth noting that the assumption of compatibility constitutes a literal and/or a selective response. As it turns out, this response is problematized by the rhetorical dimension of Tan's novel.   Moreover, responding to rhetorical structures makes possible a radical theoretico-political critique, one that functions very differently to the ideology critique of benevolent intellectuals and China specialists because it is insightful regarding the ineradicability of Orientalist ideology.   Its difference is also evidenced insofar as an attention to language, particularly tropes and figures, makes possible insights about the linguistic and by implication the ideological bases of Orientalism, both new and old. For example, inside/outside is a metaphor, functioning reliably only if benevolent intellectuals and China specialists assume an ideological understanding of the rhetorical dimension of language. A critique that addresses the part played by tropes and by figures in effecting

Orientalist stereotypes is also "a powerful and indispensable tool in the unmasking of ideological aberrations, as well as a determining factor in accounting for their occurrence." (De Man, *The Resistance to Theory*, 11)

More specifically, the turn towards language is effective for at least two reasons. First, it involves a turn away from new Orientalist "information retrieval" (Spivak, *The Post-colonial Critic*, 9), resisting the marginalization of other linguistic forms by that which apparently accords them central status. Tan elucidates this point when she comments on the way in which (American) schools and universities include 'ethnic' literature on their reading lists only to ignore its identity as literature through the assignation of a didactic function. Inclusion or centralization thus realized effectively marginalizes and, indeed, censors 'ethnic' literature, something that Tan resists by insisting that her readers respond to the literariness of *The Joy Luck Club*. As she puts it, "there's work to be done to include [other] books in American literature, so that people don't use them entirely for lessons outside of literature" (Stanton, "Breakfast," 7). Second, the fact that Orientalism has its basis in language as opposed to natural reality makes possible contestation. In other words, the assumption of a natural link between 'the Chinese' (an imagined category) and the Chinese (the literal referent) is rhetorically enabled and, as such, is unreliable regarding the latter. Moreover, the movement of language towards and away from an Orientalist meaning and an Orientalist referent makes possible other interpretations of 'the Chinese'. That 'Chineseness' resists a final interpretation is also significant as far as the questioning of racist stereotypes is concerned. With reference to *The Joy Luck Club*, it promotes an insight about the part played by rhetoric in formulating 'the Chinese' and 'the Chinese American', racial categories that are also vulnerable to undoing because tropes and figures "take you in a completely different direction." (De Man, *The Resistance to Theory*, 87) In other words, rhetoric enables the formulation of a racial identity that it simultaneously has the potential to disable. It is important to retain this two-fold perspective of 'Chineseness' insofar as it empowers a radical theoretico-political critique, one that promotes, and, indeed, cannot help but promote, a racial identity, acknowledging both its benefits and its limitations, in a manner that is vigilant regarding the issue of language. Vigilance on this count also makes possible an insight into the ineradicability of Orientalist ideology without uncritically perpetrating an essentialized understanding of 'Chineseness'. All in all, then, ideological aberrations regarding racial identity are unavoidable; at the same time, however, they are vulnerable to critique because they are rhetorically effected, which is compelling in terms of a radical challenge to Orientalism.

It is necessary to consider mainstream responses to *The Joy Luck Club* before analyzing its complex negotiation of Orientalist ideology. In other words, this discussion moves from Orientalism (old and new) to an understanding of the way in which Tan's novel, particularly its ending, "avoid[s] and resist[s] the reading [it] advocate[s]." (De Man, *The Resistance to Theory*, 19) What is more, the debate about racial identity moves from the new Orientalism of inside/outside Orientalist ideology to a properly critical inquiry, which understands 'Chineseness' as linguistically enabled (and disabled). Indeed, the latter part of this discussion offers a reading of three incidents from Jing-mei Woo's "A Pair of Tickets" in order to make the claim that their literariness, a dimension of *The Joy Luck Club* that resists marginalization because it is a literary text after all, both enables and disables 'Chineseness'. More specifically, Jing-mei's comments about "becoming Chinese" (267) on first entering China, discovering China in a packet of shampoo and identifying with her Chinese-born mother and sisters via a Polaroid photograph gesture towards essentialism. However, essentialism is undone because Jing-mei's access to 'things Chinese' happens in language, depending on a(n unreliable) tropological link between a shampoo and a country. Jing-mei's announcement that "This is China" (278) while washing her hair is therefore vulnerable to concepts of difference and deferral. The identities formulated -- individual, family, national, racial -- are simultaneously advanced and avoided, problematizing the claim that *The Joy Luck Club* unambiguously "repackag[es] Orientalism" (Wong 197). According to this reading, *The Joy Luck Club* offers representations that resist for epistemological and for ethico-political reasons an unambiguous understanding of 'Chineseness'.[4]

The Joy Luck Club apparently offers much to the Orientalist, usually receiving favourable criticisms from both popular and academic reviewers. Compliments predominate because Tan's novel seems to adequately accord with western(ized) fantasies of the east. Stereotypical representations of Asia as veiled woman and as eastern queen are transferred to a literary text by an Asian (American): "Tan's visions are rich in magic and mystery" and "She has written a jewel of a book." (Fong 123; Schell 28) It is worth noting that the supernatural east only makes sense if contrasted with an understanding of the west as natural: "From a rational, 'monological' world, otherness cannot be known or represented except as foreign, irrational, 'mad', 'bad'." (Jackson 173) Occidental magic is also left unacknowledged. For example, Christian religious ideology is marked by a supernatural dimension, as is ideology in general insofar as it " = *illusion/allusion*" (Althusser 87). Ideology is magical to the extent that it functions to create the illusion of a reliable reconciliation between linguistic and natural reality, albeit on the basis of an allusion. From this perspective, the binary opposition between the magical east and the mundane west owes much to Orientalist ideology. Moreover, representing 'things Chinese' in terms of riches concurs with the Orientalist fantasy of "Asia as an exotic woman possessing the rare perfumes, precious stones, fine silks, and spices that Europe [and America] desired." (Sharpe 149) The east is in this way objectified, as is *The Joy Luck Club* when described as a jewel. At one fell swoop, then, linguistic and natural reality are essentialized, homogenized and universalized. The emphasis on stereotypical description, coupled with a tendency to eliminate the American dimension of Tan's novel, makes possible the claim that these reviews are uncritically determined by Orientalist ideology.

Orientalism is not the prerogative of the reviewer; indeed, many academic readers affirm this racist ideology as well, whether intentionally or not. So-called radical critics, including benevolent intellectuals and China specialists, perpetrate new Orientalism. The former group, which typically comprises western(ized) thinkers, celebrate "oppressed subjects speak[ing], act[ing], and know[ing] *for themselves*" (Spivak, "Subaltern," 276). They argue for the expansion of disciplinary boundaries to include the 'racial other'. Undoubtedly, congeniality on the part of English in its relation to 'ethnic' literature constitutes something of an improvement, particularly since the transferral of the "'role of referee, judge and universal witness'" (Spivak, "Subaltern," 280) to the 'racial other' plays a significant part in post-colonial criticism. According to this viewpoint, 'ethnic' literature is assigned a critical function, delivering information that contributes to the undermining of English's assumptions about the literary object and/or the 'racial other'. On an elementary level, *The Joy Luck Club*'s dialogic form and 'ethnic' content resist appropriation, along with problematizing the boundary established by English as regards high and low art. Appealing to a diverse readership, this postmodern novel also constitutes something of a challenge to the assumption that literature is the prerogative of the privileged white male.

However, the notion that 'ethnic' literature is reliable inadvertently reinforces conventional approaches to language and to experience, approaches that were supposed to be put into question. The fact that what is radically exterior to English is formulated in terms ultimately compatible with it ensures that 'ethnic' literature barely troubles traditional approaches to scholarship and to teaching. As Gayatri Chakravorty Spivak notes in relation to benevolent intellectuals, they "have [their] cake and eat it too: [they] continue to be as [they] are, and yet be in touch with the speaking subaltern." ("Subaltern Talk" 292) Western(ized) conscience is salvaged because 'ethnic' literature is brought into English. The consciousness of western(ized) intellectuals is preserved from doubt because the ability to determine meaning and reference reliably is a possibility even in confrontation with the radically exterior. For example, a category like the "sovereign subject as author, the subject of authority, legitimacy, and power" (Spivak, *In Other Worlds*, 202) informs the self-understanding of benevolent intellectuals, which empowers them to formulate the truth about 'ethnic' literature. Moreover, sovereign subjectivity provides the 'racial other' with an understanding of identity that is worthy of appropriation, enabling 'subalterns' to intervene effectively in theoretico-political debate. However, uncritical appropriation "restores the category of the sovereign subject within the theory that seems most to question it." (Spivak, "Subaltern," 278) Restoration goes almost unnoticed because the sovereign subject is officially absent. After all, benevolent intellectuals let subalterns speak for themselves. However, the sovereign subject is unofficially present owing to the fact that subalternity is modelled on the imperialist/humanist "hero" (Spivak, *In Other Worlds*, 202).

More specifically, subalterns are formulated in terms compatible with the heroic model insofar as they seem undeceived. Full consciousness is granted to them because they are assumed to share a fundamental relationship with natural reality. An analogy is presupposed between identity and experience: "only the subaltern can know the subaltern". That affinity "is sustained by irreducible difference" notwithstanding, this analogical relationship apparently ensures that subalterns are reliable with regard to meaning and to reference (Spivak, *In Other Worlds*, 253-54). The truth that subalterns represent seems untroubled by partiality, which enables them (and benevolent intellectuals) to participate in information retrieval. However, this potentially radical operation is undermined because benevolent intellectuals affirm otherness according to the logic of new Orientalism, typically understanding the literary object and/or the 'racial other' in terms that ultimately safeguard dominant assumptions. Indeed, benevolent intellectuals need 'ethnic' literature to mean unambiguously in order to maintain their authority and the authority of the institution of which they are a part. Modifying the content of English to include 'ethnic' literature is not that risky because this institution's methods and facts typically go undisputed: "the unpresentable [is] put forward only as the missing contents; but the form, because of its recognizable consistency, continues to offer to the reader . . . matter for solace and pleasure." (Lyotard 81) In short, then, benevolence towards 'ethnic' literature uncritically endorses a 'native populism' whereby subalternity is affirmed as both good and right for reasons of appropriation.

Benevolent intellectuals assume that *The Joy Luck Club* bolsters dominant ideas about the literary object and/or the 'racial other'. From this perspective, Tan's novel reassures its audience by offering reliable information not only in terms of the text but also in terms of the context. The 'inside' of *The Joy Luck Club* is approached as an object for appropriation, generating (the) meaning via technical description. Mastery over the literary object encourages the belief that the 'outside' referent is also liable to objectification. Indeed, truth about the 'racial other' is apparently delivered via *The Joy Luck Club*. As Tan puts it, "[w]hat people read th[is] book for seems to be so much about role models, cultural explanation, historical point of view" (Stanton, "Breakfast," 7). Reliability with regard to meaning and to reference is a possibility because *The Joy Luck Club* seems to conform to traditional aesthetic categories. For example, mimesis is assumed between linguistic and natural reality, engendering certainty concerning definitions of the author, the text and the reader. Further, a didactic function is accorded to Tan's novel. It is also expected to delight its audience, pleasing both popular and academic audiences: "The nonintellectual consumer . . . can find much in *The Joy Luck Club* . . . to satisfy her curiosity about China and Chinatown; at the same time, subversions of naive voyeurism can be detected by the reader attuned to questions of cultural production." (Wong 191)

As well as seemingly sanctioning mimesis, didacticism and aestheticism, Tan's novel ends happily, "mov[ing] inevitably towards *closure* which is also disclosure, the dissolution of enigma through the re-establishment of order" (Belsey 70). Gaps appear to be unproblematically closed in *The Joy Luck Club*, which brings about a happy ending for its characters as well as for its audience. Confronted with that which is radically exterior, whether it takes the form of a Chinese mother or an American-born daughter, *The Joy Luck Club* advocates appropriation, most dramatically when Jing-mei is apparently reconciled with her dead Chinese mother through her lost Chinese sisters on a trip to the Chinese motherland. It is for this reason that Rocío G. Davis proposes that " *The Joy Luck Club* is not essentially a novel about divisions[;] it is the reconciliation between daughters and mothers" (98). As it turns out, a large number of mainstream critics imagine Tan's novel in terms of reconciliation. "[A] complete and holistic experience" (Shen 243) necessitates the recognition of identity among the women in *The Joy Luck Club*. Motherhood renders the older generation of women identical. (Ling 138) Mothers and daughters also prove difficult to differentiate. In the words of Bonnie TuSmith: they "are one and the same." (67) *The Joy Luck Club* lends support to this argument because identity is emphasized on a number of occasions with the two generations of women looking, acting and thinking like each other. From this viewpoint, a limited understanding of Chinese (and Chinese American) femininity is promoted in Tan's novel -- particularly if a selective response is privileged.[5]

It is interesting to note that China specialists also respond selectively to *The Joy Luck Club*. As critical as this group is with respect to the new Orientalism of benevolent intellectuals, China specialists also take for granted the possibility of a non-Orientalist viewpoint. Rather than arguing that Tan's novel is outside this ideology, China specialists typically claim exteriority for themselves. In other words, both forms of new Orientalism adhere to the ideological notion of "The Native [as] the Non-Duped" (Chow, *Writing Diaspora*, 52). However, a point of contention emerges inasmuch as China specialists argue that *The Joy Luck Club* misrepresents 'things Chinese'. Drawing attention to the liberties taken with Chinese myths, a number of China specialists effectively announce that "[t]he East is a career" for Tan (Benjamin Disraeli qtd. in Said xiii). Indeed, the financial return for misrepresenting Chinese myths in terms agreeable with white racism, western capitalism and first world feminism is phenomenal. As David Streitfield notes, "[a]ccording to one theory, Tan inadvertently tapped into the mentality of the baby boomer female - who also, coincidentally, forms a huge chunk of the book-buying public." (F9) It is impossible to deny that *The Joy Luck Club* has furthered Tan's career. However, it is also worth noting that other theories are possible with respect to her trafficking in Orientalism via the faking of Chinese myths.

The fact that Chinese myths change or, as Chi na specialists would argue, are changed by Tan is undeniable. Indeed, mainstream mythologists can be used to corroborate the assertion that *The Joy Luck Club* misrepresents Chinese myths. As well as mixing myths, Tan uses details that turn out to be unreliable. For instance, Ying-ying St. Clair's representation of the Moon Lady has this mythical woman steal a magic peach from the Master Archer (81). However, authoritative accounts reveal that she actually took a "magic herb" *and* "the pill of immortality" *and* the "elixir of immortality made from the fruit of a tree that only flowered once every one thousand years." (Birch and Keene 337; Werner 185; Liu 234) The implications of this discrepancy are not necessarily taken on board by China specialists. For instance, Wong's concern is with the misrepresentation of the Moon Lady myth as it occurs in *The Joy Luck Club*. Fluctuating between identifying the author and/or the audience as functionaries for Orientalist ideology, Wong proposes that the mistaken rendering of Chinese myths is inadequately explained in terms of "Tan is just writing fiction" (182). In short, literariness fails to account for the misrepresentation of the Moon Lady myth. The fact that Ying-ying's reliability as a story-teller is at issue in Tan's novel seems not to undermine Wong's argument. Further, dramatic insertions, socio-political change, memory lapses, historical limits and the movement of formal linguistic structures fail to convince her that *The Joy Luck Club* radically questions Orientalist ideology.

Misrepresentation is not explained by Ying-ying's tendency towards overdramatization as far as Wong is concerned. In the words of Lena St. Clair, "I knew [it] was not true. I knew my mother made up anything to warn me, to help me avoid some unknown danger." (105) It is therefore possible to argue that literary/ethical considerations necessitate Ying-ying's misrepresentation of the Moon Lady myth. This point is also raised by Tao Tao Liu in relation to the impact of politics on Chinese myths: "Shortly after the Communist Party took power they issued a new version of the Monkey story . . . . It was interpreted as the rebellion of the humble and the weak against the powers of the establishment." Liu also draws attention to the fact that the Moon Lady was mentioned "in sources from . . . the BC era" (246, 239). Given its history, along with the changes in the ideological configuration of China both nationally and locally, it is hardly surprising that the Moon Lady myth is susceptible to change. Moreover, it is worth noting that Ying-ying openly admits to misrepresentation in relation to the Five Evils, which is revealed to be an insect repellent. In addition to admitting her mistake, Ying-ying recalls her sleepy mind (68). Neither drowsiness nor, for that matter, memory lapses account for misrepresentation in Wong's opinion. As she remarks with respect to the latter, "[i]n the minds of many older people, recollections of remote childhood events often surpass, in clarity and specificity, those of more proximate occurrences." (187) *The Joy Luck Club* lends support to Wong's argument: "But now that I [Ying-ying] am old, moving every year closer to the end of my life, I also feel closer to the beginning. And I remember everything that happened that day" (83). At once reliable and unreliable regarding the Moon Lady myth and its accompanying festivities, *The Joy Luck Club* "avoid[s] and resist[s] the reading [it] advocate[s]." (De Man, *The Resistance to Theory*, 19) The movement of language to and fro problematizes the possibility of 'the real' and, indeed, 'the fake' in relation to Chinese myths. Following this logic, a discrepancy of the fruit-herb-pill-elixir type is something of an inevitability, occurring in both fictional and factual texts, because "the mythical concept . . . has at its disposal an unlimited mass of signifiers." Indeed, the signification of the Moon Lady myth "is constituted by a sort of constantly moving turnstile" (Barthes 120, 123).

Moving constantly, because it has its basis in language, the myth generates difficulties for China specialists. To announce that Tan fakes Chinese myths is to overlook, whether explicitly or implicitly, "the open character of the [mythical] concept; it is not at all an abstract, purified essence; it is a formless, unstable, nebulous condensation" (Barthes 119). As it turns out, Wong leaves unacknowledged the movement of myth, along with bypassing the movement of "The Moon Lady". In so doing, she embroils herself in an argument that effectively constitutes a triumph for Orientalism. As insightful as Wong is with respect to the part played by language in effecting Orientalist stereotypes, insightfulness that also takes into account the impact of reading on the production of meaning, she proclaims that *The Joy Luck Club* is in the final analysis repackaged Orientalism. More precisely, Wong proposes that Tan's novel represents itself as reliable in relation to 'things Chinese' via linguistic mechanisms, including epideixis, italicized words and pidginized 'Asian English'. These formal linguistic structures enable *The Joy Luck Club* to generate "The Oriental Effect". As Wong remarks, they "signal a reassuring affinity between the given work and American preconceptions about what the Orient is/should be." This affinity between linguistic and natural reality happens "in a discursive rather than referential dimension" (Wong 187-88). This emphasis on the linguistic is important because it generates the notion that the basis for Orientalist ideology is language as opposed to the phenomenal world. Indeed,

Wong is keen to point out the ways in which *The Joy Luck Club* depends on functions of language to effect 'Chineseness'. However, there is unwillingness on Wong's part "to progress from apparently purely linguistic analysis to questions which are really already of a political and an ideological nature." (De Man, *The Resistance to Theory*, 121)   In other words, her insights about the Oriental effect pertain only to *The Joy Luck Club*, effectively leaving unacknowledged the part played by the literary dimension of language in enabling Orientalist ideology as it operates in the political/ideological realm. 'Chineseness' not only raises problems for Chinese American literature; it also is part of the reason why in the United States "there are few Chinese in top management positions [and] in mainstream political roles." (Tan, "Discretion," 30)

Further, Wong observes that "the same narrative detail may yield widely divergent readings -- Orientalist, culturalist, essentialist, and ahistorical on the one hand, and counter-Orientalist, anticulturalist, constructionist, and historicist on the other" (192). Following this logic, it proves difficult to make the claim that *The Joy Luck Club* repackages Orientalism. However, Wong's insight as regards the influence of reading on the production of meaning is not applicable to Tan's novel because it is "epistemologically unproblematized - in [her] view, [its] narrative modality is 'declarative.'" What she means by this is that *The Joy Luck Club* refrains from radically questioning the epistemological reliability of the 'racial other'. Wong contends that the Chinese mother(land) is uncritically represented as "a locus of truth" (195, 196). On one level, *The Joy Luck Club* grants an epistemic advantage to 'things Chinese'. For example, Jing-mei concedes that her Chinese "mother was right." (267) She is not the only one to make this admission: "Collectively . . . the mothers' narratives are translated into . . . a style of domineering, a tongue for control, and a gesture for having authority" (Yuan 295). In addition, travelling to China apparently enables Jing-mei to formulate reliable insights about her identity.   On another level, however, it is possible to argue that Wong takes advantage of the fact that the Chinese mother(land) determines meaning in order to determine the way in which *The Joy Luck Club* is read. In other words, Wong confuses "reference with phenomenalism" (De Man, *The Resistance to Theory*, 11) inasmuch as she assumes that what is apparently happening 'inside' Tan's novel unproblematically affects what happens 'outside'.

Wong's vigilance as regards the part played by language, an unpredictable part at that, in effecting 'Chineseness' is not pursued in terms of a radical theoretico-political critique. Rather, she represents herself as a China specialist. This is not to overlook Wong's knowledge about Chinese culture and, indeed, about the westernization of 'things Chinese'. For example, it is difficult to disagree with Wong's critique of the mainstream in light of the Orientalist remarks made by so many of Tan's reviewers irrespective of their positions in "the worlds of 'mass' literature and 'respectable' literature" (175). However, a question arises as to whether Wong has underestimated the critical potential of *The Joy Luck Club* and its readership. Although readers like Melanie McAlister and Lisa Lowe are accorded this potential, it is "unlikely to reach the 'airport newsstand' readership of Tan's works." (Wong 193) People who buy books at airports may be prevented from hearing McAlister's and Lowe's voices, perhaps through no fault of their own. However, the notion that Tan's airport newsstand readership is uncritical cannot be guaranteed. Indeed, theorists working in Cultural Studies problematize the notion that popular culture constitutes a site that merely gives expression to dominant ideologies. Rather than addressing the possibility of critical thinking in popular culture, the Wong overdetermines Tan's readership, an overdetermination that also pertains to *The Joy Luck Club*. In addition to raising the issue of overdetermination, this emphasis allows a question to emerge regarding the basis of Wong's critique of Orientalist ideology as it operates both 'inside' and 'outside' Tan's novel.

As it turns out, the possibility of ideology critique is available to Wong because she claims exteriority in relation to Orientalism, making reliable decisions about what is Chinese and what is not Chinese. For example, Wong's argument about the removal of the veil during a Chinese wedding ceremony as "a suspiciously Western practice" (182) involves a decision as regards Chinese/non-Chinese. It is important to note that she does concede "the materiality of Westernization as an irreducible part of Asian modern self-consciousness" (Chow, "Violence," 94). The influence of the west on China, alongside the diversity within China, fails to disturb Wong's final decision about *The Joy Luck Club*'s representation of a Chinese wedding as not Chinese. [6] What is problematic about Wong's decision is *how* she formulates "'this is Chinese' and 'this is not Chinese'" (Chow, "Violence," 89). The difficulty, then, is not with *what* she decides because decisions are inescapable, together with varying in pertinence, although not to the extent of 'anything goes'. Rather, it is

Wong's inadvertent appropriation of China specialism that generates difficulties. Admittedly, China specialism is enabling, functioning as "an epistemological weapon" (Chow, "Violence," 91) *vis-à-vis* Orientalism by exposing its ideological underpinnings and by allowing China specialists to assume the privilege of a non-duped viewpoint with respect to 'things Chinese'.

However, the limitations of China specialism demand attention on a number of related counts. First, China specialists generally leave unacknowledged the ideological basis for reliable decisions about what is Chinese and what is not Chinese. The assumption of reliability, together with the binarized logic that China specialists utilize, raises the issue of ideology. Indeed, Orientalist ideology perpetrates a binary opposition between east and west. China specialists take this distinction on board, often uncritically, inasmuch as they assume that their apparent exteriority with respect to the western(ized) phenomenon of Orientalism ensures the possibility of being non-Orientalist regarding 'Chineseness'. Wong adheres to this logic to the extent that she opposes "the Amy Tan Phenomenon" to what is happening in literary studies and in cultural politics: "Asian American critics are busily engaged in defining a canon dissociated as much as possible from Orientalist concerns" (174, 202). However qualified it is, dissociation presupposes the possibility of exteriority with respect to Orientalism, which is problematic because it leaves unchallenged the Orientalist distinctions that empower Wong and her colleagues. Either east or west, either Chinese or not Chinese, either duped or non-duped, and either Orientalist or non-Orientalist: dichotomies such as these permit China specialists to oppose Orientalism without rendering it vulnerable to a radical theoretico-political critique.

Second, China specialists effectively put a stop to debate, which signals the beginning of the end for a radical theoretico-political critique of Orientalism. Not only is China specialism limited to the extent that it essentializes identity, ultimately in terms compatible with Orientalism; it also de-historicizes experience. Experience is de-historicized because self-critique on the part of western(ized) thinkers and, for that matter, China specialists is prohibited. In short, China specialists are born into structure, one that is assumed impervious to historical (ideological) reality. Similarly, as Rey Chow comments, "the moralistic charge of . . . being 'too Westernized' is devastating; it signals an attempt on the part of those who are specialists in ['her'] culture to demolish the only premises on which [she] can speak." ("Violence," 91) Critical of all 'things western', China specialists claim epistemological and ethico-political advantage in order to marginalize western(ized) thinkers irrespective of what they have to say. Third, promoting vigilance with respect to 'things Chinese' is regarded as unnecessary because there is an obviousness about what is Chinese and what is not Chinese. However, these decisions are only obvious from inside Orientalist ideology, which is experienced as truth. The difficulties involved in making decisions are in this way marginalized without adequate attention to the fact that it is precisely these difficulties that ensure that debate about racial identity has a future as opposed to ending with unambiguous, if not stereotypical, statements about 'the Chinese' and 'the Chinese American'. It is possible to argue that China specialists, along with benevolent intellectuals, affirm otherness according to the logic of new Orientalism, typically imagining 'alien territory' in accordance with aesthetic categories. Like its predecessor, new Orientalism responds literally and/or selectively to *The Joy Luck Club*, with literary metaphors apparently providing reliable information about 'Chineseness'.

What is being proposed, then, is not indecision, which is both elitist and impossible, but a vigilance with respect to *how* decisions about 'Chineseness' are effected. Vigilance concerning how involves acknowledging the instability of racial categories, an instability effected by the rhetorical or the literary dimension of language. A radical theoretico-political critique of Orientalism is in this way enabled. In marked contrast to the sort of analysis promoted by benevolent intellectuals and China specialists, a critique that engages tropes and figures radically upsets Orientalist ideology. That "[l]iterature involves the voiding, rather than the affirmation, of aesthetic categories" (De Man, *The Resistance to Theory*, 10) calls into question the assumption of reliability with respect to meaning and to reference. Reliability is questioned not only because of the difference between linguistic and natural reality, but also because rhetoric is marked by movement, a movement that resists ideological determination. This resistance "designates the impossibility for . . . language . . . to appropriate anything, be it as consciousness, as object, or as a synthesis of both." (De Man, *Allegories of Reading*, 47) Appropriation is impossible, problematizing the assumption that representation reliably functions as information retrieval. It is also worth noting the impossibility of abandoning this understanding of "linguistic structures [as] somehow truly consubstantial with the world of natural processes and forms." (Norris 14) At once impossible and ineradicable, appropriation is nevertheless "a mere *effect* that language can perfectly well achieve, but which bears no substantial relationship . . . to anything beyond that particular effect." (De Man, *The Resistance to Theory*, 10) Vigilance about the way in which rhetoric is both enabling and disabling as regards appropriation makes possible a properly critical mode of inquiry. This inquiry acknowledges that identification is "an irreducible moment in any discourse" (Spivak, *The Post-colonial Critic*, 11). More than this, the identities formulated are linguistic effects and, as such, are unreliable with respect to meaning and to reference.

What this means in relation to Tan's novel is that its negotiation of Orientalist ideology is more complex than mainstream critics are willing to admit. The ineradicability of formulating unambiguous, if not stereotypical, identities is raised in *The Joy Luck Club*. For instance, one American-born daughter, Rose Hsu Jordan, understands herself as weak and as needing western protection. Whether paternal or romantic in nature, protection is solicited from a *waigoren*: "I was victim to his hero." (118) "'[T]he ideal of cultural harmony through romance'" (Peter Hulme qtd. in Loomba 158) is sanctioned with no attention to its suspect ideological underpinnings. Another daughter, Waverly Jong, endorses homophobia by taking for granted a link between homosexuality and AIDS: "'he *is* gay . . . . He could have AIDS.'" (204) Chinese mothers also participate in stereotyping. For example, An-mei Hsu believes that M & M's and sweatshirts "would make her brother very rich and happy by communist standards." (36) Not content with these useless gifts, he betrays her 'expectation of what Communist 'ethnic specimens' ought to be." She assumes that "a 'native' of communist China ought to be faithful to [his] nation's official political ideology. Instead of 'racial' characteristics, communist beliefs become the stereotype" (Chow, *Writing Diaspora*, 27-28). Clearly, then, Chinese and Chinese American women in *The Joy Luck Club* are not beyond prejudice, rendering Tan a functionary of dominant ideologies in the opinion of many of her mainstream critics. However, to represent Chinese mothers and American-born daughters as necessarily good and right is not only to leave their ideologically suspect remarks unchallenged; it is also to perpetrate the ideological notion of the native as the non-duped. Whether the women in *The Joy Luck Club* are compliant or non-duped regarding Orientalism, Occidentalism, homophobia and so on, they are embroiled in ideological structures.

Orientalist ideology is inescapable, although not invulnerable to criticism. Criticism is unable to disengage from Orientalism, a fact that benevolent intellectuals and China specialists overlook in their discovery of its ideological underpinnings from "the vantage point of superior knowledge and insight." (Warminski 9)   However, both groups leave unacknowledged that their performance of ideology critique is effective only because its exploits the ideological notion of exteriority. Even without an outside, that is, without the possibility of disengagement, Orientalism is vulnerable to critical engagement, especially if it takes the form of a radical theoretico-political critique. More specifically, this particular critique of ideology does not work with the inside/outside model of Orientalism apart from as a rhetorical effect. It also involves "critical-linguistic analysis" or close reading, focusing on the way in which *The Joy Luck Club* "avoid[s] and resist[s] the reading [it] advocate[s]." (De Man, *The Resistance to Theory*, 121, 19) Further, close reading makes possible the claim that Tan's novel unmasks and accounts for ideological aberrations to the extent that it raises the issue of the part played by representation, particularly the literary dimension of representation, in generating 'Chineseness'. Three scenes from "A Pair of Tickets" are referenced in order to support the notion that *The Joy Luck Club* promotes insights that radically problematize essentialism/Orientalism in relation to 'things Chinese'. This last chapter is targeted because mainstream critics typically argue that *The Joy Luck Club* endorses closure, although some are untroubled by the ideological ramifications of Tan's happy ending. Others, like Wong for example, propose that "[t]he ending of the novel . . . offers a powerful essentialist proposition" (194). Following the synecdochal logic of mainstream critics, this discussion proposes that the ending of *The Joy Luck Club* gestures towards essentialism/Orientalism insofar as Jing-mei acquires insights about herself, her family and China. At the same time, however, the reliability of these insights is compromised because they have their bases in formal linguistic structures. As language is involved, enabling and disabling 'Chineseness', the possibility of resistance to ideological determination is made possible. This resistance ensures a happy ending proper.

First, Jing-mei Woo's trip to China: "The minute our train leaves the Hong Kong border and enters Shenzhen, China, I feel different . . . . I am becoming Chinese . . . . [T]oday I realize I've never really known what it means to be Chinese." (267-68)   Tan's mainstream critics refuse to let this representation of China as ultimately reassuring with respect to identity go uncriticized. They argue that it is at best naive and at worst ethnocentric. The problem with this criticism is that it does not attend to the fact that *The Joy Luck Club* "builds up the romantic concept of cultural origins and lost ethnic essence only in order to radically undermine and reconfigure the notion of an ethnic essence." (Schueller 80) On one level, then, Jing-mei's experience of becoming Chinese appeals to the notion of authenticity. However, her comment about "transforming like a werewolf" (267) puts into question the notion of authenticity because of its non-Chinese dimension. Further, Jing-mei understands her experience as "com[ing] out of popular representations." (Schueller 75) Indeed, her image of China comes from guidebooks, which promote the idea that it is made up of blue-jacketed people working in canal-flanked fields. As it turns out, imagined China fails to match up with Chinese 'reality'.[7] This gap between linguistic and natural reality thwarts Jing-mei's link with China, a situation exacerbated because not even the Chinese know China. For example, Great Auntie Aiyi is "astonished" (279) by the news that Japanese soldiers invaded Kweilin during the Sino-Japanese War. This point about invasion also draws attention to the fact that China is affected by non-Chinese influences. Jing-mei's reconciliation with the Chinese mother(land) is in this way disturbed, "undercut[ting] any notions of simple identification of origins or of a cultural 'reality' easily available for access." (Schueller 80)

Second, Jing-mei's shower scene: "The hotel has provided little packets of shampoo which, upon opening, I discover is the consistency and color of hoisin sauce. This is more like it, I think. This is China. And I rub some in my damp hair." (278) Comments like these generate a number of responses, which for the most part emphasize Jing-mei's apparently unambiguous commitment to suspect ideologies. For instance, it is possible to argue that China is objectified (as shampoo) *à la* Orientalism. Further, Jing-mei appears absolutely determined by corporate capitalism: her experience of China cannot be disengaged from the advertising industry. From this perspective, Jing-mei "betray[s] . . . expectation of what . . . 'ethnic specimens' ought to be" (Chow, *Writing Diaspora*, 28) by using shampoo in order to gain a sense of China. The advertising industry openly overdetermines the capacity for betterment that shampoo promises, engendering the possibility of more than a literal response to Jing-mei's epiphany. Perhaps (hair) roots are troped with (cultural) 'Roots' in order to problematize the ethnic specimen stereotype. Or perhaps the shower scene plays on expectations regarding 'ethnic' literature, undercutting the information retrieval approach on the part of English, for example. Indeed, information retrieval denies rhetorical movement to *The Joy Luck Club* because English "take[s] literary metaphors as Chinese facts" (Smorada 33). In so doing, it prohibits the possibility of a critical engagement with language, an engagement that raises the issue of rhetoric as effecting 'Chineseness'. On one level, then, Jing-mei's discovery of China via a packet of shampoo involves a rhetorical gesture that is difficult to take seriously. On another level, however, this rhetorical gesture is worth taking seriously inasmuch as it unmasks and accounts for ideological aberrations, generating questions about the way in which 'Chineseness' is formulated.

Third, the Polaroid photograph of Jing-mei and her Chinese sisters promotes a sense of unity not only between siblings but also between them and their dead mother: "Together we look like our mother." (288) "This composite image", remarks TuSmith, "reflects the novel's communal subtext, which works as a counterpoint to the textual surface of individualistic strife between mothers and daughters." (68) Her use of the depth-surface binary opposition generates the belief that community is more fundamental to Chinese and to Chinese American women than individuality. However, *The Joy Luck Club* problematizes this hierarchical dichotomy. It is of no small consequence that Jing-mei "see[s] no trace of [her] mother in [her sisters]." After the photograph is taken, the three sisters "watch quietly together, eager to see what develops." Significantly, oneness develops in terms of representation: "The gray-green surface changes to the bright colors of our three images, sharpening and deepening all at once." (287-288) The development of a photograph, which only afterwards seems to lend itself to the development of relationships, draws attention to the fact that familial reconciliations always already involve representation. More specifically, tropes and figures, which operate on the textual surface, generate the sense of oneness that Jing-mei experiences and that TuSmith proclaims. However, the possibility of ultimate unity among family members is compromised by the fact that tropes and figures move unreliably, compelling Jing-mei to privilege her interpretation of the photograph. In so doing, she "reveals h[er] despair when confronted with a structure of linguistic meaning that [s]he cannot control and that holds the discouraging prospect of an infinity of similar future confusions" (De Man, *Allegories of Reading*, 10).

In the final analysis, then, these three episodes generate a reading that promotes vigilance as regards the ineradicability of Orientalist ideology, a vigilance that prevents it from uncritically essentializing, homogenizing and universalizing 'Chineseness'. Unlike new Orientalism, this reading does not assume exteriority in relation to Orientalism, an exteriority that is ultimately in keeping with Orientalist ideology. Indeed, benevolent intellectuals and China specialists conduct debate about racial identity in binarized terms, uncritically sanctifying the native as the non-duped. 'Non-dupedness' is enabling, as China specialists know only too well; it is also disabling to the extent that it involves essentialism. In other words, 'the Chinese' enables theoretico-political mobilization, but its sanctification brings about "all kinds of guilt-tripping, card-naming, arrogance, self-aggrandizement and so on, [which] begin[s] to spell the beginning of the end." (Spivak, *The Post-colonial Critic*, 104) It is possible to resist this end if insights are developed as regards the underpinnings of 'Chineseness'. Indeed, an insight about the Orientalist underpinnings of this racial category, alongside an insight about the way in which 'Chineseness' is effected by the rhetorical dimension of language, makes possible a radical theoretico-political critique of Orientalism. *The Joy Luck Club* promotes these insights insofar as Jing-mei's comments about becoming Chinese and so on allow her to formulate an identity -- personal, familial, national, racial -- that she regards as enabling: "After all these years, it can finally be let go." (288) It is also important to note that the harm brought about by family reconciliation is acknowledged. Further, Jing-mei's identity 'becomes' via formal linguistic structures, whether in terms of popular representations (the werewolf myth/the shampoo advert) or a Polaroid photograph. Her reliance on these structures does not make Jing-mei's identity less real. After all, Orientalist representations limit the opportunities of the Chinese, both indigenous and diasporic. What this reliance does reveal is that identity is rhetorically constructed, moving continuously and unpredictably, if not ambiguously, which is compelling as regards resistance to Orientalist ideological determination. Rhetorical movement, then, ensures the possibility of future debate about racial identity and literature.

Bella Adams

NOTES

[1] Complimenting and condemning can happen simultaneously: "Chinese people are 'discreet and modest' . . . . I do believe anyone would take th[is] description as a compliment - at first. But after a while, it annoys" (Tan "Discretion," 30-31).

[2] Admittedly, the boundaries between 'old' and 'new' Orientalism are unstable, particularly as both Orientalisms ultimately function to legitimate a model of consciousness that accords the privilege of objectivity to the western(ized) subject. This point notwithstanding, it is possible to determine differences between these two kinds of Orientalism, as Gayatri Chakravorty Spivak has argued and from whom the concept of 'new' Orientalism derives. Indeed, Spivak contends that 'new' Orientalism reverses the hierarchy that takes for granted the superiority of the west in all matters eastern insofar as it benevolently concedes that "the other side is all unfractioned good." ("Subaltern Talk," 305) However, this reversal is achieved under the illusion that 'the east' is a more or less stable category. In so doing, 'new' Orientalism becomes what it criticizes, inadvertently participating in the perpetration of an essentialized, homogenized and universalized representation of 'the east'. Borrowing from Spivak, this paper agrees that it is possible to formulate a relationship between benevolent intellectuals and 'new' Orientalism. Moreover, it argues that China specialists are 'new' Orientalist because they too work with a fairly unproblematic binary opposition between east and west.

[3] Frank Chin is the China specialist *par excellence*, distinguishing reliably between what is the real and what is the fake regarding China. In short, Chin argues that Amy Tan's fiction is in keeping with white racism because it fakes (and feminizes) Chinese myths. Sau-ling Cynthia Wong also situates Tan in the context of white racism, particularly Orientalism, along with addressing the issues of capitalism and of feminism. Ultimately, Wong assumes the status of a China specialist, *specifically* in "'Sugar Sisterhood' Situating the Amy Tan Phenomenon." It is important not to conflate Chin and Wong because the latter responds more critically to Tan's fiction. However, they either explicitly (Chin) or implicitly (Wong) assume the possibility of a non-ideological viewpoint as regards 'Chineseness'. It is possible to argue that ideology critique does little to problematize dominant assumptions. This is because it inadvertently depends on categories (real/fake and east/west) that demand analysis in order to generate a radical theoretico-political critique of racial identity.

[4] Ambiguity constitutes something of a risk for a Chinese American because this racial group is stereotypically constructed as sly and dishonest partly because of its apparently ambivalent language. However, it is possible to resist an unambiguous racial identity without affirming this stereotype.

[5] This response is selective because it overlooks the way in which the American-born daughters in particular emphasize the harm engendered by reconciliation. For example, Jing-mei (27-29) raises the point that identification with her dead mother, Suyuan Woo, involves the loss of identity and by implication the loss of humanity. She is given the task of speaking for and about Suyuan in *The Joy Luck Club*. It is assumed - a little too easily for Jing-mei's liking - that a mother can be "shelved" in order to make way for a daughter. The problem with this arrangement is that it regards two different women as interchangeable. Interchangeability has at its basis the assumption of similarity, if not identity, between Suyuan and Jing-mei, which can be both harmful and beneficial. Interchangeable calendars and indistinguishable cities function to convey Jing-mei's sense that inter-generational reconciliation is limited, effectively reducing her to the status of an inanimate object: "It is as if we were truly those little dolls sold

in Chinatown tourist shops, heads bobbing up and down in complacent agreement to anything said!" (Tan, "Discretion," 26)

6 "[T]he inland location of the episode and the lack of corroboration in ethnographic literature (e.g., Shizhen Wang) make the kind of veil lifting . . . described by Tan an extremely unlikely occurrence." (Wong 204n)

7 Jing-mei is confronted by a country that is decidedly western: drab western clothes, railway tracks and cement buildings are in force in China. Jing-mei's hotel is equipped with an array of western consumer goods, thwarting her link with the essential China (271, 276-77).

WORKS CITED

Althusser, Louis. "Ideology and Ideological State Apparatuses." *Contemporary Literary Theory*. Ed. Dan Latimer. San Diego: Harcourt Brace Jovanovich, 1989: 60-102.

Barthes, Roland. *Mythologies*. Trans. Annette Lavers. London: Vintage, 1993.

Birch, Cyril and Donald Keene. *Anthology of Chinese Literature*. London: Penguin Books, 1965.

Belsey, Catherine. *Critical Practice*. London and New York: Routledge, 1980.

Chow, Rey. "Violence in the Other Country: China as Crisis, Spectacle, and Woman." *Third World Women and the Politics of Feminism*. Eds. Chandra Talpade Mohanty, Ann Russo and Lourdes Torres. Bloomington and Indianapolis: Indiana University Press, 1991: 81-100.

---. *Writing Diaspora: Tactics of Intervention in Contemporary Cultural Studies*. Bloomington and Indianapolis: Indiana University Press, 1993.

Davis, Rocio G.. "Wisdom (Un)heeded: Chinese Mothers and American Daughters in Amy Tan's *The Joy Luck Club*." *Cuadernos de Investigacion Filologica* 19-20 (1993-94): 89-100.

De Man, Paul. *Allegories of Reading: Figural Language in Rousseau, Nietzsche, Rilke, and Proust*. New Haven and London: Yale University Press, 1979.

---. *The Resistance to Theory*. Minneapolis: University of Minnesota Press, 1986.

Fong, Yem Sui. "Review of *The Joy Luck Club*." *Frontiers* 11. 2-3 (1990): 122-23.

Jackson, Rosemary. *Fantasy: The Literature of Subversion*. London and New York: Methuen, 1981.

Ling, Amy. *Between Worlds: Women Writers of Chinese Ancestry*. New York: Pergamon Press, 1990.

Liu, Tao Tao. "Chinese Myths and Legends." *The Feminist Companion to Mythology*. Ed. Carolyne Larrington. London: Pandora, 1992: 227-47.

Loomba, Ania. *Colonialism/Postcolonialism*. London and New York: Routledge, 1998.

Lyotard, Jean-François. *The Postmodern Condition: A Report on Knowledge*. Trans. Geoff Bennington and Brian Massumi. Fwd. Frederic Jameson. Manchester: Manchester University Press, 1984.

Norris, Christopher. "Paul de Man and the Critique of Aesthetic Ideology." *AUMLA* 69 (1988): 3-47.

Said, Edward W.. *Orientalism: Western Conceptions of the Orient*. London: Penguin Books, 1978.

Schell, Orville. "Your Mother is in Your Bones: *The Joy Luck Club*." *The New York Times Book Review* 7.3:1 (19 March 1989): 3, 28.

Schueller, Malini Johar. "Theorizing Ethnicity and Subjectivity: Maxine Hong Kingston's *Tripmaster Monkey* and Amy Tan's *The Joy Luck Club*." *GENDERS* 15 (Winter 1992): 72-85.

Sharpe, Jenny. *Allegories of Empire: The Figure of Woman in the Colonial Text*. Minneapolis: University of Minnesota Press, 1993.

Shen, Gloria. "Born of a Stranger: Mother-Daughter Relationships and Storytelling in Amy Tan's *The Joy Luck Club*." *International Women's Writing: New Landscapes of Identity*. Eds. Anne E. Browne and Marjanne E. Goozé. Westport, Connecticut and London: Greenwood Press, 1995: 233-44.

Smorada, Claudia Kovach. "Side-Stepping Death: Ethnic Identity, Contradiction, and the Mother(land) in Amy Tan's Novel," *Fu Jen Studies* 24 (1991): 31-45.

Spivak, Gayatri Chakravorty. "Can the Subaltern Speak?" *Marxism and the Interpretation of Culture*. Eds. Cary Nelson and Lawrence Grossberg. London: Macmillan Education Ltd., 1988: 271-313.

---. *In Other Worlds: Essays in Cultural Politics*. New York and London: Routledge, 1987.

---. "Neocolonialism and the Secret Agent of Knowledge." *Oxford Literary Review* 3.1-2 (1991): 220-51.

---. *Outside in the Teaching Machine*. New York and London: Routledge, 1993.

---. *The Post-colonial Critic: Interviews, Strategies, Dialogues*. New York and London: Routledge, 1990.

---. "Subaltern Talk." *The Spivak Reader: Selected Works of Gayatri Chakravorty Spivak* . Eds. Donna Landry and Gerald MacLean. New York and London: Routledge, 1996.

Stanton, David. "Breakfast with Amy Tan." *Paintbrush: A Journal of Multicultural Literature* 12 (Autumn 1995): 5-19.

Streitfield, David. "The 'Luck' of Amy Tan." *The Washington Post* 8 October 1989: F1, F8-F9.

Tan, Amy. *The Joy Luck Club*. London: Minnerva, 1989.

---. "The Language of Discretion." *The State of the Language* . Eds. C. Ricks and L. Michaels. Berkeley: University of California Press, 1990: 25-32.

TuSmith, Bonnie. *All My Relatives: Community in Contemporary Ethnic Communities* . Ann Arbor: The University of Michigan Press, 1993.

Warminski, Andrzej. "Introduction" *Aesthetic Ideology* by Paul de Man. Minneapolis and London: University of Minnesota Press, 1996: 1-33.

Werner, E. T. C.. *Myths and Legends of China*. London: Sinclair Browne, 1922.

Wong, Sau-ling Cynthia. "'Sugar Sisterhood': Situating the Amy Tan Phenomenon." *The Ethnic Canon: Histories, Institutions, and Interventions*. Ed. David Palumbo-Liu. Minneapolis and London: University of Minnesota Press, 1995: 174-210.

Yuan, Yuan. "The Semiotics of China Narratives in the Con/texts of Kingston and Tan." *Critique* 40.3 (Spring 1999): 292-303.

6.

STRATEGIC *CRÉOLITÉ*
CALIBAN AND MIRANDA AFTER EMPIRE

Postcolonial writing often springs from a confrontational impulse to reread and rewrite the European historical and fictional record by refashioning the plots, characters, or founding assumptions of European texts in order to appropriate or redirect the ascribed meaning of the original. Nowhere is this impulse exhibited more evocatively than in the works of the many postcolonial writers who have taken up Prospero's tools in response to William Shakespeare's *The Tempest*. Interpreted by many critics as a fable of the colonial experience, the play has proved a popular model for fictional re-writing of that experience and has served as a touchstone for a generation of postcolonial writers.

In tracing the trajectory of responses to *The Tempest* by writers from the Caribbean, we see that the male writers of the independence era who championed Caliban as a figure of colonial resistance reversed the manichean opposition of Prospero and Caliban, but left the essential colonizer/colonized binary intact. More recently, female writers have attempted to displace, rather than merely invert, this opposition via the character of Miranda, recast as a Creole figure through whom divisions of race, class, and culture are mediated.

Explicit identification of *The Tempest* with the Americas, rather than the Mediterranean, began in Latin American literature where Caliban was identified as a symbol of the crudity and materialism of United States imperialism and Ariel was identified with idealistic Latin American intellectuals. [1] The paradigm shift, which cast Caliban as a victim of colonial oppression and Prospero as the colonial usurper, began with the publication of D.O Mannoni's *Prospero and Caliban: The Psychology of Colonialism* (1950). Mannoni, a psychologist and former French colonial administrator in Madagascar elaborates a psychoanalytical discourse, the "Prospero/Caliban Complex," which seeks to account for the colonial uprisings in Madagascar during the 1940s. In this discourse, the colonized's "dependence complex" and the colonizer's "inferiority complex" are illustrated through reference to Caliban and Prospero. The result is an apology for colonialism that portrays Europe's rise to global hegemony and the subsequent loss of its colonies as a psychodrama played out between two different but complementary personality types: "Prosperos" who were predisposed to be colonizers and "Calibans" who had permitted themselves to be colonized.

A subsequent generation of Afro-Caribbean intellectuals wrote back to Mannoni in defense of Caliban, whose famous declaration, "This island's mine by Sycorax my mother / which thou tak'st from me" (I.ii.333-4), informs much of the work that was produced during this nationalistic period. The Martinican writer and political leader Aimé Césaire explains the motivation behind his adaptation of *The Tempest* thus: "To me, Prospero is the complete totalitarian. I am always surprised when others consider him the wise man who 'forgives.' What is most obvious, even in Shakespeare's version, is the man's absolute will to power" (Césaire qtd. in Vaughan 162). [2]   Prospero may have ruled over Caliban, but it was not, as Mannoni suggests, because of their respective personality traits; "Prospero's Magic" was nothing more than superior technology and brute force. In *Black Skin, White Masks* (1952), Frantz Fanon argues that the dependency complex Mannoni attributes to the colonized was not the *cause* of colonialism but rather its *result.*

In his important 1987 essay on Caribbean and African appropriations of *The Tempest*, Rob Nixon argues that, since the play lacks a sixth act depicting relations among Caliban, Ariel, and Prospero in a postcolonial era, its value for African and Caribbean intellectuals faded "once the plot ran out." Apparently excluding Miranda from this brave new postcolonial world, Nixon adds that "because of the difficulty in wresting from the play any role for female defiance or leadership," it was no surprise to find that all the writers to date who had "quarried from *The Tempest* an expression of their lot" (577) were men. [3] These independence-era writers, who heralded Caliban as a revolutionary figure of colonial resistance, privileged racial oppression over sexual oppression, more often than not merely *reversing* the roles of oppressor and oppressed, rather than interrogating the legitimacy of these racialized heirarchies. The anti-colonial discourse that empowers Caliban and moves him toward speech does so at the expense of Miranda, who as the "property" of her father comes to serve as a prize to be claimed by the victor of the revolutionary struggle. If the discourse of sexuality and the discursive construct of the sexually-menacing native underpinned the consolidation of colonialist authority, the fact that authors who sought to dismantle manichean colonial structures ignored the intersections of race, sexuality, and political struggle in their construction of alternative liberationist narratives remains a peculiar oversight. [4]

Where Sylvia Wynter reads Caliban's sexual desire for Miranda as the product of a fruitless search for a legitimate mate, [5] other feminist critics see misogyny, arguing that Caliban's "masculinist" stance, both in Shakespeare's play and in the work of his revisionists, "radically questions any construction of him as the homogenous colonized Other of the Prospero Complex" (Donaldson 17).[6] This does not invalidate Caliban's claim to victimhood, but it does destabilize his position within the absolute either/or binary of the Prospero/Caliban complex, for here he can be seen as both victim and potential victimizer. Similarly, Miranda's claim to victimhood through her sexual objectification is undercut, as Wynter argues, by her ultimate alignment with the forces of patriarchy and imperialism that her father and husband Ferdinand represent.

The multiplicity of often-contradictory meanings contained within the figures of Miranda and Caliban does not allow for an easy identification with either character nor do the meanings permit facile ascriptions of "victim" and "perpetrator." Rather, consideration of the ambivalent subject positions that are possible within the Caliban/Miranda dyad offers an alternative to the discursive prison of the Prospero/Caliban complex and its manichean binary opposition. Displacement of this opposition, rather than its militant inversion, enables new development, a moving beyond what Derek Walcott has called a literature of "recrimination and despair, a literature of revenge written by the descendants of slaves or a literature of remorse written by the descendants of masters" (37).

The works discussed here belong to a second generation of *Tempest*-based texts that explore relations between the descendants of Prospero, Sycorax, Caliban, and Miranda in the postcolonial era. They write back not only to the history of racism and Eurocentrism that subtended the initial colonial venture, but also to the explicit sexism found in the work of writers who, in viewing

Caliban as *the* victim of Prospero's will-to-power, were often blind to the ways in which both daughter *and* slave are subject to Prospero's authority. They seek to displace the Prospero/Caliban binary via the characters of Miranda and Caliban, who ally themselves to escape what they come to recognize as their common subjugation to Prospero. This budding affinity between Miranda and Caliban is grounded, in part, in a recognition of what I term their Creoleness. They discover that, in spite of their physiognomic differences, they have in common a Creolized culture and identity. The acknowledgement of the insurgent creativity of this shared, New World identity offers at last the possibility of displacing its brutal origins and forging hybrid alternatives to colonial stratification.

The term Creole is used by Edward Kamau Brathwaite to describe both the inhabitants of the colony as well as the new cultural and linguistic forms that developed from the juxtaposition of European and African ways. Depending on the time and the place of its use, "Creole" was also used as a racial classification signifying either full European ancestry ("white Creole") or a mixed-race identity (implying some European ancestry mixed with African or Amerindian ancestry) (Raiskin, *Snow* 3). In their 1990 manifesto, "In Praise of Creoleness," Martinicans Jean Bernabé, Patrick Chamoiseau, and Raphaël Confiant suggest that *la créolité* (creoleness) is an "interior attitude" that looks neither toward Europe nor toward Africa for self-definition, but rather connects all people of the Caribbean with one another, as well as with the various countries of their respective origins. *Créolité* is not grounded in the purities of racial or cultural identity that informed the works of earlier "white Creole authors" such as Jean Rhys or Phyllis Shand Allfrey nor is it imagined as a "melting pot" in which differences of ethnicity and class are blended into a utopian Creole "wholeness." Rather, it is a contentious process in which cultural identity must be continuously scrutinized and redefined. As Edouard Glissant states in *Caribbean Discourse,* "To assert that people are creolized, that creolization has value, is to deconstruct [a definition] of 'creolized' that is considered as halfway between two pure extremes" (141). Accordingly, the term "Creole" is not posited as an alternative center or an alternate "pure" identity; rather, it is a celebration of heterogeneity and an alternative to linear origins -- a model based in "becoming" as opposed to "being."

Michelle Cliff and Marina Warner can both be classified, loosely, under the rubric of "Creole" writers who have returned to *The Tempest* in order to displace the racially-based Prospero/Caliban binary through the character of Miranda. Of the two, Warner's purchase on Creoleness is the most tenuous. Although she was not born in the Caribbean herself, her ancestor, Sir Thomas Warner, was the founding European settler of St. Kitts, and the Warner family lived in the Caribbean for three centuries. However, in spite of her family's West Indian Creole roots, Warner rejects the designation for herself, stating that it would be "fallacious, even opportunistic, for a descendant now to grasp the label and wear it with new pride....[t]he history of denial in the past has forfeited someone like me the right to own in the present to the [Creole] inheritance, much as I should like to" (Warner, *Family* 199). Jamaican-born writer Michelle Cliff, of African, Carib, and English heritage, identifies herself as "Creole." In *Abeng* (1984), her largely autobiographical first novel, and *No Telephone to Heaven* (1987), its more fictive sequel, Cliff grapples with the construction of racial identity and with the legacy of guilt and privilege that accompanies her family's racial ascription as "Jamaica white" (Jamaicans of mostly white ancestry) in Jamaica's class and color-conscious society.

Re-writing *The Tempest* in the interests of a Creole Miranda is a literary strategy indebted to Rhys's *Wide Sargasso Sea*. Like Rhys's Antoinette Cosway Mason, the new Miranda as envisaged by Warner and Cliff is clearly defined as Creole: a child both of Europe and the Caribbean. For Rhys, the Creole is a lost woebegone figure, tragically trapped between two worlds. However, when we turn to Cliff and Warner's Creole heroines, we find nothing passive or "tragic" about their characters. Creole identity changes from an accident of birth to a strategic position that inhabits the space between colonizer and colonized, black and white. In addition, while Prospero still oppresses, the source of his "magic" is now located in class and capital, rather than in racial difference. Racial identity in the texts analyzed here is fluid and as dependent on class and wealth as it is on color. In their ability to mediate between Prospero and Caliban, these Creole heroines suggest the possibility of an identity outside of the restrictive binaries of colonialist discourse.

Indigo: or Mapping the Waters (1992) is both prequel and sequel to *The Tempest*. The novel reconstructs precolonial life on Sycorax's island and the postcolonial world of late twentieth century England, where descendants of Sycorax and Prospero grapple with, to use Wole Soyinka's term, the "burden of memory and the muse of forgiveness," colonialism's legacy of white guilt and black rage. The novel also restores the woman's part to the drama of the New

World by giving voice to Miranda and Sycorax. In an interview, Warner says of *Indigo*, "Shakespeare was writing the father's plot. Prospero works out the plot for his daughter. Prospero's wife is conspicuously absent...So I tried to write the daughter's plot, to take the story from the other side and show how the daughter extricates herself from the father's plot" (Zabus, *Yarn* 524). In Warner's case, this can be read not just as Miranda's escape from Prospero's authority, but as a literal escape from her own family past. For *Indigo*, though ostensibly a re-telling of *The Tempest*," is also a fictionalized account of the Warner family in the early days of European settlement in the New World.

A significant episode in the history of the Warners in the Caribbean is alluded to in *Wide Sargasso Sea*. Part Two of Rhys's novel begins with a journey to Granbois, Dominica, where Antoinette and her husband will spend their honeymoon. En route, they stop to rest at a village called "Massacre," and the husband asks "Who was massacred here? Slaves?" "Oh no," Antoinette replies, "shocked," "Not Slaves. Something must have happened a long time ago. Nobody remembers now" (*WSS* 38). However, as Peter Hulme notes, Antoinette, like Rhys, would have known very well that the "massacre" from which the village takes its name was the 1674 killing of Indian Warner, the half-Carib son of Sir Thomas Warner, the first English Governor of St. Kitts. [7] When Thomas Warner arrived in St. Kitts, he "married" a local woman and had several children by her, including a son named Indian Warner. When Sir Thomas died, Indian Warner was appointed Governor of Dominica and Philip Warner, Sir Thomas's son by his English wife, was appointed Deputy Governor of Antigua. The two half-brothers fought each other bitterly for dominion over the islands, a struggle that culminated in Indian Warner's murder by Philip, after Philip tricked his half-brother into believing they were meeting for peace negotiations.

The story of Indian and Phillip Warner and of the unspoken blood knot that bound colonizer and colonized, master and slave, brother and brother, became the inspiration for *Indigo*. Through "convenient acts of memory and sins of omission," Warner writes, "the story of miscegenation in the early colonies is never told" (Warner, Family 199). *Indigo* recasts Sir Thomas Warner as Sir Christopher "Kit" Everard (b. 1595), the Prospero-like "discoverer" of the Caribbean island of Liamuiga, renamed "Everhope" by Sir Christopher [later, *Enfant-Béate*, while under French rule; and finally Liamuiga again after Independence].[8] In *Indigo*, the "island wife" who bears Kit Everard's mixed-race son, Roukoubé (a name Warner translates as "Red Bear Cub"), is a young Arawak woman named Ariel.

Warner's novel interweaves narratives from different time periods: "Then," seventeenth-century Liamuiga at the time of Christopher Everard's landing, and "Now," present-day England where Miranda Everard and her family live. As the story opens, Miranda's parents, Kit and Astrid, are bickering -- having one of their "tempests" (*Indigo* 36) -- as they head off to the christening of Xanthe, Kit's much-younger half-sister by his father's English second wife. Kit, like his father, was born in the Caribbean, on *Enfant-Béate*. Kit's deceased mother was a "Creole woman," and thus racially suspect. Warner discusses the meaning of "Creole" as it functioned in relation to "Englishness" within the British colonial context, stating that although the French and the Spanish include whites in the term Creole,

> to English ears, 'Creole' sounds foreign, French or worse, native, but native of another place besides England....[T]he word connoted an Elsewhere where ...various kinds of foreigners mingled and became natives in the process. And it was of course impossible, then, for an Englishman to be a foreigner at all, and perilous (although regrettably not impossible) for an Englishman to become a native. (Warner, Family 199)

In spite of his father's illustrious pioneer forebears, a "touch of the tarbrush" from his Creole mother consigns Kit Everard to the margins of Englishness where the boundary between Englishmen and natives becomes blurred. He is taunted as 'Nigger" Everard at school, and Miranda , accordingly, is described as "high yellow" (*Indigo* 23). In addition to the present-day descendants of Sir Christopher Everard is Serafine Killebree, their housekeeper, whose family has served the Everards on *Enfant-Béate*/Liamuiga for generations.

Serafine is descended from the island's original matriarch, Sycorax, through whose narrative we learn about life on Liamuiga before the arrival of the "tallow men" from across the sea. Warner's account of pre-colonial life draws on Hulme's book *Colonial Encounters* to explain relations between the island's original inhabitants and the European interlopers. Warner's appropriation of *The Tempest* rests on Hulme's assertion that the very presence in the play of Ariel, Caliban, and, through Prospero's story, Sycorax, serves to undermine Prospero's account of how he came to possess the island: "Prospero tells Miranda (and the audience) a story in which the island is merely an interlude, a neutral ground between extirpation and resumption of power. Ariel and Caliban immediately act as reminders that Prospero's is not the only perspective, that the island is not neutral ground for them" (*Encounters* 124). Accepting as a given that Prospero's narrative is "not simply history... but a particular *version*" (*Encounters,* 124), Warner writes that she felt compelled to "imagine, in fiction, the life and culture of Sycorax, and of Ariel and Caliban...I wanted to hear their voices in the noises of the isle" (Warner, Family 203).

Rather than Shakespeare's diasporic North African Sycorax, Warner's Sycorax is a Carib Indian who restores the missing matriarchal presence to *The Tempest* by humanizing Shakespeare's blue-ey'd hag (I.ii.269) and recasting her as a life-giving force, a wise woman, to whom others in the community turn for help and advice. In addition to her skill as cloth-maker (her work with indigo dye is what colors her blue), Sycorax is also a healer who possesses "sixth sense." When the failing cargo of a slave-ship is tossed overboard and the bodies wash up on shore, Sycorax intuits that there is something still living among the corpses (*Indigo* 97). She locates the corpse of a pregnant woman and cuts from her womb a living child. Sycorax adopts the boy and names him Dulé, which we are told means grief. In giving him a name that reflects the horror of the Middle Passage and the circumstances of his birth, rather than a name that reflects European fears of cannibalism, Warner champions Caliban's claim to the island and to linguistic autonomy. Sycorax and Dulé are joined by another orphan, Ariel, an Arawak girl whose mother was kidnapped by a European expedition and whom Sycorax agrees to raise as her own. Thus, Warner recasts Ariel and Caliban as adoptive brother and sister rather than androgynous spirit and earth-bound slave. In addition to providing a missing account of Sycorax and of Caliban's claim to the island, "Dulé" solves the problem of identifying Caliban with Africa while also establishing his claim to rightful ownership of a Caribbean, rather than a Mediterranean, island.

Warner's account of the meeting between the Europeans and the islanders also revises the vision of the original colonial encounter described by Mannoni in *Prospero and Caliban.* When Sir Christopher and his landing party first stumble upon Liamuiga, they are greeted not as "long-awaited Gods," but rather as fellow humans, albeit particularly inept ones. [9] The islanders treated the Europeans in accordance with the rules of reciprocity and kinship that governed relations in pre-colonial societies. They are generous; they provide food and permit the Europeans to establish a small settlement. However, they become frustrated with the "Tallow Men's" continued inability to feed themselves and with their clearing of the forests to build a stockade. [10] The turning point comes when the native inhabitants realize that the Europeans, in spite of their promises, have no intention of leaving. Quite the contrary, Sir Christopher Everard, Gonzalo-like, means to "plant the island with people of his own kind" and establish a permanent imperial outpost on the "fair new-found land of Everhope" (*Indigo* 113,156). The natives of Liamuiga mount an attack against the invaders, but the islanders do not have guns, and their knives and poison arrows are no match for the English firearms. Many die, among them Sycorax, and the natives are eventually "subdued." Dulé survives and with his hamstrings slit, is made to serve as Sir Christopher's bondsman. In his journal Everard writes of Dulé (now called Caliban): "He has a mordant wit, 'tis plain, and it diverts me to teach him our language as he serves me. He has already learnt to curse" (*Indigo* 198).

In the "Now" section of the novel, Miranda, Xanthe and Kit, as direct descendants of the original Sir Christopher Everard, are invited to attend the 350th anniversary celebration of the founding of Liamuiga. The year is 1969, and Miranda, who is keenly aware of the rising racial tensions in England, and that "we [Black British] are here because you [Europeans] were there," feels disinclined to "celebrate" the historic Everard landing. The pragmatic Xanthe (in Greek, the gilded one), who serves as a blonde, pearlized foil to Miranda's disheveled "swarthiness" (*Indigo* 232), lectures Miranda, telling her that it's "history with a big H, you can't make it happen or unhappen as you please....this is the past that we belong to. You can't hide from it" (*Indigo* 265). Miranda, less sanguine, cannot absolve herself of her family's complicity in the slave trade so easily: "The slaves, the slaves. The sugar, the Indians who were there, the Indians who were brought there afterward. Feeny [Serafine] and Feeny's parents and grandparents and...her daughter, the one she had to leave behind. The plantations. The leg irons and the floggings. Sugar. Sugar (*Indigo* 267).[11]

Miranda's ambivalence regarding her family's past is reminiscent of Rhys's tortured Creole heroines. However, unlike Rhys's characters, who remain tragically "trapped between worlds," Miranda Everard makes a choice, electing to identify with the island, with Serafine, and with her Creole grandmother, Estelle Desjours, rather than with the class and race privilege that is her legacy as an Everard. The novel's most divided figure is Miranda's father, Kit, a man who looks like he has "somehow found his way in, but never learned the insider's ways" (*Indigo* 12). Kit becomes a casino manager on the island and finds himself "Neither boss nor worker, but somewhere in between, a lackey who is despised but also feared" (*Indigo* 344). Because he is poor, Kit's position on Liamugia is akin to that of Rhys's "white cockroach" in post-emancipation Jamaica. Without money and power, he has lost his connection with "whiteness," but his family name and history still distance him from the islanders. Also like Rhys's Creoles, when in England, in spite of his father's renown, Kit's colonial background and racial indeterminacy relegate him to second-class status.

Miranda's decision to align herself with Caliban and with the revolutionary politics of black nationalism provide Warner an opportunity to denounce the misogyny that informed much of the movement's rhetoric. The 1960s find Miranda in London, working for an alternative newspaper, *Blot*. Sent to interview an avant-garde director about the film he is shooting, she finds a naked white actress sitting on the hood of a rusted car, reading aloud from the work of "a French philosopher who later in a fit of madness, pushed his wife under the bath and held her there till there were no more bubbles (*Indigo* 250).[12] Quoting from LeRoi Jones, another actress reads "Rape the white girls. Rape/their fathers. Cut the mothers' throats" (*Indigo* 253). The director explains the film's message to Miranda, that "female sexuality and capitalist codes of production are intertwined....The difference is that women collude in their subjection. They think it's power" (*Indigo* 252). Thus, the attack on the white actresses strikes a blow against capitalism.

The director's explanation of the relationship between white women's sexuality and the magic of capitalism calls to mind Wynter's argument regarding Shakespeare's Miranda, which states that, although Miranda is subordinate to Prospero's magic, she participates "in the power and privileges generated by the empirical supremacy of her own population." Moreover, she also benefits from being the sexual "object of desire for all classes (Stephano and Trinculo) and all population groups (Caliban)" (363). Warner's solution, via a Miranda whose racial indeterminacy calls into question her absolute affiliation to Prospero, is for Miranda and Caliban to ally themselves against the forces of patriarchy and racism -- for Miranda to become Caliban's Woman.

Caliban re-appears in *Indigo* in the form of an angry, posturing Black Panther actor, who taunts Miranda, calling her "whitey" and "bourgeois liberal" (*Indigo* 256). Miranda protests weakly that she's on his side, thinking to herself, "I can't tell you how bad it feels to be one of them....she would have liked to tell him about her father, who was called Nigger Everard at school and spurned in his own family...how she herself was a musty [mixed-race], couldn't he see it?"(*Indigo* 256). The highly-charged encounter culminates in a one-night-stand, driven, for Miranda, by equal parts of guilt and lust. Afterwards, in an attempt to escape the racial guilt that accompanies her whiteness, Miranda attempts to "pass," frizzing her hair into a drooping afro so that she might "not be mistaken" again (*Indigo* 268).

The novel concludes fifteen years later with the birth of a second mixed-race child, the daughter of the angry actor (Shaka) and Miranda, whom they name Serafine. Miranda happens upon Shaka during a break in a rehersal of a production of *The Tempest.* Shaka is playing Caliban. If his earlier angry rhetoric were, indeed, Caliban's curse, then it seems that in entering into a loving relationship with Miranda, they both have at last found a measure of grace and a way to lay down the burden of memory. Shaka tells Miranda "I'm so tired...of your fucking guilt and our fucking envy.... I'm forgetting as hard as I can" (*Indigo* 373). Both estranged in England, removed from the islands that their respective families called home for generations, the two people recognize in each other a shared sense of placelessness, and a weariness with this "cowardly old world" filled with "ungoodly people." "We're maroons together now," Shaka tells Miranda, "so many of us, and we know our own..." (*Indigo* 373). Maroons, Africans who escaped slavery and established free settlements in the Blue Mountains of Jamaica, are a powerful symbol of African resistance to the totalizing authority of European imperialism and slavery. By suggesting that both Shaka and Miranda are now "maroons" together, Warner proposes a shared New World identity for Miranda and Caliban outside of the roles delineated by *The Tempest's* model of master/slave colonial relations. In her discussion of the novel's conclusion, Zabus argues that though *Indigo* remedies the lack of Caliban's woman through the union of Miranda and Shaka, "Warner does not envisage a Black mate for Caliban as suggested by Sylvia Wynter" (Zabus, WNM 88). In discounting Miranda's claim to blackness, Zabus ignores the degree to which Miranda chooses to identify with the black, diasporic elements of herself as well as the degree to which racial identity becomes a matter of political identification and alignment, rather than an accident of birth.

The Tempest is not so much a plot as a presence in Michelle Cliff's novels, *Abeng* and No *Telephone to Heaven*, allowing the author to break free from the play's limited cast of characters and configurations. Like Warner, Cliff seeks to restore the woman's part to the drama of the New World by giving voice to silenced fictional characters such as Miranda, Sycorax, and Charlotte Brontë's Mad Wife, as well as to the marginalized historical figures of Pocahontas, La Malinche, and Nanny of the Maroons. Indeed, what most distinguishes *No Telephone to Heaven* from both its colonial and postcolonial predecessors is its matriarchal focus and its rejection and denial of patriarchal authority, whether embodied in Prospero or a successfully mated and politically redeemed Caliban (Cartelli, New 96).

Cliff's novels set forth a kind of collective history of the Jamaican people, rather than a linear chronicle of a solitary hero or heroine. In an interview, Cliff has said that most of her work concerns "revising": "revising the written record, what passes as the official version of history, and inserting those lives that have been left out" (Raiskin, Art 71). For Cliff, the light-skinned daughter of middle-class privilege, revising also means re-visioning her family mythology to encompass a history as both the oppressed and the oppressor. Cliff's novels seek to reconcile Sycorax with Prospero, an Afrocentric maternal identity with the legacy of guilt that accompanies her father's European lineage of planters and slave owners. They attempt to rewrite the white Creole history of privilege and integrate it with the unwritten, unrecorded black and Amerindian histories of bondage and resistance.

The protagonist of Cliff's two novels is named Clare Savage, whom Cliff says is not an autobiographical character, but an amalgam of herself and others. Cliff self-consciously ties her project of revising the literary and historical record to that of Rhys, whom she names as a literary foremother. However, whereas Rhys defined herself in colonialist terms, marking her distance between the opposing poles of Englishness and blackness, Cliff seeks to redefine "Creole consciousness" in ways that no longer invoke the oppositional singular identities of mistress and slave or victor and victim. Cliff writes,

> I imagine I am the sister of Bertha Rochester. We are the
> remainders of slavery -- residue:

white cockroaches

white niggers

quadroons

octoroons

mulattos

creoles

white niggers.....

I also imagine I am the sister of Annie Palmer [13].

"white witch"

creole bitch

imported to the north coast of Jamaica

legend of the island

mistress of Rosehall

guilty of husband-murder three times over. (*LLB* 41,43) [14]

By claiming kinship with Annie Palmer as well as Bertha Mason, and by claiming the pejorative terms "white cockroach" and "white nigger" along with the quasi-scientific classifications "mulatto, octoroon, and quadroon," designations that spoke to an individual's admixture of "black blood," Cliff marks "Creole" as a continuum, rather than as a mid-point between two opposite extremes.

Abeng and *No Telephone to Heaven* chronicle Clare Savage's coming of age in Jamaica and in the United States, her quest to learn the suppressed history of Jamaica, and her eventual commitment to anti-colonialist politics. In her essay "Caliban's Daughter," Cliff says of Clare, "A knowledge of history, of the past has been bleached from her mind, just as the rapes of her grandmothers bleached her skin. And this bleached skin is the source of her privilege and power..." (45). Clare's father, "Boy" Savage, claims his whiteness through his great-grandfather, Judge Savage, who owned a sugar estate and a hundred slaves, whom he burned to death on the eve of emancipation in Jamaica in 1831. Boy's great-grandmother, the judge's involuntary slave-mistress, is remembered by the Savage family as "'Guatemalan' -- part Indian and part Spanish." For the Savages "[t]he definition of what a Savage was like was fixed by color, class, and religion, and over the years a carefully contrived mythology was constructed which they used to protect their identities. When they were poor, and not all of them white, the mythology persisted" (*Abeng* 29). Thus, Clare is "white" although her mother, Kitty Freeman Savage, openly acknowledges her racially-mixed background. Clare's move from aimlessness to action is marked by a growing awareness that her class and color privilege have been, as Gayatri Chakravorty Spivak says, her loss, and that achieving psychic wholeness does not mean relinquishing privilege, but rather, as Cliff explains, "grasp[ing] more of herself" by embracing the scattered fragments of a suppressed maternal identity (Schwartz 607).

Cliff locates the potential for recuperation of identity in the Jamaican landscape and, specifically, in maternal figures who are associated with the island. Cliff writes, "For me, the land is redolent of my grandmother(s) and mother" (Daughter 46). Indeed, as Belinda Edmondson notes, "all black women in [*Abeng*] are presented as having a direct linkage to a positive black history and consciousness" (188), a link that is nourished through their explicit connection to the Jamaican landscape. Clare's relationship to the land is negotiated through her mother, Kitty, who attempts to pass on to Clare her reverence for the land, for the Jamaica beneath the colonial estates and behind beach front resorts.

In spite of her husband's objections, Kitty insists that Clare spend part of every summer away from Boy and from the bourgeois world of Kingston, with Miss Mattie, her maternal grandmother, "in the bush." Clare is "given" a playmate, Zoe, the daughter of a market woman whom Miss Mattie allows to squat on her land. Clare's relationship with Zoe provides her first inkling of the privileged position she occupies within the stratified system of class, caste, and color in colonial Jamaica. Although they are friends, Zoe, the poorer, darker child, is well aware of the differences in their respective positions *vis à vis* the class and color hierarchies of Jamaica, differences that Clare takes for granted:

> Wunna is town gal, and wunna pappa is buckra [white]. Wunna talk buckra. Wunna leave here when wunna people come fe wunna. Me will be here so all me life -- me will be marketwoman....Wunna will go a England, den maybe America to university, and when we meet later we will be different smaddy. But we is different smaddy now. (*Abeng* 118)

Clare is reluctant to accept Zoe's unflinching assessment of their differences and of the divergent paths their lives will soon take. She wonders why things must be so "fixed." And she feels "split" between two identities: "white and not-white, town and country, scholarship and privilege, Boy and Kitty" (*Abeng* 119). Clare's identity crisis presupposes an inherent disjuncture within the Creole identity. In her quest for wholeness, Clare must look past her privilege as Prospero's daughter to "her real sources," which have been effaced, "whitewashed," by colonial history. Moving toward wholeness means assimilating both halves of her identity. Cliff writes, "as I grasp more of this part [the part associated with her maternal ancestry] I realize what needs to be done with the rest of my life" (*LLB* 71).

Coming-to-consciousness as a Jamaican woman, then, means distancing herself from her paternal legacy, the privilege accorded her as a light-skinned daughter of Prospero, and identifying, instead, with the island and with the maternal legacy of her "grandmothers": Bertha Mason, Pocahontas, and Sycorax. Myriam Chancy argues that Cliff affirms the need for re-connection to "fore/mothers" and to the "ancestral Afrocentric knowledge they represent." For Chancy, adopting Sycorax facilitates a reclamation of "self, spirit and body in light of a buried history" that can ameliorate Caliban's profitless appeal for "recognition and affirmation that will never, in truth, be freely granted" (168). However, championing Sycorax does not displace the colonizer/colonized binary; it merely supplants Caliban with Sycorax as Prospero's antithesis. And in spite of Cliff's ostensible rejection of linear narrative and unitary racial and sexual identities, Chancy's reading casts Clare's move toward action and speech as making a none-too-subtle choice between Father/Prospero/England, and [Grand]Mother/Sycorax/Africa. While I think that positing Clare's foremothers as an untapped, unmediated source of ancestral knowledge risks defining women in terms of a biological or cultural essence, I prefer to read replacing Prospero with Sycorax as a form of strategic essentialism, that is, a positivist essentialism that allows for the possibility of mobilizing to effect social change.[15] Like Warner's Miranda, Clare will eventually choose an identity that permits her to perform the political actions she believes in. In this respect, Clare's "strategic créolité" echoes the Creolists' manifesto, which posits créolité as a way of *becoming*, rather than a way of *being*.

No Telephone to Heaven traces the trajectory of Clare's reverse middle passage, as she travels from Jamaica, to the United States, and finally to England in search of the diasporic fragments of her colonized self. The novel opens as Clare and her family embark for New York where the profligate Boy hopes to improve his situation. When her mother dies unexpectedly, Clare finds herself stranded in Brooklyn with her father. Using "the logic of a Creole" (*NTH* 109) she decides to go to England to further her education. Alone in the "country she had been taught to call Mother" (*NTH* 111), Clare rereads *Jane Eyre* and is taken in by Brontë's heroine:

> Yes. The parallels were there. Was she not heroic Jane? Betrayed
> Left to wander. Solitary. Motherless... Converted for a time,
> [Clare] came to. Then, with a sharpness, reprimanded herself.
> No...not Jane. Small and pale. English. No, she paused. No, my
> girl, try Bertha Wild-maned Bertha...Yes, Bertha was closer to the
> mark. Captive. Ragout. Mixture. Confused. Jamaican. Caliban.
> Carib. Cannibal. Cimarron. All Bertha. All Clare. (*NTH* 116)

Here and elsewhere in Cliff's novel, Clare acts out what Rhys has previously suggested on the level of textuality. That is, she explicitly rejects identification with Jane Eyre, the "feminist, individualist, heroine of British fiction" (Spivak, TWT 270), and rewrites herself, instead, as the composite, confused, colonial other. Edmondson notes that this passage "is particularly important for the link it provides between Caliban and Bertha, the two gendered symbols of Caribbean independence and invisibility [both of whom] inhere with the identity of Clare" (184). However, rather than Caliban, Cartelli argues that "it is Miranda-- like Cliff herself a product of Western experience education, and indoctrination -- who plays a more prominent role in underwriting Clare Savage's subjective development...." (New 91). But instead of defining herself solely in terms of her relationship to Europe and to Prospero, Clare/Miranda (like Warner's Miranda Everard) deliberately divorces herself from her father and from his family's history of colonial power and privilege in favor of her matrilineal inheritance.

Clare/Miranda encounters "Caliban" in Bobby, a physically and psychologically maimed African-American veteran, whose happy childhood memories of "catching shrimp with [his] mother...gathering okra, and dodging snakes" (*NTH* 158) have been permanently supplanted by horrific visions of Viet Nam. The possibility of "peopling the isle" with the offspring of a union between Miranda and Caliban is foreclosed after Clare becomes pregnant but miscarries as a result of a malformation in the fetus, which Bobby blames on the effects of Agent Orange. A side-effect of the miscarriage is an infection that renders Clare sterile: "All that effort for naught. Lightening up. Eyes for naught. Skin for naught. Fine nose for naught. Mule--most likely" (*NTH* 169).[16]

Cliff has written that the most "whole" character in *No Telephone to Heaven* is Harry/Harriet, an androgynous Ariel-figure who can "pass" as man or woman. Harry/Harriet is the novel's most insistent voice for social change; s/he tells Clare that it's a luxury not to choose: "...[W]e will have to make the choice. Cast our lot. Cyaan live split. Not in this world" (*NTH 131*). Extending the metaphor of the Jamaican landscape as female, s/he tells Clare," Jamaica's children have to work to make her change. It will be worthwhile...believe me" (*NTH* 127). Harry/Harriet has to choose between life as a man and life as a woman and Clare must choose whether to remain adrift in Europe or to return to the island and work for social change. Raiskin argues that Harry/Harriet's and Clare's choices complicate the meaning of "identity politics" by resisting the positions they have been assigned within the colonial matrix of race, class, and gender "not to take on new 'truer positions,' but [to] choose roles that permit them to perform the political actions they believe in" (Raiskin, *Snow* 192). Clare elects to return to her grandmother's land with a guerrilla group committed to fight against the neo-colonial exploitation of Jamaica. Harry/Harriet becomes Harriet only ("the choice is mine man, is made. Harriet live and Harry be no more"), and goes forth "like Mary Seacole" to nurse the poorest of the poor in the "Dungle" (the shantytown) of Kingston (*NTH* 168, 171).

At the end of *No Telephone to Heaven*, Clare has cast her lot, but her choice results in her death. She joins a resistance movement to fight against the neocolonial destruction of Jamaica by multinational corporations. Since she is no longer able to reproduce, she donates her grandmother's land, her inheritance, to the cause. Clare's life ends literally burned into this same piece of land, when her small revolutionary band is ambushed by the mercenaries hired as protection by an American film company. Clare's comrades come from a cross-section of Jamaican society, a group who, Cliff says, have been brought up to distrust each other and to distrust light-skinned Jamaicans, who are perceived as Quashees (informers), in particular. One of Clare's last cognizant thoughts is to wonder "Who had been the quashee?" Then nothingness: "She remembered language. Then it was gone" (*NTH* 208). Clare's dying thought, *"who among us was the traitor?"* indicates that in spite of her revolutionary politics, she remains trapped by colonial thought patterns, a legacy of slavery that pit the house nigger against the field hand.

As its title suggests, there is no redemption in *No Telephone to Heaven,* no reconciliation between the descendants of Prospero and the descendants of Sycorax. Cliff describes the novel's ending as "essentially tragic," but one that completes the...triangle of [Clare's] life." Because she dies defending Jamaican autonomy and dies on her grandmother's land, Cliff argues that in death, Clare finally achieves "complete identification with her homeland"(Daughter 45). But this is a high price to pay if, like her "grandmother," Bertha Mason, identification with her homeland can only be achieved through death. Cliff's apparent inability to envisage a productive means of resistance to the forces of neocolonialism can be seen as a failure of imagination. However, rather than blaming Cliff, I take my cue here from Spivak, who suggests that instead of indicting the artist, we rage against the "abject script" of the imperialist narrative (*Critique* 116), a narrative in which both Bertha Mason and Cliff's Clare/Miranda must choose between assimilation and acceptance or resistance and death.

All the novels discussed here suggest that it is time to break with Prospero and Caliban as paradigms of the colonizer and the colonized and to look, instead, to the female figures of Sycorax, Miranda, and Bertha as models for a new, creolized, New World identity. Thus, the Creole woman moves from the pitiful "white cockroach," trapped between worlds, to a guerilla warrior who renounces her privilege as Prospero's daughter and takes her inspiration, instead, from Nanny of the Maroons, whom Cliff calls "the Jamaican Sycorax"(Cliff, Daughter 47),[17] as she casts her lot with her countrymen against the forces of neocolonialism and capitalism. No longer a passive victim or an object of exchange in a contest between Prospero and Caliban, Miranda identifies herself on her own terms and through a maternal lineage that includes Jane Eyre and Bertha, Pocahontas and Nanny, mistress and slave. As Derek Walcott writes, "revolutionary literature is a filial impulse, and...maturity is the assimilation of the features of every ancestor" (111). Both novels demand a break with Prospero and Caliban as racialized paradigms of the colonizer and the colonized; both seek to re-imagine the long-contested island space as a brave new world, neither wholly European nor wholly African, whose inhabitants must struggle to place themselves both within and against the scripts that history has written.

Jennifer Sparrow

NOTES

[1] See José Enriqué Rodó, *Ariel,* trans. Margeret Sayers Peden (1900; Austin: University of Texas Press, 1988) and Rubén Darío "the Triumph of Caliban" *Spanish American Images of the United State 1790-1960s,* ed. John T. Reid (Gainesville: University Presses of Florida, 1977): 195. The original Spanish version, "El triunfo de Caliban," is reprinted in *Escritos ineditos de Rubén Darío,* ed. E.K. Mapes (New York: Instituto de las Españas en los Estados Unidos, 1938): 160-62.

[2] A. Belhassen, "Aimé Césaire's *A Tempest,*" *Radical Perspectives in the Arts,* ed. Lee Baxandall (Middlesex UK: Penguin, 1972): 176.

[3] In English Canada, both male and female authors have found that rather than the Prospero/Caliban relationship, it is the relationship between Prospero and Miranda, between parent and dutiful daughter of the Empire, that is the most apt colonial metaphor. For discussions of these texts, see Diana Brydon, "Re-writing *The "Tempest,"* WLWE 23.1 (1984): 75-88, and Chantal Zabus, "Prospero's Progeny Curses Back: Postcolonial, Postmodern, and Postpatriarchal Rewritings of *The Tempest,*" in Theo D'Haen and Hans Bertens, *Liminal Postmodernisms: the Postmodern, the Post(-)Colonial and the Post(-)Feminist,* in *Postmodern Studies,* 8. (Asterdam and Atlanda: Rodopi):115-138. Also, Elaine Showalter argues that women writers from the US have a long history of looking to Miranda as a metaphor of the woman artist or feminist intellectual. See her discussion of Harriet Beecher Stowe, Louisa May Alcott, Katherine Anne Porter, Sylvia Plath, and Gloria Naylor in "Miranda's Story," in *Sister's Choice: Tradition and Change in American Women's Writing,* (Oxford: Clarendon Press, 1991): 22-42.

[4] Fanon, although not writing explicitly about Caliban, rhapsodizes about grasping white civilization and dignity along with white breasts (*BSWM* 56); George Lamming, after speculating on whether or not Caliban really tried to "lay her" in *The Pleasures of Exile,* answers his own question in *Water With Berries* with an obscenely violated Myra, a prostituted, suicidal Randa, and an on-stage rape committed by an erstwhile Othello. In Césaire's *Une Tempête* (1969) Miranda's character is incidental -- "hitched to Ferdinand's star" (III.v. pg 58) in the last act. His Sycorax, even more importantly, is re-cast as an idealized "Earth Mother," an abstraction of *négritude's* "Mother Africa," rather than as a viable speaking subject.

[5] See Wynter, Sylvia. "Beyond Miranda's Meanings: Un/silencing the 'Demonic Ground' of Caliban's 'Woman.'" in Davies and Fido 355-371.

[6] Donaldson refers here, not to the relationship of inferiority and dependency described by O. Mannoni, but to one that casts Prospero in the role of "omnipotent Western patriarch, and Caliban [as] the 'native' Other suffering from the cultural deracination..." wrought by deportation and slavery (16).

[7] "The Locked Heart: The Creole Family Romance of *Wide Sargasso Sea,*" *Colonial Discourse/Postcolonial Theory,* eds. Francis Barker, Peter Hulme, and Margaret Iverson (Manchester: Manchester University Press, 1993): 2-88. Abbreviated LH.

[8] Liamuiga and its smaller sister-island, Oualie (called Grand Thom' and Petit Thom' after colonization) clearly correspond to St. Kitts and Nevis, two of the Leeward islands of the Lesser Antilles.

[9] In *Prospero and Caliban: the Psychology of Colonization* Mannoni argues that "wherever Europeans have founded colonies...it can safely be said that their coming was unconsciously expected--even desired--by the future subject peoples" (*PC* 86).

[10] Hulme has noted the parallels between the Europeans' reliance on the native Americans for food and the magician Prospero's reliance on Caliban to chop wood and catch fish. Because of their technology (especially firearms) Europeans " *became* magical when introduced into a less technologically developed society, but [they] were incapable (for a variety of reasons) of feeding themselves" (*Encounters* 128).

[11] In an interview, Warner states that the "cruelty and waste" of the colonial enterprise was driven by a hunger for sugar. As such, she decided to put "something sweet" in every chapter of *Indigo* (Rich Pickings, 31).

[12] Marxist theorist Louis Althusser killed his wife in this manner in 1980. He pled insanity.

[13] Herbert deLisser's *White Witch of Rosehall* (1929) recounts the Jamaican legend of Annie Palmer, the sadistic, sexually insatiable mistress of Rosehall estate, who murdered three husbands and terrorized her slaves through the use of obeah.

[14] References to Cliff's works are incorporated in the text, keyed to the following abbreviations and editions:

> *Abeng* -- *Abeng*, (1984 *New York:* Dutton, 1990).
> *BW* -- *Bodies of Water* (New York: Dutton, 1990).
> Daughter -- "Caliban's Daughter: The Tempest an d the Teapot,"
>   *Frontiers* 12.1 (1991): 36-51.
> *LLB* -- *The Land of Look Behind* , (Ithaca: Firebrand, 1985).
> *NTH* --- *No Telephone to Heaven* , (1989 New York: Plume, 1996).

[15] For a discussion of strategic essentialism, see Gayatri Chakravorty Spivak, "In A Word," *Outside in the Teaching Machine,* (New York: Routledge, 1993): 1-24.

[16] Clare is referring to the nineteenth-century belief that different races were in fact different species and that a bi-racial individual was a hybrid species and, thus, sterile. The most commonly used example was that of the mule, a cross between a horse and a donkey. The word *mulatto* derives from a reference to the sterile hybridity of the mule.

[17] Nanny was the leader of the Windward Maroons who hid in the Blue Mountains of Jamaica and fought against the British during the War of the Maroons (1655-1740). Nanny was said to have been an obeah-woman of the Ashanti tribe, who prepared amulets and oaths for her followers that rendered the British bullets harmless (Cliff, *Abeng* 14).

WORKS CITED

Belhassen, A. "Aime Césaire's *A Tempest,* " in *Radical Perpectives in the Arts*. ed. Lee Baxandall. Middlesex UK: Penguin, 1972.

Bernabé, Jean, Patrick Chamoiseau and Raphael Confiant. "In Praise of Creoleness."

Callaloo 13 (1990) 886-909.

Brathwaite, Edward. *The Development of Creole Society in Jamaica 1770-1820* . Oxford: Clarendon Press, 1971.

Carby, Hazel. *Reconstructing Womanhood: The Emergence of the Afro-American Woman Novelist*. New York: Oxford University Press, 1987.

Cartelli, Thomas. "After the Tempest: Shakespeare, Postcoloniality, and Michelle Cliff's New, New World Miranda" *Contemporary Literature*. 36(1): 82-102.

---. *Repositioning Shakespeare: National formations, postcolonial appropriations* . New York: Routledge, 1999.

Césaire, Aimé. *A Tempest.* (1969) Trans. Richard Miller. New York: Ubu Repertory Theatre Publications, 1992.

Chancy, Myriam A. *Searching for Safe Spaces: Afro Caribbean Women Writers in Exile.* Philadelphia: Temple University Press, 1997.

Cliff, Michelle. *Abeng*. 1984. New York.· Dutton, 1990.

---. *Bodies of Water*. New York: Dutton, 1990.

---. "Caliban's Daughter: The Tempest and the Teapot." *Frontiers* 12.1 (1991): 36-51.

---. *The Land of Look Behind* . Ithaca: Firebrand, 1985.

---. *No Telephone to Heaven* . 1989. New York: Plume, 1996.

Davies, Carole Boyce and Elaine Savory Fido. *Out of the Kumbla: Caribbean   Women and Literature*. Trenton, N.J.: Africa World Press, 1990.

Donaldson, Laura E.. *Decolonizing Feminisms: Race, Gender, and Empire-Building.* Chapel Hill: University of North Carolina Press, 1992.

Edmondson, Belinda. "Race, Writing, and the Politics of (Re) Writing History: An Analysis of the Novels of Michelle Cliff." *Callaloo* 6(1): 180-191.

Fanon, Frantz. *Black Skin, White Masks.* 1967. Trans. Charles Lam Markmann. New York: Grove Weidenfeld, 1991.

Glissant, Edouard. *Caribbean Discourse.* trans. J. Michael Dash. Charlottesville: University of Virginia Press, 1989.

Hulme, Peter. *Colonial Encounters: Europe and the Native Caribbbean, 1492-1797.* New

York: Methuen, 1986.

---. "The Locked Heart: The Creole Family Romance of *Wide Sargasso Sea*" in *Colonial Discourse/Postcolonial Theory*. eds. Francis Barker, Peter Hulme, and Margaret Iverson. Manchester: Manchester University Press, 1993. 72-88.

Lamming, George. *The Pleasures of Exile*. 1960. Reprint, Fwd. Sandra Pouchet Paquet. Ann Arbor: University of Michigan Press, 1992.

Mannoni, D. O. *Prospero and Caliban: The Psychology of Colonization*. 1950. Trans. Pamela Powesland. New Forward by Maurice Bloch. Ann Arbor: University of Michigan Press, 1990.

Nixon, Rob. "African Appropriations of *The Tempest*" *Critical Inquiry*. Spring 1987 557-578.

Raiskin, Judith L. "The Art of History: An Interview with Michelle Cliff." *Kenyon Review* 15.1 (1993): 57-71

---. *Snow on the Cane Fields: Women's Writing and Creole Subjectivity*. Minneapolis: University of Minnesota Press, 1996.

Jean Rhys. *Wide Sargasso Sea*. 1966. Ed. Judith L. Raiskin. New York: Norton, 1999.

Schwartz, Meryl F. "An Interview with Michelle Cliff" *Contemporary Literature*. 34 (1993): 595-619.

Shakespeare, William. *The Tempest*. 1623. Ed. Frank Kermode. New York: Routledge, 1994.

Spivak, Gayatri Chakravorty. *A Critique of Postcolonial Reason: Toward a History of the Vanishing Present*. Cambridge: Harvard University Press, 1999.

---. *Outside in the Teaching Machine*. New York: Routedge, 1993.

---. "Three Women's Texts and a Critique of Imperialism." in *'Race,' Writing and Difference*. ed. Henry Louis Gates, Jr.. Chicago: University of Chicago Press, 1986. 262-280.

Vaughan, Alden T. and Virginia Mason. *Shakespeare's Caliban: A Cultural History*. New York: Cambridge University Press, 1991.

Walcott, Derek. *What the Twilight Says*: *Essays*. New York: Farrar, Straus, Giroux. 1998.

Warner, Marina. "Between the Colonist and the Creole: Family Bonds, Family

Boundaries." in Shirley Chew and Anna Rutherford, eds. *Unbecoming Daughters of the Empire*. Sydney: Dangaroo Press, 1993. 199-204.

---. *Indigo: or Mapping the Waters*. New York: Simon and Schuster, 1992.

---. "Rich Pickings." in *The Agony and the Ego: The Art and Strategy of Fiction Writing Explored*. Harmondsworth: Penguin, 1993. 29-34.

Wynter, Sylvia. "Beyond Miranda's Meanings: Un/silencing the 'Demonic Ground' of Caliban's 'Woman.'" in Davies and Fido 355-371.

Zabus, Chantal. "A Calabanic Tempest in Anglophone and Francophone New World Writing." *Canadian Literature* 104 (1985): 34-50.

---. "Prospero's Progeny Curses Back: Postcolonial, Postmodern, and Postpatriarchal Rewritings of *The Tempest*." in Theo D'Haen and Hans Bertens *Liminal Postmodernisms: the Postmodern, the Post(-)Colonial and the Post(-) Feminist*. Atlanta: Rodopi, 1995. 115-138.

---. "Spinning a Yarn with Marina Warner." in *Into the Nineties: Post-Colonial Women's Writing*. London: Dangaroo Press, 1994. 519-529.

---. "What Next Miranda: Marina Warner's *Indigo*." *Kunapipi* 16.3 (1994): 81-92.

7.

WHITE IDENTITY AND THE NEW ETHIC
IN FAULKNER'S *LIGHT IN AUGUST*

"What do whites talk about when they talk about racism?" The words of performance artist Robbie McCauley resonated over the heads of a silent, primarily Euro-American audience at Bowling Green State University one night. Her question struck me as a good one. While important conversations about the intersection between race issues and literature have been going on for a long time, it can be difficult for whites who want to engage these issues to avoid slipping into a posture that is either defensive or hyperapologetic--polarities that tend to curtail rather than facilitate one's ability to deepen or extend the conversation. More productive seems to be scholarly examinations of the ways in which race is constructed such as Ruth Frankenberg's *White Women, Race Matters: The Social Construction of Whiteness*. Here Frankenberg describes whiteness as "a set of linked dimensions." The first allows whiteness to function as racially conferred privilege, the next dimension is a perspective from which whites consider themselves and others, and the last allows whiteness to act as a referent to cultural practices which are most often "unmarked and unnamed" (1).

When contemplating this definition of white identity in conjunction with Faulkner's *Light in August*, one sees not only a representation of white privilege as a perspective, but also a dramatization of scapegoatism, a cultural practice integral to the maintenance of an identity that is constructed in opposition to, and at the expense of, that which falls outside it. But simply naming Joe Christmas's position as scapegoat is not enough: it is important, I believe, to try to understand how this practice operates and the psycho-social forces that put it into play as presented in this text.

I.   The Collective Shadow in *Light in August*

According to Erich Neumann, the chief difficulty raised by the typical process of forming an identity--whether it be that of an individual or a group--is that it usually depends on the rejection and often the vilification of that which falls outside it. If, for instance, one accepts the association between the color white and virtue, it may seem a logical extension to cast those with non-white features at the opposite end of a spectrum. Even if we feel ourselves to be beyond the false association of white/good and black/evil, the clean simplicity of binary classifications can be hard to resist. In *Depth Psychology and the New Ethic*, Neumann writes that such polarities are inevitable at an early stage in an individual's or society's development of consciousness, but in maturity a capacity for a more sophisticated approach to morality develops. This early method of defining morality, which depends on "the principle of opposites in conflict," is what Neumann calls the old ethic (45).

Value judgments are inherent in the old ethic. Limited by the binary system to only two poles, a social unit must consider the characteristics that suit its identity to be "good" and the characteristics that would compromise its identity to be "bad." This is an important factor in the old ethic's operation: the undesirable material cannot be acknowledged to be merely incompatible with the group's identity; the material must be denigrated as well in order to seal its rejection. Neumann applies this assignment of values to the formation of an individual's ego and to a group's "ethos," or conscious identity; indeed, one can observe many instances where "I am" is defined in opposition to "I am not." In Jungian terms, the "I am not" (a.k.a. Neumann's "Thou" or the poststructuralist's "Other") falls into the realm of the shadow, one of Jung's most fascinating and useful concepts. A most general description of the shadow can be borrowed from Marie-Louise von Franz, who writes that the shadow can be seen as "all that is within you which you do not know about"(4). Faulkner himself observes, "[I]t is a happy faculty of mind to slough that which conscience refuses to assimilate" (323). The conscience indeed has the ability to deny ownership of traits it finds challenging to its self-concept--this is what is called repression--but that which is "sloughed" does not simply disappear: it is forced into the unconscious where it contributes to the shadow.

In and of itself, the shadow is not evil, but often its contents are perceived as such because they are not acknowledged to be part of the identity, and in a binary value system that labels desirable traits as "good," rejected traits are assigned the opposing value. The shadow's most highly charged material and therefore the material that is most actively repressed is often that which the self needs in order to function but cannot incorporate within its identity without serious compromise. The repression of this material often results in its taking on a violent character. Neumann observes the danger of repressing psychic material, especially those "contents which are capable of becoming conscious but whose access to consciousness has been blocked" as they are most likely to "become evil and destructive"(49). The more repressive the self is toward these elements, the more destructive the resultant tension can become, since the alienated material must become more forceful as it struggles for its place in the psyche to be acknowledged. Pushing its way through layers of denial, the shadow provokes a corresponding counterforce in defense of the status quo.

As an individual consciousness has a personal shadow, a group has a collective shadow. Franz asserts that the collective shadow is uniquely dangerous because it is so difficult for members of the group to recognize: "[P]eople support each other in their blindness--it is only in wars, or in hate for other nations, that the collective shadow reveals itself" (6-7). This is true even if we exchange "nation" with another type of grouping, such as "gender" or "race." When a group identity embraces a set of concepts it defines as whiteness, characteristics associated with non-whiteness become loaded with negative value, and people identified as non-white are excluded from and oppressed by that community. Conflicts between relative equals in martial and political power are distressing enough; what complicates race as an identity marker is that whites' domination and exploitation of nonwhites has historically preceded definitions of whiteness. Indeed, as postcolonial scholars point out, whiteness signifies a strategically constructed rationale that attempts to justify commercial and cultural profiteering. Furthermore, many of the traits that seem to constitute whiteness are no more the province of whites than of anyone else. A propensity for violence, a certain "inscrutability," and closeness with the natural world are but a few of the traits we see associated with blackness in Faulkner's work, yet it goes without saying that there are certainly plenty of violent, inscrutable, earthy white people. Nevertheless, white can cast black as its shadow, thus consciously disassociating itself from traits some members of its community possess.

When approaching the idea of a collective white identity, one runs into the problem Adrienne Rich has found whenever one tries to speak of "we." As she says, "[T]here is no collective movement that speaks for each of us all the way through"(644). Thus any attempt to responsibly define a generic collective white identity would be a major undertaking, one outside this brief paper's scope. (Reality is shaggy; it likes to rebel against the tidy topiaries of theory.) This said, Faulkner's work strikes a resonant chord with its presentation of the distinct collective ethos that emerges in *Light in August*, an ethos which is both white and androcentric.

We glimpse the values of this community early on, when we see the pregnant Lena Grove walking with her "unflagging and tranquil faith" in search of Lucas Burch, the father of her child. We are told her path has been "a peaceful corridor paved with unflagging and tranquil faith and peopled with kind and nameless faces and voices" (4). The narrator's stance makes it clear that Lena is the one who perceives the kindness, but Armstid, the farmer who offers her shelter one night, sees the matter differently. He muses, "I reckon womenfolks are likely to be good without being very kind. Men, now, might. But it's only a bad woman herself that is likely to be very kind to another woman that needs the kindnesses' thinking" (10). Yet despite Armstid's "kindness," the reader registers that the character subscribes to his community's collective values and considers Lena to be a bad woman. Furthermore, she is a shameless one at that for getting into, as Armstid says, "what she don't even call trouble" (12). We can expect that he, like Lena's brother, considers her "a whore" (4).

Lena is not the only unmarried pregnant woman to traverse these pages. We later learn that Joe Christmas's mother, Milly Hines, also became pregnant out of wedlock. Though Mrs. Hines would accept her daughter Milly and the baby, Doc Hines seems to feel his daughter and her child represent an unacceptable rupture in his value system. This drives the unstable man to prevent Milly's elopement by murdering the child's father and to later cause her death in childbed by preventing a doctor's attendance. Significantly, his expressions of outrage are laden with pseudo-Christian rhetoric, as the multi-valenced use of Christianity in the novel is a strong clue to the dilemma created whenever anyone clasps an ideological pole too tightly. In this passage, he describes his discovery of Milly's condition to Reverend Hightower, referring to himself in the third person:

> He ought to knowed God's abomination of womanflesh; he should have
> knowed the walking shape of bitchery and abomination already stinking

in God's sight. Telling old Doc Hines, that knowed better, that he was a
Mexican. When old Doc Hines could see in his face the black curse of
God Almighty. (353-54)

Doc Hines's murderous response to his daughter's sexual liberality is an
extreme reaction to the judgment levied against women who don't play by the
rules--that is, whose actions threaten the established Judeo-Christian ethos in
which female chastity is valued and its opposite is "sin and bitchery." That Doc
Hines believes Milly's lover to have been of African, rather than the presumably
less egregious Mexican descent, is not offered as textual proof that this was so. It
is clear through Hines's obvious madness and the lack of credible corroboration
that Faulkner intends to leave this point ambiguous. And yet the old man fixates
on the suitor's "nigger blood" to fuel the rage which he carries over into his
insane persecution of his grandson, Joe Christmas.

Here, we see the anxiety provoked by the lover's dubious race mixed
with the judgment against Milly's sexual freedom in such a way that the former-
-whether true or not--forms a massive projection of the white male ethos against
all activities that are a threat to its identity, including those attached to race as
obviously as promiscuity is here. Philip Weinstein says that in Joe Christmas
Faulkner found that "racial difference, gender distinction, and sexual desire fuse
into a single magnetic field[...]" (52-53). I would extend this observation to
include the characters that surround Joe. There are many such moments in Light
in August where that which is black is associated with the feminine--as, for
example, in the Faulknerian blur "womanshenegro" (47)--both of which are in
turn made to carry associations to physical passion, animalism, fecundity, the
natural world, and paganism. Blackness in Light in August is not a state limited
to having African ancestry. Instead, it is a container for all the shadow contents
of the white, male, Judeo-Christian identity, an identity which, because formed
according to the old ethic, must maintain itself through acts of internal
repression and external oppression against those upon whom it can project the
threatening material--those who seem to deny the dominant ethos.

Though the two identities sometimes overlap, blackness and femaleness
are not interchangeable in this novel. Still, in the sense that both carry part of the
white, androcentric community's shadow in this novel, they certainly have
something in common, a commonality important in considering this novel in
terms of the old and new ethics.

II. Joe Christmas, Scapegoatism, and the Old Ethic

The "Us" versus "Them" mentality of the old ethic results in the accumulation of tension between the collective consciousness and its shadow. According to Jungian analyst Sylvia Brinton Perera, these tensions once found expression and temporary resolution in periodic enactments of religious rituals, such as the ancient Hebrew rite described in Leviticus from which we inherit the term "scapegoat." For this ritual, two goats were chosen. One was sacrificed to propitiate Yahweh; the other was symbolically heaped with the sins of the tribe and then driven into the wilderness where, it was believed, it would be devoured by a divine being called Azazel who would digest the sin. In the ritual, the heavy burden of the toxic collective shadow, interpreted as sin, was magically transferred to and symbolically grounded in a tangible creature (the goat) so that the vague and fearsome anxieties that haunted the collective unconscious could be driven off to a being far better equipped--because of its divine, rather than mortal, status--to handle sin without becoming contaminated by it. The wandering goat, "the chosen and over-burdened carrier of collective guilt," is "analogous to the libido of impulses which originally threatened or challenged the ideals of the status quo and were called sinful" (22-23). Perera explains that there came to be a crucial alteration in Azazel's character: though he began as a chthonic god for a herding people, he evolved (or devolved) into an accusatory demon, becoming "Yahweh's scapegoat" when he was "redefined [...] simplified, made opposite and evil in order to excise Yahweh's shadow" (19). In other words, an infallibly righteous divinity must have its ballast at the other end of the moral spectrum.

Psychologically, a demonized Azazel cannot perform his original function as "divine source and carrier":

> In the modern [psychological] complex, Azazel is a condemning judge.[...] Since he represents a negativized spirit that will not accept or recognize any wayward impulsivity, the wandering goat becomes a symbol of dissociated, hence demonic, energies that have lost their connection to a transpersonal, neutral libido source. They cannot find the matrix in which they can be put to rest, and they cannot be admitted into consciousness at all while the sadistic accuser controls what is acceptable. (Perera 23)

It is thus a demonic version of the ancient rite we see Faulkner evoke in *Light in August*. Clearly, Joe Christmas becomes the goat which must be sacrificed in order to maintain the boundary between the conscious collective of white identity and its collective shadow, but he also internalizes and reinforces the voice of the "sadistic accuser." Joe is often read as a Christ figure, but one with a complicated martyrdom. Faulkner's biblical allusions and the likenesses between Joe and Christianity's holiest martyr have been so well documented that I will light on only a few points. Next to the name and their age at their deaths, both Joe and Christ agree on some level to travel a fixed trajectory toward their fates. But, unlike Jesus Christ, Joe is not divine, and where Christian mythology holds that the former was charged by God to carry his burden, the mortal Joe has been singled out for his travails by the human representative of the demonic "sadistic accuser," God's shadow: Azazel.

Joe is groomed for his role in this demonic scapegoat ritual from birth. The initial gestures that mark his supposed blackness are his associations with female "sin and bitchery," first through his premarital conception and then by the dietitian's fear of exposure for an amorous escapade. We are told that Joe is singled out from the other children in the white orphanage not because he is essentially unique but because Doc Hines manufactures a difference by staring at him "with a profound and unflagging attention." Faulkner writes,

> If the child had been older he would perhaps have thought He hates me
> and fears me. So much so that he cannot let me out of his sight.[...] That is
> why I am different from the others: because he is watching me all the
> time. (129)

A conspiracy between Doc Hines and the dietitian ends in Joe's adoption by the dour and oppressive MacEachern. Joe resents his treatment at his foster father's hands but becomes accustomed to it. By the time he's eight, he learns to accept MacEachern's beatings "with a rapt, calm expression like a monk in a picture" (140). He is more comfortable with the abuse than with Mrs. MacEachern's attempts at kindness. For example, after the beating Joe receives for failing to memorize the Presbyterian catechism, Mrs. MacEachern brings a tray of food to his room which he overturns on the floor. Later, he crawls to the corner and "above the outraged food kneeling, with his hands ate, like a savage, like a dog" (146). Jessie McGuire Coffee identifies these and other food-related episodes as evidence of Joe's "attitude toward a kind of communion, the breaking of bread with other people" in way that contrasts markedly with Christ's (44). Indeed the religious references implicate the sacred, but Joe's inability to accept unspoiled nourishment is an indication of the profane. Later, when Joanna Burden leaves out food for Joe after their first encounter, he throws the dishes in a reprise of the earlier scene with Mrs. MacEachern. Though Joe has escaped the presence of MacEachern and the other accusers from his childhood, he is locked on the scapegoat's path and can embrace only that which reinforces his identification with negative, transpersonal powers.

What makes Joe a particularly interesting scapegoat in this racially-charged drama is his ambiguous racial status. Not only can Joe "pass," but his blackness is based on such unreliable knowledge of his parentage that it's conceivable one in his situation could choose to shrug off the black identity. But this is not possible for Joe. MacEachern's abuse provokes the behavior that convinces Joe of his badness, and once this is done, Joe cannot help but suspect his blackness as well. This conflation of morality and race is created by the white ethos's dependence on a binary system to determine relative value. If good and white are placed at one pole, then not-good and not-white are required to fall at the other. Not only do multiple terms at a pole implicate one another, the placement of the negative values as diametric opposites to the positive forces a conceptual slippage. Not-white becomes black, and not-good becomes bad.

Joe is compelled to bear out a life that supports his belief that he is bad (black) as if this were the only way to exorcise the transpersonal guilt, the collective sin, that has been projected upon him by Doc Hines, the dietitian, MacEachern, and the rest. Vulnerable in innocence and isolation as an orphan, Joe Christmas accepts the weight of the collective, transpersonal shadow. In other words, he colludes with his white judges so he can become a tangible expression of the negative force of the white collective shadow, and provoke the violence that resolves the otherwise free-floating tensions created by the white ethos. As long as there are blacks to scapegoat, the community can be identified by its whiteness. Faulkner makes this important point by keeping Joe's race ambiguous: the white ethos is so dependent on having a black scapegoat, that it can and will invent one if need be. It does not actually matter whether Joe is part African. In truth this would not be the source of his blackness, only an explanation for his badness which allows whiteness to remain aligned at the pole of good. If the collective forms its identity through the old ethic, then the scapegoat ritual will be performed-- through oblivious compulsion if not conscious ritual.

Joe, MacEachern, and Doc Hines are but three of several characters who provide both the machinery and the dramatic progression of the scapegoat ritual in the novel. Another key figure is the Reverend Hightower, who provides a crucial bridge between the Joe Christmas and the Lena Grove storylines and is also trapped within the rigid parameters of the old ethic's binaries. Like the Christianity of MacEachern and Hines, Hightower's religion is pointed like the accusing finger of a wrathful god. Though Hightower earns a sort of redemption in the end, Faulkner positions him carefully at the hypermoralistic end of the old ethic binary where, with his less conscious brethren, he can serve as the ballast to Christmas. The connection between the two characters is underscored when Hightower relates the treatment he received during his public shaming to the treatment of Joe Christmas:

> Not of my own choice that I am no longer a man of God. It was by the
> will, the more than behest, of them like you and like her and like him in
> the jail yonder and like them who put him there to do their will upon, as
> they did upon me, with insult and violence upon those who like them
> were created by the same God and were driven by them to do that which
> they now turn and rend them for having done it. (345)

This passage suggests a sort of mirroring relationship between the "black" criminal and the "white" ex-minister. Hightower continues to deny his responsibility for his disgrace as vehemently as Joe rejects his innocence and embraces instead the inevitability--and the inevitable consequences--of blackness. Though Hightower and Joe are ostensibly situated at opposite poles, both are so split off from what Perera calls a "transpersonal, neutral libido source" (23) that they both become demonic. Azazel-as-demon walks through Light in August; we can track his movement through those characters whose inflexible and extreme moral positions result in their alienation and psychosis. It is not insignificant that Hightower is an outcast, that Doc Hines is considered a kook, and that MacEachern lives on an isolated farm in the country. Though these figures are integral to the action in the novel and the operations of the old ethic, they are positioned on the physical and/or social fringe of the towns in which they live. Hightower is even described as being "oblivious of the odor in which he lives--that smell of people who no longer live in life" (300). Percy

Grimm, another figure aligned with the self-righteous, is seen by the sheriff (representing the town) as a benign and ridiculous loser. These characters allow the community that occupies the moderate center of the ethos to remain oblivious to the extremes it engenders; meanwhile, the split off energies accumulate tension until the Azazel-like Accusers and the Sacrifice they have created are mutually provoked to complete the ritual drama and reject, on the community's behalf, the collective shadow material. A violent showdown in which Accusers expunge the Sacrifice will be the only way for the white community to neutralize the tumultuous energies that would force recognition and ownership of its shadow.

As others have observed, the novel contains several dyads. One we've already noted is between Joe and Hightower. The simplest and most comic is that of Byron Bunch and Lucas Burch. The text also invites comparisons between Milly and Lena and Joanna and Lena. Yet it is not inconsistent to consider the juxtaposition of Lena's and Joe's stories to elevate her status from a background figure in Joe's story to being another element in a shared story. As others have noted, Lena and Joe are united by common motifs: both climbed from bedroom windows to enter new lives, both are offered food, both have traveled a long way. Joe was a bastard; Lena's child is a bastard. In one view, it's possible that either one of them might have taken on the role of scapegoat in a society where blackness and female sexual promiscuity were both conditions that would land one on the fringe.

Again, we should note that despite similarities, we cannot overlook the importance of the characters' racial identities and the relevant socio-political forces evoked by the setting. Though Faulkner does not make the racial comparison between Joe and Lena explicit, it cannot be insignificant that Lena, whose fate is so different from Joe's, is presumed white. Though Joe's racial position seems to follow rather than precede his isolation from the white tribe, and it is predicated by feminine "sin and bitchery," we must consider that the psychodrama presented in Faulkner's novel does not depend simply on any abused person's susceptibility to becoming a scapegoat. Rather, the author refers to the real-world politics and oppression that have formulated a blackness that could signify unworthiness in the white schema. The effects of the scapegoating mechanism in this novel would be no less tragic if it was made certain that Joe's father was African-American, but this point of ambiguity allows us to recognize how persistent and insidious the old ethic's operations can be and that, operating in the white collective, it cannot allow there to be a Joe that is both good and bad, a white Joe that is bad, or a black Joe that is good. Instead, the old ethic and all those who subscribe to it will insist on what allows the white community to retain its morally privileged identity: a Joe that is black, evil, and expendable.

III. Movement and the New Ethic

In a sense, the key difference between Joe and Lena is not racial, but lies in Joe's subscription to the very ethos that strangles him. He isn't doomed because he thinks he's of African descent--as he admits to Joanna, he doesn't know this to be true (240). Rather, he is doomed by his inability to operate outside the binary value system of the old ethic. Like his accusers, Joe lacks connection to the neutral source of life energy and creative exchanges, a source located in the space Lena Grove personifies. Not only is her body where new life happens, but her very name suggests the broad multiplicity of a stand of trees rather than the singular point of a "Hightower."

We may speculate that Lena succeeds in eluding the forces that tear Joe apart because her apparent whiteness makes her task much, much easier. Because Faulkner does not make race an issue for Lena and does not make Lena's race an issue for other characters in the novel, we may be tempted to overlook another important factor that Faulkner seems to insist upon: the ability to travel in mind as well as body. Though Joe's feet may travel, his mind stays stuck. As an adult, he recreates his difficulties wherever he goes. Lena, however, can mentally as well as physically leave the position others have left her in. Her change of scenery introduces her to new possibilities, such as the option to marry Byron Bunch. Richard Adams discusses the problem of inflexibility in *Faulkner: Myth and Motion*, where he observes that the most tragic characters in Faulkner's novels

> go down because they are fundamentally opposed to life. They try to find something unchanging to stand on, motionless in the midst of change.[...]They are not vital spirits crushed by the inert weight of matter. On the contrary, they are desperate because a living world keeps forcing them into action in spite of their desire for security, peace, and stasis.[...] [B]y Faulkner's logic, the only way to be motionless is to be dead. (13)

One might claim that a reason Lena Grove survives is that, as Adams notes, she is "so much in harmony with motion"(13). Faulkner does use her as a symbolic property for life's perpetual movement and cycles, but she relates to movement in the sense that she does not seem to identify herself in the inflexible terms of the old ethic's binary code as Joe does. Unlike Joe, she neither flaunts nor tries to hide her marginalizing condition, and it appears that for her, single motherhood is neither virtue nor vice. This placid self-acceptance, this "unflagging faith," seems to serve a protective function, shielding her from an outcast's consuming loneliness, moving her beyond the range of the accusatory voices. Consider what sets her in motion: Lucas has fathered her child and has abandoned her to be branded a whore by her brother, yet instead of accepting that identity, Lena hits the road to look for one she likes better. Is she a bad person? A good person? Though Faulkner gives little from her perspective, this question doesn't seem to concern her much. When she lies to Martha, she confesses her lie in her next breath (14-15). And while other characters make much of the dogged pursuit of Lucas that she seems to intend to carry through indefinitely, she cries when it seems Byron has left her (390), and it is suggested that her new intention is to settle with him after she enjoys a bit more traveling (479-80). As far as we can see, there is room for changing perspectives and conflicting desires in Lena's character. She's a grove, not a tower.

Another dynamic character is Byron Bunch, who shifts allegiance from Hightower and the old ethic to Lena and the new. If Lena's strength against the forces of the old ethic is characterized by her ability to be unashamed, then Byron Bunch's lies in his ability to reconfigure his identity without needing to shame or blame others. Described as the sort of man nobody notices, Byron is a virgin in his thirties whose punctilious honesty is almost humorous. When he takes a five minute break at the mill to talk to Lena, he clocks it carefully to avoid claiming pay for a minute he has not labored (47). His exactitude with time here is indicative of a rigid obedience to an ethical code he shares with his mentor, Hightower --an obedience that dissolves when Byron meets Lena.

Byron's transition from choir boy to love slave is not immediate, nor does it lack a certain amount of flailing on his part. His desire to please Hightower is evident in their many exchanges as he tries to rationalize taking care of Lena. Yet, ultimately, Byron is transformed. In the course of the novel, he develops his own moral compass and becomes better able to consciously accept behaviors in himself that would be antithetical to his former persona. This process is what Jungians call individuation, and, as Gerhard Adler punctuates in his foreword to *Depth Psychology and a New Ethic*, individuation is required if an ethical attitude toward an Other is to be attained. Adler notes that assimilating material that has been part of the shadow into one's persona can shift one's locus for "ethical authority" from "collective values of good and evil" (represented to Byron by his mentor, Hightower) to "an inner 'Voice'--a constant challenge to individual decision and responsibility, even where it might lead to a rejection of collective morality"(8).

In order to act on the love he feels for Lena, Byron must turn away from the judgmental interpretations of the situation represented by Hightower's morality and his internalized notions of what the town might say about him-- that he's a sinner or a fool for tending "another man's laidby crop" (394). After Hightower fails to dissuade Byron from the plan to care for Lena, the mentor remarks that Byron's carriage is confident and upright, and, for the first time ever, the younger man does not stumble on Hightower's bottom step (294). It is as though Faulkner is saying that listening to one's inner voice rather than the condemning judgments of the accusers can grant one confidence and a form of grace.

Refreshingly, milquetoast Bunch does not need to bolster his conviction to follow his inner voice with invective against Hightower (and, by extension, the accusatory forces Hightower represents). Instead of projecting negative judgment onto Hightower, Bunch states, "[I]t aint for me to say that you are wrong," yet neither does he choose to carry the weight of Hightower's judgment: "And I dont reckon it's for you to say that I am wrong, even if I am" (299). On the other hand, while Byron slips loose the hold of the old ethic, Hightower struggles to force Byron to continue to think in binary terms. First, he insists that there are two logical contradictories, sin and marriage (298), then he asserts that women like Lena must choose between two categories of men, Lucas Burches and Byron Bunches. "[N]o Lena, no woman, deserves more than one of them," he insists. "No woman" (299). Hightower feels that Lena has made what should be an irrevocable choice between one pole (Lucas) and the other (Byron) and is clearly irked by Lena's and Bunch's refusal to cooperate with this schema.

Faulkner undermines the old ethic in a number of ways, but nowhere more blatantly than with Hightower's epiphanic moment near the end, in which the character considers his share of responsibility in his wife's adultery and his subsequent disgrace. This is in stark contrast to Hightower's earlier cut-and-dried assertions to Byron in which he pits sin against marriage--now it occurs to him that a man can remain within the boundaries of his marriage commitment and still sin against that commitment. Realizing he might have betrayed his wife before she betrayed him, he admits the possibility that he "became her seducer and her murderer, author and instrument of her shame and death" (462). This paradoxical concept--that a cuckolded man could be responsible for adultery--collapses the oppositions in the old ethic and brings a moment of humility to this self-righteous, fixed character. Interestingly, this realization contains his sense of having acted by compulsion. He confesses that if he was the instrument of his wife's fate, then he was "in turn instrument of someone outside myself" (465). This force outside him is represented by the glamour of his grandfather's self-righteous violence--an inherited desire to damn others correspondent with Joe's internalized tendency to damn himself.

In this novel, we see Lena and Byron move physically and symbolically away from the stagnant machinations of the old ethic and its inevitable outcome of scapegoatism. Because these characters do not need to define themselves in opposition to others, the end of *Light in August* suggests a possible movement toward an alternative, the "new ethic" of Neumann's title.

IV. The Subject of the Fictive Dream

Faulkner's use of characters such as Joe and Lena as carriers of the collective white shadow is politically provocative. Many critics find Faulkner's representations of characters that are not white, not male, or both to be seriously flawed. Not only are "blackness" and "womaness" signifiers for whatever is not allowed to be whiteness and maleness, but his black characters are so often clearly undynamic, elemental background figures designed to perform symbolic functions that critics point to them as proof that Faulkner's fictive scope is confined to only a (racist and sexist) white man's perspective. According to Craig Werner, James Baldwin once complained, "Faulkner could see Negroes only as they related to him, not as they related to each other." Werner himself charges Faulkner with the failure "to excavate Afro-American history as thoroughly as he excavates Euro-American male history" (40). We can say much the same of Faulkner's female characters. I agree that Faulkner's essentializing depictions of African-American and female characters are troubling, even distressing, and it seems small consolation to say the novel reflects not how one might want things to be, but only interprets them from a particular point of view. Still, this is the nature of a fiction writer's task. Toni Morrison explains that her "early assumptions as a reader were that black people signified little or nothing in the imagination of white American writers," but that her opinion changed when she started to "read as a writer." Doing this led to a desire to consider what the absence, presence, and representations of black characters in American fiction say about the writer's labor of imagining. She writes,

> As a writer reading, I came to realize the obvious: the subject of the dream is the dreamer. The fabrication of an Africanist persona is reflexive; an extraordinary meditation on the self; a powerful exploration of the fear and desires that reside in writerly consciousness. It is an astonishing revelation of longing, of terror, of perplexity, of shame, of magnanimity. (929)

It's certainly possible for writers to create believable characters that do not share their race, class, and/or sex, but if it happens that the subject of the dream is the dreamer, and the dreamer is preoccupied with his whiteness, and his maleness, and the work reflects this, can we say he has failed at anything except not writing someone else's dream?

As Weinstein notes, the strength of Faulkner's racial representations rests in the "extraordinary depiction of turmoil and hatred that the notion of black can unleash in the white male mind" (64). In spite of Faulkner's limitations, he seems to embrace the weighty task of telling the truth that he knows and of acknowledging the oppositional forces which white identity manufactures yet would deny. His South is not a black south, nor a white woman's south, but a particular white man's dream--and sometimes nightmare--of the south. In this light, one may consider the figures of the dream, including the black characters, to be permutations of a white male's repressed versions of himself. The implications may make us uncomfortable, but overall, *Light in August* says less about relations between the races than it says about the white male psyche torn between its collective ethos and the shadow it casts.

Jennifer Gibbs

WORKS CITED

Adams, Richard P. *Faulkner: Myth and Motion*. New Jersey: Princeton UP, 1968.

Adler, Gerhard. Foreword. *Depth Psychology and a New Ethic* . By Erich Neumann. Trans. Eugene Rolf. New York: Harper Torchbooks, 1969.

Coffee, Jessie McGuire. *Faulkner's Un-Christlike Christians: Biblical Allusions in the Novels*. Ann Arbor: UMI Research Press, 1983.

Frankenberg, Ruth. *White Women, Race Matters: The Social Construction of Whiteness*. Minneapolis: University of Minnesota Press, 1994.

Faulkner, William. *Light in August*. New York: Vintage Books, 1972.

McCauley, Robbie. "Regenerating Cultural Presence: Tuning in Through Performance." Citizenship and Diaspora. Provost's Lecture Series. Bowling Green State University, Ohio. 18 Mar. 1999.

Morrison, Toni. "Playing in the Dark." *Literary Theory: An Anthology.* Eds. Julie Rivkin and Michael Ryan. Massachusetts: Blackwell Publishers, 1998. 923-35.

Neumann, Erich. *Depth Psychology and the New Ethic* . Trans. Eugene Rolfe. New York: Harper Torchbooks, 1969.

Perera, Sylvia Brinton. *The Scapegoat Complex: Toward a Mythology of Shadow and Guilt* . Toronto: Inner City Books, 1986.

Rich, Adrienne. "Notes Toward a Politics of Location." *Literary Theory: An Anthology*. 637-49.

von Franz, Marie-Louise. *Shadow and Evil in Fairy Tales: Revised Edition* . Boston: Shambala, 1995.

Weinstein, Philip M. *Faulkner's Subject: A Cosmos No One Owns*. Cambridge: Cambridge UP, 1992.

Werner, Craig. "Minstrel Nightmares: Black Dreams of Faulkner's Dreams of Blacks." *Faulkner and Race: Faulkner and Yoknapatawpha, 1986* . Jackson: University Press of Mississippi, 1987. 35-57.

8.

WHITE FATHERS, BROWN DAUGHTERS:
THE FRISBIE FAMILY ROMANCE
AND THE AMERICAN PACIFIC

This article examines an important moment in the formation of Pacific Island literature by engaging with two biomythographies: *Miss Ulysses from Puka-Puka* (1948), a text published by Florence Johnny Frisbie, the fourteen year-old daughter of a white American trader and Cook Islander, and her later work, *The Frisbies of the South Seas* (1959).[1] Robert Dean Frisbie, the literary and biological "creator" of --although not the first--certainly the youngest Pacific Island writer, was a novelist who had lived in the Pacific Islands for nearly three decades before the literary emergence of *Miss Ulysses*, significantly published the year of his death. *Miss Ulysses*, edited and translated by Frisbie senior, bears the complex markings of a family caught between racial, national, and cultural narratives at the advent of the Second World War, evidenced by their erratic travels across a Pacific which was rapidly becoming a battleground between two hemispheric imperialisms. Yet the narrative subsumes many of the international political maneuverings of the time into a conflicted celebration of a multicultural, domestic family romance. By comparing Frisbie senior's novels, personal correspondence, and his daughter's subsequent biomythography with the ideologies at work in *Miss Ulysses*, I conclude that what is generally perceived as one of the first Pacific Island literary texts[2] is primarily the production of a white American who had *literally* "gone native." This destabilization of authorship could easily dovetail with similar debates concerning the "authenticity" of ethnic autobiographies by Rigoberta Menchú, Poppie Nongena, and Forrest Carter. In fact, Robert Dean Frisbie's introduction to *Miss Ulysses* begins by calling it "an authentic autobiography of a South Sea trader's daughter" (vii) and his daughter insists it is not a "'fake' book" (117). But I would like to complicate the erected binary in some of these discussions

between "ethnic" versus "white" authenticity and examine the deeply conflicted
literary performance of what I term "white nativism" as it appears in this family
work. It is only by reading Johnny Frisbie's sequel in conjunction with the
former text that the guiding hand of white American masculine narrative
convention becomes apparent. This is not to deny Johnny's own contributions to
Miss Ulysses or Pacific literature in general; her second biomythography is
unique for being one of the first 'postcolonial' works to deconstruct its western
inheritance along epistemological and biological genealogies. I read Johnny's
contributions to *Miss Ulysses* as deeply subsumed by her father's editing hand;
as such they are not the primary focus here. Given the very limited amount of
critical attention paid to indigenous Pacific literature by the larger academic
community, my reading of "white nativism" has troubled me and has raised
important questions about recuperating the legacy of a white American trader in
a "native" text. Anne McClintock's nuanced reading of Poppie Nongena's
autobiography is helpful here. In her discussion of this heavily mediated South
African text, McClintock explains that:

> to will away (the white writer's) voice and yearn for the (colonial
> subject's) unmediated voice is to hanker after an anachronistic Western
> notion of individual purity and creative singularity. We may balk at
> being refused identification with a single self, but through this refusal we
> are invited into an altogether different notion of identity, community,
> narrative power and political change (328). [3]

Like Johnny Frisbie's complicated familial and cultural genealogies, I read *Miss
Ulysses* as a complex, collaborative father/daughter literary production, which
cannot be segregated into the camps of "white" (South Sea) versus "Polynesian"
(indigenous) literary works.[4] My paper seeks to elucidate the ways in which, as
a "white native" text, it straddles both literary genres, just as both father and
daughter negotiate complex international and multi-ethnic identities. In fact,
Miss Ulysses' subtitle, *The Autobiography of a South Sea Trader's Daughter*, and the
words "Edited and Translated by Her Father, Robert Dean Frisbie" on the cover
mark the work from the outset as an unevenly collaborative effort that
complicates and highlights racial and cultural boundaries. That the work is
collaborative does not necessarily mean an equal distribution of social and
textual power—clearly Frisbie senior, as a white American father of a mixed-
race Cook Island daughter, dominates the text in ways that resonate with
missionary or ethnographic works which drew upon 'native informants' in

order to promote the publishing careers of their European and American writers. In fact, Johnny's textual relegation to "a South Sea Trader's Daughter" suggests her intrusion into a patriarchal literary tradition that is bolstered and sustained by colonial trade relations. Yet one remarkable difference from the 'native informant' tradition is that the writer-daughter constantly draws attention to the process of collaboration where the textual process is made visible. As a result, "identity, community, narrative power and political change" continually shift and become entangled in a complex and often contradictory depiction of a Pacific family romance.

In keeping with the objectives of this volume, my work emphasizes how Robert Dean Frisbie's collaborative text complicates the literary production of whiteness in the region. Although recent scholarship has interrogated whiteness for its performative transparency and suggests "that the formation of specifically white subject positions has in fact been key...to the sociopolitical process inherent in taking land and making nations" (Frankenberg 2), most of this research focuses on white-majority nations. The terms associated with whiteness in this context such as "invisibility," "normalcy," and "transparency" (Frankenberg 6) do not easily apply to someone like Robert Dean Frisbie, the only white man residing for fifteen years on an island with six hundred Pukapukans[5] who adopted local customs, clothing, and spoke and thought in the local language (Frisbie qtd. in Hall 172). This is not to imply that Frisbie senior did not have access to and draw upon British and American colonial and economic powers in the region; in fact, he received a U.S. Government pension and fashioned specific national claims to this collaborative text. Rather, I suggest that *transparent* forms of whiteness require the continual maintenance of institutions, visual and print media, trade, language, and food among other things to maintain any supposed "normalcy."[6] Since he resided longer in the Pacific Islands than in the United States, Frisbie's American whiteness was constantly re-performed, challenged and altered — it was anything but transparent. Although Frisbie insisted he had not "gone native" (Frisbie qtd. in Hall 209-10), it is clear from his work on *Miss Ulysses* that he had helped initiate a new genre, which sits uneasily alongside popular "South Sea" heterosexual romance narratives, and while upholding American presence in the Pacific, also offered scathing critiques of the colonial center. I conclude that Frisbie senior, a white immigrant, anticipated many of the current inscriptions of indigenous Pacific literature. This "white nativism," the literary hybridization of multiple

ethnicities, is entangled in our definitions of (white) American, Pacific Island —
and by extension — postcolonial literature.

Inscribing the South Seas

The Pacific Island region has long been the template upon which
European male writers have grafted their philosophical, ethnographic, and
imperial ideologies. The early narrative writings of and about James Cook,
Joseph Banks, Louis de Bougainville, Pierre Loti and many others marked a
literary space where Rousseau's concept of the *homme naturale* was woven
alongside the often violent practices of European imperialism in the scramble
for colonial power over trade and resources.[7] The Pacific Ocean, long depicted
by writers like Herman Melville as a blank, unknowable expanse (a depiction
which suppresses ancient and extensive Polynesian mappings), has functioned
as a convenient "blank slate" upon which to graft U.S. and European male
markings.[8] Perhaps not surprisingly given the highly intertextual narratives of
this region, there are few thematic differences between 18th and 19th century
masculine European inscriptions of the Pacific world and their 20th century U.S.
counterparts. This is not to suggest that South Sea texts and their writers are
homogenous (even if many of these authors were middle-class military
servicemen), but that, given the large cultural and historical distances between
European and American writers, their productions circulate around persistently
rigid tropes. The South Sea genre becomes entrapped in a hermeneutic circle
because "(o)ne decade's literary pioneer became the next decade's hero and
model. This frontier seemed to serve as its own self-perpetuating inspiration"
(Whitehead 406).[9] A few of the thematic similarities across the centuries can be
listed as follows: the inevitable sexual arrival scene (where scantily clad women
"swarm" a male-occupied ship); an idealization of the so-called Pacific Paradise
(seen most obviously in eroticized, passive Polynesian bodies); the romance of
heterosexually available "dusky maidens;" the writer's abhorrence of certain
forms of western modernity (excluding his own imports like books and radios);
and contemptuous depictions of missionaries, unscrupulous beachcombers,
traders and sailors who contribute to the "fatal impact" of local Pacific culture.
These romantic narratives, usually travelogues, criticize westerners for bringing
about environmental, cultural, and moral Pacific decay through "unnatural"
western perversion while erasing the consequences of the writer's own physical

and textual presence in the Pacific. This is seen most obviously in Melville's *Typee;* the narrative idealizes non-violent Marquesans yet uncritically concludes with a remarkable act of violence in the text—that of the white beachcomber Tommo against his own host community. Generally South Sea writers, while crying out against western 'invasions' of their adopted homes, consistently observe that it was their literary predecessors who brought them to the South Seas and yet rarely make the connection between their own literary productions and subsequent visitors. This creates a textual contradiction: like early anthropological texts, South Sea writing depends upon the erasure of both local native subjectivity *and* the writer's continuing textual and economic relationship to the metropolitan center. This places both writer-observer and native-observed into a presumed cultural and historical vacuum, even as the material production of the text creates further contact histories by perpetuating additional migrant-writers.[10] With the exception of perhaps the Caribbean, nowhere else is there a more interdependent relationship (even as it attempts to erase itself) between textual, imperial, and tourist production than in Pacific Island historiography.

Robert Dean Frisbie is somewhat of an exception in that he was forthcoming with his critiques of American and European writerly migrations to the Pacific. In a 1931 article called "Americans in the South Seas," he complains that these writers are simply concerned with "debunking" or upholding the South Sea myth:

> It seems not to occur to any of them to write a simple and factual account
> of life in the islands. There is a reason for this: the reading public
> demands one of the two, and if a South Seas author would see his work
> in print, he must follow either the old Melville-Stevenson-Grimshaw
> romance and glamour line, or the blatant debunking line (157).

Having just published *The Book of Puka-Puka* three years before, a collection of anecdotal stories about his experience as a trader on the island, Frisbie presumably categorizes his work as "simple and factual," therefore exempting himself from his following critique: "The glamourists do the greater harm, they bring Americans to the South Seas to write more books to bring more Americans to write more books" (157-8). Frisbie's anxiety about American migration should be read not only as a concern with literary 'occupations' but with the increasing militarization of the region. By the publication of *Miss Ulysses* in 1948, the establishment of U.S. air, communication and supply bases across the Pacific region revealed that "simple and factual" as well as "story-book pictures of the South Seas" (155) were obsolete.

The increasing Americanization of the Pacific and the Frisbie's participation in U.S. publishing circuits lend colonial and national contours to *Miss Ulysses* which mark the text as a specifically historical production. Following the lead of Paul Sharrad, I read the Frisbies' text not as an anomalous "emergence" out of centuries of European literary practice (often symbolized by westerners as the oceanic cultural "void" where the young Frisbie's ahistorical production would presumably rise from the depths) but a significant moment in a long process whereby father and daughter engage with Pacific Island, American, and European literary and cultural genealogies in a rapidly changing Pacific. As Sharrad points out, the first biomythography begins with Frisbie senior's discussions with acclaimed writer James Norman Hall in Tahiti and concludes with a meeting with James Michener in American-occupied Samoa ("Beginnings" 134-5). Thus, *Miss Ulysses'* frame is rich with colonial and literary resonance; the father's frame for his daughter's voice is in turn circumscribed by a long history of literary and military occupation of the Pacific. Tahiti first entered European narrative history as the idyllic "Nouvelle Cythére" when Louis de Bougainville visited in 1768 and represents a persistent textual space of European desire as well as France and England's first colonial acquisition in the Pacific. American Samoa became one of the United States' early Pacific territories in 1899; like Tahiti, it remains to this day under colonial administration. The geographic and historical imaginary invoked by this frame also gestures to the specific literary production of Frisbie's era, symbolized by Hall and Michener. The presence of these two literary figures signifies an important transition in military occupation and writing about the South Seas: Hall, Frisbie, and Charles Nordhoff represent the wave of former U.S. military men who, after WWI, migrated to a Pacific which was predominantly ruled by Great Britain and France; Michener, author of the Pulitzer-prize winning *Tales of the South Pacific,* represents the second wave of American occupancy and military writing about the region during and after WWII.[11] Wedged between these military and literary occupations appears *Miss Ulysses,* a literal production of multiple ethnic, national and cultural histories, which signals a transition in the production of a contested American Pacific.

This essay addresses two separate strands woven into these complicated biomythographies. First I map out the inscriptions of the South Sea genre at work in *Miss Ulysses* that bear the obvious imprint of Robert Dean Frisbie and which signify his ambivalent relationship to the trope of heterosexual romance in this genre. Reading Johnny's second biomythography in conjunction with the first reveals the ways in which Frisbie senior was cognizant of his American audience and their post-war nationalism, so he fabricated and exaggerated events to satisfy the American literary palate and to earn a living with which to support himself and his children. These textual strategies (intrinsic to all autobiographies) were not only geared to American publisher and audience expectations but also reflect Frisbie senior's inability to graft a South Sea heterosexual narrative onto a work which was co-authored with his own daughter. Doris Sommer and Mary Louise Pratt have theorized the ways in which cross-cultural romance narratives mystify unequal colonial relations; although this has not been applied to the South Sea genre, there are striking resonances. Since Frisbie's Pukapukan wife had died early in their marriage, leaving him with the responsibility of raising five young children, Frisbie found himself unable to enter the well-marked textual space of the swinging single white traveller who seeks the company of obliging "dusky maidens." Instead, in *Miss Ulysses*, he refashions the genre into a multicultural travelling family romance in order to integrate his mixed-race children into the segregationist American imaginary. The final part of this paper delves into the critiques of colonialism embedded in *Miss Ulysses*—not, as one might expect, to reveal the ways in which the "half-caste" daughter simply foreshadows the Pacific Island literary production that followed her, but to highlight the ways in which this double-voiced collaboration with her father anticipates some aspects of native literary production and, by extension, its postcolonial tropes.

South Sea Colonial 'Yarns'

Miss Ulysses from Puka-Puka, when read alongside the later text, *The Frisbies of the South Seas* contains outright fabrications—"yarns" that are prevalent in both Pacific oral tradition as well as the South Sea lore of traders and sailors. In fact "Puka Puka" is not only the name for one of the Cook Islands but in Maori means to chatter or gossip. But since these tales are refuted or absent from the subsequent work they can be attributed to Frisbie senior's editing hand—as I explain later, the misrepresentations highlight aspects of the South Sea genre that he attempted to reconcile with the authorship of a native text. The first biomythbiography begins with Johnny's Cook Island ancestry, her father's life as a trader in the Cooks, her mother's death after an illness introduced to the island by a European ship, Johnny's travels all over the Pacific with her father, her ethnographic observations of Pacific songs and cultural practices, and concludes with Johnny and her siblings' first airplane flight to American Samoa to visit their hospitalized father. *Miss Ulysses* ultimately charts the family's journeys across space and time as the children are "whisked ...out of the primitive South Sea Islands to one of our Uncle Sam's naval bases!" (239) [12] As I will explain in more detail later, the text struggles to pave a trajectory between the children's "savage" existence in Pukapuka to their acculturation into the English language and American imaginary.

Miss Ulysses consciously draws attention to its own contribution to the history of travel narratives; interspersed through the text are references to Johnny's namesake Ulysses, James Cook, Robert Louis Stevenson (a long time resident and writer in Samoa), children's adventure novels, and a section describing their experience on Suwarrow entitled "The Treasure Island" where, significantly, the children find the bones of European traders and unearth an 18th century treasure chest. There are other, more subtle intertextual allusions to Frederick O'Brien (whose *White Shadows in the South Seas* inspired Frisbie to migrate to the region), Stevenson's travelogue *In the South Seas*, as well as references to Charles Nordhoff, James Norman Hall, and Frisbie's own novels. The biomythography is consciously enmeshed with its literary predecessors to the extent that Frisbie senior makes textuality a corporeal experience: in one of their adventures the children find "a dead man" (137)--the grave of Stevenson's friend Jack Buckland. Frisbie senior tells the children, "'(s)ome day you will read Robert Louis Stevenson's novel *The Wrecker*. Then you will meet Jack Buckland under the name of Tommy Haddon'" (137). This chapter, entitled "Night on a Haunted Island," is peppered with the imagined ghosts of previous traders, writers, castaways, and natives in a way that suggests the family and the text are entertained, informed, and haunted by Pacific historiography. Significantly, the chapter closes with the children watching the lights of the ship the *Taipi* (Typee) blinking off the shore.

The same chapter is also enmeshed, perhaps less consciously, with western imperialism and the U.S. frontier legacy. By "western" I mean both the European-American occupation of the region and the teleological U.S. frontier where discourses of manifest destiny were used to justify occupation of the

Pacific in terms that were cartographically and ideologically naturalized. Christopher Connery remarks, "(t)he Pacific Ocean as temporal destiny is an American idea; Western history as constant westward motion would of course not appeal to any countries east of the Atlantic" (299). Since "(t)he globe's finite circularity made the expansion into the final frontier (the Pacific) also a return to putative origins" (299), it is no surprise that it is Frisbie's children who, at their father's suggestion, identify themselves as "cowboys." In *Miss Ulysses*, the U.S. frontier myth merges with Greek epic and the Frisbie family's conquering of a deserted Pacific isle. After framing her experience *vis a vis* the *Odyssey*, young Johnny exclaims "Uninhabited island! I have told you what a thrill I feel on stepping ashore in a strange port; but it is nothing to standing for the first time on the beach of a desert island, with the jungle before you, wondering what adventures await you!" (129) In one chapter, the children assist in the construction of a "wigwam" (136), fish, collect coconuts, and make "Indian trails" (131) to find their way back to the shore. The Cowboy/Indian dyad, a residue of U.S. imperialism, has been imported by Frisbie senior and refashioned and adopted without irony by his part-native children. This raises an important trope of racial hybridity in that the children are both aligned with the western frontier *and* its conquered others. By literally expanding the U.S. frontier into the Pacific, Frisbie and his colleagues are implicated in the naturalization of a South Sea "literary frontier" that "maintained American interest in the Pacific and helped lead to the eventual Americanization of Hawai'i and its admission" to the union (Whitehead 380). The western narrative tropes mentioned thus far mark Frisbie's cognizance of the haunting of 19th century European imperial history and his complicity with its 20th century American counterpart. But the imperial underbelly of the text is cloaked by the trope of domestic South Sea romance; in this case cross-cultural heterosexual relations are substituted by a benign American paternalism. *Miss Ulysses* asserts an economically impoverished yet creatively potent, hybrid, "happy family"(161); despite their trials and tribulations, the narrative attests that the children are looked after and cherished by their devoted father.

Johnny Frisbie's second work, *The Frisbies,* depicts a radically different parent — the narrative debunks the romance of the family by revealing an alcoholic, temperamental, and occasionally violent and neglectful man who forces his children to type his manuscripts (215), "slapped (his children's) faces until (they) could hear the ringing of distant bells" (116), and brings them unwillingly with him on his Pacific travels. The second work admits that "(w)e kids did not have the faintest idea of how to make an Indian trail" (163) and that it was Frisbie senior who called their tent a "'wigwam'" (155). What is striking about this second work, published well after her father's death, is that it relies — and quotes extensively--from Frisbie senior's letters to James Norman Hall and his earlier novels to frame the chapters and flesh out scenes and events that are dimly remembered in Johnny's memory. In her second biomythography she adopts the structure of her father's work *The Book of Puka-Puka*, yet while her father's work framed each chapter with a relevant chant or song (in Pukapukan and English), Johnny's second work frames each chapter with her father's letters and published writing. Between these two works, the subject slips from an American male inscribing Pukapukan culture to his daughter using the "master's tools" to dismantle the written legacy of "A South Seas White Man" (*The Frisbies* 139). The transition in subject is highlighted by the second text's introduction of the Rarotongan term "Papa'á" (white man), which suggests a semiotic resonance with her name for her father: "Papa." Significantly, *The Frisbies* retells many of the exact same events from *Miss Ulysses* but with radically different perspectives; this marks it as one of the earliest written works to decolonize a western patriarchal text along the writer's literal genealogy. In the 1950s, Johnny Frisbie prefigured what Samoan writer Albert Wendt would assert twenty years later: "(o)ur dead are woven into our souls like the hypnotic music of bone flutes: we can never escape them" ("Oceania" 10). Johnny Frisbie's notable difference lies not only in her attempt to inscribe the impact of her white heritage, but also the fierce paternal conflicts waged within and outside the texts over her developing sexuality. As such, Johnny's texts deconstruct the objectification of Pacific Island women far earlier than most scholars have recognized.

White Fathers, Brown Daughters

The ideological gaps between *Miss Ulysses* and *The Frisbies* highlight the uneven and often contradictory aspects of travelling masculine whiteness. This formulation of whiteness is tied to imperial constructions of western men (whose heterosexuality is sanctified by colonial structures) but more important is its performative textual historiography. Like his fellow South Sea authors, Frisbie depicts himself as "chest-thumpingly heterosexual" (Roulston 34). His published works depict a sexually active American male who has many affairs

with Pacific Island women until, as *Miss Ulysses* documents, he settles down
with his wife Ngatokorua a Mataá. After her death he is transformed into the
devoted father who is pursued by other women but remarries merely for the
sake of the children. Like 18th century cross-cultural sentimental fiction, Frisbie
attempts "to cast the political as erotic and to seek to resolve political
uncertainties in the sphere of family and reproduction" (Pratt 101). In each case,
the women who pursue Frisbie show agency only in their desire for white men;
ultimately Frisbie's masculinity is upheld by his decision to terminate these
relationships based on various legitimizing reasons. In one case Frisbie ends his
marriage with a woman "when she grew fat and lazy" (*Miss Ulysses* 3). In
Manihiki, "the siren isle of the South Seas" (186), he is pursued by and
eventually marries "poor lovesick Calypso" (198) but later sends her home from
Rarotonga. Johnny comments "my father was not much of a woman chaser…but
Calypso was a number-one man chaser" (198). This racialized heterosexual
trope, integral to the South Sea genre, holds Pacific Island women complicit in
their own (sexual) colonization. Although this has escaped the attention of many
scholars, in the South Sea and beachcomber genre it is Pacific Island women
who facilitate western male acculturation to the region by proffering 'natural'
and/or sexual resources in exchange for manufactured products and
masculinist administration.13 One can trace a clear trajectory between the early
contact narratives that repeatedly depicted Pacific women 'swarming' European
military ships in order to exchange sexual favors for nails to its depoliticized
and romanticized counterpart when an individual "lovesick Calypso" pursues
an expatriate American male.

      In contrast to her father's sexual "yarns," Johnny Frisbie's later work
depicts the repeated failure of white American heterosexuality in the Pacific. In
the second work, Frisbie senior is not actively pursued by Polynesian women
whom he later abandons; instead, he pursues numerous women in Tahiti,
Tongareva, and Manihiki and each one abandons him for relationships with
native men (27, 35, 182). Given the three hundred-year written history of
depicting Polynesian women as sexually available to white men, one can see
how Frisbie senior's rejections had to be excised from the first text in a way that
ultimately employs his daughter's complicity with the romantic South Sea
genre. Johnny does her own "debunking" of her father's sexual myths in *The
Frisbies* by framing the chapter on Calypso's infidelity to her father with a
statement from his novel *Mr. Moonlight's Island*:

> In the land of the Anglo-Saxons there is a heritage of greed and jealousy
> which makes objectionable the thought of marrying a woman who has
> been loved by other men...Civilized man has idolized private property;
> "mine" has become a sacred word to him...His monogamic marriage is a
> direct reflection of his attitude towards property (179).

Clearly Frisbie senior was trying to reconcile his own personal need for "monogamic" relations while upholding the myth of "sexual paradise" in print. Calypso's sexual autonomy undermines not only Frisbie's individual virility but destabilizes the textual representation of romantic, economic and colonial exchange in the region. In this context it's significant that the name "Calypso" derives from the Greek word to "cover" or "hide" (Knox 34).

Because of its collaborative packaging, *Miss Ulysses* remains deeply conflicted about the depiction of Pacific women in a way that one would not ordinarily see in the South Sea genre. In Manihiki, ten-year old Johnny observes, "the women were soft, purring creatures, with Mongolian eyes, pouting lips (...), wide hips, big breasts, yielding bodies and minds, and, like kittens, they were so full of the joy of life that it was impossible for them to relax" (186). Clearly this is not the observation of young Cook Island girl who had never been out of the Pacific but reflects her father's sexual and textual orientalism. The inability to transform the South Sea romance trope to the voice of a Pacific Island girl is highlighted by the following passage: Young Johnny remarks, "As for me, I was Miss Ulysses from Puka-Puka. I had broken the ropes that bound me to the mast; I had taken the wax from my sailors' ears; ashore I saw the sirens beckoning and I heard their song. For Manihiki is the siren isle of the South Seas" (186). As much as *Miss Ulysses* strives to depict a young woman traveler, a "half-caste" subject with agency amidst a white male-dominated region and genre, the western frame employed by her father is so relentlessly heterosexual that the metaphor of a young Pacific girl perceiving her fellow islanders as sexually tempting "sirens" collapses. The biomythography cannot seamlessly rescript Homer's *Odyssey* because this Greek travel narrative and the South Sea genre that was modeled upon it privilege a transient and heterosexual male subject who encounters and must resist alternative, feminized islands. *Miss Ulysses* attempts to adopt the *Odyssey*'s teleology by sanctifying the traveler's reunion with home and family but as a father-daughter collaboration it cannot be effected along the lines of heterosexuality without coming dangerously close to incest.

The title of this paper, "White Fathers, Brown Daughters," deliberately plays with the textual contradictions that arise when the South Sea racial and heterosexual exotic of "White Man, Brown Woman"[14] becomes transposed onto a similarly racialized father/daughter relationship. Unlike the cross-cultural, national romances of the early colonial Americas, the South Sea genre allows little textual or social space for the mixed-race offspring of white male travelers.[15] This is remarkable given the history of sexual exchange in the Pacific, and the ways in which the growing population of "half-caste" and illegitimate children caused significant political and social tensions in occupied islands such as Tahiti and American Samoa.[16] In his study of 18th and early 19th century white beachcombers, H.E. Maude cites numerous polygamist men who recognized as many as fifty children. He explains that these men left two important legacies: written representations of the early "contact zone" and such complex demographies that Maude deduces that there are no "pure-blooded natives" left in the region (166-67). Maude's conclusion is debatable, but it does gesture towards a tangible legacy of white presence in the Pacific. The literary suppression of this reproductive legacy cannot be addressed in all its complexity here. But generally stated, the product of cross-cultural sexual alliances not only threaten the western mythology of paradisiacal and hermetically sealed 'islands of culture' (prevalent in colonial travel writing about the region and its own epistemological offspring, anthropology), but challenge the discourse of temporary colonial 'visitation' with a corporeal, and firmly delegitimized legacy of international expansion and (re)production. If, as Sommer so convincingly argues, the 19th century nation-building novels of the Americas sought to legitimize and homogenize multicultural entanglements under the rubric of family reproduction as it was rooted to a particular national soil, the South Sea romance resists this localizing nationalist strategy and renders its own reproductive future either invisible or illegitimate. As such, this genre has more in common with the 18th century contact narratives addressed in Pratt's *Imperial Eyes*, where the depiction of cross-cultural sexual allegiances suppress political and social relations under the rubric of nonreproductive sentimental romance. Although many of the American South Sea writers cited here did establish families in the Pacific, as migrants from a segregated U.S., most chose not to explore the repercussions of their presence, finding it easier to woo their audience with the romanticization of young "dusky maidens" rather than their own hybrid offspring.

Miss Ulysses is unique in that it attempts to naturalize a multicultural family without genealogical claims to one national soil but, when read alongside Frisbie's other writing, the transition between heterosexual romance to family romance is decidedly contested. Frisbie senior's novels and personal letters are filled with conflicted representations of Pacific heterosexuality and reflect his inability to perceive any young Pacific women, including his daughters, as anything but sexually promiscuous. In *The Book of Puka-Puka,* Frisbie senior narrates a chapter about Pacific sexuality called "The Young Unmarried" where he explains that young Pukapukans are allowed unlimited sexual freedom before settling down. Frisbie finds the missionaries' and colonial officials' attempts to stop this unpalatable. He explains, "I urged that the Puka-Puka love fests are of great antiquity and cause no harm whatever on an island where there are no diseases to be transmitted and where unmarried mothers lose no social standing" (83). He complains that the western impositions of sexual morality are eroding "more healthful habits of life" (85). Of course, like any South Sea author worth his salt, Frisbie attests to his participation in these healthy "love fests." Yet Johnny's second biomythography calls attention to her father's gendered and racial double standards by asserting her own perspective on these community gatherings. In this section, Johnny and her siblings are told by their father "never to play with the Puka-Pukans again" since they are "lice breeders" (118). Later, Johnny and her siblings sneak out at night to play games with the village children and return to their father who is "red with anger" and spanks them. Johnny is isolated from her siblings and punished the longest. Even though she has not met with any boys, she supposes her father's "thoughts then were similar to those when he wrote James Norman Hall: 'I am afraid she might turn into a good-for-nothing whore if she stays here too long.' And to Uncle Charles: 'I hope she will keep her stinking virginity for another three years.'"(120)[17] He later warns her that "the boys here are so full of diseases" and advises her to keep her virginity until she is "nineteen or twenty" when in "a more civilized country" (121). [18]

The preceding section highlights the ways in which white male heterosexuality is naturalized in South Sea discourse but when "half-caste" daughters embrace the same "free-love" Pacific they must be physically quarantined from their fellow villagers. The village community slips from being represented as isolated and disease-free (when perceived as exotic women) to a group of (male) syphilitic "lice breeders." Robert Dean Frisbie's texts are filled with images of "corrupting" western imports, so it's remarkable that when it's time to advise Johnny about her virginity he suggests a "civilized country" would be safer from disease. Of course, implicit in this suggestion is that she find a "civilized" (read: white) boy. In this case Frisbie is not unlike his literary predecessor and idol, Robert Louis Stevenson, whose *The Beach of Falesá* ends with the narrator's lament that even though his son "is being schooled with the best":

> what bothers me is the girls. They're only half-castes, of course; I know that as well as you do, and there's nobody thinks less of half-castes than I do; but they're mine, and about all I've got. I can't reconcile my mind to their taking up with Kanakas, and I'd like to know where I'm to find the whites? (98)

These texts suggest that miscegenation becomes problematic only when the fathers of mixed-race *female* offspring realize that their own sexualizing activities have repercussions for their daughters who have limited access to white male privilege. For these writers, there is no textual way to reconcile the "chest-thumpingly heterosexual" white male who pursues Pacific women with the role as a father whose female progeny will inherit the same sexualization. But ultimately both positions are based on a totalizing claim to all women's bodies; any autonomy exhibited by Pacific women, including their daughters, causes a masculine colonial crisis.

(E)Racing a National Pacific

Paul Sharrad's article on *Miss Ulysses* finds it remarkable for its untroubled rendering of miscegenation during a racially turbulent era in American history. I agree given the popularity of Michener's *Tales of the South Pacific* (published a year later) and its subsequent musical, which dramatized a white American nurse's dilemma over not marrying an actual Pacific Islander but a French man whose former wife was. Yet Frisbie's correspondence and other publications that follow *Miss Ulysses* reflect that he was deeply conflicted about the social position of his "half-caste" children--especially his daughters. As a text dictated by "the familiar spirit of place" (77), it's significant that *Miss Ulysses* mentions Johnny's inability to gain entrance to British-owned Fijian hotels due to her 'color' (90). With the exception of this brief scene, Frisbie senior suppresses colonial racialization presumably to naturalize his multicultural family. This parallels racial erasures in the British colonial administration of the time: in a letter to Sir Harry Luke, the Governor of the Fiji Islands, Frisbie remarks that "(b)ecause I am travelling with my half-caste daughter...I am of course not signing the Government House Book" (Luke 172). After their visit Luke recorded in his diary, "Frisbie came to tea and discussed the future of his children. We all thought...that they should be brought up wholly as Europeans or wholly as Puka-Pukans, but that to give them a taste of both worlds would be certain to make for misery" (174). The miscegenation dilemma arises much like Ulysses' choice between Scylla and Charybdis. Frisbie's correspondence allows us to see that the Pacific was circumscribed by racial boundaries that were not easily permeated by his complex family.

Although colonial "one-drop" prejudices are almost entirely suppressed in *Miss Ulysses*, Johnny Frisbie subtly addresses these western-imposed racial boundaries in her second work. The cognizance of the children's racialization becomes apparent in *The Frisbies* when the children ask their father if his brother is "'black like us, or white as flour like you?'"(196) Although Frisbie senior clearly wanted to promote the romance of racial democracy for his mixed-race family, the second work suggests that the children were well aware of their own racialization and the socio-cultural gaps between them and their father. In *The Frisbies,* the children perceive their father as a colonial "African hunter," a "great king, followed by submissive...(native) subjects" (128). Consciousness of their negative racialization is the most likely reason for the fact that, where *Miss Ulysses* is filled with constant reference to the children as "savages," in *The Frisbies* this term appears infrequently and only in the mouths of colonial whites. This includes Johnny's father who calls her brother a "'goddamn Puka-Pukan savage!'"(167)

The difficulties of marketing a multiracial Pacific family to a white American audience cause a number of contradictions in *Miss Ulysses*, a text which otherwise strives to reproduce a Ulysses-like teleology of home, family and nation. We know from Johnny's second work that her father feared that his parents would perceive his wife as a "savage" (23).[19] In his collaboration with his daughter, Frisbie was unable to erase or homogenize her racial difference from mainstream America. During their erratic "island hopping," a term which derived from American occupation of the Pacific, Frisbie attempts to give a patriotic cast to his family's travels. Johnny asserts that they left Pukapuka "to help our Uncle (Sam) win the war" (112). The text claims that the family's travel itinerary is reflective of a gestation period of American military patriotism; they had been "nine months on (their) way to the gates of Tokyo" (205). Frisbie senior feels he "could be of service in a literary way" (206) to the war effort but is rejected. Of course, his publications, including *Miss Ulysses*, were already central to the production of an American Pacific. But the children's desire to become "our Uncle's warriors" (181) seems disingenuous because none of their itineraries include any of the American bases in the Pacific; in fact, Frisbie senior directs them away from occupied islands. Overall Johnny comments that "we were silly enough mooncalves to believe that (the U.S. military) might take some notice of us" (205). The term "mooncalves" resonates with English literature's most famous "mooncalf," Caliban. As native subjects of a colonized island, or as "Indians" amidst white, gun-toting "cowboys," the text's racial positioning of the Frisbie children prevents them from entering American patriotic and military fervor.

Miss Ulysses' nationalist framework is fractured due to its inability to imagine Pukapukan "savages" as American subjects; as a result, Frisbie senior reverts to the South Sea genre's trope of transcultural sexual contract. If romance narratives function to domesticize complex international relations under the banner of national belonging, and American citizenship defines *Miss Ulysses'* teleology, then Johnny's racial positioning must be subverted in favor of her sexual exchange to a military representative of her father's nation. Frisbie's desire to construct his children as Cook Island *Americans* becomes apparent when *Miss Ulysses* enacts a transcultural sexual exchange. Johnny asserts that her father "is taking no chances of...me becoming the mistress of some soldier" who will quickly abandon her in favor of a white American wife (110), yet by the end of the biomythography Johnny is paired with an American pilot whom she calls her "boyfriend." This brings us back to Frisbie's desire to find Johnny a "civilized" boy. The last chapter of *Miss Ulysses*, notably titled "The Bomber, the Commandant, and the Jeep," details the children's flight in a Navy bomber to American Samoa to join their father. While her siblings sleep, Johnny observes the Pacific Ocean below which has become "a sheet of galvanized iron, corrugated, brand-new, and dazzling" (233). Johnny has now "grown into a big girl" (234) who fancies that the pilot, a "good-looking young man, clean-faced, (and) boyish, (is) really in love" with her (235). The pilot feeds Johnny American products such as apples and sandwiches and "trie(s) to teach (her) about the dials and levers" in the cockpit (236). When she looks below onto her Cook Island home, Johnny imagines that "those green isles had never belonged to the world; they had been dreamed out of nothingness and set adrift among the clouds" (237). Where racial difference alone may complicate Johnny's entrance into American national belonging, her racialized sexuality, precoded in the familiar trope of "white man, brown woman," prevails. The text sanctifies Johnny's ultimate seduction by young white military men, technology, American food, and the English language. As if arrival to American Samoa were not enough to signal the family's entrance into the U.S. military nation state, Frisbie senior tells them that they are departing for "Honolulu tomorrow" because the family has "a job there with the navy!" (241). This would conveniently situate the Frisbie family in Hawai'i roughly a decade before it became part of the union. *Miss Ulysses*, which begins with Johnny's Cook Island genealogy, concludes with her father whisking them away in a military vehicle. Unlike her namesake, Johnny does not return to her original home or 'motherland' which has just faded into "nothingness"; the text's teleology attempts to assert her cultural and national migration from a feminized "South Seas to one of our Uncle Sam's military bases!" (239). The entrance into masculinized American soil and national belonging is purchased by Johnny's sexual contract with an American soldier. I mentioned earlier that this father/daughter text must submerge the trope of South Sea romance to suppress incest. But since transcultural romance is the most obvious way of marking the colonized woman's entrance into the imperialist nation, Johnny must become a "big girl" and make a sexual allegiance with a white boyfriend (rather than her father) in order to facilitate her entrance into her father's and "Uncle's" national territory. Not surprisingly, there never was a military boyfriend or any sexualized national exchange--Johnny's second biomythography explains that she slept through the entire flight.[20] Furthermore, Johnny's family never made it to Honolulu but returned to her mother's land: the Cook Islands.

Father-lands and National Ambiguity

Although Johnny claims "I've never known a native who wouldn't prefer his country run by the Americans" (90), and the text outlines a teleology of American citizenship, *Miss Ulysses* indicates profound ambiguity about the relationship between these multicultural children and their 'father's land.' Frisbie senior was as unable to reconcile the two cultural heritages of his children as he was unable to integrate their multiple claims to national territories. In *Miss Ulysses,* the nation, like Frisbie himself, is a jealous patriarch. Although the Cook Islands are a sovereign territory under New Zealand administration, the region experienced significant nationalist movements during the production of *Miss Ulysses* that had to be suppressed in order to facilitate the children's entrance into an imagined American citizenship. Ironically, the presence of American troops was a catalyst to Cook Island proto-nationalist agitation; Frisbie senior had to critique U.S. military presence in the Pacific in order to suppress Cook Island sovereignty, while simultaneously inscribing his daughter's sexual exchange into a masculine, militarized America.

Just as 18th century sentimental and later South Sea narratives suppressed the exploitation of native labor and sovereignty, Frisbie senior's domestic mystifications include the erasure of one of the most important proto-nationalist movements in the Cook Islands. In 1943, the pro-labour Cook Islands Progressive Association (CIPA) was (re)initiated by native Cook Islanders concerned about highly questionable market conditions inflicted by an unsympathetic New Zealand Administration. The primary New Zealand-based monopolist was A.B. Donald Ltd., Frisbie's employer on Pukapuka.[21] Unionizing agitation began after U.S soldiers stationed at Aitutaki hired native laborers at much higher wages than were ever received from British/NZ employers and provided islanders with health care and library access. Some of the U.S. troops were African-American, unionized, and vocal in critiquing the NZ Administration, which contributed to an already present anti-colonial sentiment (Scott 232). The 1940s, when most of *Miss Ulysses* takes place, was a tumultuous time period including multiple CIPA-backed labor strikes, waterside demonstrations, and petitions against the appointment of Resident Commissioner William Tailby, a man who consistently suppressed labor agitation and had married into the dominant trading company family. The Frisbie family visited Aitutaki the same year the CIPA was established there, but there is no mention of any labor disputes. Instead, the island's difficult history is described: 19th century blackbirding (kidnapping laborers), unscrupulous western traders, and western government systems are critiqued for testing Aitutaki's "happy spirit" (225). Despite this long and troubled history, the island only "lost its soul" when American soldiers appeared and prevented the islanders from returning "to their old way of life" (225). *Miss Ulysses* presents a picture of gum-chewing, cigarette-smoking, swearing native women the sight of whom "sicken" the narrator (226). Since Johnny's second work testifies to the joys of smoking and gum chewing, this is clearly the voice of her father. This critique of a culture destroyed by American commercialism given by a self-described American "South Seas trader" is somewhat disingenuous. But more disturbing is Frisbie's primitivist ideological stance, which insists that the trappings of modernity (including capital) "corrupt" native culture while erasing the fact that the CIPA in Aitutaki was agitating against considerable resistance for compensation for their already modern society. One of the text's more insidious forms of romance is that the focus on the Frisbie family deflects attention from the domestic and broader imperial concerns of Cook Islanders. In *Miss Ulysses*, family romance cannot be aligned with the familial structures of early Cook Island nationalism because, as an anticolonial sentiment, proto-nationalism cannot be easily reconciled with (Frisbie's) paternalist nation-state. It's not that Frisbie was unaware of the CIPA's highly publicized struggle: he spent the last year of his life on Rarotonga where the CIPA was holding month-long executive meetings and organizing strikes on the waterside. Significantly, this excision erupts in one of the closing chapters of Johnny Frisbie's second text, suggestively titled "A Big Man-of-War." Johnny narrates her tour of the New Zealand military ship and her fear that she would be kidnapped (225). As the Cooks' colonial administrator, New Zealand had "kidnapped" local labor much like the blackbirders of the previous century with the notable difference that local labor was now exploited at home rather than abroad. The chapter closes with Johnny accompanying her "papa" to a function held at Resident Commissioner Tailby's home. Although she does not directly link Tailby to his anti-labor politics, in describing her first interaction with the colonial "elite" Johnny states, "'it wasn't very much fun'" (221).

Because of *Miss Ulysses'* competing claims to national belonging the text suppresses the labor movements that were the backbone of Pacific nationalism. Yet the distance erected in this first text between political versus domestic formulations of labor collapses when Johnny's second work debunks her father's romance of the kind, American trader. In other words, Johnny's second work, by focusing on power in the familial realm, suggests that national domestic hierarchies are implicated in this multicultural family. Frisbie senior's attempt "to resolve political uncertainties in the sphere of family" is turned on its head by Johnny whose text inscribes a highly politicized domestic sphere. In *The Frisbies*, her father cheats the locals by manipulating the copra scales (126), plans an "expedition" to "discover" "two rich, uninhabited islands belonging to no country" where he will "hoist the American flag" (25), and treats his children, as the title of one of her chapters indicates, as a "slave-labor gang"

(183). The exploitation of familial labor is also tied firmly to American literary production. According to Johnny, she had typed her father's last novel, *Dawn Sails North* at least six times during his tumultuous revision process.

Unlike her father who projected sources of sexual contagion onto the indigenous realm, Johnny's second work relocates the discourse of military and colonial pollution as a family tragedy. Among the most devastating blows to the Frisbie family romance is the suggestion that Frisbie probably contributed to the death of his own beloved wife. Although *Miss Ulysses* clearly insinuates that a trading ship brought tuberculosis to Pukapuka and caused his wife's early death from the disease (33), Johnny's second text reveals that Frisbie senior brought the illness from the United States — it was the cause of his medical discharge from the military (10). Thus, a domestic tragedy emerges from her father's political one: it seems that it was not only U.S. troops in Aitutaki who "contaminated" the local population. Her father's charge, discussed earlier, that male Pukapukans are contagious "lice-breeders" is deconstructed. Her second biomythography does little to debunk rumours that Frisbie was a substance abuser[22] by concluding with her father's alcoholism, his reliance on his children to carry him home from bars and to care for him during his poignant dying hours. In an ironic twist that suggests military and colonial pollution of local resources, Johnny explains that her father's death was precipitated by "drinking homebrew made in an unclean kerosene can" (232). Robert Dean Frisbie died a few months after the publication of *Miss Ulysses*, deeply in debt and leaving his children penniless.[23]

Robert Dean Frisbie's family romance is indebted to a long colonial narrative history that is in no way limited to the Pacific region. Peter Hulme and Mary Louise Pratt have already noted the persistence of romantic love narratives in the early contact literature of the Americas and point out the ways in which social and economic relations are disguised by the romantic "mystique of reciprocity" (Pratt 97). This also applies to the legacy of the South Sea genre. As the author of novels such as *Amaru:A Romance of the South Seas* and *Island of Desire*, the very titles of Frisbie's works suggest that he was deeply committed to narrating "'cultural harmony through romance'" (Hulme qtd. in Pratt 97). Frisbie perpetuates this "mystique" in his narrative relations with Pacific Island women and in his self-ascription as an honest trader and devoted father, because "(a)s an ideology, romantic love, like capitalist commerce, understands itself as reciprocal" (Pratt 97). His daughter's second work lays bare the foundations of American paternalism by complicating her father's national and domestic mystifications. Ultimately she reveals the ways in which nationalist and domestic exchanges in the Pacific were hardly reciprocal.

From the South Seas to White Nativism

Reading the textual historiography of whiteness in Robert Dean Frisbie's works can be a facile task in a critical climate that is focused on deconstructing colonial genres. A much more difficult and perhaps problematic task now that Frisbie has "died' in this essay is to "revive" his legacy by concluding with additional aspects of "white nativism," specifically the components of *Miss Ulysses* which gesture towards a sensitivity to colonial issues and a recognition of native subjectivity. This double voice of "white nativism" has relevance for the themes and concerns of later indigenous Pacific literature.

Miss Ulysses refutes the colonial gaze in myriad ways and as such can be read simultaneously as a South Sea and a "white native" text. For instance, the text positions the European as object and re-fashions the European arrival scene from a native viewpoint; Johnny observes that in Puka Puka, white "passengers would jump ashore, grinning and self-conscious—and how strange, if not ridiculous they looked" (28-9), and follows with a mocking description of their clothing. Noticeably absent are the naked women who, in South Sea narratives, "swarm" these boats. The visitors become the object of the larger community's gaze: "a hundred tongues muttered how astonishing were the ways of white men" (29). *Miss Ulysses* also documents exploitative aspects of Pacific history that are usually suppressed by the romantic South Sea genre. The text inscribes native oral traditions about the experiences of 19th century "blackbirding," or the practice of kidnapping islanders to work in the Chincha Islands guano industry, incorporates an "old sailor song" about the trip to Callao (9), and the Pukapukan "King Pereto's" escape and return (24)[24] The text draws extensively upon Pukapukan oral traditions (14, 23, 62), celebrates the various forms of island dancing that the children learn on their travels (63, 190, 104), critiques the imposition of Christian morality upon Pacific sexualities (67), and calls attention to the lack of contact reciprocity when Euro-American traders "cheat my people...get drunk and spoil the young girls" (185).

In its validation of Pacific oral epistemologies, traditions, and subjectivities, *Miss Ulysses* marks a break from its South Sea counterparts. It anticipates other tropes that are common to contemporary Pacific and broader postcolonial literature. The text parodies colonial education by describing the schoolteacher as the "Hitler of Puka-Puka," a man who teaches English out of "vanity" (43) and preaches fidelity yet is "the worst adulterer on the island" (44).[25] The children enjoy "mimicking" the English language of authority figures on the island such as the schoolteacher's wife and the local reverend (44). The text is deeply rooted in the discourse of family and local community, while also making gestures towards a broader Pacific regionalism. I've only mentioned a few of the counter-discursive tropes implemented in the work, but already thematic parallels can be made to other contemporary Pacific authors.[26]

Paul Sharrad has already addressed some thematic aspects of *Miss Ulysses* that anticipate later indigenous Pacific writing. He notes that it adopts the structure of Pacific oral traditions by beginning with Johnny's Cook Islands' genealogy and it includes a long critique of European discovery narratives. Sharrad finds *Miss Ulysses* to be a dialogic and communal-based text that highlights the process of adapting to multiple language systems (written and oral) and testifies to the complex hybridity of the Pacific region. Johnny continually breaks the narrative to comment about her experience while writing (39), describes the multiplicity of narratives she will be drawing upon (which include Pukapukan legends, her diary, her father's journals and the *Odyssey)* and consistently interacts with her presumed (American) reader. As such the text separates itself from its South Sea counterparts and struggles to break the boundaries between written and oral traditions. Ultimately Johnny is fashioned as the progeny of two important storytellers in her genealogy—her father and "Wué, the great navigator of ancient times who told such tall tales of his travels that even today people say of a liar: 'He has the tongue of Wué!'" (107).

I'd like to turn to one final scene in *Miss Ulysses,* which I believe addresses the vexed question of multiple authorship in this text. In this scene, Johnny, her father, and Araipu are attending a New Year's Eve celebration in a Fijian church; the visiting men are invited to preach a sermon to the gathered community. Araipu speaks first in Pukapukan, Frisbie senior translates this into English, and their guide "Mohammedan Joe" translates the English into Fijian. Johnny is the only one who "understood all the languages pretty well" (88), so she is able to witness the process of translation. Araipu's original speech would be perceived as insulting, so her father alters the message and "spun it out" (89). When it "came to Mohammedan Joe's turn to translate he spun it out" (89) even farther, "though Lord knows that it wasn't Christianity—maybe something out of the Koran" (89). No matter how far this speech was "spun out," it ends up condensed and summarized, in English, in *Miss Ulysses*. The scene calls attention to the ruptures, alterations, and gaps in complex, multi-layered linguistic translation—as well as the complicated process of translating formalized speeches in three different languages to one written counterpart. Frisbie senior, who translated Johnny's writing from Rarotongan and Pukapukan and edited her English in order to produce *Miss Ulysses*, was well aware of the problematic process of multi-cultural translation and calls attention to this in his introduction to the work. The characters in this scene are as circumscribed by the church and their expectant audience as the Frisbies were by language and genre. Frisbie once wrote to Hall, "if I bared my soul it would not be a printable book," (228) but evidently he found a satisfactory medium— that of collaborating with a "Pukapukan anthropologist"--when he admitted "it is only the keen interest in Johnny's book that keeps me going" (238). Even though "speaking through the voice of the disempowered becomes, in part, a way of lessening the marginalization of privilege" (McClintock 304), Frisbie's collaboration also allowed him to address some of the "marginalization" of Pacific Islanders under colonial rule and to explore the textual repercussions of native subjectivity.

Coda: White Natives and Postcolonial Writing

The structure of Johnny Frisbie's second biomythography calls attention to itself as a variation "spun out" from an indefinable origin. Although it incorporates a deeply masked critique of her father and continues in the first text's tradition by describing children's games, the activities of her village peers, and asserts her revision of family events, it does not *directly* engage with the critiques of the colonial center that are so apparent in *Miss Ulysses*.[27] The proto-postcolonial aspects of *Miss Ulysses*—such as parody and mimicry; the critiques of missionaries, colonial occupation, and education; the revision of European narratives of discovery and arrival; the foregrounding of Pacific genealogy; the metafictional narrative structure; the gesture towards Pacific regionalism and cosmopolitanism; and the intertextual entanglement with the South Sea genre and Pukapukan oral tradition---are noticeably absent in *The Frisbies*. Presumably Frisbie senior, by utilizing his own "white nativism," had drawn upon these elements because of his conflicted position as a white native with familial ties to the region. More conversant at that time with the South Sea genre, Frisbie senior "wrote back" to the very center that he helped perpetuate.

Johnny Frisbie's biomythographies reflect a deep entanglement with the legacy of her father and her own western/literary genealogy. As the father of a "South Seas Daughter," Frisbie senior was also concerned with literary and familial genealogies. While Johnny Frisbie can be readily integrated into the corpus of modern Pacific literature based on her Cook Islands' heritage and literary contributions, the interjection of a "white native" amidst the historical trajectory of contemporary writing in the Pacific might be viewed as problematic but, to return to Wendt's theory of the Pacific imagination: "our dead are woven into our souls…we can never escape them." [28]

At the present time, Fiji is reeling from the repercussions of its latest racially-motivated coup. The tensions between "Indians" and "indigenous" Fijians revolve around competing definitions of ethnic, national and cultural belonging. Like many postcolonial regions, and like *Miss Ulysses* itself, the Pacific is still entangled in the complex implications of past and present colonial presence. These questions about genealogy, historiography, colonial contact, language, and ethnic belonging in the tumultuous period after the second World War were anticipated by the double-voiced, conflicted narratives of Robert Dean and Johnny Frisbie. Both biomythographies gesture towards the "racial ambiguity" of Pacific literature in a way that complicates and mitigates inscriptions of hybrid, nationalist, and ethnic identities.

Elizabeth Deloughrey

NOTES

I'm indebted to thank Chris Harbrant, Paul Sharrad and the editors of this volume for their thoughtful feedback on this article.
[1] Johnny Frisbie's first work was completed when she was fourteen; the second was published when she was twenty-seven. I borrow the term "biomythography" from Audre Lorde's well-known work, *Zami*. I prefer the term since there is no unified authorial subject in *Miss Ulysses*.

"Mythography" suggests the centrality of the past and calls attention to the process of narrative invention.

2 See Subramani *South Pacific Literature* for a brief comment on Johnny Frisbie and other Pacific autobiographies of the time (14). In "Autobiography in the Pacific" Michael Hayes outlines a much longer Pacific writing tradition by indigenous missionaries. See also Majorie Crocombe for the Cook Islands' context.

3 Pratt reminds us that "transcultural...relations of subordination and resistance" are present in contemporary autobiography; to read them simply as "authentic" or "inauthentic" suppresses transcultural dialogics (102).

4 The term "Polynesian" is vexed by its problematic colonial history but generally refers to the triangular region between Hawai'i, Aotearoa/New Zealand and Rapanui/Easter Island. Johnny's ancestry is not merely bicultural—it also involves Mangaian (of the southern Cook Islands) genealogy.

5 I've adopted the more contemporary spelling of the island.

6 The Cook Islands have a long history of contact with Europeans, beginning with Spanish arrival in 1595. James Cook visited and charted the islands in the late 18 th century, followed by British missionaries who settled in the 1820s. The islands became a British protectorate in 1888 and a New Zealand colony in 1901. The islands achieved self-government (in association with New Zealand) in 1965. I mention this to highlight the fact that this island region has been subjected to various forms of western institutional rule—this certainly has propagated some aspects of white "normalcy" (in religion, language, education, dress, trade and written law). But Euro-Americans have never represented a demographic majority—much of the islands' governance was conducted from overseas.

7 See the works of Rod Edmond and Bernard Smith for analyses of textual and artistic 'Orientalism' in the Pacific.

8 See Paul Sharrad's "Imagining the Pacific" and Chris Connery's "The Oceanic Feeling" for interrogations into the ways in which European and American writers have depicted the Pacific Ocean as a cultural void.

9 Contemporary Samoan writer Albert Wendt complains that this Pacific Orientalism contributes to "literary straightjackets" from which indigenous Pacific Island writers must extricate themselves (28).

10 Although this relationship between native and wr.ter has been extensively critiqued in anthropological studies (see Fabian), it has not to my knowledge been adequately applied to 20th century South Sea writers.

11 These early 20th-century "waves" of American male migrants (including anthropologists, beachcombers, and authors) to the Pacific Islands have received strikingly little critical attention—particularly in relation to their contributions to modernist primitivism. Their emigrations suggest that modernist writers seeking out the "primitive" were as dependent upon the South Seas as Africa, Asia, and the Caribbean.

12 Like anthropologists of his time, Frisbie segregates western temporality from particular Pacific spaces. Pacific primitivism "is constructed as a system of coordinates (emanating of course from a real center--the Western metropolis) in which given societies of all time and places may be plotted in terms of relative distance from the present" (Fabian 26).

13 See H. E. Maude's insightful chapter "Beachcombers and Castaways" in *Of Islands and Men* which details the impact of early beachcombers in the region but neglects the obvious

relationship between these arrivants' polygamy and their acculturation to local societies. Campbell's *Gone Native* briefly mentions how Polynesian women were central to the assimilation process for white beachcombers.

[14] *White Man, Brown Woman: The Life Story of a Trader in the South Seas* by Tom A. Richards is one of the many similarly titled works of his genre. Paul Sharrad notes that this text comments on Frisbie and Ngatokorua. See Sharrad 136 and Richards' negative comments on Frisbie's "dusky wife" page 188.

[15] Rod Edmond remarks, "For all the sexual commerce across the beach in Pacific romances there are curiously few offspring" (176).

[16] See for instance David Chappell's "The Forgotten *Mau*" which describes Samoan resistance to U.S. naval occupation, which produced over 500 'illegitimate' mixed-race children in late 1920s Pago Pago (250).

[17] This was a recurrent fear on Frisbie's part since his health was failing. He wrote to that in the case he died in American Samoa "it is appalling to think of my beloved Johnny becoming a little whore on the streets of Pago Pago" (qtd. in Hall 234).

[18] In my forthcoming interview with Johnny Frisbie she says of her father, "other than his white skin, there were no other white man's jewels that he wanted me to inherit or that he believed would be of value in my future life, other than to learn to be a lady and not lose my virginity before marriage."

[19] It is probably no coincidence that Frisbie's last published novel, *Dawn Sails North,* is heavily invested in untangling complicated racial genealogies and concludes by erasing the Pacific Island heritage of one of its main "half-caste" female characters so that she may marry the white protagonist.

[20] This text also explains that when dining later in the "officers' mess" Johnny felt shy and "could barely speak" (209); as a result, she "ate little of the rare American food" (209).

[21] A.B. Donald Ltd. did much to contribute to Cook Island poverty for two decades by enforcing low wages, monopolizing trade, recruiting islanders for slave-like labor in the phosphate mining of Makatea Island, and by consistently resisting any local unionization. They sold the Pukapuka station to a similar company, Burns Philp. The station was closed in the mid 1930s during the worst depression in Cook Island history.

[22] In *Return to Paradise,* Michener suggests that Frisbie was a morphine addict who "had been responsible for his own death. He had used once too often a rusty hypodermic needle" (18). James Ramsey Ullman is less subtle: "He became a drunkard, a drug addict, a derelict beachcomber, and when he died, still a comparatively young man, it was in squalor and misery" (229).

[23] Ironically, it was not the proceeds from his South Sea novels that helped ensure the future of his children. James Norman Hall published Frisbie's edited personal correspondence as a series of articles in *The Atlantic Monthly* and donated the proceeds to Frisbie's children.

[24] One hundred and forty-five Pukapukans were kidnapped (24% of the population) and at least half died before they reached Peru (Maude 51).

[25] The critique is somewhat problematic given the fact that it is of Geoffrey Henry, whose son was one of the most prominent members of the CIPA.

[26] See the works of Sia Figiel, Albert Leomala, Ruperake Petaia, Teresia Teaiwa and Konai Helu Thaman Some of these writers can be found in Albert Wendt's anthologies, *Lali* and

Nuanua. Subramani, Sharrad, Hereniko and Wendt are some of the more prolific writers about Pacific literature and address many of these themes.

[27] Johnny's second work is also deeply relevant to later Pacific writing but the narrative structure she has chosen remains more deeply coded, more focused on the subjectivity of children, and fashions a much more horizontal, "local" community than her father's cosmopolitanism. Her authorship reflects a moment in a long Cook Islands literary history that includes ample predecessors such as Ta'unga, Maretu, Teaia, Tom Davis and many others (See Crocombe). Like Maretu, the 19th century Rarotongan missionary who also travelled extensively through the Cook Islands and completed his autobiographical manuscript with guidance from his (Christian missionary) "father," Johnny Frisbie was enmeshed in a similar type of deeply mediated authorship. Maretu and Frisbie both obtained their literacy through the intervention of westerners; inscribed oral traditions, songs, and western impact on dynamic local cultures; and weaved historiography alongside auto-ethnography while writing within rigid western genre structures. Maretu framed his work by the Bible, Frisbie around the South Sea genre. Sadly, both authors' works have been out of print for much of the 20th century.

[28] Wendt's poem uncannily echoes the complexities of the Frisbie family when he weaves together an equally complex Pacific historiography that includes "polynesian fathers," missionary "Sky-Piercers," a lost mother, and a European trader who "reaped a brood/of 'half-castes' and then fled/for the last atoll and a whisky death" (287).

WORKS CITED

Chappell, David. "The Forgotten *Mau:* Anti-Navy Protest in American Samoa, 1920-1935." *Pacific Historical Review.* 69:2 (May 2000): 217-260.

Connery, Christopher. "The Oceanic Feeling and the Regional Imaginary." *Global/Local: Cultural Production and the Transnational Imaginary.* Ed. Rob Wilson and Wimal Dissanayake. Durham and London: Duke UP, 1996. 284-311.

Crocombe, Marjorie Tuainekore. Ed. and Trans. *Cannibals and Converts: Radical Change in the Cook Islands by Maretu.* Suva: Institute of Pacific Studies, 1983.

Edmond, Rod. *Representing the South Pacific: Colonial discourse from Cook to Gauguin.* Cambridge: Cambridge UP, 1997.

Fabian, Johannes. *Time and the Other: How Anthropology Makes its Object.* New York: Columbia University Press, 1983.

Frisbie, Florence Johnny. *The Frisbies of the South Seas.* Garden City, NY: Doubleday, 1959.

---. *Miss Ulysses from Puka-Puka.* New York: Macmillan, 1948.

Frisbie, Robert Dean. *Amaru: A Romance of the South Seas*. Garden City, New York: Doubleday, 1945.

---. "Americans in the South Seas." *American Mercury* 24.94 (1931): 154-160.

---. *The Book of Puka-Puka*. New York: The Century Company, 1928.

---. *Mr. Moonlight's Island*. New York: Macmillan, 1939.

Hall, James Norman. *The Forgotten One and Other True Tales of the Pacific*. Boston: Little, Brown, 1952.

Hayes, Michael. "Autobiography in the Pacific: Changing Functions of Self, Writing and Nation." *New Literature Review* 27 (1994): 29-44.

Knox, Bernard. Ed. *The Odyssey*. New York, Penguin Group, 1996.

Luke, Sir Harry. *From a South Seas Diary 1938-1942*. London: Nicholson & Watson, 1945.

Maude, H.E. *Of Islands and Men*. Melbourne: Oxford UP, 1968.

---. *Slavers in Paradise: The Peruvian Slave Trade in Polynesian, 1862-1864*. Stanford: Stanford UP, 1981.

Michener, James. *Return to Paradise*. Greenwich: Fawcett, 1951.

Pratt, Mary Louise. *Imperial Eyes: Travel Writing and Transculturation*. London and New York: Routledge, 1992.

Richards, Tom A. *White Man, Brown Woman: The Life Story of a Trader in the South Seas*. With Stuart Gurr. London: Hutchinson & Co., 1933.

Roulston, Charles Robert. "Eden and the Lotus Eaters: A Critical Study of the South Sea Island Writing of Frederick O'Brien, James Norman Hall, and Robert Dean Frisbie." Diss. U Maryland, 1965.

Sharrad, Paul. "Imagining the Pacific." *Meanjin* 49:4 (Summer 1990): 597-606.

---. "Making Beginnings: Johnny Frisbie and Pacific Literature." *New Literary History* 25 (1994): 121-136.

Stevenson, Robert Louis. *The Beach of Falesá*. 1892. Ed. Barry Menikoff. Stanford: Stanford UP, 1987.

Subramani. *South Pacific Literature: From Myth to Fabulation*. Rev. ed. Suva: Institute of Pacific

Studies, 1992.

Ullman, James Ramsey. *Where the Bong Tree Grows: The Log of One Man's Journey in the South Pacific.* Cleveland and New York: World Publishing, 1963.

Wendt, Albert. "In a Stone Castle in the South Seas." *Mana Review* 1:2 (1976): 27-32.

---. "Inside us the Dead." *Lali: A Pacific Anthology*. Ed. Albert Wendt. Auckland: Longman Paul, 1980. 284-290.

---. ed. *Lali: A Pacific Anthology*. Auckland: Longman Paul, 1980.

---."Towards a New Oceania." *Readings in Pacific Literature*. Ed. Paul Sharrad. Wollongong: New Literatures Research Centre, U Wollongong, 1993. 9-19.

Whitehead, John S. "Writers as Pioneers." *Yankees in Paradise: The Pacific Basin Frontier*. Ed. Arrell Morgan Gibson and John Whitehead. Albuquerque: U of New Mexico Press, 1993. 379-410.

9.

WRITING CULTURE AND PERFORMING RACE
IN MOURNING DOVE'S *COGEWEA, THE HALF-BLOOD* (1927)

He [Alfred Densmore] was hardly satisfied with his surroundings.
Where were those picturesque Indians that he was promised to meet?
Instead, he had been lured into a nest of half-bloods, whom he had
always understood to be the inferior degenerates of the two races. (48)
--Mourning Dove, *Cogewea, The Half-Blood*

In the following essay I examine how Mourning Dove imagines and
textually performs the dilemmas of cultural hybridization and racial ambiguity
in her ethnic modernist novel, *Cogewea, The Half-Blood: A Depiction of the Great
Montana Cattle Range* (1927). By calling Mourning Dove's novel "ethnic
modernist," I suggest that there is a coherent body of ethnic modernist texts that
functions as a counter-discourse to the high modernist Anglo-American literary
production between the World Wars.[1] In their texts American ethnic modernist
writers specifically bring to surface and debate such issues as cultural, ethnic
and/or racial belonging—as well as the issues of gender and class—through
their usage and appropriation of the narrative modes and techniques of what
Judith Butler calls "subversive repetition" and "discursive resignification."[2]
Such texts question the assumed authenticity of national, cultural, ethnic or
racial, gendered, and class-stratified bodies within the bureaucratized and
segregated units of political organizations. Their characters "perform" and re-
signify identities that are produced and "interpellated" by specific ethnic, racial,
or cultural communities that defy the naming, signifying, and
inclusionary/exclusionary authority of political institutions.

In *Gender Trouble* and in the later *Bodies that Matter*--two of the founding
texts of gender studies--Judith Butler treats gender as "performative." While
Butler almost exclusively uses the notion of performativity to destabilize

essentialist and binary notions about gender she considers troubling in contemporary feminist discourse, indirectly—by virtue of association—she extends her category to also include the performativity of racial identity. For example, in *Bodies that Matter*—Butler's follow-up and extension to her previous argument in *Gender Trouble*—she dedicates a chapter to Nella Larsen's novel, *Passing*. In that chapter, titled "Passing, Queering: Nella Larsen's Psychoanalytic Challenge," Butler connects the performativity of gender to the performativity of racial identity when she associates "queering" with "passing." In Butler's view "queering" is an expression of homoerotic desire that presupposes sexual and gender ambiguity, while "passing" involves heterosexual desire that implicitly mandates the prerequisite of racial passing. However, in her argument concerning the parallels between "queering" and "passing," Butler downplays the racial aspects of homoerotic desire between the two female characters of Larsen's novel. Thus, in Butler's analysis the racial passing of the two women is actually the foil for the possibility of sexual transgression in the form of homoerotic desire. According to that logic, both queering and passing crack open illicit spaces for greater freedom and social mobility for women of color within the matrix of compulsive heterosexuality and white hegemony. Even though the issue of racism is still submerged under the weight of compulsory heterosexism, Butler's interpretation of Larsen's novel leaves the door open for making the leap from the performativity of gender to the performativity and ambiguity of racial identity. In the following argument I borrow Butler's notion of performativity in order to examine under what circumstances it is or it is not possible to extend her category of performativity from gender to racial identity. While Butler views the performativity of gender and, possibly, of racial identity as a universally available tool for subverting sexually and, to a lesser degree, racially confining social institutions, I examine some of the instances when racial passing is not uniformly available to everyone--regardless of class status and racial, cultural, or ethnic belonging--as Butler's category of performativity might suggest.

In an interview Butler distinguishes the category of "performance" from that of "performativity": whereas the "former presumes a subject . . . the latter contests the very notion of the subject" (see Osborne and Segal 33). Butler defines performativity as a "discursive resignification," which works through the bodily mechanisms of "subversive repetition." In developing the notion of identity as performative, she relies on the "Foucauldian premise that power works in part through discourse and it works in part to produce and destabilise subjects" (33). In Butler's epistemology gender constructs sex--or, by way of analogy, bureaucratized institutions and cultures construct rigid categories and discourses of racial, ethnic, or cultural identity. Thus gender is produced by the "heterosexual matrix," which prescribes a "casual continuity among sex, gender, and desire" (*Gender Trouble* 22). To defy, that is to re-signify and subvert, the "structuring structures" of gendered--or, for our purposes here, the "structuring structures" of racially determined--binaries, Butler suggests that gender is a performative entity.[3] Thus, she rejects the exclusionary and bureaucratized notions of sexual, differential, and possibly racial constructions of identity. Performativity, then, destabilizes the binary and oppositional categories of gender and race, more specifically, those of male versus female and/or white versus non-white. A performative approach to gender and race then allows for a pluralistic and more fluid envisioning of sexuality and cultural as well as racial belonging. Since socially and culturally determined configurations of gender--and of race or ethnicity--have seized a hegemonic hold within bureaucratized Western societies, rather than proposing nostalgic or utopic resistances that disregard the very real and oppressive powers at work in modern societies, Butler calls for subversive action in the present. She calls for "gender trouble," the mobilization, subversive confusion, and proliferation of genders--and racial as well as cultural identities. To extend her argument concerning the performativity of gender to issues of race, culture, and ethnicity, we could also include, beside the narrative and political strategy of "gender trouble," the strategies of passing and mixedblood identity.

In this essay I focus on Mourning Dove's *Cogewea, The Half-Blood: A Depiction of the Great Montana Cattle Range* (1927) in order to examine how the author imagines the limits and possibilities of the performativity of racial identity through the narrative strategies of "discursive resignification" and "subversive repetition." Written during the heyday of high modernism, Mourning Dove recycled the traditional genre of the western romance and used it to rephrase the narrative of historical "tragedy" as a melodramatic "farce" and to re-imagine modernist urban centers in the peripheries of the cattle ranches in Montana.[4] But her main concern is with mixedblood identity--with racial ambiguity and cultural hybridity--at a time of widespread and intense anxiety over American national identity on behalf of American-born and white-identified, what Walter Benn Michaels calls "nativist," groups.[5]

"Mourning Dove," which is the English translation from the Okanogan (also called Salish) language of the name *Hum-ishu-ma*, is the pen name of Christine Quintasket who grew up among the Okanogans of the Colville Confederated Tribes of eastern Washington State. She later moved to the Flathead Reservation in Montana. Mourning Dove was only the second Native American woman to publish a novel.[6] She wrote *Cogewea, The Half-Blood* around 1912, but it was not published until 1927. As the novel's subtitle suggests, the text focuses on the problematic of *métis, mestizo*, or mulatto, in particular, mixedblood Indian identity. She both engages with and questions the cliched figure of the "tragic mulatto" popular in American fiction. She also argues against the sentimental and biased depictions of Native Americans by white ethnographers whose narratives proliferated during the first few decades of the twentieth century.

Mourning Dove, like several other ethnic modernist writers, engages with the modernist practice of textual borrowing, as well as with the narrative strategies of "discursive resignification" and "subversive repetition." She ironically rewrites an earlier text, Therese Broderick's *The Brand, a Tale of the Flathead Reservation* (1909),[7] which one-sidedly dramatized the early twentieth-century literary and popular cliché of the "Vanishing American." Mourning Dove revises this cliché through the trope of the legendary rounding-up and corralling of the last free-ranging Michel Pablo buffalo herd in 1908:

> "It was a grand and never to be forgotten sight," replied Cogewea sadly.
> "But it was pitiful to see the animals fight so desperately for freedom.
> Although I participated in a way, it brought a dimness to my eyes. They
> seemed to realize that they were leaving their native haunts for all time.
> To the Indian, they were the last link connecting him with the past, and
> when one of the animals burst through the car, falling to the tracks and
> breaking its neck, I saw some of the older people shedding silent tears.
> But what else could the owner do than sell them? The reservation had
> been thrown open to settlement and the range all taken by homesteaders.
> Pablo had to make some kind of disposition, so he sold his herd to the
> Canadian Government. The few too wild to corral, were killed. They
> were considered too dangerous for the white settlers, but we never found
> them dangerous when we were here alone. (*Cogewea* 148)

Mourning Dove tells this story not once but twice. While Broderick's text reiterates the notion that Native Americans are a "vanishing race," Mourning Dove's novel rejects the white ethnographer's melodramatic reading of Native American culture. Thus in *Cogewea* the author subverts the stereotypes of Indians by retelling the story of the "vanishing" buffalo herd as a farce:

> Cogewea then told of an amusing incident in that connection. The irrepressible camera man was there and he thought to obtain a rare picture of a band of stampeding buffaloes, bearing directly down upon him. He secured his negative alright, but with lowered horns the animals charged and he had scant time to spring into the branches of a nearby tree, where he hung thus narrowly escaping with his life. A noted "Cowboy Artist" was in close proximity and he drew a sketch of the discomfited man swinging to the tree with the rushing buffaloes passing under him. It was, perhaps, a more interesting picture than the camera could have secured. (149)

The image of the Cowboy Artist drawing the portrait of a photographer, who is taking a picture of the last "authentic" buffalo roundup––moreover, it is retold by Cogewea in Mourning Dove's novel–– is a highly ironic commentary on the general modernist dilemmas of authenticity and the originality of artistic representation. The simulacrum of the last "authentic" free-ranging buffalo that Broderick associates with the figure of the "Vanishing American" is, then, the "original" sign eternally deferred in Mourning Dove's novel. She subverts the cliched association of the buffalo with the Indian by making tragedy into its own farce––what Judith Butler calls the narrative strategy of "discursive resignification" through the technique of "subversive repetition." Similarly, Mourning Dove defers the essentializing notion of authentic Indian identity, and, instead, she foregrounds culturally hybrid or mixedblood characters.

Much work has been done lately on the issue of mixedblood identity by both Native and non-Native critics. For example, Louis Owens dedicates two of his critical books, *Other Destinies* and *Mixedblood Messages*, to examining mixedblood characters and identity in Native American, or in his terms American Indian, literature. Recently, Arnold Krupat has discussed the development of racial discourse concerning mixed-descent identity from the early decades of the twentieth century until the present.[8] Both Owens and Krupat read Mourning Dove's novel as a bittersweet celebration of mixedblood identity that leaves the issue of racial belonging in a limbo and the narrative in a stasis. Krupat quotes Owens that "the novel concludes ambiguously with the prospect of a wealthy Cogewea and Jim living happily ever after, a matched pair of mixedbloods in the lap of luxury" (*Other Destinies* 47). Krupat agrees with Owens that *Cogewea* leaves the dilemma of mixed descent unsolved. I suggest that while Mourning Dove's novel leaves the dilemma of mixedblood *racial* identity open to ironic and sometimes tragic interpretations and appropriations, ultimately, her narrative does support a less ambiguous Indian *cultural* identification. At the level of the plot—the main device for exegesis for both Owens and Krupat who exemplify the crucial scene of the two horse "races" during the July Fourth celebrations—the heroine does remain in a cataleptic stasis between white Anglo and traditional Indian worlds without hope for a resolution. But following the ethnographic thread of the novel--represented by the repeated retellings of the round-up of the last free-ranging buffalo herd and the interpolated story of the white female ethnographer's visit to the H-B ranch that produces the much reviled book, *The Brand*--it is clear that Cogewea's identification is not with the white outsiders but with the culture of her grandmother or Stemteemä. Moreover, Cogewea strives to become an "authoress" in order to record and preserve her tribal culture instead of leaving the task to white ethnographers. In that sense, Mourning Dove's novel is a subversive fictionalized critique of white anthropology in favor of leaving the task of preserving traditional cultures to their members. Thus, Cogewea should write the story of the Flathead and Okanogan tribes as opposed to Therese Broderick (a.k.a. Tin Schreiner); or to make Mourning Dove's critique more encompassing, she suggests leaving ethnographic study to members of an ethnic, racial, or tribal group and not to outsiders. Similarly, Mourning Dove's contemporaries, the Yankton Sioux Ella Cara Deloria and the African American Zora Neale Hurston—both of whom studied with Franz Boas-- subversively reworked the "facts" of ethnographic "science" into what Arnold Krupat calls "ethnographic fiction" (see *Ethnocriticism*).

Mourning Dove specifically responds to Therese Broderick's novel, *The Brand, a Tale of the Flathead Reservation* (1909). In *Cogewea*, she turns Broderick into a ridiculous character: she is the white ethnographer who tries to collect "authentic" information about the buffalo roundup but only gets misinformation. Cogewea paraphrases *The Brand* as follows:

> With a frown, she [Cogewea] picked up the book and began perusing it
> again. The story, interesting to the whites, was worm-wood to her Indian
> spleen. However, she determined to see how much of an ape the author
> had made of her breed-hero.
>> By adroit sketching, she had, in a short time the gist of the plot.
>> The scene opened on the Flathead, where a half-blood "brave" is
> in love with a white girl; the heroine of the story. He dares not make a
> declaration of his affection, because of his Indian blood. He curses his
> own mother for this heritage, hates his American parent for the sake of
> the girl of his heart. He deems himself beneath her; not good enough for
> her. But to cap the absurdity of the story, he weds the white "princess"
> and slaves for her the rest of his life. (91)

Mourning Dove's *Cogewea* is a subversive reversal––to use Judith Butler's terms,
a "discursive resignification" and a "subversive repetition"––of Broderick's
melodramatic romance: the mixedblood heroine rejects her white (and deceitful)
suitor, Alfred Densmore, who only seeks her inheritance; instead, she marries
her mixed-descent (and honest) fellow "cowpuncher," Jim LaGrinder, at the end
of the novel. In the last chapter Cogewea finds out that she has inherited a large
sum of money from her estranged white father who went to Alaska in search of
gold, because of a clerical error in the will. Thus, she becomes a woman of
substantial means who can afford to have a room––or ranch––of her own and
pursue her dream of becoming an "authoress." Nonetheless, according to the
narrative conventions of the romance genre, she marries Jim at the end of the
story:

> The curse of the Shoyahpee [white man] seems to go with every thing
> that he touches. We despised *breeds* are in a zone of our own and when
> we break from the corral erected about us, we meet up with trouble. I
> only wish that the fence could not be scaled by the soulless creatures who
> have ever preyed upon us. (283)

According to the narrative, Native Americans and the free-roaming buffaloes
are corralled into reservations and reserves, and Native women must give up
their dreams of independence and hopes for a career in writing and settle for
personal fulfillment in marriage, even though it is a marriage to a fellow "half-
blood." Jim's response to Cogewea's desperate words about Native peoples
being corralled and forced into reservations by whites is a marriage offer––being

corralled together: "S'pose we remain together in that there corral you spoke of as bein' built 'round us by the Shoyahpee? I ain't never had no ropes on no gal but you" (283).

Susan K. Bernardin suggests that Cogewea's situation of being in-between white and Indian worlds, being a "half-breed," mirrors the condition of Native Americans at the beginning of the twentieth century. She says, "Despite the semblance of freedom, the H-B ranch is confined within the Flathead Reservation [in Montana], which is hemmed in by surrounding Anglo settlements. Moreover, as an Okanogan whose land allotment is located in Washington, Cogewea is geographically displaced" (497). Historically, Mourning Dove's novel is a fictional response to the so-called "assimilation period" of the 1880s through 1934 when the U.S. government forced Indians to sell their allotments of reservation land to white settlers. [9]

If we read the novel as a western romance, then its plot culminates with Cogewea's marriage to Jim, with the patriarchal paradigm of compulsory heterosexuality. But, if we extend our examination of the novel's ending from reading it exclusively within the gendered paradigm of a color-blind patriarchy to a more racially as well as culturally sensitive reading, then the union between the two mixedblood characters is an affirmation of Cogewea's choice to stay close to her tribal heritage. By rejecting her white suitor, Alfred Densmore, who physically abuses and financially tries to exploit her, she finally comes to appreciate not only the kindness of kin in Jim but also his assurance that she could maintain her Okanogan heritage in their marriage. Mourning Dove affirms Cogewea's resolution of the dilemma of the "half-breed" by her acceptance and claiming of her "Indianness" as opposed to the culture of her white father.

In another instance, the author resolves the dilemma of cultural—though not of racial—ambiguity, when she juxtaposes the white ethnographer's approach to recording the language and culture of the Flatheads with Cogewea's own intentions to preserve her tribal heritage. After summing up the plot of *The Brand* Cogewea, who nurtures ambitions of becoming an "authoress" (33) herself, delivers a critique of Broderick's novel:

> Cogewea leaned back in her chair with a sigh. "Bosh!" she mused half
> aloud. "Show me the Red 'buck' who would *slave* for the most exclusive

white 'princess' that lives. Such hash may go with the whites, but the Indian, both full bloods and the despised *breeds* know differently. And, that a 'hero' should be depicted as hating his own mother for the flesh and heart that she gave his miserable frame. What a figure to be held up for laudation by either novelist or historian! No *man*, whether First American, Caucasian or of any other race, could be so beastly inhuman in real life; so low and ungratefully base as to want to hide his own mother. The lower animals respond to this instinct, and can people suppose that the Indian, who is of the heroic, has not the manhood accredited to even the most commercialized of nations? The truth is, he has more love of the undying type than his 'superior' brother ever possessed." (91)

Thus, Cogewea's devastating reading of Broderick's novel is reiterated through Mourning Dove's plot, which concludes with Cogewea's choice to marry a fellow mixedblood cowboy. Arnold Krupat reads the romantic union between Cogewea and Jim less as a resolution than as a suspended ambiguity between white and traditional tribal cultures:

Cogewea, as Mrs. James LaGrinder and, like her sister, Mrs. John Carter, will probably preside as the homespun hostess of a great ranch. Unlike her sister, she will probably not allow her assimilated life to be purchased at the cost of a wholesale "blotting out" of her Indian culture. But she most certainly will not follow Stemteemä back to the reservation, to live in a teepee, or, as the condemnatory phrase for Carlisle backsliders had it, return "to the blanket." ("From 'Half-blood' to 'Mixedblood'" 132)

But to read Indian identity within the binaries of either being "assimilated" or "returning to the blanket," as does Krupat, reiterates the very stereotypes of Indian identity that Mourning Dove's narrative critiques so clearly. Here Judith Butler's notion of the "performative" comes in handy, because it leaves space for ambiguous identities that do not re-inscribe the exclusionary binary categories of gender or racial identity. It is possible to take a stand on the side of Indian culture and identity without having to "return to the blanket." Here the discourse of race or blood diverges from the discourse of cultural identification: Cogewea will never become a fullblood Okanogan but she can still culturally identify with her tribal heritage.

Besides reworking the romance plot, Mourning Dove's novel also rewrites the white ethnographer's story from within Native culture itself. Cogewea rejects the option of assimilating into white culture, and she also rejects the mistreatment of Native Americans—in this case of the Okanogans (the Salish) within the Flatheads tribe--by the penmanship of white anthropology. In a memorable scene, in Chapter X titled "Lo! The Poor 'Breed'," Jim LaGrinder recalls the actual event of Broderick conducting field research:

> I was there when the boys was a stuffin' one poor woman. It was at the
> first buffalo roundup when lots of people come to see the sight. A bunch
> of us riders was together when this here lady come up and begins askin'
> questions 'bout the buffaloes; and Injun names of flyin', walkin', and
> swimmin' things and a lot of bunk. Well, you know how the boys are.
> They sure locoed that there gal to a finish; and while she was dashin' the
> information down in her little tablet, we was a thinkin' up more lies to
> tell her. We didn't savey she was writin' a real book, or maybe we would
> a been more careful. Yes, *maybe*! Why, then there writin' folks is dead
> easy pickin' for the cowpunchers. (93-94)

Jim LaGrinder is a trickster figure who teases and dupes the unsuspecting outsider, the white ethnographer Therese Broderick, who indeed published her book in 1909.   Jim and the rest of the cowboys enact the "discursive resignification" of Indian culture and identity through the narrative technique of "subversive of repetition": they make up words and misinformation about Flathead culture according to the white ethnographer's expectations. They tell her what she wants to hear and feed back to her the very misinformation that sounds "authentic," based on her cliched expectations.

Mourning Dove fixes and re-writers Broderick's mistranslation of Okanogan (Salishan) words and customs in her own book, when she comments on an outsider's efforts to give an "authentic" account of tribal life:

> "There you have it! But that is only a glimpse of the real situation; of
> what the tribesmen give would-be writers. You now understand why I
> contend that the whites can not authentically chronicle our habits and
> customs. They can hardly get at the truth. A promulgator of the law of
> requital--good and bad--he [a tribesman] is aware of how he has ever
> been deceived and taken advantage of, and he has no scruples in

> returning, as he thinks, some of the coin. Of course he does not
> understand the true situation; and when the ridiculous 'facts' which he
> narrates are once in print, he has the worst of it. I have heard the Indian
> boast of the absurdities told to the white 'investigator'. It is practically
> impossible for the alien to get at our correct legendary lore." (94)

Mourning Dove's narrator suggests that even though Natives—as well as
mixedbloods who culturally identify with their tribes--have the upper hand in
feeding white ethnographers lies, because of the structure of white hegemony,
the initially "subversive repetition" of their words comes back to haunt them in
the form of Broderick's novel spreading more misinformation about Indians.
The solution then is to give Native Americans control over their stories. In
Mourning Dove's novel Cogewea listens to the stories of her Stemteemä and
writes them down. This is the instance Mourning Dove comes the closest to
identifying with her fictional character: Cogewea plans to get Broderick's story
right, and the author does publish the novel, *Cogewea*. Mourning Dove writes
down her own insider's and supposedly "authentic" version of the story.[10]
Here, of course, by "authentic" I do not mean an absolute in some binary
relation of the "true" and the "false" but that Mourning Dove's perspective
allows her to escape the traps Broderick falls into.

Cogewea--and Mourning Dove--give voice to the Okanogan members
of the Flathead tribe who were merely exotic objects, the icons of the "Vanishing
American," of ethnographic scrutiny in Broderick's text. Mourning Dove turns
the table on the ethnographer and makes Therese Broderick into an object of
Native scrutiny.[11] A contemporary of Mourning Dove, the anthropologist Franz
Boas, developed the "modern" ethnographic methodology of the "participant-
observer." Indirectly, Mourning Dove criticizes that methodology usually
deployed by white ethnographers. A similar sentiment can be observed in the
works of Zora Neale Hurston, who was one of Boas's students at Barnard
College. In her "Introduction" to *Mules and Men* (1935), Hurston comments on
her experiences of going back to Eatonville, Florida as one of Boas's
ethnographers:

> Folklore is not as easy to collect as it sounds. The best source is where
> there are the least outside influences and these people, being usually
> under-privileged, are the shyest. They are most reluctant at times to
> reveal that which the soul lives by. And the Negro in spite of his open-

faced laughter, his seeming acquiescence, is particularly evasive. You see
we are a polite people and we do not say to our questioner, "Get out of
here!" We smile and tell him or her something that satisfies the white
person because, knowing so little about us, he doesn't know what he is
missing. The Indian resists curiosity by a stony silence. The Negro offers
a feather-bed resistance. That is, we let the probe enter, but it never
comes out. It gets smothered under a lot of laugher and pleasantries.

The theory behind our tactics: "The white man is always trying
to know into somebody else's business. All right, I'll set something
outside the door of my mind for him to play with and handle. He can
read my writing but he sho' can't read my mind. I'll put this play toy in
his hand, and he will seize it and go away. Then I'll say my say and sing
my song." (2-3)

Because the role of "participant" cannot be easily separated from the role of the
"observer," Hurston subverts the scientific methodology of ethnography and
creates a new hybrid, rather literary, genre, that of "ethnographic fiction." [12]
Thus, through the narrative techniques of "discursive resignification" and
"subversive repetition," ethnic writers appropriate and then transpose the
discourse of ethnography from the realm of science into the world of fiction, and
they also delegate the role of the cultural informant to members of the observed
group.

Nostalgia for traditional or vanished cultures is one of the founding
pillars of ethnography. Such cultures are always deferred to the safe distance of
a mythic past preserved in oral culture that allows them to take on such
unquestioned attributes as those of the "authentic," the "primitive," and/or of
the "communal." James Clifford suggests that "salvage" ethnography has
historically worked under the assumptions that "the other is lost, in dissipating
time and space, but saved in the text" ("On Ethnographic Allegory" 112).
Therefore, the recording and cataloging of "vanishing" cultures are not only
justified but necessary. He states, "Ethnography's disappearing object is, then,
in significant degree, a rhetorical construct legitimating a representational
practice: 'salvage' ethnography in its widest sense" (112). Thus, Clifford
questions

> [T]he assumption that with rapid change something essential ("culture"),
> a coherent differential identity, vanishes. And I [Clifford] question too,

the mode of scientific and moral authority associated with salvage, or redemptive, ethnography. It is assumed that the other society is weak and "needs" to be represented by an outsider (and that what matters in its life is the past, not present or future). The recorder and interpreter of fragile custom is custodian of an essence, unimpeachable witness to an authenticity. (Moreover, since the "true" culture has always vanished, the salvaged version cannot be easily refuted.) (113)

The ethnographic process of "inscription"--as opposed to the more desirable processes of "transcription" or "dialogue"--creates an allegorical ethnographic structure, which is marked by the essentialist language of binary oppositions, such as civilized versus primitive, or written versus oral (113). In Clifford's definition of ethnographic allegory, "culture [is] described from a specific temporal distance with a presumption of [its] transience" (114). That is, ethnographic allegory is the result of "historical worlds salvaged as textual fabrications disconnected from ongoing lived milieux and suitable for moral, allegorical appropriation by individual readers" (114). Clifford concludes, "the cultures studied by anthropologists are always already writing themselves" (118). Since the transcribing of culture is a collaborative effort between informants and researchers, the writing of culture is always a process of "re-writing," because the field of ethnography is "already filled with texts"--what Clifford calls the "intertextual predicament" of culture (116-17).

Besides the epistemological explanation of culture as always already intertextual, elsewhere Clifford describes culture at the juxtapositions of actual physical encounters, of "traveling cultures":

My own attempt to multiply the hands and discourses involved in "writing culture" is not to assert a naïve democracy of plural authorship, but to loosen at least somewhat the monological control of the executive writer/anthropologist and to open for discussion ethnography's hierarchy and negotiation of discourses in power-changed, unequal situations. ("Traveling Cultures" 100)

Clifford views the genre of the ethnographic narrative as an historical construct and as a product of hegemonic discourses. No culture is in permanent stasis or isolation, rather, cultures, especially under the conditions of modernization, colonization, and globalization, are constantly in the process of transformation.

For that reason Clifford associates culture with travel--with "ways of looking at culture (along with tradition and identity) in terms of travel relations" (101). Clifford emphasizes the hybrid qualities and global influences in each of these categories--in culture, in tradition, and in cultural identity. He suggest that we rethink culture in terms of travel, allowing for the possibility that "[c]onstructed and disputed *historicities*, sites of displacement, interference, and interaction, come more sharply into view" (101). Thus, Clifford rejects the neocolonial assumption that a culture can be transcribed by outsiders: "If the ethnographer reads culture over the native's shoulder, the native also reads over the ethnographer's shoulder as he or she writes each cultural description" ("On Ethnographic Allegory" 119). Ethnographic narratives exist in a palimpsest of competing interpretations and within the discursive web of the Foucauldian "power/knowledge" paradigm.

Mourning Dove's critique of Broderick's book, contained and challenged by Cogewea's ambition to become an "authoress," is an affective example of Okanogan culture writing itself while being observed. In Mourning Dove's representation Cogewea's character reconciles two cultural identities by being both white and Indian. The heroine must also contend with two opposing purposes: she is one of the "cowpunchers" on the "H-B" ranch who ultimately marries a fellow cowboy at the end of the story but who is also a well-educated and literary woman of means, through inheritance, who wants to write, transcribe and dialogue with her own culture. Cogewea's two sisters, Mary and Julia, represent--in terms of cultural identification--two possibilities for women of mixed descent. Mary marries a white man, while Julia, who is the more "traditional" of the sisters, lives with their grandmother, the Stemteemä:

> This younger sister [Mary], like Julia, had imbibed more of the primitive Indian
> nature, absorbed from the centuries-old legends as told them by the Stemteemä.
> Recognizing the new order of things, Cogewea realized that these threads in the
> woof of her people's philosophy, must be irretrievably lost unless speedily placed on
> record. . . . "I [Cogewea] was contemplating the possibilities of becoming an
> authoress, of writing a book. I have the theme all right and there is plenty of
> material yet available." (33).

Although Cogewea's speech fluctuates between the literary and the colloquial, between the speech of an inspiring "authoress" and the speech of a "cowpuncher," her worldview ties her to the Stemteemä consistently throughout the novel.

As a challenge to Broderick's ethnographic account, Mourning Dove transcribes traditional Okanogan stories, such as "The Story of Green-Blanket Feet," Chapter XIX, in her novel. The story of Green-Blanket feet was originally told to Cogewea by her grandmother and the narrative functions as a counter-discourse to the outsider's rendition of the "tragic mulatto" theme, the cliched and allegorized story of miscegenation. Thus, the text simultaneously performs "culture writing itself" and the critique of white outsider ethnographic practices that merely inscribe and exoticize cultures. Mourning Dove puts the two practices into a dialogue—thereby the Okanogan culture maintains agency and control over its transcription, instead of passively yielding itself to salvage. Cogewea's character—that is both white and Native, both an educated "authoress" and a cowgirl—poses a challenge to Broderick's position as a cultural outsider. Cogewea takes over the role of the ethnographer, but instead of freezing her culture in the fragile icon of ethnographic allegory, she depicts the parallel processes of recovery and change, of authenticity and cultural encounter with others. Cogewea re-writes the traditional stories of the Okanogans, but she also infuses them with other stories of cultural change and travel/encounter. Mourning Dove does not merely salvage her culture from a mythical past but "transcribes" her tribal customs and traditions as being alive and in transition. Thereby she evades the trappings of ethnographic allegory and authentic identity. In her transcription Okanogan culture becomes a story, a dialogic narrative discourse, which is influenced by encounters with other tribes, such as the Flathead (Kootenai), and with whites. Okanogan culture is both traditional and modern, both authentic and in transition. By incorporating both fullblood and mixedblood characters, traditional narratives and outsider accounts, and past and present events, the novel depicts a culture that is very much alive: it is a rich text of past traditions and present and future changes.

Mourning Dove discursively resignifies the early twentieth-century ethnographic trope of the "Vanishing American" through the narrative technique of subversive repetition. The "Ladies" and the "Squaw" races of the Independence Day celebrations demonstrate her subversive narrative gesture early on in the novel:

> "I'm going over to the Kootenais and rent a buckskin dress. I have no native costume and this garb would be a dead give away; for they may kick on me riding this race."

> Then mounting, Cogewea cantered to the Kootenai camp, where
> she had but little difficulty in securing a complete tribal dress. Very soon
> she came from the tepee in full regalia, her face artistically decorated
> with varied paints. The Indian children saw and giggled among
> themselves. Remounting, she doubled the bright shawl over her knees,
> lapping it securely. When she rode back to the track, the "H-B" boys
> recognized her only by the horse. (64-65)

Cogewea wins both the "Ladies" and "Squaw" races. She is an intruder in both:
as a mixedblood character she challenges both the Kootenai (or Flathead)
"Squaw" races—she is an Okanogan on Flathead territory––and the white
"Ladies" races. By focusing on the in-between status of cultural hybridity or
racial ambiguity, Mourning Dove poses a double challenge: she challenges the
authenticity of a culture and the fixity of racial or ethnic identity. She critiques
the Kootenai for claiming superiority over a mixed-decent Okanogan and the
white community for racial discrimination. Indirectly, Mourning Dove also
critiques the outsider and hegemonic stance of white ethnography, which claims
entitlement to recording "primitive" cultures. Cogewea's character subverts the
hierarchies and taxonomies of white ethnography, which deems one culture, the
Flatheads or Kootenai, more "authentic" than another represented by an
educated and literate mixedblood Okanogan.

Mourning Dove writes against a long line of nostalgic textual renditions
of Native Americans. In such context, her choice of mixedblood characters, for
herself[13] and for her heroine, is a modern critique of the white ethnographers'
construct of the authentic "aborigine": in her interpretation Native American
identity is a performative and dynamic, as opposed to fixed or "salvaged,"
entity. Indians have been written up, painted, and photographed so much that
there is only the "aura" of a "collective perception" left, which we have all
"agreed to be part of," to use Don DeLillo's proto-postmodern words (12). With
the thick layers of already-there textual and visual images of Native Americans,
the "ab/original" becomes invisible, leaving only commodified images behind
for collective consumption. In the "Fourth of July" horse races (Chapters VI-VII)
Cogewea subverts the rigid terms of race relations. By donning an appropriate
costume for each race, she participates in both the "Ladies" and the "Squaw"
races, winning both but upsetting both whites and the Kootenais (Flatheads) in
the process. In the end, she is denied both prizes. Cogewea's character upsets
the carefully guarded boundaries of racial and cultural belonging:

> A riding habit of blue corduroy fitted her slender form admirably. Red,
> white and blue ribbons fastened her hair, which streaming to the racer's
> back, lent a picturesque wilderness to her figure. Securing the stirrups,
> she requested Jim to tighten her spur-straps, as they seemed a trifle loose,
> adding:
>> "We just must win this race from the whites. See!" (62) . . .
>> "Why is this *squaw* permitted to ride? This is a *ladies* race!" (63)

During the "Squaw" race her reception by the fullblood Kootenais is not much
more favorable:

> One of the Kootenai girls turned to her and spoke sharply in
> good English:
>> "You have no right to be here! You are half-white! This race is
> for Indians and not for *breeds*!" (66)

However, in the end, Cogewea triumphs over both: the white villain Alfred
Densmore and the fullblood members of the Flathead reservation who rejected
her during the "Squaw" race.   Indirectly, she also triumphs over the white
ethnographer's attempt to record a "vanishing" culture, since Cogewea's story
overwhelms and ruthlessly deconstructs Broderick's ethnographic narrative.
Mourning Dove also celebrates hybridity over white cultural domination or
fullblood cultural or racial resentment. Thus the novel avoids the nostalgic
tones of the ideology of the "Vanishing American," and it also evades the traps
of trying to fix Native American culture in the past and through the
essentializing binaries of both fullblood Natives or white ethnographers.

Mourning Dove transcribes the narrative conventions of homogeneous
racial and cultural nostalgia and the monologic language of the patriarchal
structuring structure of mandatory marriage through a modern and melancholic
rendition of displaced lives and missed opportunities. Mourning Dove's novel
thus discursively resignifies the essentializing tendencies of pseudo-scientific
racialized discourses through the narrative technique of subversive
repetitions—achieving a narrative that celebrates hybridity and racial
ambiguity, even though it commits itself culturally.   As Judith Butler
destabilizes the discourse of gender or race through the more fluid category of
perfomativity, or as James Clifford critiques the fixing of a culture in the past

through "salvage" ethnography and ethnographic allegory, in *Cogewea* Mourning Dove also suggests that--through the hybrid genre of ethnographic fiction--we rethink our monologic notions of racial identity and cultural authenticity.

Rita Keresztesi Treat

NOTES

I would like to thank the editors of this volume, Neil Brooks and Teresa Hubel, as well as my colleagues, Ronald Schleifer and Catherine John, for their thoughtful comments on earlier versions of this essay.

[1] I use the term "ethnic modernism" strategically in order to incorporate multicultural texts in the canon of American "high modernism." I appropriate Werner Sollors' term "ethnic modernism," which best describes the twofold direction of my future larger project. Ethnic modernism implies the converging of two literary traditions usually considered separate: the peripheral field of ethnic and minority literatures and the literary production of high modernist writers. Ethnic modernism signals congruencies between the modernist project and ethnic writings in the first half of the twentieth century. Sollors suggests that "if ethnicity and modernity go well together, there are also important modernist writers who challenge all the clichés of ethnic discourse, if not ethnicity itself" (255). However, the challenge moves in both directions. By turning the "camera eye" from its object to its holder (a gesture taken literally in Mourning Dove's novel), from high modernism to its peripheral other, ethnic discourse also challenges the clichés of modernism.

[2] Judith Butler uses these two terms to define how "gender trouble," the "performativity" of gender, disrupts hegemonic structures within the heterosexual matrix. Her example for discursive disruption is the performativity of gender in drag. See *Gender Trouble*.

[3] For an overview of Judith Butler's works concerning performativity as a politically subversive category, see Disch.

[4] Historically Mourning Dove's novel depicts the era and consequences of the General Allotment or Dawes Act of 1887. As Louis Owens explains,

> The second historical catastrophe [the first one was the Indian removal Act of 1830] for the American Indian came with the General Allotment Act (Dawes Act) of 1887, an act designed to end traditional ways of life for Indian tribes by breaking communal tribal land into individual allotments of 160 acres for each family head, 80 acres to single persons over eighteen and orphans under that age, and 40 acres to each tribal member under eighteen. Indians who accepted allotment or agreed to

adopt "the habits of civilized life" were granted citizenship, something most native
Americans would not enjoy until 1924. A key provision of the Dawes Act allowed
the federal government to purchase 'surplus' Indian lands––what was left over after
all eligible individuals received their allotted shares. The major effect of allotment
was to take land away from Indians so effectively that in the forty-five years
following the Dawes Act's passage 90 million acres passed from Indian ownership.
(*Other Destinies* 30)

[5] In *Our America*, Walter Benn Michaels examines how the notion of American identity
changed from its racialized meaning in the Progressive era between the world wars to a
culturally determined term during the literary period of "nativist modernism." He suggests
that in the 1920s American modernists were preoccupied with redefining American identity in
response to a reshuffling of the racial and cultural make-up of the nation. White Anglo-
American hostility to strangers was brought to the surface by the simultaneous events of
northward African American migration from the South and the Caribbean, legal restrictions
on immigration put into law in 1924, and the decision to turn Native Americans into "legal"
citizens in the same year. See also an earlier version of his argument in the founding issue of
Modernism/Modernity (1993).

[6] The first known novel written by a Native American woman is S. Alice Callahan's *Wynema*
(1891). See Ruoff and Ward, Jr., eds.

[7] For a discussion on Mourning Dove's interpretation of Broderick's text, see Beidler, Viehman.

[8] Arnold Krupat "expands upon" Owens's reading of *Cogewea*, and he also gives an overview
of the history of the present-day proliferation of critical discussions on mixedblood identity in
his article, "From 'Half-blood' to 'Mixedblood'."

[9] During the assimilation period mission schools and boarding schools operated by the Bureau
of Indian Affairs violently propagated white values and culture to "eradicate Native tribal
identities" (see Brown 274). Native Americans did not gain American citizenship until 1924,
which was a direct response to Indians' growing enlistment in the military. The Indian
Reorganization Act of 1934, also called the Indian New Deal, meant to reverse the Dawes
Severalty Act of 1887 by promoting more extensive self-government through tribal councils
and constitutions. With the appointment of John Collier to direct the Bureau of Indian Affairs
in 1934, more humane federal Indian policies were enacted. Another Native American author,
D'Arcy McNickle, also responds to the assimilation period in his novel, *The Surrounded* (1936).
But, for the protagonist, Archilde Leon, the corralling of the buffalo and the enclosing of
Indian communities within reservations is already an event of the past:

> Actually, in the way he was learning the world, neither Modeste nor his mother was
> important. They were not real people. Buffaloes were not real to him either, yet he
> could go and look at the buffaloes every day if he wished, behind the wire enclosure
> of the Biological Survey reserve. He knew that buffaloes had been real things to his
> mother, and to the old people who had come to eat with her tonight. To him they
> were just fenced up animals that couldn't be shot, though you could take
> photographs of them. (62)

In McNickle's narrative economy the commodification of the buffalo has turned a way of life
into a photo opportunity.

[10] *Cogewea* is the result of collaboration between Mourning Dove and her white male mentor-

editor. Because of her limited knowledge of English and her desire to have her manuscript published, Mourning Dove welcomed the assistance of Lucullus Virgil McWhorter, whom she met in 1914 at a Walla Walla, Washington Frontier Days celebration. McWhorter was an amateur ethnographer with a commitment to Indian affairs. The collaboration between Mourning Dove and McWhorter resulted in a book that bears the weight of his anthropological intervention in Mourning Dove's romantic story. When she received the final product from the publisher, she wrote to McWhorter: "I have just got through going over the book *Cogewea*, and am surprised at the changes that you made. I think they are fine, and you made a tasty dressing like a cook would do with a fine meal. I sure was interested in the book, and hubby read it over and also all the rest of the family neglected their housework till they read it cover to cover. I felt like it was some one elses [sic] book and not mine at all. In fact the finishing touches are put there by you, and I have never seen it" (Fisher xv). The story of the novel's editorial revision and of its publication, and the collaboration between Mourning Dove and her white editor, Lucullus Virgil McWhorter, have been already well documented.

11 In his article, "From 'Half-blood' to 'Mixedblood'," Arnold Krupat critiques Cogewea's erroneous reading of Broderick's *The Brand* in Mourning Dove's novel (see 133-34).

12 For a more detailed discussion on the convergence between ethnography and literature in general, see Arnold Krupat's *Ethnocriticism*.

13 In her autobiography, the Okanogan (or Salishan) Mourning Dove imagines herself as a mixedblood. In the posthumously published *Mourning Dove: A Salishan Autobiography* she describes herself as of two worlds:

> Father's mother was a Nicola Indian, with a strain of Okanagan [Canadian side of Okanogans] in her family. His father was a white man, a Scot named Andrew, who at one time was in the employ of the Hudson Bay Company. (4) . . .
>
> My mother, Lucy Stui-kin (Sna'itckstw), was born a fullblood. She was born about 1868 at Kettle Falls, which we call Swah-netk-qhu, meaning Big Falls or Big Water, also our name for the Columbia River. (6)

In his introduction to Mourning Dove's autobiography Jay Miller points out that since Mourning Dove's father was an orphan she could invent a Scottish white grandfather, even though "his other children and the census records deny this" (xvi). In her supposedly "factual" autobiography Mourning Dove reinvents herself as a "half-blood" character, much like Cogewea, her heroine in the novel with the same title.

WORKS CITED

Beidler, Peter G. "Literary Criticism in *Cogewea*: Mourning Dove's Protagonist Reads *The Brand*." *American Indian Culture and Research Journal*, Los Angeles, v. 19, no. 2 (1995): 45-65.

Bernardin, Susan K.. "Mixed Messages: Authority and Authorship in Mourning Dove's *Cogewea, The Half-Blood: The Depiction of the Great Montana Cattle Range* ." *American Literature* 67 (1995): 487-509.

Bloom, Harold, ed. *Native American Writers*. Philadelphia: Chelsea, 1998.

Broderick, Therese (Tin Schreiner). *The Brand, a Tale of the Flathead Reservation* . Seattle: The Alice Harriman Company, 1909.

Brown, Alanna Kathleen. "Looking though the Glass Darkly: The Editorialized Mourning Dove." Arnold Krupat, ed., *New Voices in Native American Literary Criticism* .

Butler, Judith. *Bodies that Matter: On the Discursive Limits of "Sex."* New York: Routledge, 1993.

_____. *Gender Trouble: Feminism and the Subversion of Identity* . New York: Routledge, 1990.

Clifford, James. "On Ethnographic Allegory." James Clifford and George E. Marcus, eds., *Writing Culture: The Poetics and Politics of Ethnography* .

_____. "Traveling Cultures." Lawrence Grossberg, et al. eds. *Cultural Studies*. New York: Routledge, 1992.

_____ and George E. Marcus, eds., *Writing Culture: The Poetics and Politics of Ethnography* . Berkeley: University of California Press, 1986.

DeLillo, Don. *White Noise*. New York: Penguin Books, 1985.

Disch, Lisa. "Judith Butler and the Politics of the Performative." *Political Theory* 27:4 (August 1999): 545-559.

Fisher, Dexter. "Introduction." Mourning Dove, *Cogewea, The Half-Blood*.

Hurston, Zora Neale. *Mules and Men*. New York: HarperCollins, 1990.

Krupat, Arnold. *Ethnocriticism: Ethnography, History, Literature* . Berkeley: University of California Press, 1992.

_____. "From 'Half-blood' to 'Mixedblood': *Cogewea* and the Discourse of Indian Blood." *Modern Fiction Studies* 45.1 (1999): 120-145.

_____, ed., *New Voices in Native American Literary Criticism* . Washington: Smithsonian, 1993.

McNickle, D'Arcy. *The Surrounded*. Albuquerque: University of New Mexico Press, [1936] 1964.

Michaels, Walter Benn. "American Modernism and the Poetics of Identity." *Modernism/Modernity* 1.1 (1993): 38-56.

_____. *Our America: Nativism, Modernism, and Pluralism* . Durham: Duke University Press, 1995.

Miller, Jay. "Introduction." Mourning Dove. *Mourning Dove: A Salishan Autobiography* .

Mourning Dove. *Cogewea, The Half-Blood: A Depiction of the Great Montana Cattle Range* . Lincoln: University of Nebraska Press, [1927] 1981.

_____. *Mourning Dove: A Salishan Autobiography* . Ed. Jay Miller. Lincoln: University of Nebraska Press, 1990.

Osborne, Peter and Lynne Segal, "Gender as Performance: An Interview with Judith Butler," London, October 1993, *Radical Philosophy* 67 (Summer 1994): 32-39.

Owens, Louis. *Mixedblood Messages: Literature, Film, Family, Place* . Norman: University of Oklahoma Press, 1998.

_____. *Other Destinies: Understanding the American Indian Novel* . Norman: University of Oklahoma Press, 1992.

Ruoff, A. LaVonne Brown and Jerry W. Ward, Jr., eds., *Redefining American Literary History* . New York: Modern Language Association, 1990.

Sollors, Werner. *Beyond Ethnicity: Consent and Descent in American Culture* . New York: Oxford University Press, 1986.

Viehman, Martha L. "'My People . . . My Kind': Mourning Dove's *Cogewea, The Half-Blood* as a Narrative of Mixed Descent." Harold Bloom, ed. *Native American Writers* .

10.

VISIBLE DIFFERENCES: VIEWING
RACIAL IDENTITY IN TONI MORRISON'S *PARADISE*
AND "RECITATIF"

> Deep within the word 'American' is its association with race. To identify
> someone as South African is to say very little; we need the adjective
> 'white' or 'black' or 'colored' to make our meaning clear. In this country
> it is quite the reverse. American means white, and Africanist people
> struggle to make the term applicable to themselves with ethnicity and
> hyphen after hyphen after hyphen. (Morrison, *Playing in the Dark* 47)

This passage, from Toni Morrison's *Playing in the Dark: Whiteness and the Literary Imagination*, provides a succinct account of the nature of racial identity in America[1]. The construction of racial identity is a matter of national and linguistic difference, of historical and geographic difference, as well as racial difference. Similarly, racial difference is not a single difference, but contested between several possible racial positions and alternative economies of identity. In addition, this contestation does not take place within a unified system of difference; some people struggle more than others.

This extract of Morrison's work allows me to situate this paper with some specificity. In its linguistic emphasis, it reminds me that the question of "literature and racial ambiguity" places the question of racial identity in a particular frame: while the textuality of racial identity remains a crucial issue in all accounts of racial identity, this paper aims toward a detailed examination of racial identity as represented in two literary texts, and by extension, in the specific textuality of literary works. By this, I mean that the literary is not to be taken simply as a "document" or historical source, but as a text constructed in particular ways around particular questions. In Morrison's texts, the questions of racial identity deliberately place the reader in a position of doubt rather than mastery, a position which forces self-consciousness into the reading process. This, in turn, acts to de-naturalise questions of identity formation beyond the text. Morrison's use of the contrasting national situations of the USA and South Africa also leads me to state my own position; while attempting to gesture to questions of racial identity "in general," this paper focuses on authors and theorists of the United States, taking into account the embedded "whiteness" of American identity, noted by Morrison, which spills over into legal, economic and class difference.

Initially I will provide a brief overview of the theoretical questions brought into play by the production of racial identity and the possibility of racial ambiguity. Then I will go on to discuss the treatment of racially ambiguous characters in two works by Toni Morrison, the short story "Recitatif", first published in 1983, and the novel *Paradise*, published in 1997. These texts, and the critical readings of these texts, display the limits of thinking racial identity as an essential or inessential identity.

Morrison's reading of race begins with the problems of naming race, the ambiguities and silences in national and racial discourse where language struggles to fully name identity. This is also the point at which I wish to start, by beginning with the notion of race as an identity that is represented rather than naturally embodied, to investigate the strategies by which "race" is at once constructed and rendered ambiguous in racial discourse and the implications of a racially ambiguous identity for our notions of "race" as a useful term for discussion.

The idea of "race" as the representation of racial identity attempts to dislocate the meaning of race from the racialised body as a source of racial "truth" and moves towards the inscription of race as a position in language. To quote Richard Dyer, "since race in itself – insofar as it is anything in itself – refers to some intrinsically insignificant geographical/physical differences between people, it is the imagery of race that is in play" (539). Emphasis is removed from the recording of physical and experiential difference and transferred to the formation of racial meaning through language. Race, in this formulation, no longer has meaning in "in itself". However, this move away from essentialism cannot be read as necessarily as step towards anti-essentialism; anti-essentialism, the step beyond the limit of identity as such, cannot be assumed to be the result of attempts to read racial essentialism critically[2]. While the focus of meaning may move from the physicality of the body, the imagery of the body, the now racialised rather than racial body, remains in play. While we may no longer argue the biological determinism of race, we must continue to uncover the work of meaning construction carried out by racial imagery[3]. "Ambiguity" is a strategically important term in this discussion; ambiguity does not sit in a direct opposition to essentialism but disrupts the subject/object relation of the gaze that identifies "race" by positing a racial identity which may or may not exist, but which cannot be read.

One problem of essentialism, or essentialising language in the formation of identity can be found beyond the persistence of the imagery of race, through the presence of racial discourses in society that are not themselves constructed in simple oppositional terms of the essential or inessential nature of racial identity. Racial discourse, or a "body of knowledge" on race can be seen in a range of social discourses including literature, sociology, history, and politics, and if America remains a racialised society, as I think we must admit that it does, then the discourse of race remains a "social fact" (Winant 183). To be without a racial identity, in this society, is to be without an identity at all[4]. The representation of race in these discourses, even when recognised as representation, continues to construct a "truth" of race, even if this truth is now situated in a multitude of overlapping, heterogeneous positions in language. "The truth of race is not apparent, natural racial identities that form the foundation of social order; rather, it is the possibility that any apparent truth is not true, that because race is a nothing, it can never in fact be what it appears to be" (Kawash 164). Crucially, we cannot overestimate the impact of theoretical interventions into these discourses of race, and we must bear in mind that no "ledger" publically records the deconstruction of binary oppositions (Elam 21). Further, racial discourse has never been a singular, unified and coherent subject; although potentially organised in terms of political strategy and towards the end of maintaining a racial hierarchy, it is the constitutive ambiguity of racial discourse that has provided its operational usefulness to contestants in inter-racial conflict[5]. This is the situation recognized in Anthony Appiah's claim that the "label" of race "works despite the absence of an essence" (82). Indeed, to suggest that the edifice of racial discourse could be displaced by the revelation that "race" may not be "true" may place too much faith in the idea that racial discourse was founded on the truth of race in the first place.

    While the opposition between essentialist and anti-essentialist identities may not function straightforwardly in racial discourses, attempts to place, or displace race through alternative discursive strategies also prove to be problematic. Several Black American critics have noted with disquiet attempts to negate what is seen an essentialist racial rhetoric by the effacement of the term "race" or "racial", and its replacement with alternative terms such as culture (particularly multiculturalism) and ethnicity[6]. Werner Sollors's *Beyond Ethnicity* acts as a useful example. Sollors's stated aim is to reread American literary history, to rewrite an American canon which represents the diversity of American history and society. In this new literary history, race is but one difference among many: "I think it is most useful not to be confused by the heavily charged term 'race' and to keep looking at race as one aspect of ethnicity" (39). In Sollors's America, everyone is "ethnic" and takes part in the "voluntary ethnicity" (33) that makes up the distinguishing experience of American society, where identity is not national and inherited, but formed through a system of "consent and descent." Although Sollors acknowledges that not every ethnic position is open to all, the emphasis this places on freedom to construct identities that disrupt a single line of descent necessarily displaces the specific history of race, which would radically disrupt this notion of freedom by bringing into question American identities founded neither in descent or consent but on forceful extraction from other nations.

    This reading of "ethnicity" explicitly removes its attention from racial identity seen through the history of racial identification, to an attempt to locate identity through cultural difference and to produce culture as a locatable source of difference. Hence, though this culturalism may provide detailed and nuanced accounts of cultural inheritances, there is a danger that "culture" may simply replace "race" as a source of prescriptive and restrictive identity codes under which personal experience and action must be reconstructed in ways which conform with and confirm cultural images, or more negatively, stereotypes[7]. Multiculturalism, in turn, may be criticised as subsuming the specific difference of racial identity within a generalised difference, which celebrates diversity as a position beyond identity. "The narrative of the beyond – beyond identity, beyond race, beyond racism – is in many ways a revision of the Enlightenment narrative of the universal subject which gradually sheds all particularity and contingency to emerge into the light of its true being, with the signal difference that this has now been recast as essentially hybrid rather than essentially singular" (Kawash 20).

In each of these cases, the problem of reading the representation of race returns to us as the problem of reinscribing relations of power, where the inscription of power reminds us of the ever-present gaze of the reader. Franz Fanon's celebrated essay "The Fact of Blackness" provides a brief and illuminating example. The opening of the essay replays this argument dramatically: " 'Dirty Nigger!' Or simply, 'Look, a Negro!'" (Fanon 109). Fanon's identity is inscribed by the gaze and voice of the white colonist, and this inscription precedes his own words, his own self description. One of the key issues in "The Fact of Blackness" is the inequality of power revealed by this episode. Fanon's reaction is violent: "I was indignant; I demanded and explanation. Nothing happened. I burst apart" (109); yet this violence, this breaking and restructuring, take place on only one side of the object/subject relationship; there is no reciprocal violence felt on the side of the white observer. Fanon reads this relationship as the imposition of perpetual object status on those positioned as black within white discourse: "For not only must the black man be black; he must be black in relation to the white man. Some critics will take it on themselves to remind us that this proposition has a converse. I say this is false. The black man has no ontological resistance in the eyes of the white man" (110). This not only suggests the reification of blackness in white discourse, but a lack of access to black subjecthood through this system of representation felt by Fanon, a lack of subjecthood which cannot be reintroduced through the erasure of race in a system where identity is fundamentally racialised.

This reading of representation by Fanon has led others to question the possibility of representing black subjecthood through mimetic language (Fuss 24). However, this reading of racial discourse, which suggests the impossibility of black subjecthood in language, where language creates "black" as the "Other of the same" (Whitford 24) of "white" identity, must be acknowledged as a reading of racial discourse within a particular rather than universalised system of representation. Discourse operates upon context (the ways in which context can be recognised/expressed) but also operates within contexts, and much Black American critical work can be read as attempting to resist or overturn the (white) majority contexts in which racial discourse operates. An example of this can be seen if we return to Morrison's *Playing in the Dark*. Here, Morrison resituates classic United States literary texts to reveal the racial discourse that has operated within them, highlighting the strategic part that race has played in the construction of "white" (read "non-raced") literature. This reveals the construction of race within these texts, "the denotative and connotative blackness that African peoples have come to signify, as well as the entire range of views, assumptions, readings and misreadings that accompany Eurocentric learning about these people" (6-7). Morrison's move to relocate race in white discourse reveals the construction and confirmation of knowledges about Africanist peoples through literature and the possibility of the racialisation of whiteness through the reinscription of a speaking black presence. "Naming 'whiteness' displaces it from the unmarked, unnamed status that is itself an effect of its dominance. Among the effects on white people both of race privilege and of the dominance of whiteness are their seeming normativity, their structural invisibility" (Frankenberg 451). To reconstitute and revisualise this structural invisibility, white identity must be written as a racial identity rather than the norm from which other identities differ, not in an effort to find a racial essence in white identity, but to recognise racial identity as a process of differentiation.

Morrison explores this process in the short story "Recitatif," which focuses on a series of meetings between two female characters, one black, one white, at several stages in their life, moving from a shared childhood in a state institution to conflict and reconciliation as adults. The racial difference of the characters is made clear from the beginning when the narrator, Twyla, describes her new roommate Roberta as "a girl from a whole other race" (210), and later looks back on their relationship as "A black girl and a white girl" (218). However, the actual identity of each, as black or white, remains concealed through the text's refusal to make explicit the skin colour of either character. By this textual omission, Morrison is able to comment effectively on the overdetermind operation of race in forming identity in the presence of racial difference.

Race, and the difference of race, marks the relationship between the characters in crucial ways; conflict between them arises from apparently racial issues, the integration of segregated schools, cultural separatism and their shared relationship to an indeterminately raced figure in their past. By removing the reassuring markers of black and white physicalities through which racial identity would normally be settled, Morrison reveals the extent to which differences potentially read as racial may also be read through other discourses of difference, particularly class. Through this, the explanatory power of "race" as an identity is questioned. In adulthood, Twyla lives an apparently working-class existence, her husband is a fireman and the couple live in a neighbourhood alongside his extended family. Roberta, meanwhile, displays the trappings of wealth and success with a chauffeur driven car, expensive clothes and expensive tastes. When the two meet, Twyla's reaction reads, "Everything is so easy for them. They think they own the world" (217). This statement reduces Roberta to a social identity, as one of them, figured as those with privileges, yet we cannot securely separate the possibility of racial privileges from class privilege in Twyla's reading of Roberta's status (Abel 103).

Reading racial identity is not only complicated by the presence of class difference, but racial identity is also clearly marked as differential, where the attribution of meaning to "black" or "white" rests on the discovery of differences between characters potentially identified as "black" or "white," differences which can then be assigned a racial significance, to suggest that one character is "more" black, "more" white than an other. The lack of a confirming structure of skin colour difference forces us to recognise that these apparently potentially racial characteristics are such only in their inclusion in racial stereotyping.

The interdependence of identity is dramatically reconstructed in the episode on the conflict over the integration of schools attended by the characters' children, where Twyla and Roberta find themselves on opposing picket lines. In official discourse the terms of the conflict have already been set. The protest over the school has already been predetermined as racial conflict, both for Twlya and the reader, and the section opens with the lines: "Strife came to us that fall. At least that's what the paper called it. Strife. Racial strife" (220). Twyla reimagines "racial strife" as a predatory creature with a life of its own. "Racial strife. The word made me think of a bird – a big shrieking bird out of 1,000,000,000 B.C. Flapping its wings and cawing. Its eye with no lid always bearing down on you. All day it screeched and at night it slept on the rooftops. It woke you in the morning, and from the Today show to the eleven o'clock news it kept you an awful company" (220). Here, the discourse of race deployed by the media is de-naturalised through an alternative, equally unreal construction. This undermines the definitive terms set down by the media, a definition which is further undermined by the uncertain racial positions of Roberta and Twyla. Roberta apparently protests against the desegregation of the school, an action which in normative terms would mark her as white. However, we must also consider the possibility that her protest is based on class, rather than race, and is against the mixing of a middle class school with a working class school, rather than a white school with a black school (Abel 106). Through her racial ambiguity, Roberta occupies a position beyond the deterministic alternatives offered by the media.

Twyla initially has little interest in the debate, and only becomes motivated to take part after a confrontation with Roberta, where Roberta constructs their personal conflict in terms of racial difference, accusing Twyla of attacking an old black lady when she was a child, an act which marks her not as violent as such, but as a bigot, a perpetrator of a specifically racial violence (222). Twyla's reaction to this, and to the protest as a whole, is to turn from the abstractions of racial or class difference to a personal protest that must also be a personal dialogue. Roberta is initially seen carrying a placard that reads "MOTHERS HAVE RIGHTS TOO!" (220), a sign which contrasts the political demands of the civil rights movement for integration with the personal and individual rights of mothers to send their children to the school of their choice. When Twyla joins the picket line she brings a series of her own signs which respond literally and personally to Roberta's, the first reading "AND SO DO CHILDREN****" (222), the next, commenting on Roberta's own absent mother, "HOW WOULD YOU KNOW?" (222). Twyla's signs make no sense without Roberta's corresponding sign; they can only be read, if reading means understanding, when Roberta is present.

Twyla's reaction to the politicization of their personal relationship, through her signmaking, refuses to conform to the laws of political protest where political demands are made on an abstract authority, and her signs function as art as well as protest (223). Rather, Twyla's disjunctive signs demand nothing but a continued dialogue with the sources of opposition and reveal that the foundation of political protest may not be in the abstraction of liberal demands, but in conflict itself. When Twyla leaves the demonstration, it is not because her side has been victorious, but because Roberta's withdrawal has made her presence nonsensical. "Two days later I stopped going too and couldn't have been missed because nobody understood my signs anyway"(223).

Identity is not only dependent on the context of other competing and comparative identities, but also on the contexts of temporality and particular languages. "Recitatif" charts a relationship that covers a number of years, but each episode in this is presented as a present, rather than a retrospective. The orchard, later to be remembered as the scene of the most significant experiences shared by Twyla and Roberta, is introduced as a place where "Nothing really happened . . . Nothing all that important, I mean" (211). One of these experiences is Twyla and Roberta's encounter with the "gar girls", the older girls of the institution against whom they form a protective bond. These girls are variously represented throughout the story, through shifting perspectives over time and memory and through several languages. Their multiple identities are signaled immediately, through Twyla's childhood perception and later adult reasoning: "They were put-out girls, scared runaways most of them. Poor little girls who fought off their uncles but looked tough to us, and mean. God, did they look mean" (211). This perspectival understanding undergoes another change when Roberta translates this into the language of psychology, the official discourse of personality order/disorder, suggesting that Twyla has "blocked" her memories and that "Those girls had behaviour problems" (219). This doubled and tripled identity is given another layer by Twyla and Roberta's use of a personal language to describe not the girls themselves, but the significance of the older girls in their shared past, by reactivating a childhood term, "gar girls" (218) – a mishearing of "gargoyles." This term is only used when their childhood is remembered retrospectively, not during the episodes actually set in that time, and here the older girls' identity is displaced so that their image may function in Twyla and Roberta's attempts to remember their past and identify themselves as like, or not like, the "gar girls" (219,223,224).

The orchard is also the site of a second, and more significant, episode, which introduces Maggie, an elderly mute woman who is "old and sandy-colored" (211). This is the only mention of skin colour in the story, yet Maggie's identity is racially undecidable and the nature of her racial identity becomes a question of increasing concern throughout the story. Here, the apparently consoling knowledge of skin colour, withheld in the cases of Roberta and Twyla, is revealed to only act as a source of knowledge when that colour conforms to the gradated differences of "black" and "white." Yet Maggie's identity is never simply a question of race, but always also entwined in a question of violence. While Roberta and Twyla argue over her racial identity, this identity only becomes important when deployed as part of an argument on violence – the violence they may or may not have done to Maggie as children, a violence which is initially hidden beneath the question of Maggie's race, but which resurfaces repeatedly and insistently. Arguing over the episode where Maggie "falls down" in the orchard, Roberta and Twyla both place the question of Maggie's racial identity on top of the question of violence:

> 'Maybe I am different now, Twyla. But you're not. You're
> the same little state kid who kicked a poor old black lady when she was
> down on the ground. You kicked a black lady and you have the nerve to
> call me a bigot.'
>
> The coupons were everywhere and the guts of my purse
> were bunched under the dashboard. What was she saying? Black?
> Maggie wasn't black.
>
> 'She wasn't black,' I said.
>
> 'Like hell she wasn't, and you kicked her. We both did. You
> kicked a black lady who couldn't even scream.' (222)

Later, Twyla reconsiders the argument:

> It didn't trouble me much what she had said to me in the car. I mean the
> kicking part. I know I didn't do that, I couldn't do that. But I was puzzled
> by her telling me Maggie was black. When I though about it I actually
> couldn't be certain. She wasn't pitch-black, I knew, or I would have
> remembered that. . . I tried to reassure myself about the race thing for a
> long time until it dawned on me that the truth was already there, and
> Roberta knew it. I didn't kick her, I didn't join in with the gar girls and
> kick that lady. But I sure did want to. (223)

Here, the significance of Maggie's racial ambiguity at first preoccupies Twyla; it is the "race thing" that troubles her. However, the truth Twyla eventually reaches, which ends her uncertainty, is not the truth of Maggie's race but the more pressing truth of the violence done against her. Maggie may be racially indeterminate, but her position as poor (one could also suggest disabled) places her in a position where violence can be done against her, violence without consequences to others. This is not to elide the specificity of different social positions – to suggest that race, poverty and relative ability add up to the same thing – but to suggest that each can be made part of the others by the imposition of the dominant gaze. Hence also Roberta's last words in the story are concerned not with Maggie's race, but with her fate, not with the existential uncertainty of identity, but with the real impact of physical violence: "Oh, shit, Twyla. Shit, shit, shit. What the hell happened to Maggie?" (225).

I wish to turn from the question of the construction of identity within the text to the construction of identity outside the text by the reader/critic, through the notion of racial "passing": passing from, or for, one race to another. While the notion of passing disrupts straightforward racial identifications – the identity of the individual must first be in question – passing itself does not necessarily disrupt racial discourse. As Appiah points out, "The very concept of passing implies that, if the relevant fact about the ancestry of these individuals had been known, most people would have taken them to be traveling under the wrong badge" (76-7). To construct racial identity as one that passes for another continues to posit an underlying "true" but concealed identity. However, the notion of passing is illuminating, and I think potentially disruptive, when read in terms of the location of racial identity rather than racial essence, and the way in which passing's traditional exposition (from black to white) reveals the unequal relations of racial discourse in the United States. By using passing as a motif through which to read "Recitatif," I hope to uncover ways in which racial identity, though stable in terms of the characters perceptions of themselves and each other, is radically disrupted for the *reader*. In effect, racial passing is not performed by one character to another, but by the text to the reader. In addition, the text disrupts the normative reading of passing as "passing for white" by rendering white identity unstable.

In many accounts of passing, the subject of passing has been anxiety over the identification of racially mixed people, or rather of bodies whose racially mixed origin can no longer be physically detected[8]. Again, this points to the reinscription of racial authenticity – there is "something" to be detected – and in this context, "white purity" has always been privileged over "black purity." However, within this essentialising discourse, a rupture does occur between the body as site and guarantee of racial identity and the possibility of a racially mixed body that no longer signifies clearly or coherently within this system of identification; there is a collapse in continuity between "appearing" and "being" which must force us to ask how being is constituted. This rupture goes beyond the case of the racially mixed body to the centre of racial identity and identification. Kawash states the point thus: "The very visibility of blackness, a visibility that seems so commonsensical in the modern world as to need no explanation, is itself a part of, not prior to, the epistemology of racial difference. If the figure of passing challenges the principles and the power of this racial epistemology, then the implications of this challenge are not limited only to those in between" (134). Passing then disrupts the discourse of race by its focus on the visibility of racial identity and the knowledge of race precariously guaranteed by this system of visible signs. "Within a Western metaphysical tradition that has naturalised visibility as the locus of ontological truth-claims about the subject, vision masquerades as the agent of unmediated facticity" (Robinson 719). Hence passing denaturalises this function of visibility as guarantor of "truth" and refocuses attention not only on the visible, but on the perspective from which the visible is viewed. Once again, the critical value of ambiguity is its focus on the problem of identity, or "facticity," as viewed.

Within many literary accounts of racial passing, particularly white-authored accounts, this gap between the viewer and their unstable visual objects is closed by the device of the "tell," a physical signal available to the informed spectator, which (re)orders and stabilises racial identity by realigning bodily and legal definitions of race. While discussing narratives of passing in *Neither Black Nor White Yet Both*, Werner Sollors recounts many such instances of this, including a usefully representative quote from Victor Hugo's *Bug-Jargal*. Discussing a racially ambiguous character, the narrator confides that "We are assured, however, that there is always perceptible on a particular part of the body the ineffaceable trace of its origins" (Sollors *Neither* 120). This "trace" provides a link to an origin in an oppressed group which cannot be overcome, and which continues to render the individual a part of the group.

As this demonstrates, narratives of passing are ultimately narratives of failures to pass, even if this failure is only recognised by the "in-group" (Robinson 715) who may have consented with and supported the passing individual. This failure to pass, which involves the acknowledgement of an identity which, if not necessarily "black," is "not-white," is the necessary condition and operative contradiction of passing. In "Recitatif" Morrison rewrites the terms of passing to create a "successful" pass. The reader is specifically situated by the text as a reader of racial ambiguity whose always only partial knowledge of the "truth" of racial identity ultimately frustrates any search for a racial "truth," or a "tell" which will disclose the truth, no matter how skilled the reader (Abel 102-8).

Therefore, racial identity is disrupted because, against most narratives of passing, the reader is no longer privileged with access to a reassuring knowledge of racial identity, even if this identity is put into question. A crucial second element of this disruption is the attendant refusal to privilege white racial "purity" over black. Throughout traditional narratives of passing, passing is almost always a transition from a black identity to a "perceived-as" white identity, where "black" stand also for mixed race identities, as famously demonstrated by the "one-drop" rule. Therefore the discourse of passing functions not on the possibility of passing from a black identity to a white identity, but in fact on the impossibility of this transition. Hence the "tell" which marks the limits of racial discourse in traditional narratives of passing acts as a signifier for the impossibility of the truly passing body – the body which is not "passing" but has passed and is no longer in question. I would argue that the impossibility of this transition is not simply a matter of racial hierarchy, but the persistent inscription of "white" as a position which is not racially marked. Hence the impossibility of passing is not of moving from a black identity to a white identity, but of moving from a racial identity to a non-racial identity. In "Recitatif," the immediate and telling omission appears to be the omission of the "facts" of race. Yet, as Morrison demonstrates in *Playing in the Dark*, similar omissions in white literature and with regard to white characters are absolutely common, even usual. In her reading of the representation of race in Hemingway's *To Have and Have Not*, she contrasts the racial presentation of two characters, concluding that "Eddy is white, and we know he is because nobody says so" (72).

By rendering white identity, in "Recitatif," as a racial identity among other racial identities, Morrison disrupts the white/non-white opposition of normative racial discourse to reinscribe the multiple boundaries of race and the multiple sites of potential racial boundary crossing, where crossing occurs in terms of racial imagery and representation as well as the body. Through the motif of "passing", we can see the ways in which Morrison's refusal to privilege the reader with knowledge on which to secure otherwise ambiguous racial identities undermines the reader's desire to continue to fix racial identity into stable categories, even if the contents of these categories are contested.

Morrison revisits some of these issues in the 1999 novel, *Paradise*. In *Turning Back: The Retreat from Racial Justice in American Thought and Policy*, Stephen Steinberg recounts the history of the migration of freed slave sharecroppers west to Kansas from 1879, in search of free land and the opportunity to found new black communities. In the 20th century, the communities created through this exodus[9] were affected by the Depression, which in most cases led to depopulation and abandonment. Steinberg relates a visit made by him in 1975 to the last remaining population whose foundation could be traced back to this movement, a community he describes as "a living symbol of 'what might have been' if blacks had been masters of their own destiny. . . 'what might have been' – if more blacks had been able to escape the yoke of southern oppression, if they had been free to own land and develop their own communities, if Reconstruction had not wound up a broken promise" (207-9). In the novel *Paradise*, Toni Morrison imaginatively reconstructs this history. She does this not through a reinvestment in the "broken promises" of Reconstruction, but through the story of an independent black town whose reaction to the Depression is to move further west, to continue the migration and re-found their community. By writing from within black history, and setting the story within a strongly black-identified community, Morrison reverses the normative terms of racial ascription and creates a literary text where to be white is to be the racialised Other.

The novel opens with the eruption of conflict between the town, Ruby, and the Convent, the town's closest neighbour that has become a refuge for a group of women, all from outside the town. This conflict begins, in the opening of the text, with the question of "the white girl." "They shoot the white girl first" (3) – but the identity of the white girl is not disclosed and remains uncertain throughout the text. The immediacy and apparent importance of this identity sets the reader on a racial investigation, looking for the textual or bodily "tell" which will disclose which of the Convent women is in fact white. Suggestive details can be found throughout the text. Members of the town fear that a relationship between one of the townsmen and Gigi, a woman of the Convent, will produce a "mixed-up child" (279), but Gigi is also said to take an active role in the civil rights movement and politically certainly seems to position herself as "black" (68). Palla's father is said to have married "outside his own race" (254) but "race" cannot be read only as the difference between black and white. Connie, the oldest member of the Convent community, is almost certainly South American, and so potentially "not-black," but is also the only member of the Convent identified alongside "the white girl" (289) While these details encourage the reader to search for evidence of racial identity among the women, I would argue that this search is ultimately and deliberately frustrated by the omission of positive proof of identity in the text. The question that should be asked is not the question of the identity of the white girl, but the question of who identifies her as white, and why.

The Convent is repeatedly figured not as a neighbour, but as an invader, both of the town itself and of the town's image of itself. In their justification of the attack on the Convent, the townsmen argue, "If they stayed to themselves, that'd be something. But they don't. They meddle. Drawing folks out there like flies to shit and everybody who goes near them is maimed somehow and the mess is seeping back into our homes, our families. We can't have it, you all. Can't have it at all" (276). Similarly, during the attack on the Convent, one of the townsmen recalls an idyllic childhood scene of beautiful:

> [n]egro ladies . . . scheduled to live forever in pastel shaded dreams, [who] were now doomed to extinction by the new and obscene breed of female. He could not abide them for sullying his personal history with their streetwalkers' clothes and whores' appetites; mocking and desecrating the vision that carried him and his brother through the war, that imbued their marriages and strengthened their efforts to build a town where the vision could flourish. (279)

Although the townsmen at this point are the hostile, invading force, their position is conceptualised as one of defence, a defence against a difference which threatens socially and psychically to disturb the town's knowledge of itself.

In part, this difference is identified in terms of gender difference, and through permissable and impermissable femininity, as seem in the excerpt above. Within the town, women are an unseen domestic presence (60), identified as wives and daughters within a system where inheritances pass from father to son (187-8). The Convent women disrupt this system, and are identified through those other female cyphers: "Bitches. More like witches" (276). "Not women locked safely away from men; but worse, women who choose themselves for company, which is to say not a Convent but a coven" (276). This gender difference, or difference of acceptable gender roles, indicates the "doubly different" identity of the "white girl," and the linkage between the town's racial difference and its protection of this through a system of gender difference.

These differences can be traced through the double-voiced identity of the town. The "official" discourse of the town leaders identifies Ruby through a pure and singular racial lineage, passed from father to son, and through a mythic history inscribed in public symbols and ritual. At the same time, a private and personal account of the town's history, often spoken by women, highlights the silences within this official discourse and exposes the violence through which the myth of a pure origin is imposed.

The official discourse of the town is largely controlled by the Morgan twins, Deacon and Steward, whose names echo their guardianship of the town, and the apparent pre-destination of this guardianship. The "history" of the town is located in their memories and rememories of the founding of Ruby and Haven, the original settlement of their fathers, and these memories are repeatedly referred to in their attempts to construct a stable identity in Ruby. The origins of the town are contained in the story of the removal from Haven, which itself is haunted by the story of the "great walk," and the settling of Haven itself. But the historical in these stories cannot be separated from the mythic. In the memories of the Morgan twins, the transference of this story from tale to memory to rememory is clear: "The twins were born in 1924 and heard for twenty years about what the previous forty had been like. They listened to, imagined and remembered" (16). Their memories are memories of a story, not even an experience, and memories of an imagined history.

The significance of this history is invested in symbolic objects and rituals in Ruby. The clearest of these is the Oven, a large communal oven first built in the centre of Haven and then transported to Ruby, where it no longer serves a domestic purpose but functions as an informal meeting place and as a symbol of the town's identity. This symbolic identity is located in the place the Oven holds in the history of the town and by the inscription of a religious dictum inside its rim, placed there by the original builders. Therefore the Oven functions as a guarantee of continuity between the first settlement and the second, between different generations of the black community (85-6). However, the Oven itself is of divided significance, and we are reminded that the Oven will always have divided origins, domestic and symbolic, as "a utility become a shrine" (104). Origins do not "speak for themselves"; rather, meaning is read back towards an origin that apparently confirms its own truth. While other public artifacts, such as the children's play which recounts the settling of Haven in a ritual reminiscent of the Nativity (208-11), remain largely under the control of the town fathers, the Oven becomes a site of conflict for competing versions of the town's (black) identity. This conflict focuses on the scriptural words inscribed on the Oven: "Beware the Furrow of His Brow" (86). The decay of this inscription, to the point where the words can no longer be clearly read, literalises the change in meaning over time of such rhetorical and symbolic devices.

The official discourse of the town is challenged most clearly in the section titled "Patricia," where the singular and linear history of Ruby and Haven is offset by a complex and multiple genealogy. Here, the town schoolteacher writes an unofficial history of the town which uncovers the silences upon which the official discourse is constructed. She constructs complex genealogical tables, and this attempt to scientifically and objectively reconstruct the lineage of the town is set alongside long, highly personal and speculative footnotes, which address the questions that cannot be contained in the official history of the town or in the names of ancestors and descendants (187-202). Through this, Pat uncovers what she believes to be the underlying truth of the town, the "8-rock theory" (193) of racial purity, which is not based on black / white difference but on black as a "pure" limit position within a continuum of colour difference.

Here, Morrison overturns the "one-drop" theory of white racist discourse to position white ancestry as the inheritance which causes deviation from the racial norm. Pat, herself the daughter of a light-skinned mother apparently shunned by the community (196-7), believes that the identity of the town as purely black is protected by both a biological system of unspoken control over marriage and by the repression of otherness in the town's history. Crucially, this identity is not only formed through conflict with dominating ideas of whiteness, but also through conflict with other Black Americans. The original migration is a migration from the violence of white segregation, but during this journey, the founders of Haven are also rejected by a coloured town. This rejection – biblically recalled as the Disallowing (189) – is motivated in part by economic difference, but is read in terms of a racial difference that goes beyond black/white difference to an unnamable conflict between Black Americans. "Their horror of whites was convulsive but abstract. They saved the clarity of their hatred for men who had insulted them in ways too confounding for language" (189). The complexities of colour difference rather than straightforward "racial" difference cannot be contained in normative racial discourse, yet it is this complexity, rather than a white-centering black / white difference, which drives the racial identification of Ruby.

Through their identification of the "white girl," the townsmen identify the Convent, the town's Other, not only through gender, but also through race. The whiteness of the white girl operates here as an empty signifier, a sign through which the townsmen can express the difference of the Convent women, and the "white girl" is only seen as distinctly white under the gaze of the townspeople who come to the Convent during and in the wake of the attack (3,4,289). The "white girl" acts not as a character, but as a symbol of the interlinked gender and racial difference of the Convent, and so the danger this presents to a town that attempts to stabilise these categories of identity, both in terms of appropriate and inappropriate feminimity and a distinct racial difference whose categories "black" and "white" can be maintained. Therefore, the question may not be which of the Convent women is white. Rather, the reader is positioned outside the racial discourse used by the townsmen, which defines the identity of the "white girl." Though we know that they see the "white girl," the reader cannot see her because of the racial ambiguity through which the Convent women are otherwise presented. Hence we not only cannot identify the "white girl", but we may not even be in a position to say whether there is a "white girl" at all. Through the insertion of racial ambiguity among the Convent women, the complexities of the racial discourse of the town, which cannot be overcome by the insertion of a straightforward black/white difference, or by the gaze of the reader, are revealed.

Throughout this essay I have tried to describe racial identity through the problems associated with dividing racial identity between the "essential" and "inessential," arguing for a recognition of the persistence of essentialising racial discourses beyond the criticism of scientific or bodily essentialism, but also highlighting the dangers of attempting to silence race as a category of identity in critical discourse. My readings of *Paradise* and "Recitatif" argue that Morrison's fiction rewrites the question of racial identity by refusing to read racial identity as a choice between an essential or inessential identity and by constructing racially ambiguous characters whose ambiguities stem not from a question of essence or authenticity, but from the always limited positions from which identity can be read.

Each of these texts, however, reveals a further difficult y in the insertion of racial ambiguity into texts, and a necessary coda to this argument – the problem of *maintaining* ambiguity. This difficulty arises both in the production of critical readings – how can we recognise ambiguity and still keep reading – and in the need for resolution, particularly in relation to racial politics.

One critical reading of "Recitatif," an essay by Elizabeth Abel entitled "Black Writing, White Reading: Race and the Politics of Feminist Interpretation," highlights this difficulty. This essay discusses the problem of white feminist critical appropriations of black women's texts, a problem she sees as the use of black women's texts as the literal which grounds white critical theory. This essay begins with a complex and detailed reading of "Recitatif," a reading that has informed many points of my earlier argument. However, during her discussion of feminist politics, Abel closes the question of racial ambiguity in the text by turning to Morrison, as the author, to confirm the racial identity of her characters[10]. Through this move, Abel is able to diagnose her reading of the text as a symptom of "white critical desire" (107), which marks white feminist appropriations of black women's texts. To reach this conclusion, her reading of the story must be acknowledged as right or wrong, or in this case "right for the wrong reasons" (107), and this "rightness" or "wrongness" must be marked in terms of her own racial position. Just as Abel's own position as a white critic must be foregrounded, the racial identities of the characters must be secured in order that the racial basis of the critical reading remains stable, and can in turn be criticised. Abel argues that while racial identity may be ambiguous within a text, to read race as figurative outside the text, and hence to efface white critical racial positioning may open the black text up to appropriations of white critics in ways which reinscribe a black/white power differential. Therefore, while the ambiguity of racial identity within the text works to destabilise racial identity, and to undermine the processes through which different racial identities acquire meaning, the ambiguity of the text apparently must be closed before it can provide critical meaning, when this critical meaning requires that the racial identities of the author and critic be known.

A similar problem occurs in the resolution of *Paradise*, where the problems of the town are in some sense also the problems faced in constructing black political unity: hence, the resolution of these problems is crucial to the political potential of the town as a black community. It would be possible to argue that the Convent, in terms of its relationship with the town, acts a symbolic and idealised Other, whose identity serves the purpose of illuminating the town itself, This would certainly seem to be the case in the potentially problematic ending of the novel, where the apparent deaths of the white girl and Connie are magically averted (292) and the Convent women transcend both their treatment by the town and the town itself (308-17). Through this transcendence, the violence done against the women has symbolic rather than legal or political consequences for the townsfolk, and restitution can be made through an equally symbolic act – the "barefoot walk" (300) taken by Deacon Morgan. While this event does politically alter the town – change becomes possible – this possibility (and possibility for the future) in some sense only comes through the sacrifice of the Convent women and their radical challenge to the stable gender and racial identities of the town.

In each of these instances, then, ambiguity is revealed not simply as the liberation of identity, but as a strategy still open to the domination of the critical gaze and the pressing questions of political ideology. While the insertion of racial ambiguity into the text may radicalise questions of identity and the stability of identity, and disrupt the subject/object relationship of the text and the reader, ambiguity is still liable to closure in the face of continuing demands for racial meanings.

Kathryn Nicol

NOTES

[1] Here I follow Morrison's use of "American" rather than "North American" or "United States Citizen".

[2] Samira Kawash's notion of the persistance of the color line informs this argument throughout. "The stubborn persistence of the color line in representation and experience is not a problem of false consciousness or anachronistic thinking; rather, it indicates the power and continuity of the cognitive, discursive, and institutional workings of the color line as simultaneously the limit and constitutive condition for cultural and social life" (Kawash 6).

[3] Throughout this essay I will attempt to follow the agenda set by Michael Omi and Howard Winant in *Racial Formation in the United States*: "There is a continuous temptation to think of race as an essence, as something fixed, concrete, and objective. And there is also an opposite temptation to imagine race as a mere illusion, a purely ideological construct which some ideal non-racist social order would eliminate. It is necessary to challenge both of these positions, to

disrupt and reframe the rigid and bipolar manner in which they are posed and debated, and to transcend the presumably irreconcilable relationship between them" (54).

[4] This may seem contrary to the notion that "white" acts as a non-racialised position in mainstream discourse. However, I would argue that in the context of American society, white may not be racialised "as white", but identifies itself through a majority (or centre) position where race is an important marker in identitfying the Other, and therefore the Self.

[5] For a discussion of "constitutive ambiguity" in a different context, see Deutscher. In the context of race, I take her suggestion that constitutive ambiguity both stabilizes and destabilizes a discourse as a useful way of registering the operational rather than essential nature of racial discourse.

[6] See for example hooks "Postmodern Blackness" *Yearning: Race, Gender and Cultural Politics*, Awkward *Negotiating Difference*, Appiah *Color Conscious*, West *Race Matters*.

[7] Tzvetan Todorov states this argument at greater length: "The term 'race', having already outlived its usefulness, will be replaced by the much more appropriate term 'culture'; declarations of superiority and inferiority, the residue of an attachment to a universalist framework, will be set aside in favour of a glorification of difference (a difference that is not valorised in itself). What will remain unchanged, on the other hand, is the rigidity of determinism (cultural rather than physical, now) and the discontinuity of humanity compartmentalised into cultures that cannot and must not communicate with each other effectively. The period of classical racism seems definitely behind us now [. . .]. Modern racialism, which is better known as 'culturalism' [. . .] replaces physical race with linguistic, historical or psychological race. It shares certain features with its anscestor, but not all; this has allowed it to abandon the compromising term 'race' (and thus the first 'proposition' of classical racism). Nevertheless, it can continue to play the role formerly assumed by racialism. In our day, racist behaviours have clearly not disappeared, or even changed, but the discourse that legitimates them is no longer the same; rather than appealing to racialism, it appeals to nationalist or culturalist doctrine, or the 'right to difference'"(70).

[8] It should be noted that for the purposes of this discussion I am privileging aspects of passing related to the conceptual construction of identity. In many instances, passing in black literature is not simply concerned with the possibility of changed racial identities, but also with segregation, economic discrimination, and class difference constructed on racial lines.

[9] Steinberg notes that such Biblical imagery was frequently applied to these migrations, whose leaders at times were referred to as the "Moses of the colored people" (207). Similar Biblical imagery is also incorporated into *Paradise*.

[10] Abel introduces this interjection of authorial authority in a way that marks it off from the rest of the essay. Describing her inability to close the question of racial identity, she explains her action: "Propelled by this irresolution to suspend my commitment to the intentional fallacy, I wrote to Toni Morrison" (106). The half-humorous tone of this comment sets it apart from the "serious work" of the rest of the essay, suggesting that this action should also be read "in suspension." Despite the invisible parentheses that seem to surround this critical move, this addition to the essay is crucial to Abel's further argument.

WORKS CITED

Abel, Elizabeth. "Black Writing, White Reading: Rave and the Politics of Feminist Interpretation." *Female Subjects in Black and White.* Eds. Elizabeth Abel, Barbara Christian and Helene Moglen. California: University of California Press, 1997. 102-31

Appia, K. Anthony, and Amy Gutmann. *Color Conscious: The Political Morality of Race .* New Jersey: Princeton University Press, 1996.

Awkward, Michael. *Negotiating Difference: race, gender and the politics of positionality.* Chicago and London: Chicago University Press, 1995.

Deutscher, Penelope. *Yielding Gender: Feminism, Deconstruction and the History of Philosophy .* New York and London: Routledge, 1998.

Dyer, Richard. "The Matter of Whiteness." *Theories of Race and Racism: A Reader.* Eds. Les Black and John Solomos. New York and London: Routledge, 2000. 539-548

Elam, Diane. *Feminism and Deconstruction: Ms. en abyme.* New York and London: Routledge, 1996.

Fanon, Frantz: *Black Skin, White Masks.* Trans. Charles Lam Markmann. London: Pluto Press, 1967.

Frankenburg, Ruth. "White Woman, Race Matters." *Theories of Race and Racism: A Reader.* Eds. Les Black and John Solomos. New York and London: Routledge, 2000. 447-461

Fuss, Diane. "Interior Colonies: Frantz Fanon and the Politics of Identification." *Diacritics* 24 (1994): 20-42

Hooks, Bell. *Yearning: Race, Gender and Cultural Politics .* Boston: South End Press, 1990.

Kawash, Samira. *Dislocating the Color Line: Identity, Hybridity and Singularity in African American Narrative.* California: Stanford University Press, 1997.

Morrison, Toni. *Paradise.* London: Vintage, 1999.

-----. *Playing In The Dark: Whiteness and the Literary Imagination .* Cambridge, Massachusetts and London: Harvard University Press, 1992.

-----. "Recitatif." *African American Literature: A Brief Introduction and Anthology .* Ed. Al Young. New York: HarperCollins College Publishers, 1996. 209-225.

Omi, Michael and Howard Winant. *Racial Formation in the United States: From the 1960's to the 1990's.* 2nd ed. New York and London, Routledge, 1994.

Robinson, Amy. "It Takes One To Know One: Passing and Communities of Common Interest." *Critical Inquiry* 20 (1993-4): 715-736

Sollors, Werner. *Neither Black nor White but Both*. Cambridge and London: Harvard University Press, 1999.

-----. *Beyond Ethnicity: Consent and Descent in American Culture*. New York and Oxford: Oxford University Press, 1986.

Steinberg, Stephen. *Turning Back: The Retreat from Racial Justice in American Thought and Policy*. Boston: Beacon Press, 1995.

Todorov, Tzvetan. "Race and Racism." *Theories of Race and Racism: A Reader*. Eds. Les Black and John Solomos. New York and London: Routledge, 2000. 64-70

West, Cornel. *Race Matters*. Boston: Beacon Press, 1993.

Whitford, Margaret. Introduction. *The Irigaray Reader*. Ed. Margaret Whitford. Oxford: Blackwell, 1991.

Winant, Howard. "The Theoretical State of the Concept of Race." *Theories of Race and Racism: A Reader*. Eds. Les Black and John Solomos. New York and London: Routledge, 2000. 181-190

11
LOOKING DIFFERENT/RE-THINKING DIFFERENCE: GLOBAL CONSTRAINTS AND/OR CONTRADICTORY CHARACTERISTICS IN YASMINE GOONERATNE'S *A CHANGE OF SKIES* AND ADIB KHAN'S *SEASONAL ADJUSTMENTS*

In his novel *Seasonal Adjustments,* Asian-Australian author Adib Khan makes the observation that "human strengths and failures are global constants" (Khan 143). Khan's statement draws attention to the homogenous humanity that exists behind the trappings of cultural differences in Australia. These "global constants," however, are contradicted and challenged by precisely the same unwieldy cultural differences that are definitive for "Asian-Australian" identities. This paper will explore this paradox as it is portrayed in Khan's novel as well as in Yasmine Gooneratne's *A Change of Skies*.

This paradox exists within "the multicultural complexity of Australia" (Khan 56). In Khan's and Gooneratne's multicultural Australia, race, class, cultural background and religion not merely intersect but collide. How do these conflicting aspects contribute to the current debate on the politics of difference? It would be useful to re-think the idea of difference: to think of difference in relation to being similar. Difference is irrevocably dependent on similarity. We notice difference because there is similarity. Both *A Change of Skies* and *Seasonal Adjustments* feature a compelling juxapositioning of Australia and Asia. In addition, several parallels are drawn between the two continents as well as between the two novels. In this paper, I will focus on how Khan and Gooneratne manipulate the means of othering and how in the process, the characters in *Seasonal Adjustments* and *A Change of Skies* become incommensurably different and similar.

A Change of Skies and *Seasonal Adjustments* undertake the deconstruction of the discourses that articulate 'difference' and set the context for a critique and commentary about multiculturalism, Australia, and Australians. Khan and Gooneratne consciously point out the commonalities within difference. The necessity and significance of recognising specificities in the midst of the postmodern flux of diasporic subjectivities is also clearly established in their novels. Both authors also explore the limitations of oppositional constructions. A dualistic system of representations - national/ethnic, modern/traditional, metropolitan/colonial is examined in both novels, with the master-binary of 'Western' versus 'Asian' dominating the discussion. These ideas illuminate the fascinating links and fissures in the formation of Asian-Australian identities. For Gooneratne and Khan, coming to grips with the dynamics of difference, multiculturalism, and identity means exploring the ever-changing nexus of representation, discourse, and power. By their inversion of representational and hegemonic 'norms' in their novels, they also call into question the very idea of a definitive centre of cultural reference and authority.

The politics of multiculturalism and anti-racism, which accepts 'the West' as its boundaries, are inadequate to address the complexity of dilemmas faced by Australians and in particular Asian-Australians. The privileged homogeneity of the nation-state can no longer be assumed, since contemporary multiculturalism in Australia is broadly understood as the recognition of co-existence of a plurality of cultures within the nation (Stratton and Ang 124). But as Khachig Tololyan notes, the definition of people within Australia in increasingly diasporic terms raises awkward questions about the state of intercultural and interracial relations (cited in Ang "On Not Speaking Chinese 15). The struggle for belonging is particularly poignant for non-white Australians.

It is ironic that Australian multiculturalism was an idea developed from a racist past. The Australian nation created at Federation was itself defined in racial terms, that is the Immigration Restriction Bill of 1901, which established the policy of White Australia for the new Commonwealth. This policy placed distinct boundaries between those of European heritage and the non-white 'Other'. Racism has certainly left its imprint on institutions, social practices, intellectual discourses, popular ideas and national cultures in Australia as well as elsewhere. The irony is that the *unity of racism* as a process of social differentiation has played a central role in Western/Australian society since the beginnings of modernity and colonialism. Stuart Hall points out that racism, of course, functions by drawing impassable symbolic boundaries between racially constituted categories:

> Its typically binary system of representation constantly marks and
> attempts to fix and naturalise the difference between belongingness and
> otherness. Along this frontier there emerges what Gayatri Spivak calls
> the 'epistemic violence' of the discourses of the Other – of imperialism,
> the colonised, orientalism, the exotic, the primitive, the anthropological
> and the folkloric (255).

In the Australian context, the non-white minority have been subjected to
processes of "racialisation" as a means of controlling them and subordinating
them to the interests of the dominant group (Castles and Vasta 5-6). As
Sunvendrini Perera remarks the term 'migrant' in Australia functions as a
racialised term for "'not (quite) white'" since whiteness is an attribute of power
and dominance ("Whiteness and its Discontents"). The term 'racialisation'
points to the existing, hierarchical system of othering in Australia.

There is no single form of racism in Australia, but rather a range of
racisms, which affects different groups in different contexts. *Seasonal
Adjustments* and *A Change of Skies* address the considerable subjectivity involved
in naming, positioning and constructing of the Other, that is the Orient
constructed as Europe's 'Other', and conversely of Europe/Australia as Asia's
'Other. Racism is thus a product of bigoted ignorance and xenophobic
intolerance of otherness. In both Khan's and Goonernatne's novels, Asian
characters are pitted against racist Australian characters. Both are racist because
of their own colonial hang-ups (Rama 4). Victims of the cultural cringe, both the
Asian and Australian characters in these novels are themselves perpetrators of
the "racism learned from the British in [the] colonial days" (Gooneratne 119).
They have yet to discard it totally. However, their racism is a form of
neocolonialism, which applies and imposes an artificial hierarchy of importance
and values on others.

Eminent 'Asianist' Alison Broinowski says in her paper "The No-Name
Australians and the Missing Subaltern: Asian Australian Fiction" that

> [r]ecent fiction about Australia shows *us* as we may not realise how *others*
> choose to see us. Large lumpen, white, hypocritical and unsubtle if not
> downright thick, is how Australians often appear in these books, and
> racist with a multicultural figleaf. In Asian Australian fiction, *racism
> rules, but whose?*[1]

Broinowski's comments insidiously reproduce the damaging dichotomy of "us" versus "others". They also highlight the fact that representation can be interpreted as a powerful form of resistance on the part of the 'subjugated (Asian/Asian-Australian) other'. In *Seasonal Adjustments* and *A Change of Skies*, subversive representation is a means of abrogating the centre. It is a subversion not "of language alone, but of the entire system of cultural assumptions" (Ashcroft et al 48). Through the careful construction of their characters and the rich textual diversity of their novels, Khan and Gooneratne effectively reflect multiple perspectives, voices and experiences. The authors' engagement with post-colonial themes also challenges established literary canons and all forms of cultural dominance, as well as numerous "cultural assumptions" about colour, race and nationality.

In the novels, otherness (Asian or Australian) is constructed by the range of discourses as well as from within a framework of socio-political and cultural assumptions. The precarious relationship between (Anglo-) Australians and Asians (Asian-Australians) is further complicated and jeopardised by each side's fundamental self-righteousness. As Stuart Hall illuminates, the play of identity and difference constructing racism is powered by the positioning of "others" as the inferior species (255). This can be seen in Keith, Iqbal's white Australian father-in-law in *Seasonal Adjustments*, who has an "inherent belief in Anglo-Saxon superiority" (163). Keith "attended one of those joyless and snobbish Melbourne private schools which desperately treats itself as hybrid of the British public school system, aping its customs, bigotry and its condescending view of the rest of the world" (Khan 163). In *A Change of Skies*, Jean[2] faces a barrage of anti-Australian sentiment when she tells her friends of her impending move to Australia:

> "Australians?" inquired Rohini [one of Jean's classmates with whom she
> was having lunch].
> "Raj and I saw plenty of Australians while we were living in London . . .
> Drunken, foul-mouthed and crude" (Gooneratne 18).

Rohini goes on to remark with great disdain and indignation that Australians are "totally uncivilised". They tramp around Colombo dressed in their "frightful shorts and skimpy sundresses" having "[n]o idea how to dress or behave in someone else's capital city" (18). It is interesting to note that in

Seasonal Adjustments and in *A Change of Skies*, both the Australian and the Sri Lankan characters are afflicted/inflicted with/by an enduring colonial legacy, namely British bigotry. Keith's willing complicity with the imperialist project perpetuates the erroneous conviction about the superiority of his British/European ancestry. Rohini's disparaging commentary about Australians' uncultured ways echoes the negative opinion that the British have of the 'colonials' from Down Under.

In the novels, a way of resisting and recreating limiting and limited binaries is created through the representation of affinity among and within subjects. In Khan's novel, he says "Australia [is] learning about the commonality of the human flaws it shares with the rest of humanity" (114). The unity and sameness of human emotions strike Khan as most enthralling. In both *Seasonal Adjustments* and in *A Change of Skies*, we see Australia and Asia conceptualised in an unusual union: *"Australians are true Orientals at heart"* (Gooneratne 129). Gooneratne's female protagonist, Jean, in *A Change of Skies* remarks with full conviction that "Australians are true Orientals, they feel so deeply, so intensely, that words aren't always adequate to express their emotions" (129). Contrary to the conventional perception of Australia as the antithesis of Asia, here Australia is equated with Asia. Australia is endowed, or some would say encumbered, with Orientalist constructions of the "East."

Gooneratne's Australia is derived from the Orientalist perception in which the East-West difference is constructed along gender lines – East or Asia as feminine and West or Australia as masculine. The Australia in *A Change of Skies* is equated with the "Asian" side of this binary: Australia is depicted with a feminine soul and is therefore seen as emotional and intuitive, but also irrational and inarticulate. Indeed, these irrational and inarticulate feelings, namely racism and prejudice, are not particular to just Australia or Asia but widely pervasive. They constitute just one of the global constants that Khan has identified, as his protagonist Iqbal wryly notes, "a Bengali can be just as indifferent, mean, egotistical, loving, creative, heroic, generous, humane, cruel and greedy as an Australian. It makes you appreciate the homogenous blueprint of human life" (143). Human characteristics are here seen as universal and consistently common. "Asian" values and "Western" values[3] are seen to conflict and contradict each other, yet ironically speak of the same intrinsic "human" values. All of Khan's and Goonerantne's characters, whatever their colour or culture, Western or Asian, possess "human" values such as honesty, compassion, loyalty and a sense of justice and are also all capable of racism, prejudice, cruelty and hate.   This similarity suggests that given this understanding of basic human nature, there should be greater open-mindedness and empathy between different peoples.

According to Anthony Milner, many so-called 'Asian values' are equally Western values ("What's Happening to Asian Values?").   Do these "values" actually mean cultural identity?   If we take cultural values to mean cultural identity, then to suggest that that they are mutually exclusive and a threat to each other is to take for granted two things: first, that there *is* an 'Asian' cultural identity potentially able to overwhelm the 'Australian' one; and, second, that 'Asian identity' and 'Australian identity' are "formed, fixed and final" (Stuart-Fox 97).   Australia and Asia are therefore similar in that they are "imagined communities" (Anderson).   A deconstruction of the discourses that construct the concept of values lays bare the assumptions of dominance and worth, as well as "the fallacy of cultural superiority" (Khan 33).   Values, like cultures, are contingent things; they are constructed or invented to serve the specific purposes of their inventors.

In *A Change of Skies*, the Koyakos, Barry and Jean's compatriots, are obsessed with upholding Sri Lankan nationalism and maintaining Sri Lankan "moral values and traditions" (88).   They are fanatical that their children, Palitha and Lassana, growing up in an "alien society," should not become "infected with Australian values" and "lose touch with the traditions of their forefathers" (88, 92-93).   The Koyakos' anxiety about the possible loss of tradition betrays an ethnocentric attitude that sees any Australian influence as inferior and corrupting.   What is foreign is presented rigidly as contaminated, threatening, and dangerous.   This resistance against and opposition to the influence of "Australian values" can be seen as a determined attempt to, in the words of the influential Indian commentor, Partha Chatterjee, "resurrect the virtues of the fragmentary, the local and the subjugated" (qtd in Milner "Why we should not swagger").   Traditions and beliefs are represented as "invaluable buffers" to the threat of identity loss which is part of the migrant's experience of cultural and geographical displacement in Australia (Bramston 20).

In *Seasonal Adjustments*, Keith too is zealous about preserving 'tradition'. With his parochial sense of 'Australian nationalism', he views all Asians as enemy aliens with the potential to destroy (Eurocentric) cultural values.   Iqbal's

sarcastic diatribe in chapter four is directed at his pompous father-in-law and
his pro-establishment arrogance:

> Tradition! Tradition! Back to the basics. Loyalty to the crown. Honesty.
> Hard work. Christian morality. Let us not forget the pioneering spirit
> and those who built the nation. The digger's courage and the spirit of
> Gallipoli. We must revive this great country of ours! Meanwhile, we
> must keep foreigners out of the club (32).

Keith's colonial cringe here is acutely mocked. The author draws attention to
Keith's archaic and absurd "belief that Australia should continue to draw all its
spiritual and cultural sustenance from Europe, even in the distant future" (86).

It is clear that Australia has a painful history of subjection to
colonial/imperial power. That painful history is something Australians have in
common with many Asian nations such as Malaysia, Singapore, India, Sri
Lanka, Myanmar, Indonesia, and the Philippines, yet a shared ethnic relationship
with Britain appears to have often "obscured, and even romanticised, the pain"
(Gooneratne "Postcolonial Papers" 3). Being a *settler* colony (originally settled by
predominantly British migrants), Australia clearly wishes to establish itself as
eminently distinct from Britain's other colonies in Asia. Desperate to assert
herself as the bastion of 'Western civilisation' in Asia, Australia's "divisive
attitudes towards Asia and Asians" can be seen as a potent aspect of the cultural
cringe (Gooneratne "Asian Culture"). It becomes clear that underpinning the
icons of White Australia, such as "the digger's courage and the spirit of
Gallipoli," is the notion of whiteness itself. As Fazal Rizvi points out in
Australia, racism is manifest under the guise of nationhood, patriotism and
nationalism ("Asia" 25). Such human failings are found not just in attitudes, but
in the discourses that shape societal reality. Racism is fear fed by atavistic
territoriality and an ignorance of the other (Stuart-Fox 98).

In this thoroughly interdependent and volatile postmodern world,
holding fast to traditions and a primordial notion of ethnic identity is a way for
displaced peoples to find a secure sense of origin and belonging. Iqbal in
Seasonal Adjustments argues that "[t]radition has to do with a sense of
belonging" (117). It is unfortunate, however, that such a 'solution' is complicit
with, and carries through, the effects of the divide-and-rule politics of colonial
modernity and its aftermath, where categorical 'ethnicity' has been produced to

control and contain peoples (Chakrabrarty 1-16). As Iqbal's friend Iiftiqar in Bangladesh astutely comments,

> Tradition is . . . [a] concept that is not easy to understand. It can impute stagnation and exclude change. It may suggest fear and insecurity. The desire to cling to a past may be an admission of an inability to change, or it could indicate a wish to escape unhappiness by reverting to a world we once knew. It is so easy to evoke the past as a stable routine of familiar practices and call it tradition (Khan 116-117).

In *A Change of Skies*, racism masks itself behind tradition and long-standing social conventions, in which "race and caste and colour . . . have their appointed place in a divine scheme of things" (119). Gooneratne is deliberate in highlighting the fact that racism has its roots in religious and colonial discourses. This is apparent through the serendipitous musings of her protagonist Jean, "My husband (Barry) says that we Asians are racist about colour. Well, he couldn't be more wrong. Our people aren't racist about colour, they just honour a very ancient and holy tradition that has clear rules about what's beautiful and what's not" (Gooneratne 119-120). Indeed, Gooneratne's novel (and Khan's as well) draws attention to the colour hierarchies in Sri Lanka and India, which are implicitly subjected to multifarious class and regional factors.

In the multicultural Australia that Barry and Jean now call home, it is not ethnicity but still race and colour, the so-called *visible difference,* that is objectionable. The discourse of tolerance and acceptance in Khan's and Gooneratne's version of multicultural Australia is only skin-deep. "The dominance of white Australians is reinscribed within Australian multiculturalism, and is reproduced by the advocation of tolerance and cultural pluralism, ideologies that ostensibly deny this dominance" (Stephenson 3). According to Stephen Castles and Ellie Vasta, these ideologies mask the existing reality of differentiation and discrimination based on biological and cultural markers, which are linked to discourses of race and ethnicity (4-5). Thus, lying at the heart of Australian multiculturalism is the power-laden division between the tolerating and the tolerated (Hage). It is a distinction that is all the more pernicious since it generally remains unacknowledged and unrecognised. In other words, while overt and explicit expressions of racism are no longer condoned, the effort to eliminate such expressions by advocating tolerance "paradoxically perpetuates the self-other divide, which is the epistemological basis of the very possibility for racism in the first place" (Ang "The Curse of the Smile" 40).

According to Ien Ang, "the politics of diaspora serves as a ploy to keep non-white, non-western elements from full admittance, and therefore preventing a contamination of the white, western cultural centre" ("On Not Speaking Chinese" 10). Chandani Lokuge points out that, in *A Change of Skies*, Barry's sense of self heightens as his time in Australia lengthens. When Barry first leaves Sri Lanka for Australia, his status was that of an "honourary white" (Gooneratne 33). Now in Australia, Barry becomes increasing conscious of his 'minority/coloured' status. "'Look', [he snaps at Jean]. *'We're Asians. They're Australians. When Australians meet us, that's what they notice first. Difference'* "(Gooneratne 118). Ang observes that no matter how long Asian people have lived in the West, they can only become westernised, never pure and simply 'western'. She asserts that imposing a fetishised and overly idealised 'Asianess' effect such exclusion. This is personified in Barry and Jean's kindly neighbour, Maureen Trevally, who perpetually thinks of them "as exotics who [have] difficulty sending roots into alien ground" (Gooneratne 87).

In *Seasonal Adjustments*, Iqbal is extremely irate that all the Australians he meets have a "prototype image" of him as "an Indian". He notes that "it is laundered and made acceptable in their (Australians') own minds. Everything, from language to food, religion, and accent, has been moulded into a composition to fit a uniform view about an Indian" (147-8). This is especially infuriating for Iqbal since he is from Bangladesh and not India. Iqbal vehemently declares that "[he] is fed up with being treated as an oddity, a stray from the forbidding darkness of the world up there. [He] is tired of misconceptions and assumptions, of being an object of curiosity!" (149) Here, Khan uses the "politics of diaspora" to demonstrate how his character is kept a permanent outsider, who is never regarded as Australian, but always non-white and non-western.

Khan and Gooneratne emphasise that differences, such as distinctions of colour are always relational rather than inherent. Colour words such as 'black' or 'white' lack accuracy and specificity. But like a 'colour barcode', they function as the means of ascribing an automatic value or pre-determined worth. In Khan's novel, what is deemed acceptable and esteemed is subjective and culturally relative. Iqbal suspects that his mother's hostility towards his estranged wife Michelle, "a white girl", "a foreigner" is "based on colour rather than religious differences" (162). He is aware that Michelle is also subject to a similar sort of colour prejudice from her father, Keith, for marrying a " *black man*" (238; 149).

Colour has an intangible worth attached to it. But, as Linda Carroli has observed, the concept of worth or "value is an item that is highly changeable, depending from where you are speaking" (333). In Gooneratne's *A Change of Skies*, Jean remarks that "Westerners and . . . Far Easterners really do look rather alike – so pale and . . . well sallow – a bit like the way raw shellfish look, before they are curried, and get some colour and taste into them" (Gooneratne 119). To suggest that "Far Easterners" could be lumped together in the same category as Europeans is boldly subversive. Gooneratne provokes the reader with this unusual and extraordinary paradigm, that is, the notion that "Far Easterners" and Europeans look similar in terms of colour. She demonstrates how value judgements based on colour can only be arbitrary. After all, even within a single racial group there are already many distinctions.

In *A Change of Skies*, a distinction is made between the " *real* Asians" and the rest, set apart by "race[4] and caste and [in particular] colour." Jean in her naïvety, oblivious to her own racism, comments that "at home in Sri Lanka, and I suppose in India too, which is the centre, after all, of the *real* Asian world, we always called Far Eastern people 'Ching-Chongs'" (Gooneratne 119). In her satirical and ironic comedy, Gooneratne's post-colonial and intra-cultural challenge to traditional hierarchies is acute and deliberate. By positioning Sri Lanka and India as the centre (rather than Britain or America as is usual), Gooneratne makes an incisive commentary about how the discourses of authenticity and ancestral certainties are never fixed. The author draws attention to how contemporary, post-colonial societies such as India, Sri Lanka as well as Australia have gradually begun to see Britain itself as just another point on the periphery.

Gooneratne and Khan challenge their readers by highlighting the diversity of 'Asian' culture, even within the 'East Asian' community in Australia. But, as both *A Change of Skies* and *Seasonal Adjustments* show, the authenticity of what comprises the *real* Asia remains contentious. The concept of 'Asia' is problematised along with the ensuing difficulty in defining the category 'Asian'. The diversity and 'vari-asians' (variations) amongst and within the Asian region makes it vital to deconstruct the monolithic concept of "Asia" and to make an effort to desegregate the group "Asian." Both are constructs created as generic categories. Deconstruction of these categories is necessary because they are highly inadequate in conveying the depth and diversity that comprise "Asia" and "Asian." Writers such as Gooneatne and Khan play a vital role in educating their readers in making them mindful of cultural differences as well as the similarities.

In Gooneratne's *A Change of Skies*, Dr Iyer, one of Barry's Indian friends, comments "'All of us are one. What is this talk of war and cultural difference? India and Sri Lanka, Barry-ji . . . All one. What is the difference?'" Barry and Jean are incensed by what they regard as a very insensitive comment to a very sensitive issue. They have to work very hard to restrain themselves from leaping up and shouting in unison that "Two thousand years of history! That's the difference!" (Gooneratne 307). Barry and Jean are also particularly angry at Dr Iyer at this time because an Indian peace-keeping force had occupied Jaffna at the Sri-Lankan Government's invitation. Barry vehemently believed that

> India had absolutely no business sorting out the problems of her tiny neighbour, however corrupt or incompetent she might imagine that neighbour's politicans might be . . . When the news broke that India had actually financed the Tamil militants all along, trained them in camps in South India, and furnished them with weapons with which to fight their own people, Barry was furious. [He was convinced that Sri Lanka] had been cynically used by India as a pawn in its Big Power exercises (305-306).

This episode with Dr Iyer is especially consequential because it is evident that historical specificities can never be ignored or overlooked.

Indeed, it is obvious that judicial attention to racial or cultural specificities is important. In *Seasonal Adjustments*, the policeman who stops Iqbal for a traffic violation sneers: "You darkies are all the same, aren't you?" "No we are not" he replies, "There's mahogany, walnut, teak, ebony. The variety is great" (Khan 144). In place here is the imposed visual stereotype that all Asians "are indistinguishable" (147). Such suggestions of a false homogeneity obscure important differences. The unity of often-disparate communities implied by the term "Asian" does not exist, nor is there an "Asianness. In *A Change of Skies*, Barry is agitated that "Australians can't make fine distinction between one kind of Asian and another" (118). However, he is equally guilty when he makes an incriminating comment about the 'homogeneity' of Westerners: "What's the difference? . . . Americans, South Africans, Britons, Canadians, Australians, New Zealanders – they are all the same, aren't they?" (Gooneratne 28). The 'Orient' and the 'Occident' are configured as necessary fictions for discursive convenience, but they are undoubtedly misleading and indeterminate.

In Gooneratne's Sri Lanka, Australia has earned notoriety and a dubious reputation for being racist; the White Australia Policy (WAP) is regarded as the ultimate display of Australian racist doctrine. Before her departure for Australia, Jean is told by a concerned Sri Lankan friend Charmaine, that "the WAP acts as a brake on the entrance of all Orientals to Australia" (19). Khan's and Gooneratne's novels ask if things have altered much in multicultural Australia? In *Seasonal Adjustments*, Iqbal is aware of the "tensions of being a child from a mixed marriage" and is anxious to shield his daughter, Nadine, from "experiencing ridicule and the pains of non-acceptance" (161). He desperately hopes that Nadine will achieve self-definition through hybridity. However, he realises that it is not as easy as it seems. He remains somewhat skeptical about the viability of hybridity and is apprehensive about the "exacting and sometimes cruel demands of cultural dualism" (161). Iqbal echoes Khan's own convictions when he asserts that "Nadine's most important identity is that of a human being" (250). Iqbal is aware of the difficulties already present "in being human" and does not want to burden Nadine with the insistence that she speaks two languages or learn two cultures (Khan qtd. in Griffin 7). He firmly believes that Nadine is Australian and therefore should be allowed to choose for herself when she is older. In his novel, Khan acknowledges the intrinsic complexity inherent in cultural identification, particularly for people of mixed ancestry.

On the other hand, hybridity in *A Change of Skies* is seemingly uncomplicated. It is personified in Barry and Jean's Sri Lankan-Australian daughter, Edwina, who is seen as Gooneratne's glowing vision for the new future. The author's unproblematised representation of Asian-Australians and Asian-Australian identit(ies), however, *is* problematic and highly disconcerting. The certainty she exercises in this representation is deceptive because "the fundamental *precariousness* of diasporic identity construction" is obscured and romanticised (Ang "Migration" 9).   Edwina is depicted as cheerfully, confidently and effortlessly negotiating her multiple identities: "Beautiful-Sri Lankan on the outside, and bloody-minded Aussie to her bootstraps" (Gooneratne "Constructing the Characters" 19).

Identity is always "conjunctural" rather than "stable and unified (Bahri and Vasudeva 14). It is a "dynamic process of inclusion, innovation, of selection and assimilation that does not stop at some point" (Stuart-Fox 97). "[E]very child is born into a tradition"; the Asian-Australian children in *A Change of Skies* and *Seasonal Adjustments* are caught in the cultural and often contradictory cross-currents of societal pressures, parental expectations, and individual desires (Khan 85). But for the Asian-Australian children in both novels, to confine themselves to "narrowness of life within a single tradition" may be a major handicap (Khan 85). In Gooneratne's and Khan's multicultural Australia, this new generation of Asian-Australians are called upon to assist in the reconciliation of differences. After all, the hybridity they embody is what Brian Castro calls a kind of bridging (qtd in Daniel 8). These young Asian-Australians therefore emerge as "a slowly growing minority which will learn how to combine traditions" (Khan 85).

The young "hyphenated Australian[s]" in *A Change of Skies* and *Seasonal Adjustments* are also examples of the cosmopolitans, who are products of hybridity and of cultures coming out of long histories based on the interaction between imperial powers and their colonies or ex-colonies (Gooneratne 312). Indeed in the postcolonial present, "a rethinking of identity requires openness to new forms of global identity or citizenship" (Cvetkovich and Kellner 12). As Cathy Van Der Driesen says, "[w]ith the Australian birthright comes a hybridity of perception, an acquisition of an Australasian gaze" (21).   For Asian-Australians, it is the differences that define them in multicultural Australia, the differences that make them highly visible, distinctive and that give them agency. They are as Salman Rushdie says, "a radically new types of human being: people who root themselves in ideas rather than in places . . . a people who have been obliged to define themselves – because they are so defined by others – by their otherness" (124-5).

For the Asian characters in both novels, "[t]o be Asian in Australia is to have choices that can change not only [the ensuing generation] but also what we call Australian" (Stone 2). Asians in Australia should be able to call themselves 'Australians' without the need for additional qualifiers. All Australians, of European or Asian descent, are a diasporic people with multiple consciousnesses and identities[5]. Australia is an imagined community. The transnational nature of diaspora unsettles the notion of 'national culture' or 'national identity' and disrupts the presumption of static roots in geography and history (Ang "On Not Speaking Chinese" 16). Embracing hybridity within both 'tradition' and 'modernity' is a reality in Asian-Australian futures. Postmodern ethnicity can no longer be experienced as naturally based upon tradition and ancestry; rather it is experienced as a provisional and partial site of identity, which might be constantly (re)invented and (re)negogiated (Ang "On Not Speaking Chinese" 18).

The ideas in this paper serve as a point of departure rather than arrival. Gooneratne and Khan attempt to provoke their readers to rethink difference. In *A Change of Skies* and *Seasonal Adjustments*, the paradox of being similar because of difference is possible within the diversity of multicultural Australia. We are the same in different ways; we are also different in the same ways. Foong Ling Kong has suggested that "in moving away from an identity politics that establishes definitions and identities in opposition, perhaps one option is to amplify and make use of the affinity in representation that allows for multiple differences among and within subjects" (94). This "affinity in representation" forges anti-racist possibilities because it emphasises a universal human experience which is independent of colour, race or religion. As Yasmine Gooneratne says, "[f]iction is a great way to find out about other cultures. It is very often deals with the same family situations, with emotions we all share" (qtd in Susskind 39). Therefore, the invariable similarities between Asians and Australians, Europeans or Far-Easterners make the call for greater racial/cultural understanding all the more obligatory. In their novels, Gooneratne and Khan issue the challenge to live in an interconnected way with our fellow humans.

The post-colonial approach adopted by Yasmine Gooneratne and Adib Khan is vital because it posits a speaking space for the Other and a genuinely radical concept of society as inevitably hybrid and multi-discursive (Dale and Gilbert 47). The very act of writing *A Change of Skies* and *Seasonal Adjustments* constitutes an act of interrogation of the Orientalist discourse, which up to now has 'spoken' for the Orient. They represent the acquisition of a voice, which must inevitably diminish the alienness of the 'other' (Van Der Driesen 27). Khan and Gooneratne achieve this by illuminating the parallels between the Asian and the Australian characters in both *Seasonal Adjustments* and *A Change of Skies*. One prominent and powerful parallel is how these characters live on and between the borders as "postcolonials. Through their respective protagonists, the authors are able to perceptively expose and scrutinise existing colonial and neocolonial mentalities in Australia and Asia. Both Australia and Asia are uncovered as the subjects and objects of colonial scrutiny. It is clear that colonial traditions rooted in discourse have shaped Australian/Asian society and attitudes, be they patronisingly tolerant, racist, fearful, contemptuous or discriminatory.

Australia, the nation of migrants and refugees, is "well known by many and no less understood" (Liberman 13). While Gooneratne's novel, *A Change of Skies,* speaks optimistically about the possibilities that exist in intercultural exchange and are borne of the shared human experience, Khan's *Seasonal Adjustments* regards this project with much more cynicism. His angst-ridden protagonist Iqbal concludes with profound insight:

> You can never call anything your own. But out of this deprivation emerges an understanding of humanity unstifled by genetic barriers . . . my prejudices [are] trimmed to manageable proportions. You realise behind the trappings of cultural differences, human strengths and failures are a global constant. This is a very precious knowledge . . . It is this impossible mixture which binds humanity and I am a part of it. No better or worse than anyone, but an equal. An equal because I know I am a composite of all those contradictory characteristics which are far stronger than any racial or religious differences. (Khan 143)

Indeed, while his "festerings" may be those of many, each must nonetheless bear them alone. Perhaps, knowing this, one may yet find human, global, solidarity in the fact (Liberman 13).

Yvette Tan

NOTES

[1] Words in italics my own emphasis. It is interesting to note that Broinowski's comments verge on the defensive. She makes an obvious distinction between the "us" and the "others". Her reference to the "us" is assumed to mean white 'Anglo/Celtic Australians' and the 'them' or "others" assumed to be other non-whites. Broinowski's comments are also problematic since she seems to be insinuating that non-white "others" in Australia are not or cannot be really Australians. Where do Asian-Australians fit into this continuum? Otherness is reinforced and perpetuated. This is ironic for someone whose highly acclaimed book *The Yellow Lady – Australian Impressions of Asia* sought to "provoke [her readers] into rethinking a lot about unconsciously attitudes to things Asian and alien, along with the reasons [that] shap[e] perceptions of [Asia and Asians]" (Jamie Mackie "Foreword". *The Yellow Lady*. Melbourne: Melbourne UP, 1996, 2nd edition, vii).

[2] In this paper, I refer to Gooneratne's main protagonists by their 'Aussie names', Barry and Jean Mundy, instead of their given names, Bharat and Navaranjini Mangala-Davasinha. Barry and Jean 'aussify' their names because in "[s]eeking ways to assimilate, they [discover] the time-honoured Australian custom of name swapping" (122).

[3] In general political discourse, "Asian" values and "Western" values are conceptualised as diametric oppositions. These paradigms invoke and thrive on stereotypes. Within the "Asian" values paradigm, the emphasis is on community rather than the individual, the privileging of order and harmony over personal freedom and the refusal to compartmentalise religion away from other spheres of life. Other so-called typical "Asian" qualities are thriftiness, industriousness, the respect for political leadership, the belief that government and business need not necessarily be natural adversaries as well as the stress on family loyalty. "Western" values, on the other hand, give precedence to individualism and personal liberty as well as making clear distinctions between state and industry. See Anthony Milner. "What's Happened to Asian Values? <http://www.anu.edu.au/asianstudies/values.html. 20 March 2000.

[4] Race here is conceptualised as "an unstable and 'decentred' complex of social meanings constantly being transformed by political struggle" (See Omi, N, and H. Winant. *Racial Formation in the United States*. London and New York: Routledge and Kegan Paul, 1986, 68).

[5] "Diasporas are a transnational, spatially and temporally sprawling sociocultural formations of people, creating imagined communities whose blurred and fluctuating boundaries are sustained by real and/or symbolic ties to some original 'homeland', that is Europe (most often Britain) or 'Asia' (Ang "On Not Speaking Chinese 5).

WORKS CITED

Anderson, Benedict. *Imagined Communities: Reflections on the Origin and Spread of Nationalism* . 2nd ed. London:Verso: 1991.

Ashcroft, Bill, Gareth Griffiths and Helen Tiffin. *The Empire Writes Back – Theory and Practice in Post-Colonial Literatures*. London: Routledge, 1994.

Ang, Ien. "Migration of Chineseness." *SPAN: Journal of the South Pacific Association for Commonwealth Literature and Language Studies – Diasporas*. 34-35 (1993): 3-15.

----------, "On Not Speaking Chinese." Postmodern Ethnicity and the Politics of Diaspora. *New Formations* 24 (1994): 1-18.

----------, "The Curse of the Smile: Ambivalence and the 'Asian' Woman in Australian Multiculturalism." *Feminist Review* 52 (1995): 36-49.

Bahri, Deepika and Mary Vasudeva, eds. Introduction. *Between the Lines: South Asians and Postcoloniality*. Philadelphia: Temple UP, 1996.

Bramston, Dorothy. "A Sri Lankan Writer in Australia: Yasmine Gooneratne's *A Change of Skies*." *New Literatures Review* 31 (1996): 19-32.

Broinowski, Alison. *The Yellow Lady: Australian Impressions of Asia*. 2nd edition. Melbourne: Oxford UP, 1996.

----------, "The No-Name Australians and the Missing Subaltern: Asian Australian Fiction." Online. Internet. 20 Mar. 2000.

Carroli, Linda. "Out of the Melting Pot, into the Fire – Writing Cultural Diversity into the Arts." *Meanjin* 53.2 (1994): 327-36.

Castles, Stephen and Ellie Vasta, eds. Introduction: Multicultural or Multi-racial Australia? *The Teeth are Smiling: The Persistence of Racism in Multicultural Australia*. St Leonards, NSW: Allen & Unwin, 1996.

Chakrabrarty, Dipesh. "Modernity and Ethnicity in India." *Communal/Plural 1: Identity/Community/Change*. Nepean: U of Western Sydney P, 1993.

Cvetkovich, Ann and Douglas Kellner, eds. *Articulating the Global and the Local – Globalization and Cultural Studies*. Colorado and Oxford: Westview Press, 1997.

Dale, Leigh and Helen Gilbert. "Looking the Same? A Preliminary (Post-Colonial) Discussion of Orientalism and Occidentalism in Australia and Japan." *Yearbook of Comparative and General Literature*. Bloomington: Indiana UP, 1993.

Daniel, Helen. "Double Cover." *The Age*. 17 Feb. (1996): 8.

Foong Ling Kong. "Postcards from a Yellow Lady." *Meridien: Asian and Pacific Inscriptions: Identities, Ethnicities and Nationalities (special book issue)*. Ed. Suvendrini Perara. 14:2 (1995): 83-97.

Griffin, Michelle. "Home and Away." *The Sunday Age*. 24 Nov. (1996): Agenda7.

Gooneratne, Yasmine. *A Change of Skies*. Sydney: Picador, 1992.

----------, "Constructing the Characters of Women in *A Change of Skies*." *Australian Women's Book Review* 4.3 (1992): 13-19.

----------, "Postcolonial Papers." *Notes and Furphies* 20 (1992): 3-5.

----------, "Asian Culture and Australian Identity." *Hecate* 22.2 (1996): 47(7). *Expanded Academic Index*. Online. 23 Mar.1999.

Hage, Ghassan. "Locating Multiculturalism' Other: A Critique of Practical Tolerance." *New Formations* 24 Winter (1994): 19-34.

Hall, Stuart. "New Ethnicities." *'Race', Culture and Difference*. Eds. James Donald and Ali Rattansi. London: Sage Publications, 1992.

Hawkins, Gay. "The Politics of Chineseness and Value in SBS." *Alter Asians: Exploring Asian/Australian Identities, Cultures and Politics in an Age of Crisis* (18-20 February 1999). Conference Abstracts. Internet. 2 July 1999.

Heiddegger, Martin. *Basic Writing*. London: Routledge & Kegan Paul, 1978.

Khan, Adib. *Seasonal Adjustments*. St. Leonards, NSW: Allen & Unwin, 1994.

Liberman, Serge. "Strength from Confusion." *Australian Book Review* 160 May (1994): 12-15.

Lokuge, Chandani. "'We Must Laugh at One Another, or Die.' Yasmine Goonerneratne's *A Change of Skies* and South Asian Migrant Identities." *Shifting Continents/Colliding Cultures" Diaspora Writing of the Indian Subcontinent*. Eds. Ralph J. Crane and Radhika Mohanram. Amsterdam/ Atlanta: Editions Rodopi b.v., 2000.

Milner, Anthony. "What Happening to Asian Values?" Faculty of Asian Studies, Australian National University. Internet. 20 Mar. 2000.

----------, "Why We Should Not Swagger." Faculty of Asian Studies, Australian National University. Internet. 20 Mar. 2000.

Omi, N, and H. Winant. *Racial Formation in the United States*. London and New York: Routledge and Kegan Paul, 1986.

Perera, Suvendrini. "Whiteness and its Discontents." *Journal of Intercultural Studies* 20.2 (1999): 183. *Expanded Academic Index*. Online. 21 Aug. 2000.

Rama, R. P. "A Conversation with Yasmine Gooneratne." *SPAN: Journal of the South Pacific Association for Commonwealth Literature and Language Studies* 38 (1994): 1-18.

Rizvi, Fazal. "Asia and the Search for an Australian Identity." *Social Alternatives* 12:1 (1993): 23-26.

----------. "Racism, Reorientation and the Cultural Politics of Asia-Australia Relations." *The Teeth are Smiling – The Persistence of Racism in Mutlicultural Australia*. Eds. Ellie Vasta and Stephen Castles. St. Leonards, NSW: Allen & Unwin, 1996.

Rushdie, Salman, *Imaginary Homelands*. London:Granta, 1991.

Stephenson, Peta. "The Triangulation of Whiteness, Ethnicity and Aboriginality in Australian Multiculturalism." Paper presented at "Re-Imagining Multiculturalism Conference," 1-3 October 1999, Melbourne Convention Centre.

Stone, Deborah. "The Asian Experience." *The Sunday Age* 13 Nov. (1994): Agenda2.

Stratton, Jon and Ien Ang. "Multicultural Imagined Communities: Cultural Diversity and National Identity in Australia and the United States." *Continuum* 9.2 (1994): 124-158.

Stuart-Fox, Martin. "Engaging Asia." *Asian Studies Review* 16:3 (1993): 95-99.

Susskind, Anne. "A Woman in a Sari." *Sydney Morning Herald* 23 July 1991: Books39.

Van Der Driesen, Cathy. "Asian Writing in Australia – Towards an Australasian Identity." *Literary Criterion* 30.1&2 (1995): 17-29.

12.

JESSIE FAUSET'S FICTION: RECONSIDERING RACE
AND REVISING AESTHETICISM

Jessie Redmon Fauset, writer of the Harlem Renaissance, begins *The Chinaberry Tree* with a Foreword that announces an apolitical literary agenda for her novel. As the opening sentence declares, "Nothing,--and the Muses themselves would bear witness to this,--has ever been farther from my thought than writing to establish a thesis." By the time she has arrived, however, at the conclusion of that Foreword (a mere five paragraphs later), she has offered a loving defense of what she calls the "homelife of the colored American" with its "joy and rue" and must admit, though with an air of pride in her apparent self-contradiction, "So in spite of other intentions I seem to have pointed a moral" (*Chinaberry* ix-x). But she has done more than merely end with an ethical statement of the sort implied by the word "moral." In the racist climate of the 1930s, to offer such a defense of African American life was also to create a political manifesto, the very antithesis of what an invocation of "Muses" might suggest.

Like the Foreword that introduces it, the *The Chinaberry Tree*--as the mixed character of her authorial pronouncement signals--is a work of self-conscious ambivalence and duality that foregrounds its own contradictoriness. As such, it reflects the divisions that run throughout her fictional *oeuvre* in general. In each of her four major novels-- *There is Confusion* (1924); *Plum Bun: A Novel Without a Moral* (1929); *The Chinaberry Tree* (1931); and *Comedy, American Style* (1933)--Fauset depicts the ambiguities associated with race in early-twentieth-century America through a literary methodology that is itself rife with ambiguities of other sorts. In her role as novelist, she assumes the position simultaneously of a political moralist and a devotee of "Muses"; a historically precise recorder of contemporary social injustice and a devotee of so-called timeless dreams; a realist engaged in exposing the ugliness of gender and racial hierarchies and an apostle of the Beautiful; a feminist proponent of civil rights for both African-American women and men and also an Aesthete, consumed by the immediacy of her impressions of the sensuous world.

That Fauset's narratives should be marked by contradiction is no surprise. Patricia Hill Collins has reminded audiences that "contradiction" and "dissonance" have been and continue to be the distinguishing features of African American experience--doubly so for Black women, as they move between and among various kinds of "segregated spaces" that are also hierarchical ones, ranked according to gender and class, as well as by race (Collins). Yet the philosophical movement with which Fauset allied herself, in order to explore and express these contradictions, proved an unexpected choice nevertheless. Given its associations with an exploded and discarded Victorian past, aestheticism was rarely the preferred allegiance of the white male Moderns of her day and, to put it bluntly, even more rarely the vehicle for Black women.

How was it possible for Jessie Fauset to be a politically astute figure in the first decades of the twentieth century and still to consider herself an Aesthete? I would like to raise the issue of how Fauset adapted and revised aestheticism, a movement first conceived to meet the needs of white male Europeans, to make it valuable to herself as an African American woman. But what I shall offer here is not a study of how one writer merely sought an individualistic solution to a personal artistic dilemma. Instead, I hope to suggest that in fashioning her own new definitions of the twin cornerstones of aestheticism--that is, its theories regarding the function of art and the nature of beauty--Fauset was also striving to open a way for all Black women to participate in the aesthetic experience. To the stirring challenge that W. E. B. DuBois had thrown out to his listeners in "Criteria of Negro Art," a speech published in *The Crisis* in 1926--"Thus it is the bounden duty of black America to begin this great work of the creation of Beauty, of the preservation of Beauty, of the realization of Beauty" (Du Bois 488)--Jessie Fauset responded by demonstrating that art and beauty were indeed already present and had been present all along, but in the circumstances, cultural productions, and also the bodies of Black women. They were there despite having always been overlooked, and a perspective derived from aestheticism could help to uncover this truth. Such a perspective could, moreover, both embrace and reveal the contradictoriness of Black women's situations, for aestheticism itself was a movement characterized by its contradictions.

Although some of Fauset's white modernist contemporaties denied its hold, the legacy of aestheticism proved more lasting and widely diffused than its late-nineteenth century adherents could have imagined. Seemingly an elitist philosophy by definition, aestheticism posited among its first principles the class-based conviction that "Art is not the common possession of the whole human race--the only inheritance common to all humanity is vulgarity; and those who claim a share in art for everyone only show themselves to be ignorant of its true nature, and condemn themselves to remain for ever outside with the vulgar" (Hough 183). Some Aesthetes insisted, moreover, that art and morality were "entirely separable categories of thought, that art should suffer no incursions from the moral sphere" (Small xii). Aestheticism "sought to place the work of art in an ideal world existing beyond or outside the social realm" (Freedman 47)--a counter-realm founded upon the principle of the artist as an "enclosed consciousness," unaffected by "politics and economic production" (Psomiades 9). Pursuing art merely for its own sake, an Aesthete allegedly could live "in a sphere removed from ordinary ethical choices" (Small xxvi), as well as from political exigencies and even from historical contingencies. Aestheticism offered its followers not only a location outside of the turmoil of the present day, but an escape into the past (at least of Western civilization), to the supposedly halcyon days of mediaeval France or Renaissance Italy. Through worship, moreover, of ancient Greece and promotion of Hellenism as the ultimate expression of beauty, it encouraged in some male artists and readers the fantasy of a male homoerotic paradise from which women conveniently would be absent--even though, as Yopie Prins has pointed out, a number of British women scholar-poets also "disovered in ancient Greek a new language of desire" that allowed for a female-centered eros (43).

Yet the doctrine of *l'art pour art* from France was only one strand of aestheticism, especially in England. Another simultaneously existing line of it connected directly to the socialist theories and practices of Walter Crane and, most notably, William Morris, who argued for the direct intervention of art in the political realm. This second strain linked the aesthetic movement not merely to the immaterial sphere of poetry, but to the sensuous and particular sphere of handicrafts and to the decoration of interior spaces. Through an emphasis upon "furniture-making, tapestries, textiles, and carpets" as aesthetic categories (Gagnier 136), it aligned itself with the labors of the working classes and with the world of the "feminine" arts associated with the domestic lives of women.

It is, in fact, nearly impossible to fix upon a single definition of aestheticism, except as a movement that embodied and revelled in its own oppositions and oppositionality. Such is the conclusion of Jonathan Freedman when examining aestheticism's manifestations in England: "I would suggest that the definining quality of British aestheticism . . . is the desire to embrace contradictions" (6). So too is its endpoint open to question. Although some critics continue to see aestheticism as moribund by 1900, others claim that it flourished well into the 1930s (Schaffer and Psomiades, "Introduction" to *Women and British Aestheticism* 4). Thus, its characteristic rhetoric, as well as its philosophical underpinnings, still would have been readily available to Jessie Fauset in the 1920s.

Though much about the aestheticism that Jessie Fauset inherited from her European predecessors demonstrated a deliberate indefiniteness and resistance to unitary notions, especially regarding gender, the racism was clearcut. If the centerpiece of aestheticism was the worship of the Beautiful, the Beautiful was white. Narrowly defined catalogues of physical features pervaded the work of earlier aesthetic artists, even in situations where the gender lines grew ambiguous. Although aestheticism "tended to attract precisely those writers whose gender ideas were in flux" (Schaffer, *Forgotten Female Aesthetes* 5), it nevertheless inscribed indubitably Anglo-Saxon characteristics upon their representations of androgynous figures. Even when neither identifiably male nor female, the bodies idealized by the aesthetic movement still displayed "conventions applied in the first instance to beautiful women--red lips, ivory flesh, golden curls" (Psomiades, *Beauty's Body* 6)-- conventions that reinforced a racial norm.

Such an obvious contradiction between the ambiguity that aestheticism embodied in other areas and its singleminded insistence upon ideals of whiteness may have suggested to Fauset, as it did to other African American contemporaries, that the movement presented a space that could be claimed and opened up for her own purposes. In Harlem and other strongholds of Black intellectuals in the 1920s, earlier productions of aestheticism haunted the imaginations of male and female artists alike. So great was their appeal that it reached out even to the far-from-privileged Zora Neale Hurston, who, in *Dust Tracks on a Road*, recalled her delight in reading and learning by heart Oscar Wilde's "The Ballad of Reading Gaol" (1898), a poetically aestheticized account of passion, murder, and punishment (Hurston 149).

Part of aestheticism's attractiveness to a new community in a different time lay in its emphasis on the senses--on the cultivation and enjoyment of smell and touch and, especially, of sight. To experience life through the lens of aestheticism was to see it in a heightened form: as brighter, stranger, and more vivid. For the Aesthetes, art was best. But if one had to live in the world, then one should do so intensely, in passionate pursuit of the most exquisite sensations. The Aesthete's task was "to be present always at the focus where the greatest number of vital forces unite in their purest energy" (Pater 550). The Aesthete's promised reward was a perpetual state of "ecstasy" that would lift him or her out of the mundane.

This desire for escape from the mundane, fuelled also by the desire to flee the limitations imposed by racist laws and social codes, is part of what draws Jessie Fauset's fictional protagonists toward aestheticism--toward its demanding artistic creed, but also toward the privileged, decorative way of life associated with it. Her head filled with the ambition to create "queer beautiful things that are different from what we see around here" (*Confusion* 45), Joanna Marshall, the misguided heroine of Jessie Fauset's first novel, *There is Confusion* (1924), looks with disdain upon the lives of most Black women as examples of "mediocrity" of the sort despised by her white aesthetic predecessors:

> Joanna hated the word [mediocrity]; with her visual mind she saw it embodied in broken chairs, cold gravy, dingy linen, sticky children. She would never mind poverty half so much; she would contrive somehow to climb out of that. But ordinary tame mediocrity!
>
>   Besides, colored people had had enough of that. Not for Joanna!
> (146)

Similarly, transfixed by the spell of the art classes in which she studies drawing and by the glimpses she has enjoyed of upper-middle-class white life in Philadelphia and New York, Angela Murray, heroine of Fauset's second novel, *Plum Bun* (1929), dreams of presiding over an aesthetic salon:

> Her fancy envisaged a comfortable drawing-room (there *were* folks who
> used that term), peopled with distinguished men and women who did
> things, wrote and painted and acted,--people with a broad, cultural
> background behind them, or, lacking that, with the originality of thought
> and speech which comes from failing, deliberately failing, to conform to
> the pattern. Somewhere, she supposed, there must be coloured people like
> that. But she didn't know any of them. (*Plum Bun* 67).

Angela Murray's aesthetic impulses-- her cravings for "excitement," on the one
hand, and "refinement," on the other--lead her to a posture of social revolt. As
she declares one day to her horrified sister, Jinny,

> "I guess really I've had it in my mind for a long time, but last night it
> seemed to stand right out in my consciousness. Why should I shut myself
> off from all the things I want most,--clever people, people who do things,
> Art,--" her voice spelt it with a capital,--"travel and a lot of things which
> are in the world for everybody really but which only white people, as far
> as I can see, get their hands on." (78)

But as Fauset's protagonist soon discovers, to participate in the realm
of Art "with a capital" and to revel in the aesthetic fancy of living a life of
sensory self-indulgence, in deliberate rebellion against "the pattern," she must
be white. She must, moreover, give up all personal ties, as well as all political
allegiances, to the Black community that has nurtured and supported her. For
much of *Plum Bun*, Angela Murray does just that. Light-skinned enough to pass
for white, she goes so far, one day, as to deny her own darker-skinned sister in
a public place. Following the example of the Aesthetes, she disclaims any
connection between the sphere of beauty and sensation and the sphere of
ethical responsibility.

Angela has, in fact, taken her instruction in "passing" since childhood
from her mother, who has used her own light coloring as a way to enjoy the
sphere of bourgeois feminine consumerism, with its department-store shopping
and meals in hotel tearooms, from which she otherwise would be barred. But
Fauset's narrative is quick to absolve Mrs. Murray's occasional excursions as a
form of Black humor (so to speak)--as mere exercises in witty masquerade at
the expense of the white people around her--and to label these as "harmless,"
"charming," and "innocent, childish pleasures" (16)[1]. The narrator's judgment

upon Angela Murray is quite different, for the daughter's behavior does not signify a wish to add to the range of experiences available to Black women, so much as to deny and supposedly transcend such experiences, replacing them entirely with the opportunities reserved for a white elite. Angela pursues a sexual relationship with a rich white man, in the vain hope of persuading him to marry her. Later, she nearly accepts her art school's scholarship prize for study in Paris, even after a Black woman artist, whose work she respects, has been rudely turned down for the award on racist grounds. She has so thoroughly absorbed the standards of white aestheticism, which relieve the artist from ethical accountability, that the pain she causes to the Black women around her quite literally *pales* in importance, compared to the pleasure she reaps from contact with the world of beauty defined by and reserved exclusively for white women and for white artists.

Yet the plot of Fauset's novel is not a downward spiral. Through bitter lessons, Angela Murray does learn that there are types of beauty that transcend those to be found in a "drawing-room," and that there are more kinds of art than the one spelled "with a capital," as imagined by the Aesthetes. Fauset uses the gradual education of her heroine to encourage her own readers, whether African American or not, to see the bodies, the spirits, and the lives of Black women as artistic achievements--creations as monumental as any works produced by white European male aesthetic culture.

At a crucial juncture in the narrative, Angela Murray achieves a sort of epiphany--a descendant of those moments of revelation, at once sensuous and intellectual, experienced by the heroes of earlier aesthetic texts, such as Pater's *Marius the Epicurean* (1885). She observes Miss Powell, her Black classmate in art school, holding her own amid a circle of hostile white newspaper journalists, who are baiting her over the lost scholarship:

> Angela thought she had never seen the girl one half so attractive
> and exotic. She was wearing a thin silk dress, plainly made but of a
> flaming red from which the satin blackness of her neck rose, a straight
> column topped by her squarish, somewhat massive head. Her thin, rather
> flat dark lips brought into sharp contrast the dazzling perfection of her
> teeth; her high cheek bones showed a touch of red. To anyone whose
> ideals of beauty were not already set and sharply limited, she must have
> made a breathtaking appeal. As long as she sat quiescent in her rather

sulky reticence she made a marvellous figure of repose; focussing all the
attention of the little assemblage even as her dark skin and hair drew into
themselves and retained the brightness which the sun, streaming through
three windows, showered upon her. (*Plum Bun* 342)

The moment is significant, for Angela Murray's vision here celebrates the often-
denied physical beauty of the dark-skinned woman of color--the figure who
stands outside the ideal of "ivory flesh, [and] golden curls." But it matters for
other reasons. At this crisis in the text, it is in fact the protagonist's aesthetic
apprehension and appreciation of the scene that leads both to moral
identification with Miss Powell and, more important, to direct political action.
Fauset's artist-heroine--and indeed, Fauset herself as a novelist--gives a new
value to the Beautiful, yet does not reproduce the objectification of the beautiful
woman practiced by white male painters and writers. Rather, Angela Murray
progresses beyond the detachment of what feminist critics call the "male gaze"
and, struck by the "dignity. . . poise and aloofness" with which Miss Powell
holds the attacking white reporters at bay, makes the leap into both emotional
and political solidarity with another Black woman. As a result, Angela Murray
scornfully turns down the scholarship herself and then informs the shocked
crowd that she, too, is Black, doing so because she has been stirred on an
aesthetic and an ethical level. Indeed, this ethical movement has occurred
through, not despite, the agency of her aesthetics.

Just as in Jessie Fauset's own statement of principle in the Foreword to
The Chinaberry Tree, her next novel, what is present here are fruitful
contradictions held in a kind of tension, rather than self-cancelling
propositions. Angela Murray simultaneously apprehends both Miss Powell and
her political stand, in aesthetic terms, as beautiful and, in moral terms, as just.
In a place where no white male European aesthete would have looked for it--in
a scene of racial pride and of resistance on the part of an African American
woman--Fauset's protagonist locates her own "focus where the greatest number
of vital forces unite in their purest energy," as described in Pater's famous 1873
"Conclusion." To do so enables her to live more fully at that moment; yet,
unlike the "focus" imagined in Pater's dictum, this new version will also help
to ensure a fuller life for others. Newly inspired by her revelation, Angela
returns for a visit to Philadelphia, the site of her youth, and to the once-
despised culture of her African American neighborhood. There she feels an
attraction that is both a projection of nostalgia and an expression of reformed

aesthetic principles, as she remembers "the simple, stable fixtures of family life, the appetizing breakfast, the music, the church with its interesting, paintable types" (361). Her parents' house, too--the center of Black family life and of her own moral education--has become invested with the glamor formerly associated with the white salon or atelier. Even its daily routines now seem to the artist to be "beautiful" (366). As she confesses to Matthew, a Black former suitor, "'Funny how I almost pounded down the walls once upon a time trying to get away. Now I can't think of anything more marvellous than having such a place as this, here, there, anywhere, to return to'" (366).

Justice and the Beautiful come together for Angela Murray, as well as for the reader of the text, as though demonstrating the propositions raised by W. E. B. Du Bois in "Criteria of Negro Art." As Du Bois asked in 1926, three years before the publication of Fauset's *Plum Bun*,

> What has this Beauty to do with the world? What has Beauty to do with Truth and Goodness--with the facts of the world and the right actions of men? . . . . I am one who tells the truth and exposes evil and seeks with Beauty and for Beauty to set the world right. That somehow, somewhere eternal and perfect Beauty sits above Truth and Right I can conceive, but here and now and in the world in which I work they are for me unseparated and inseparable. (Du Bois 445-46)

It is hardly surprising that Fauset would have been conscious of Du Bois's pronouncements as she wrote her fiction, or that she would have felt impelled to respond to them. Throughout much of her literary career, he was her mentor, publishing some of her earliest stories in *The Crisis*. In 1919, he appointed Fauset as literary editor of *The Crisis*, the periodical most central to the Harlem Renaissance, and she continued working on it with him until 1926. Indeed, Fauset pays tribute to Du Bois in *Plum Bun* by sending her heroine off to Harlem, to attend a lecture by a Black intellectual named "Van Meier"--a respectful portrait of Du Bois himself. In that speech, as we are told by the narrator, the fictional character of Van Meier argues in favor of

> the deliberate introduction of beauty and pleasure into the difficult life of the American Negro . . . [and for] the acquisition . . . [of] a racial pride. A pride that enables us to find our own beautiful and praiseworthy, an intense chauvinism that is content with its own types . . . that loves its own

as the French love their country, because it is their own. (*Plum Bun* 218-
19)

In the context of Fauset's aestheticism, the mention of the French here is
significant. France was, of course, by tradition the spiritual homeland of
Aesthetes everywhere--a fact on which Oscar Wilde played in *A Woman of No
Importance* (1893), by suggesting "that when good Americans die they go to
Paris" and "when bad Americans die. . . they go to America." But in the
Twenties and Thirties, African-American artists and intellectuals were
following the lure of France and abandoning their more harshly racist
homeland in ever-growing numbers. Some went abroad in search of escape
from the grosser forms of oppression, such as segregation and lynching; others
went to achieve the public recognition denied them in their own country.

French culture in general, as well as Parisian society in particular, held
out a special promise of refuge, especially to artistically-minded, middle-class
women such as Fauset. During her career as an undergraduate at Cornell
University and then at the University of Pennsylvania, from which she received
an M.A. degree in 1919, Fauset studied French. She did additional coursework
at the Alliance Française and, on one of her trips to Europe, at the Sorbonne.
After her stint as a literary editor, moreover, she supported herself for many
years by teaching French in high schools, first in Washington, D.C.--until she
"tired of the growing racial discrimination shown there" (Kunitz 441)--and later
in New York City. The urge to abandon America, the country that had already
abandoned her in so many ways, and to explore the beauty of Blackness in
another setting was as strong in Jessie Fauset as in any of her Harlem
Renaissance associates.

Yet Paris did not equal paradise. Although female painters such as Lois
Mailou Jones, who was also laboring in Washington, DC (as a teacher of art at
Howard University), would enjoy increased opportunities in Paris to display
their work in galleries and to be recognized as important artists, other women,
such as Josephine Baker, would find themselves treated as exotic, scarcely
human spectacles. In a brief study of Jessie Fauset's career, Cheryl Wall does
cite Fauset's postive comments about France from a 1925 interview for the
Herald Tribune: "I like Paris because I find something here, something of
integrity, which I seem to have strangely lost in my own country" (Wall 71).
Flight to Paris, however, was not a permanent answer for Fauset, any more

than for her male contemporary, Langston Hughes. Both were struck by the sterility they quickly uncovered in European culture, as well as by the richness they continued to unearth in African American society. For Langston Hughes, this aesthetic revelation led to the publication in 1930 of a seven-line poem called, appropriately enough, "Aesthete in Harlem." It read in its entirety:

> Strange,
> That in this nigger place
> I should meet life face to face,
> When for years, I had been seeking
> Life in places gentler speaking
> Until I came to this near street
> And found Life--stepping on my feet.
>   (Hughes 182)

It is true that, in the poem's final line, "Life" (like Angela Murray's notion of "Art") is spelled with a capital letter. But the rather remote and hollow ideal implied by such a capitalization is transformed, when juxtaposed with the words "stepping on my feet." Hughes breaks through and out of the kind of artistic solipsism seemingly advocated by one of the dominant strands of European aestheticism. His reward for doing so comes with the discovery that by putting himself "face to face" with his own community and by refusing to distance himself from struggle, he can actually experience sensations more powerful and more intense than any that the world of white High Culture has to offer.

As both Hughes and Fauset agreed at the same juncture in history, if the Black artist wished to embrace aestheticism and (to paraphrase Walter Pater) to burn with "a hard, gemlike flame," that flame would burn harder and brighter in Harlem than in Paris, or those other "places gentler speaking." To avoid either confrontation and engagement with injustice or solidarity with one's racial community and to flee instead to the illusory panacea of France was to doom oneself to an irreversible state of loss and lack--to discover, as Angela Murray does in *Plum Bun*, when she finally pays her own way to Paris, "that she had never felt so lonely in her life" (375).

There is no more tragic character in any of Jessie Fauset's four novels than Teresa Cary of the ironically-titled *Comedy: American Style* (1933), who arrives far too late at similar conclusions about the impossibility of locating what she needs in those places of "gentler speaking." Influenced by her mother's acceptance of the prevailing ideologies of middle-class society-- notions, especially, of the superiority of white skin, of European culture, and of masculine models of high Art ("spelt," as Fauset says, "with a capital")--the light-skinned Teresa opts for a career of "passing" and thus of of unproductive imitation.   She abandons America for France and for a Frenchman who chauvinistically instructs her in how to appreciate, in the Paterian sense, the ancient "beauties" of Toulouse:

> He took . . . [her] to see the marvellous Church of St. Sernin, which dates
> from the third century, and showed. . . [her] the tombs of the early counts
> of Toulouse. . . . It was he who opened . . . [her] eyes to the beauties of
> those fine old Renaissance buildings . . . . (*Comedy* 174-75)

But this performance of married life as a "white" woman in France turns out to be unsatisfactory in every respect. Cut off emotionally through a union with a   bloodless and undemonstrative husband, cut off intellectually from the current of ideas of the day and confined to the narrow sphere of the proper petit-bourgeois housewife, and cut off socially from her own family members, who can never visit because they are dark-skinned enough to give her away, Teresa falls into despair. Her story concludes, in the words of the narrator, as "Gradually her expectation of a change died away and she settled into an existence that was colorless, bleak and futile" (183). This absence of color in Teresa's life has been rendered inevitable, not so much by her choice of a particular French husband, but by her earlier capitulation to her mother's demand that she pass as white and move in circles where she can do so with the least danger of exposure. Teresa does encounter "color"-- indeed, both aesthetic and emotional excitement in France--but it is among the "great, black Senegalese quartered there [in Toulon], speaking in some instances, beautiful, unaccented French, [who] stirred her imagination" (182). As she cannot, of course, risk her own precarious identity as a white woman by associating more intimately with these Africans, her freedom to enjoy the aesthetic pleasure of "colorful" contact is doubly restricted.

Against the "colorless" ends of those who deny their color, Fauset juxtaposes the career of a very different protagonist, such as Laurentine Strange from her third novel, *The Chinaberry Tree* (1931). Subtitled *A Novel of American*

Life and set in small-town New Jersey, Fauset's text is in part a celebration of the beauty of rootedness--both as a figurative and a literal concept--through the image of the connection between Laurentine and the chinaberry tree growing on the land where she was born. Like other figures in Fauset's fictional narratives, Laurentine, too, is temperamentally an Aesthete, who feels the pull of sensation and excitement and who says to herself, "Give me life, give me contacts, give me the good times which are every young girl's due. Don't leave me here to perish, to dry, to wither" (*Chinaberry* 12). Yet, unlike the unfortunate Teresa Cary, Laurentine learns early to feed her own roots upon the nourishment of her environment and heritage. She draws strength and inspiration from the largely female community that surrounds her. In becoming, moreover, a brilliant designer and maker of dresses, Laurentine discovers an aesthetic outlet that not only offers a satisfying alternative to high Art "with a capital," but that allows her to give something back to this community--especially, to the many Black women whose beauty she acknowledges and enhances through her designs. As one of her friends and customers gushes, "enraptured," while Laurentine places "the cloth up against Mrs. Ismay's skin and drape[s] with her magic fingers the stuff into marvelous fold and line" to make a somewhat decadent, androgynously-cut pair of lounging pajamas, "Oh, Laurentine, it'll be wonderful! Nobody thinks of such delightful color combinations as you, or gets such lovely lines" (146-47). Her praise could apply just as well, however, not merely to Laurentine but to Jessie Fauset herself, a prose artist of "color combinations" and of "lovely lines" throughout her fictions. Such diverse and imaginative "combinations" are only possible, of course, in a context where racial differences are acknowledged and embraced as material of equal aesthetic value, rather than as the stuff of hierarchical rankings. In the worlds of misguided Aesthetes, such as Angela Murray or Teresa Cary, who shrink from the full spectrum of color that includes blackness, art itself (whether "with a capital" or without) must ultimately be the loser.

Over the almost ten-year course of producing her four novels, Fauset repeatedly reworked aestheticism to turn it into a concept newly applicable to and useful for Black women in the United States, perhaps doing so with greatest success in *Plum Bun*. There, she forged both a creed and a practice for the artist-protagonist that would unite activism with Paterian "appreciation"-- that would acknowledge the spectacular pleasures of the idealized feminine body, yet make these the accompaniment to political struggle. In achieving this,

Fauset created a version of aestheticism that was no longer "pure" in its function or goals, but "mixed."

Plum Bun would, for instance, draw upon the form of the fairy tale, as commentators such as Jacquelyn Y. McLendon--who has called it a "bad," or anti-romantic, fairy tale-- have often noted (McLendon 28-49). In doing so, it would build upon a narrative strategy pioneered by an earlier Aesthete, Oscar Wilde, who was famous for deploying fairy-tale structures ironically for the purposes of social criticism and social satire in *The Happy Prince and Other Tales* (1888) and in *A House of Pomegranates* (1891). Yet, in an example of striking "color combination," Fauset's novel would bring together this frame of self-conscious aesthetic irony, which it owed to Wilde's influence, with passages that erased all distance and forswore the pose of detachment, in order to create direct engagement with Black cultural issues and generate political movement. This was especially true in the section which dramatized the public lecture by Van Meier (the character based on Du Bois), with its call for a new "racial pride" among Black people. Here, Fauset showed the effect of such ideas upon the audience in terms that echoed both the European aesthetic fairy-tale formulae and the very different rhetorical traditions of African American sermons and political speeches, which emphasized inspiration for the sake of action: "Dark, drooping faces took on an expression of ecstatic uplift, it was as though they suddenly saw themselves, transformed by racial pride as princes in a strange land in temporary serfdom, princes whose children would know freedom" (*Plum Bun*, 218-19).

Embracing these disparate and contradictory traditions, Fauset's aestheticism (unlike earlier manifestations of the aesthetic movement) also addressed directly the contradictions of race, a category that may sometimes be constructed as absolute, but is never actually so. At the very moment when the light-skinned Angela Murray apprehends a dark-skinned woman engaged in an act of political resistance as the Beautiful and, through this apprehension, enters into a position of resistance herself, all the boundaries blur that neatly divide blackness from whiteness, American from European locations, and masculine gazes from feminist perspectives. In appropriating and revising aestheticism, Jessie Fauset was actually keeping alive a female counter-tradition that had made itself known earlier within the aesthetic movement, particularly in the 1890s. Her predecessors in redefining "art" and "beauty" were late-Victorian feminists whose published texts had, by the 1920s, fallen into nearly total neglect and obscurity. Their efforts were unlikely to be known by Fauset. These writers had, nevertheless, laid a groundwork for the reconsideration of aesthetic practice through their own attempts "to rescue the worship of beauty, so prominent in aesthetic doctrine, from its association with the exploitation of women as nothing more than beautiful 'occasions' for masculine discovery, theorizing, and reverie" (Stetz 31) and, in a number of cases, to expose the gender hierarchies of male aesthetes. But what they had done only rarely, if at all, was to confront the subject of race, in relation either to "art" or to the Beautiful.

"Art," as Jessie Fauset demonstrated to her early-twentieth-century American readers, need not be limited to what the narrator of *The Chinaberry Tree* labels "the rather obvious poetry of beauty and of romance, Tennyson, Rossetti and Swinburne . . . [or] the intensely masculine emotionalism of Browning, the divine nebulousness of the Ode on the Intimations of Immortality" (139), as recited by the confused and still questing young Black man, Malory Forten. Instead, art, as practiced by *The Chinaberry Tree*'s Laurentine Strange, can also take such material, concrete expressions as dressmaking and room-decoration--those often despised feminine accomplishments that are part of what Bettina Aptheker terms "the dailiness of women's lives" (Aptheker 39-74). Clearly, Fauset's preferred strain of nineteenth-century aestheticism was the one that had emphasized the importance of handicrafts and of domestic furnishings. In Fauset's novels, the Beautiful, moreover, can locate itself in the tones, shadings, and highlights of Black women's skin--what, in *Comedy: American Style*, Fauset's narrator describes as "the rich mingling and contrast of coloring not only in clothing but in faces . . . the vividness of Marise's nut-brown skin. . . beside the lemon-clear skin of Sylvia Raymond" (57-58).

Long before Alice Walker found, in the essay "In Search of Our Mothers' Gardens" (1974), the equivalent of a museum hung with masterpieces in the flowerbeds behind her mother's house, Jessie Fauset paved the way toward Walker's discovery by insisting that communities of Black women were in themselves masterpieces, as well as the producers of masterpieces. Hers was in many ways a forward-looking, indeed an avant-garde position. Yet, because of the problematic nature of the materials she employed in making this point, it has often been easy to discount Fauset's work. After all, her fiction was largely aimed at and chiefly accessible to middle-class Black readers, who were familiar with the tenets of white aestheticism and who could appreciate the radical swerves and transformations of its conventions that she was offering. Her literary imagination, moreover, could be termed retrogressive, for it remained in dialogue with an earlier generation of writers who were rapidly being discarded by Twenties and Thirties modernists.

Thus, important African American critics, such as Deborah McDowell, still feel the need to bemoan Fauset's over-reliance upon "familiar genres and their conventions," even as they laud the novelist for deploying some of those genres to "subversive purposes: (McDowell xvii). For other critics, even that supposed effect of subversion is in doubt. In "The Quicksands of Representation," Hazel V. Carby asserts that "ultimately the conservatism of Fauset's ideology dominates her texts," and that Fauset's is an ideology of "black middle-class morality" (Carby 80-81) as constricting and as limited in its applications as its white counterpart.

I do not wish to minimize these obstacles to reconsidering the nature of Fauset's work or to revaluing her appropriations and adaptations of aestheticism. Nonetheless, I would juxtapose such critiques as Carby's with what the novelist Alice Walker has said of another problematic and sometimes disappointing figure, Phillis Wheatley, who has also been accused of conservatism and of over-dependence upon the literary traditions of the white oppressors:

> But at last, Phillis, we understand. No more snickering when your stiff,
> struggling, ambivalent lines are forced on us. . . . It is not so much what
> you sang, as that you kept alive, in so many of our ancestors, *the notion of
> song*. (Author's own emphasis) (Walker 237)

Jessie Fauset employed the materials which, as a writer laboring at a particular cultural moment, she found ready to hand; chief among these was the legacy of aestheticism. Using its philosophy and practices as a starting point, she took up the challenge that W. E. B. Du Bois had issued to the artists of the Harlem Renaissance and tried to keep alive the *notion of beauty* for her Black audiences. That the results illuminated for readers then and now the ambiguous and contradictory position of the Black woman--as simultaneously the site, the perceiver, and the creator of the Beautiful, while also an active political agent--should be something to acknowledge with gratitude, rather than to deplore.

Margaret D. Stetz

NOTES

[1]For an alternative interpretation of Mattie Murray's passing see Teresa Zackodnik's essay on page 57 of this volume.

WORKS CITED

Aptheker, Bettina. *Tapestries of Life: Women's Work, Women's Consciousness, and the Meaning of Daily Experience.* Amherst: U of Massachusetts P, 1989.

Carby, Hazel V. "The Quicksands of Representation: Rethinking Black Cultural Politics." In *Reading Black, Reading Feminist: A Critical Anthology* . Ed. Henry Louis Gates, Jr. New York: Meridian, 1990, 76-90.

Collins, Patricia Hill. "The Politics of Diversity: Issues and Challenges." Keynote Address. Making Connections V. Conference of the National Association for Women in Catholic Higher Education. Boston   College. 30 June 2000.

Du Bois, W. E. B. "Criteria of Negro Art." In *Writings in Periodicals Edited by W. E. B. Du Bois: Selections from THE CRISIS*. Vol. 2, 1926-1934 of *The Complete Published Works of W. E. B. Du Bois*. Ed. Herbert Aptheker. New York: Kraus-Thomson, 1983.

Fauset, Jessie Redmond. *The Chinaberry Tree*. New York: Frederick A. Stokes, 1931.

-----. *Comedy, American Style*. New York: Frederick A. Stokes, 1933.

-----. *Plum Bun: A Novel Without a Moral* . 1929; rpt. Boston: Beacon, 1990.

-----. *There Is Confusion*. 1924; rpt. Boston: Northeastern U P, 1989.

Freedman, Jonathan. *Professions of Taste: Henry James, British Aestheticism, and Commodity Culture*. Stanford: Stanford UP, 1990.

Gagnier, Regenia. "Production, Reproduction, and Pleasure in Victorian Aesthetics and Economics." In *Victorian Sexual Dissidence*. Ed.   Richard Dellamora. Chicago: U of Chicago P, 1999. 127-145.

Hough, Graham. *The Last Romantics*. 1947; rpt. London: Methuen, 1961.

Hughes, Langston. "Aesthete in Harlem." *Opportunity* (June 1930): 182.

Hurston, Zora Neale. *Dust Tracks on a Road: An Autobiography*. Ed. Robert E. Hemenway. 2nd ed. Urbana and Chicago: U of Illinois P, 1984.

Kunitz, Stanley J. and Howard Haycraft, eds. *Twentieth Century Authors: A Biographical Dictionary of Modern Literature*. New York: H. W. Wilson, 1942. 441-42.

McDowell, Deborah E. "Introduction: Regulating Midwives." *Plum Bun: A Novel Without a Moral*. 1929; rpt. Boston, Beacon, 1990. ix-xxxiii.

McLendon, Jacquelyn Y. *The Politics of Color in the Fiction of Jessie Fauset and Nella Larsen* . Charlottesville and London: U P of Virginia, 1995.

Pater, Walter. "Conclusion to *Studies in the History of the Renaissance*." In *Prose of the Victorian Period*. Ed. William E. Buckler. Boston: Houghton Mifflin, 1958. 550-553.

Prins, Yopie. "Greek Maenads, Victorian Spinsters." In *Victorian Sexual Dissidence*. Ed. Richard Dellamora. Chicago: U of Chicago P, 1999. 43- 81.

Psomiades, Kathy Alexis. *Beauty's Body: Femininity and Representation in British Aestheticism* . Stanford: Stanford U P, 1997.

Schaffer, Talia. *The Forgotten Female Aesthetes: Literary Culture in Late-Victorian England* . Charlottesville: U P of Virginia, 2000.

Schaffer, Talia and Kathy Alexis Psomiades. "Introduction." *Women and British Aestheticism*. Eds. Talia Schaffer and Kathy Alexis Psomiades. Charlottesville: U P of Virginia, 1999. 1-22.

Small, Ian. "Introduction." *The Aesthetes: A Sourcebook*. London: Routledge & Kegan Paul, 1979. xi-xxix.

Stetz, Margaret D. "Debating Aestheticism from a Feminist Perspective." In *Women and British Aestheticism*. Eds. Talia Schaffer and Kathy Alexis Psomiades. Charlottesville: U P of Virginia, 1999. 25-43.

Walker, Alice. "In Search of Our Mother's Gardens." In *In Search of Our Mothers' Gardens*. New York: Harcourt Brace Jovanovich, 1983. 231-243.

Wall, Cheryl A. "Jessie Redmon Fauset: Traveling in Place." *Women of the Harlem Renaissance*. Bloomington & Indianapolis: Indiana U P, 1995. 33-84.

13.

"I MAY CREATE A MONSTER": CHERRÍE MORAGA'S TRANSCULTURAL CONUNDRUM[1]

Cherríe Moraga's celebrated and influential contribution to Chicana and Mexican American identity debates, *Loving in the War Years: lo que nunca pasó por sus labios* (1983), constructs a journey from being closeted, both as a lesbian and a Chicana, to a public identification as a Chicana lesbian. Moraga deploys the coming-out trope to imply the physical as well as identificatory endspace in which she can "be" a Chicana lesbian, and be safely. At the same time Moraga emphasizes that her sexualized status is engendered and qualified by the conjunction of Americas analogized and literalized by her parents' union: "I am the daughter of a Chicana and anglo" (vi). Indeed, Moraga claims that the bridging of rival, clearly differentiated Anglo and Chicano value systems is fundamental to her securing of a Chicana lesbian identity inside the U.S.A.'s borders: "I think: what is my responsibility to my roots: both white and brown, Spanish-speaking and English? I am a woman with a foot in both worlds. I refuse the split. I feel the necessity for dialogue" (58).

However, Moraga's quest for dialogic bridging is not without risk. In a poem that appears shortly after she disavows "the split," a rather less confident Moraga writes:

> To gain the word to describe the loss,
> I risk losing everything.
> I may create a monster . . . (63)

The Moraga of this poem does not quite figure herself as the embodied bridge between rival racial, cultural, linguistic, and gender-sexual taxonomies. This Moraga is fearful. Indeed, as her book's title suggests, this is the Moraga around and over whom ethnic, linguistic, and sexual classifications battle. The bridge she seeks may not reconcile Anglo and Chicano; rather, it may engender a neocultural identification that is potentially inimical to, yet fundamentally modulated by, both Anglo and Chicano.

A document of Moraga's ontogenesis as a Chicana lesbian, *Loving in the War Years* thus reveals a fundamental difficulty — a transcultural conundrum[2] — in the ongoing, "necessary dialogue[s]" between Chicano/a and Anglo, Chicano and Chicana, Chicana and Chicana, heterosexual and lesbian, and between and within subjects who straddle or confound such categories. The dialogues are as necessary and risky now as they were when Moraga's book first appeared. According to Susana Chávez-Silverman, Chicana writers concerned to counter hegemonic Chicano and Anglo stereotyping of the Chicana lesbian often require their readers and critics to "acknowledg[e] the tension between the temptation of the transgressive and the refusal to allow the figure of the lesbian to completely inhabit an essentialized exteriority to the dominant discourse" (39). In Moraga's case, that tension impels a bipartite journey into identity. On the one hand, she wants eventually to embody a cultural, racial and sexual bridge between Anglo and Chicano. On the other hand, she also desires a return to a "feminine" space of certainty as her Mexican mother's brown, lesbian, Spanish-speaking daughter. In my response to this doubled, troubled quest, I am interested in how Moraga manages the names accruing to her racialized body, sexuality, and transculturated place. Does Moraga regard "Anglo" and "Chicana" as natural, immutable, uncontaminated, and mutually exclusive categories? If so, does she find refuge in fixity rather than contradiction because she feels that those categories might, in fact, be best left unbridged, given that the alternative may be an unforseen, potentially "monstrous" Chicana lesbian neoculturation? In Chávez-Silverman's words, does Moraga aim to "reverse the valency" of Anglo and Chicana and other dichotomized identifications "without problematizing the underpinning structure" of domination, thus "risk[ing] inevitable containment" by such categories? (38).

Passing *la güera*[white ruling class] back into the generic Chicana

The difficulties that beset Moraga's writerly project in *Loving in the War Years* are apparent in the introductory "Amar en los años de guerra," the Spanish words replicating the English of her book's title. Here Moraga describes how her grandmother's death signifies a closure that blocks the quest for identity she wants to document: "And what goes with her? My claim to an internal dialogue where el gringo does not penetrate? Su memoria de noventa y seis años [her memory of ninety-six years] going back to a time where 'nuestra cultura' [our culture] was not the subject of debate. *I write this book because we are losing ourselves to the gavacho* [gringo]. *I mourn my brother in this*" (italics hers, iii). If Moraga's brother has already sold out to the gringo and thus precluded a Chicano-inflected Anglo status on his part, Moraga is already pointing to a counter-reactive bridge-burning to prevent the gringo from modulating her own view of self. The trouble for Moraga is that a somatic sign of those modulations is to be found in the paleness that has enabled her to pass as white.

According to Harryette Mullen's analysis of African-American identity tactics in the highly charged racialized terrains of the U.S.A., passing is a pivotal mechanism in "the cultural production of whiteness" (72). The adoption of a white persona "requires an active denial of black identity . . . by the individual who passes from black to white, while the chosen white identities are strengthened . . . by the presumption that white identities are racially pure" (72). Mullen regards such passings as performances aimed at "mov[ing] from the margin to the center of American identity" (77), with the consequence that African-American passers are often accused of racial treachery, dishonesty, and complicity with a racialized white hegemony (73). Such accusations are dependent on definitions of white and black racialized categories as mutually exclusive, immutable, and knowable facts (73). Moreover, as Valerie Smith has shown, the "consequences" of passing are "distributed differentially on the basis of gender"; passing women receive more punitive attention than men (43). Marjorie Garber pushes this point to describe the history of racial passings in the United States as one of double "drag," nineteenth-century slave narratives, for example, providing many instances of passings over racial and gender lines. While such passings were "a necessity, not a pleasure" (284), they nonetheless "reveal[ed] the masquerade that is already in place" (282). For Garber, the wilful disregard of racial and gendered conventions betrays the *"structuring and confounding"* of both race and gender, with the result that the categories are confirmed to be provisional rather than fixed, knowable only as simulations that conceal as natural the production of gendered and racialized values over time and in different places (italics hers, 17). If "brown" is substituted for "black," these observations about racial passing have implications for Moraga's account in which, moreover, passing as a white woman is complicated by the sexual passing announced by Moraga's occupancy of the closet.

Moraga defines herself as an oxymoronic representative of "a colored kind of white people" (74), a statement that would seem to acknowledge the inherent instability of racialized designations. Alongside lesbian sexuality, race features in *Loving in the War Years* as a problematics of identity played out on and "under the skin" (54). As a light-skinned Chicana, *una güera*, she could and did pass as white. Passing allowed her class and educational advantages denied to darker, working-class Chicanos/as. Thus, although Moraga points out that throughout her studies at a private Los Angelean college she was both alienated from and fearful of the "white and rich" students around her because her family's class and cultural background were decidedly less privileged, such alienation and fear also led her to regard education, and the upward-class mobility she attributed to it, as a secure route by which "whiteness" could be consolidated: "White was right. Period. I could pass. If I got educated enough, there would never be no telling" (55). Passing also enabled Moraga to move within a white-dominated feminist culture as a "lesbian." In Moraga's early adulthood, whiteness thus metaphorized the attractions of economic security and sexual solidarity:

> *It was whiteness and . . . safety.*
> Old lovers that carried their whiteness like freedom/ and breath/ and
> light. Their shoulders, always straight-backed and sweetly oiled for color.
> In their faces, the luxury of trust.
> *It was whiteness and money.*
> In this way, she had learned to be a lesbian. (italics hers, 39)

These learned meanings of whiteness — sexual identity, social power, class privilege and security — were even more attractive for Moraga given that her paleness, her lesbianism, and her deculturated Spanish, precluded involvement in Chicano activism and identification as a Chicana: "No soy tonta [I'm not stupid]. I would have been murdered in El Movimiento — light-skinned, unable to speak Spanish well enough to hang; miserably attracted to women and fighting it; and constantly questioning all authority, including men's. I felt I did not belong there" (113).

Yet, Moraga's inculcation into the power of whiteness began earlier than the above outline would suggest. In her poem "Later, She Met Joyce," she describes her school friendship with Joyce, the first girl Moraga kissed, and with whom Moraga as Cecilia,

> . . . formed their own
> girls' gang with code words & rhymes
> that played itself cooly [sic]
> on *this* side of trouble
> they got separated by the summer. (19)

The summer marks a temporal barrier between adolescent intimacy and the parameters of divergent Chicana adulthoods. When Cecilia again meets up with her old friend, she realizes that Joyce has become a street-wise *pachuca*, a member of what "Cecilia's momma called/ *a difernt claz o' people*" (20). Joyce's skin has fixed her social position, "wearing/ shiny clothes and never getting/ to college," in direct opposition to Moraga's own dryly noted class progress: "Later that year/ Cecilia was picked/ by the smart/ white girls/ for president" (21). Moraga calls this form of passing "bleaching," or a becoming Anglo enabled by upward class mobility. Since her Mexican mother strove to "protect her children from poverty and illiteracy," Moraga was bleached, for "the more effectively we could pass in the white world, the better guaranteed our future" (51). Bleaching signified the mother's repression of the Mexican under the whitening aegis of the father's surname, "a badge of membership to the white open-door policy club" (96-97). But this account of class and racialized mobility is tempered by the fact that Moraga willingly bleached herself to gain both an education and a lesbian persona, the latter a possibility that Moraga claims is inconceivable in her mother's culture.

Nonetheless, Moraga attempts to critique the narrative of whiteness-equals-success by revealing how that equation is perpetuated, yet undercut, performatively. As she sees it, passing is often an economically motivated strategy requiring denial. It may be justified as a defensive strategy undertaken in compliance with discourses that negativize darkness: "once my light skin and good English saved me and my lover from arrest. And I'd use it again . . . to save our skins" (97). The embraces of whiteness does not, however, protect her from violence: "the joys of looking like a white girl ain't so great since I realized I could be beaten on the street for being a dyke" (52). For Moraga, the contradictory motivations for racial passing are always related to her marginalization as a lesbian. Differently regulated racial and sexual knowledges make certain bodies and desires invisible and fix them in the social margins beyond knowing: "What I never quite understood until this writing is that to be without a sex—to be bodiless—as I sought to be to escape the burgeoning sexuality of my adolescence, my confused early days of active heterosexuality, and later my panicked lesbianism, means also to be without a race" (125). Similar to Fanon's idea of "putting on the white world" (27), racelessness here refers to an accession to a whiteness consolidated by the denial of non-white ancestry. "Putting on" whiteness also signifies an occupation of the sexualized closet, the implication being that passing as white is paralleled by the denial of lesbian desire. To undo the effects of "bleaching," then, Moraga decides that she has to put off the Anglo in order to claim the brown Chicana as the basis for her identity. Moraga must "work to remember" the real Chicananess hidden beneath the masquerade of whiteness:

> I cannot
> choose nor forget
> how simple
> to fall back
> upon rehearsed racial memory.
> I work to remember
> what I never dreamed possible (75)

Moraga thus characterizes her reclamation of an authentic brownness in terms of a shift from being a *"white girl gone brown to the blood color of my mother"* until she reaches the point when, "as it should be, dark women come to me" (italics hers, 61).

The irrepressible desire to permanently pass *la güera* back into the generic dark Chicana provides the theme for "Feed the Mexican Back Into Her." In this poetic dialogue with her cousin, Moraga attempts to dispense with "the difference between us," between a dark and a pale Chicana (146). She strives to goad her cousin's rage against discursive legislations of their skins: "I meant to tell her how I thought of her as not brown at all, but black—an english-speaking dark-girl, wanting to spit the white words out of her— be black angry. I meant to encourage" (146). Moraga then recalls a childhood photograph of the two girls and its negative in which

I am dark
and profane/ you light & bleached-boned
my guts are grey & black coals glowing. (147)

By means of this inversion Moraga literally exposes the repressions and silences that perpetuate the dark-light dichotomy so that, in the poem's last stanza, she may come out as a *mestiza*, a woman of mixed race, and the cousins may unite under that collective rubric:

> *Call it the darkness you still wear*
> *on the edge of your skin*
> *the light you reach for*
> *across the table*
> *and into my heart.* (147)

But what does this passing back to dark(er) Chicananess imply for that category? To transcend whiteness and become brown, Moraga must make a stand on one side of each binarized link in a chain of discretely imagined racialized (white-brown/ *mestiza*), cultural (Anglo-Chicano), gendered (male-female), and sexualized (heterosexual-lesbian) entities, thus fulfilling her contention that "To be a woman fully necessitated my claiming the race of my mother. My brother's sex was white. Mine, brown" (94). But Moraga fails to extrapolate from her knowledge of her rehearsed whitenesses, or from her learned lesbianism, that putting on a brown persona confirms that guise as similarly provisional and discursively modulated. Passing herself back into the generic Chicana, Moraga appears to discount how her move inaugurates what Garber calls a "category crisis," a "failure of definitional distinction, a borderline that becomes permeable, that permits of border crossings from one (apparently distinct category to another)" (16). Although her own *mestizaje* spoils white and brown distinctions, Moraga needs the *mestiza* Chicana to be a coherent category. But she does not quite "work with 'race' as a political concept *knowing* it is a biological fiction" (Fuss 91). The racialized trouble of Moraga's "work" is marked by a double, but wilfully maintained, misrecognition: of the biological fiction of whiteness as dispensable to the *mestiza* category; and of the *mestiza* as non-fiction, as a transcendent signifier rather than a discursively impelled brown rival to her white appearances. Moraga claims that the pale Anglo self can be put on or off at will, but she does not admit that her Chicana self at once confirms the same self-interest and enjoys the same mutability, even if that Chicana self aims for—and rightfully so—political ends at the expense of the discursive powers of whiteness and homophobia.

Those ends, in this instance, are not quite strategically justified by Moraga's apparent embrace of essentialism. Rather, this scenario of jettisoning and adopting rival racialized selfhoods requires of Moraga a faith in what John Beverley calls the liberal assumption "that 'conversation' is possible across power/exploitation divides that radically differentiate the participants" (39). In Moraga's case, the racialized shift from "untrue" white to "truer" brown, a move intended as a political gesture of affiliation with the brown Chicana, betrays an unacknowledged self-subalternization. That is, Moraga rhetorically disavows her access to an array of privileges (educational and intellectual, class, somatic paleness) in order to ally herself with the Chicana subaltern against patriarchal, heteronormative and racist hegemonies. Nonetheless, those privileges, most notably what Beverley calls "the very mechanism of formal education" (139) that has enabled Moraga to write and publish, inevitably confirm Moraga's intellectual, class and transcultural distance from her desired brown Chicana identification. Her "return" to brownness occludes the challenge posed by her passing history to "her initial class or group base" (139). Moraga cannot simply be "one of them," for she "is in fact speaking in the place of the subaltern—speaking a necessarily different language" (139). Determined, in Chow's words, "to *unlearn*" her submission to fixity (25), Moraga nonetheless claims to pass into an untransculturated place where she will be known only in terms of an authentic and fixed Chicananess, now defined against and beyond the very privileges that have always already problematized her relation to that identification.

Moraga's own private Aztlán

By 1983 there was another place of authenticated Chicanoness into which Moraga might have passed: Aztlán, the mythical homeland appropriated by the Chicano movement in the 1960s, and identified with the U.S. Southwest. Aztlán also signified a utopian future destination, metaphorizing the Chicano struggle by joining a nativist past, current activism, and a liberated future into a teleology of collective resistance. Ten years after the publication of *Loving in the War Years,* Moraga celebrated her sense of belonging to this mythical and geocultural space. In her essay "Queer Aztlán: The Reformation of the Chicano Tribe," Aztlán is resignified to admit its 1990s queer sons and daughters (*Last Generation* 145-74).[3] Although the essay admonished Chicanos for their continuing fear of Chicano/a queers and chastised Chicano queers for continuing to benefit from Chicano male privilege, its celebratory account of Moraga's spiritual bonding with the landscape conveyed a clear message: Moraga had found her rightful place in a newly queered Chicano imaginary. In *Loving in the War Years*, however, Aztlán is a decidedly less attractive destination. Aztlán cannot be extricated from an androcentric, homophobic nationalist discourse that Moraga feels has hitherto neither overcome its mythical blindness, nor accorded her lesbianism a space or voice. In fact, in the years leading up to 1983, Aztlán was an authenticating place to which Moraga could only have gained admission as a straight and dark-skinned Chicana.

In "A Long Line of Vendidas [Traitors]," Moraga's refutation of the Chicano Movement is unequivocal. She berates proponents of Aztlán for "believing in this ideal past or imagined future so thoroughly and single-mindedly that finding solutions to present-day inequities" was neglected (129). This dispute resurfaces in her poem "Passage" where she distances herself from the Chicano liberatory agenda:

> there is a very old wound in me
> between my legs
> where I have bled, not to birth
> pueblos or revolutionary
> concepts or simple
> sucking children (44)

In these lines Moraga's sexed status, marked by menstruation, cannot be aligned with the Mexican ideals of "woman" as national or familial mother, or even as an *Adelita*, female agent of the Mexican revolution.[4] Not only does Moraga lack common experiences with these women, but within Chicano and Mexican cultures her lesbianism is regarded as a sign of treachery against gender and sexual conventions. As a traitor, Moraga becomes a modern-day Malinche. I examine Moraga's treatment of this oppressive gender paradigm later, while noting here how awareness of "a memory/ of some ancient/ betrayal" leads Moraga to dispute the Chicano movement's rhetorical reclamation of the U.S. Southwest as a homeland:

your mouth opens, I long for dryness.
The desert, untouched.
Sands swept without sweat.

Aztlan. [sic] (44)

For Moraga, Aztlán's redemptive promise, "This safety of the desert," signifies a myth with no relation to material conditions or struggles, let alone to lesbian desires: "My country was not like that/ Neither was yours" (45). Moraga later elaborates on this point by arguing that Aztlán's proponents have excluded lesbian Chicanas by consolidating the Chicano male control of "the family unit . . . to safeguard it from the death-dealings of the anglo" (110). Chicano militants merely replicated the logic by which the traditional Chicano patriarch struggles to "determine how, when, and with whom his women—mother, wife, and daughter—are sexual." According to that logic, since "lesbianism . . . challenges the very foundation of la familia," lesbians are stigmatized, suppressed, or most commonly, simply overlooked in a culture that either disparages or disregards sexual desires not centred on and defined by men (110-11).

Nonetheless, in *Loving in the War Years* it is possible to recognize Moraga's nascent moves to reimagine Aztlán in lesbian-friendly, if not yet queer-friendly, terms. Having rejected the Chican*o* Aztlán, Moraga advocates a liberatory restructuring of her family into her own private Aztlán so that it may accommodate its Chican*a* lesbian daughter. Curiously, this lesbianization of the family is shadowed by a wistful romanticization of the very Chicano patriarch Moraga critiques throughout her book: "I sometimes fantasized some imaginary father, dark and benevolent, who might . . . remind us that we still *were* a family" (93). Moraga's Anglo father, it seems, was of a different paternal species. He permitted Moraga the opportunities for public movement and individual assertion that were denied to, and unthinkable for, the female children of traditional Chicano patriarchs. As Moraga says, "Had I been born of a Chicano father, I sometimes think I never would have been able to write a line or participate in a demonstration, having to repress all questioning in order that the ultimate question of my sexuality would never emerge" (112-13).

The tension revealed between the wistful desire for a "real" Chicano patriarch father and this admission of paternally tolerated public mobility is revelatory in another sense. It signals a crisis of authenticity directly related to the fact that Moraga had an Anglo father and thus may be regarded by herself and others as never quite Chicana enough. While this fraught situation understandably leads Moraga down contradictory paths, it has also engendered misreadings of Moraga's identity manoeuvres. For example, Leigh Gilmore has stated, "In the family home, Moraga learned the sexual and gender politics of Chicano culture. Relentlessly patriarchal and homophobic, the home was represented through these oppressions as the last stand against assimilation" (193). Ostensibly motivated by an admiration for Moraga's "guerilla autobiographical" interventions into Chicana identity debates, Gilmore's thesis can be sustained only by ignoring two facts. First, as already noted, Moraga's mother actively encouraged her children to pass as white, speak English, and gain an "Anglo" education, in short, to become Anglo. These imperatives indicate that Moraga's family home was not organised unequivocally to resist assimilation. Second, Moraga's challenge to Chicano patriarchy is based on a family, her own family, with a phantom Chicano patriarch. Paradoxically, this very patriarchal lack is embodied and confirmed by her Anglo father, a presence who also indicates that, at least for Moraga's mother, the home does not signify a bulwark against Anglo hegemony. At the same time, however, the power to interpellate the family's children into Chicano bodily logics is invested in the mother, and to some degree, in the extended family of women (aunts, cousins) on the mother's side. The women Moraga claims taught her "about loving, singing, crying, telling stories, speaking with the heart and hands, even having a sense of my own soul" (54), are also the women through whom Moraga learns and experiences the gendered hierarchies of Chicano patriarchy and homophobia.

Such tensions between the matrilineal transmission of Chicano bodily logics and the consequences of the mother's desires for her children to pass as Anglo are evident throughout Moraga's book. Yet Moraga insists that her lesbian identity is antithetical to Anglo values and is best affirmed by a tripartite denial of her white side, of Anglo-American culture, and of her father. The contradictions between liberatory intention and effect that result from these denials are evident in "What Kind of Lover Have You Made Me Mother?" In this combination of prose and poetry Moraga attempts to reconfigure the family's gender and sexual terrain, her principal target being her father: *"this queer I run from.* This white man in me" (italics hers, 8). Moraga describes the gulf between her father's "Anglo" nature and her Chicana mother's unmet expectations of a "real" man-husband-lover. Recognizing that her daughter is "worldly and full of knowledge when something goes queer," and yet queerly "different" like her father, Moraga's mother assigns Cherríe the task of talking to her father "man to man," of determining what his queerness might actually mean:

> I am driving his car. Feeling more man than my father. The car is entrusted to me to handle. I am on a mission. I am man enough to handle the situation, having a sex-talk with my father. But I can't say anything decent to the man; I'm not supposed to know. I must only be a son to him, supportive, encouraging, reliable — stroking and coaxing the subject.
> How to advise a man to keep his manliness intact? (11-12)

In the conversation that follows, neither emasculated father nor masculinized daughter are able to complete questions or answers, or indeed to communicate fruitfully. Likening the conversation to "beating a dead horse" (13), Moraga then dispenses with her father and appropriates his paternal function for herself, thus redefining her relationship with her mother:

> the damage
> has defined me
> as the space you provide
> for me in your bed (16)

Now that she has figuratively replaced her (not Chicano) father in familial space and in the parental bed, Moraga is liberated to disarm the memories of being beaten, or "damaged," by a Chicana mother concerned with her youthful daughter's lesbian non-conformity (14). Moraga attempts to overcome conflict by redefining the family as lesbian-centred. In fact, she appropriates (Anglo) paternal rights in order to make her (not Anglo) mother's sex, body, and disciplinarian will the objects of her desire, to

> Strip the belt from your hands
>
> and take you
> into
> my arms. (16)

In this way, Moraga rhetorically interpolates both her lesbianism and her body into the gender and sexual structures of her Borderlands family.

However, while the strategic queering of the family space allows Moraga to dispense with the sexual closet as it pertains to her, she also reinforces another closet, the one occupied by her "queer" (not Chicano) father. For the reader he appears as an epistemological conundrum. His queerness slips between a homosexual identity in an Anglo-American sense and a behavioural passivity — impotence, sexlessness, disinterest, inaction — considered unsuitable for men in what Roger Lancaster has called a Latin(o) "political economy of the [macho] body" (146-47).[5] Moraga's equations that "Anglo" equals "passivity," that "passivity" equals "queerness," and that this "queerness" equals "whiteness," have the effect of disparaging her (not Chicano) father from a machista Chicano perspective. At the same time, distancing herself from the Anglo father and culture that has in part produced her, Moraga downplays knowledge of her adoption of a lesbian identity in middle-class and white Anglo-American terms. Indeed, she accredits to her lesbianism the positive, active, and masculine Chicano values her father is imputed to lack. As she puts it elsewhere in her book, she would prefer death to "being fucked" (118). With the disparagement of the queer father, the move to neoculturate the (not quite Chicano) family home into a space safe for the lesbian daughter is achieved. The queer daughter simply replaces her queerly disparaged (not Chicano) father in a family conceived in accord with a stigmatizing bodily logic. That logic betrays not only a conventional Chicano male demonization and fear of sexual passivity but also a conception of the lesbian as a symbolic male (the penetrator or *chingón*), hence the rhetorical and conceptual ease by which Moraga can substitute her father's body with her own.

Moraga's lesbianizing call would thus suggest a wilful embrace of Chicano androcentric and homophobic rhetoric, presented and legitimated as an ostensibly anti-Anglo, anti-white stance, and manifested in complicity with the logic of the mother who first drew Moraga's attention to the father's "queerly" passive self. Only through that disparaging logic can Moraga's Anglo-Chicano family be de-Anglicized and thus resemanticized into a symbolic Aztlán secured for the lesbian (now only Chicana) daughter. Given Moraga's career-long advocacy of a desimplified notion of queerness, the political purchase enabled by the queer disparagement of the not-macho-enough father must be questioned: what sort of identification is enabled by a denial of the messy transculturation of Chicano and Anglo-American bodily economies in Moraga's perception of either her queer father or her differently queer self?

Unspeakable recognition, tenuous reconciliation

In her moves to reconvert both Aztlán and her family into a Chicana lesbian space unmodulated by the presence of the Anglo father, Moraga appears to be unconcerned by her compliance with a homophobic logic in order to do away with the "queerness" signified by the passive, weak, unmanly, not-Chicano she "runs from." While the move has not attracted comment in the critical responses to Moraga's book, this is not something that can be said of Moraga's widely cited and laudable Chicana lesbian intervention into the Mexican and Chicano discourse of treachery centred on Malinche and her always already "fucked" and "fuckable" synonym, *la Chingada*. Indeed, Moraga's reputation in large part rests on her valuable lesbian contribution to a feminist tradition that has countered the narrative that labels Chicanas as betrayers, or rescripted Malinche as a positive model rather than exemplary victim.[6]

Moraga's engagement with the Malinche-as-*Chingada* script appears as a dialogue with her mother in "A Long Line of Vendidas," an intermixture of essayistic, autobiographical, historical, feminist, and poetic modes. In this section of her book, Moraga observes how the notion of female treachery reinforces the subordinacy of mother and daughters before the family men, particularly her brother, making Moraga acutely aware that unlike the son, "the daughter must constantly earn the mother's love, prove her fidelity to her" (102). Moraga's dispute with Malinche discourse here translates as a grievance with her mother: "What I wanted from my mother was impossible. It would have meant her going against Mexican/Chicano tradition in a very fundamental way. You are a traitor to your race if you do not put the man first" (103). Moraga concludes that her mother, like the mother of Malinche reported to have sold her daughter into slavery, had only "been doing her Mexican wifely duty: *putting the male first"* (italics hers, 101). In this way, the chain of treachery is perpetuated. If Moraga's mother becomes a "modern-day . . . Malinche [by] marrying a white man," then Cherríe, "a half-breed," betrays conventional Chicano bodily scripts by embracing the white "disease" of lesbianism (114). Moraga's dilemma lies in the following painful equation: "if lesbianism is white, then the women I am faithful to can never be my own. And we are forced to move away from our people" (116). Throughout *Loving in the War Years* Moraga attempts to bridge the gap between the stigmatization of the lesbian that impels leaving the Chicano community and the desire for a place within that community. The bridging has two aspects: to render as possible and secure rather than as antagonistic the conjunction of Chicana and lesbian; and to reconcile mother and daughter.

In her book's final sections, Moraga describes the resemanticization of Malinche from a symbol of maternal treachery to a symbol of productive genealogical connections. This shift is linked to the culmination of a personal journey in which Moraga moves from her Borderlands family to radical feminist and then "women of color" political movements until, finally, she finds her real family with other lesbians of color, other betrayers of gender scripts. Only then does Moraga claim to be reconciled with both mother and maternal culture as a Chicana lesbian. The reconciliation depends, as Yvonne Yarbro-Bejarano recognizes, on a "translation of the concept of 'faith' from one context to another" (600). Faith serves "as a counterbalance to the fear of betrayal by women"; it permits "the possibility of faithfulness to one another as women, as Chicanas" (600). Faith is also characterized as a confirmation of women's strength, epitomized by black-clad women on their knees in a Mexican cathedral (ii) and by politicized women of color (132). Moraga claims that such manifestations of women's commitment to each other parallel the genealogical bonds between *Chingadas* "as paramount and essential in our lives [since] It is the daughters . . . who remain faithful a la madre, a la madre de la madre" [to the mother, to the mother of the mother] (139). This assertion, made after noting that Moraga's mother was always faithful to her son and not to her daughters (102), follows a scene in which Moraga's "mother told me that she felt in some ways that I was choosing my 'friends' (she meant lesbian lovers) over her. She said, 'No one is ever going to love you as much as I do. No one.' We were both crying by then and I responded, 'I know that . . . I know how strong your love is. Why do you think I am a lesbian?'" (138). The response is "Dead silence." But for Moraga it is a definitive and long sought moment of reconciliation: "But I knew, I felt in the air, that it was the silence of an unspeakable recognition. Of understanding finally, what my being a lesbian meant to me. I had been 'out' to my mother for years, but not like this" (138-39).

Yet, as already noted, the outness described here requires, in part, a stigmatizing logic to know the queerly passive father in order to figuratively absent him from the family. According to Frances Negrón-Muntaner, that denial enables Moraga to assert, "at least textually," her place in the newly fatherless family home in the hope of making her mother avow her love for her daughter and her daughter's lesbianism (257). The poignancy and pain of this scene does not, however, counter the fact that mother and daughter are only linked in a rare moment framed by "the silence of an unspeakable recognition." The subject of Moraga's lesbianism never unequivocally emerges into speech. Moraga may always be frustrated by the unspeakably brief breaches of her lesbianism into her mother's consciousness and conversation.

This tenuousness is also at odds with the affirmative rhetoric of one of Moraga's final poems, addressed to her mother, in which she writes about loving another Chicana:

> For you, mamá, I have unclothed myself before a woman
> have laid wide the space between my thighs
> straining open the strings held there
> taut and ready to fight. (140)

The poem is intended to celebrate the end of "the secret agenda of denial which has so often turned the relationships between mother and daughter, sister and sister, and compañeras into battlegrounds" (140). Desire between Chicanas is figured as a force capable of transforming the years of war and silence into years of love and speech: "her arms/ her kiss, all the parts of her open/ like lips moving, talking me into loving" (140). This form of loving, Moraga asserts, heals the mother-daughter divide by evoking the maternal as racial and sensual home. In the poem the mother once again appears as Moraga's primary focus of desire:

> I remember this common skin, mamá,
> oiled by work and worry.
> hers is a used body like yours
> one that carries the same scent
> of silence   I call it home. (140)

Here "the unspeakable recognition" that characterized the silence of the earlier scene of reconciliation between mother and daughter has been bypassed.

Silence now signifies safety, belonging and rightfulness. With that shift Moraga redefines the maternal as her authentic, sole origin: *"El regreso a mi pueblo. A la Mujer Mestiza"* [The return to my people. To the *Mestiza* Woman] (italics hers, 140). But the *mestiza* enabled by this logic can only be conceived by wilfully deculturating the Anglo in the neocultural body produced by the crossing of Anglo and Mexican. Moreover, despite refusing to sell out to "el gringo" (iii), Moraga attempts to carry back an Anglo-American construct of lesbian identity into the very spaces where "el gringo does not penetrate" (iii). Claiming to be a "woman with a foot in both worlds" who "refuses[s] the split" (58), she nonetheless aligns herself with the latter halves of a warring series of binaries: white-brown, Anglo-Mexican, father-mother, and heterosexual-lesbian. Moraga makes her "Chicana lesbian" self monological and unsullied. She does not conceive of the alternative transcultural possibility that rival sexual and racialized knowledges continue to antagonistically, uneasily, contradictorily, and yet fruitfully, meet on her Chicana lesbian body, and in her writing and speech.

Of cunts and tongues

Moraga likens writing to a coming "out-to-the world" (ii), a public admission of lesbian desire as ontologically definitive: "The freedom to want passionately. To live it out in the body of the poem, in the body of the woman" (v). The links between the bodies of author and text, and between lesbian desire and speech, are explicit: "The mouth is a cunt" (142). She emphasizes this point with recurring images of the mouth, the lips (oral and genital), and the tongue, *la lengua*, language. Moraga's position recalls Heléne Cixous's cry, "Your body must be heard" (880). But because Moraga's body has been a "lesbian" body she claims her body has been silenced and threatened: "If they hurt me, they will hurt me in that place. The place where I open my mouth to kiss and something primordial draws the lips back, cause a woman to defend herself against the love of a woman" (137). And because Moraga has striven to avoid sexual censorship by passing as Anglo, in English, she also claims that her Spanish has been silenced. Not privy to the heteroglossic choices available to many other Chicana writers, Moraga describes her lack of confidence and fluency in Spanish as a loss, a partial deculturation in which she was complicit: "I had disowned the language I knew best - ignored the words and rhythms that were closest to me. The sounds of my mother and aunts gossiping — half in English, half in Spanish — while drinking cerveza [beer] in the kitchen. And the hands — I had cut off the hands in my poems" (55-56).

Despite this complicity, and that of her mother in making English the primary language of her children, Moraga has elsewhere characterized as Calibanic her ambivalence towards the language of her father that she has always spoken. For example, in her essay "Art in America Con Acento," she asserts, "I am the product of invasion . . . the result of the dissolution of bloodlines and the theft of language; and yet, I am a testimony to the failure of the United States to wholly anglicize its mestizo citizens" (*Last Generation* 54). The Calibanic theme — the taking away of what Moraga romanticizes as "her mothertongue," the Spanish that has never been Moraga's first or only language (141) — appears throughout Moraga's book as the battle between English and Spanish idioms. The stake in this contest is Moraga's ability to textually represent the desired conjunction of lesbian and Chicana categories. This, she insists, is the crux of her project: "The right to passion expressed in our own cultural tongue and movements" (136). However, the thesis that her language was stolen from her is predicated on the denial of bilingual and bicultural origins. The thesis, reminiscent of the claims made by Alfred Arteaga (68-75), regards Spanish and *caló*, or Spanglish, as the true Chicano languages and linguistic deculturation as always synonymous with assimilation or americanization. In short, only by denying the transcultural evidence that English is also a Chicano language can the monolingual English-speaking Chicana be denied her Chicananess.

Defining her predicament in terms of binarized linguistic conflict, Moraga claims this as the reason she feels distanced from her mother. "Words are a war to me/ They threaten my family," she says in her poem "It's The Poverty" (63). But these lines also indicate the irreversible distance between mother and daughter caused by the daughter's Anglo-American education, class mobility, and feminist world-view. The gulf between working-class mother and middle-class, university-educated feminist daughter persists as a problem not only of translation, but of communication across class and ideological divides:

> To gain the word to describe the loss,
> I risk losing everything.
> I may create a monster,
> the word's length and body

swelling up colorful and thrilling
looming over my *mother*, characterized.
Her voice in the distance
unintelligible   illiterate. (63)

In this poem Moraga recoils from monstrous possibility. This is a vision of the monster to be added to those Chávez-Silverman identifies in the work of two other Chicana writers: "For [Alicia] Gaspar de Alba, the violent monster is a sign of inauthenticity, closetedness, whereas for [Sandra] Cisneros, the beast signifies positive, transgressive power" (41, n.7). Moraga's monster, by contrast, is a sign of semiotic and ideological unintelligibility. The codes she uses and her political stance are liable to be misunderstood by a mother who, while unable to read English, also operates according to different cultural and class values. The monstrosity of Moraga's predicament arises because her writerly message won't be read or comprehended by the person Moraga most wants to reach.

Faced with this irresolvable linguistic-cum-ideological conundrum, Moraga seeks other audiences for her text: Chicana lesbian "daughters" like herself (vii); and white feminists, "particularly those that claim to be speaking for all women," so that they "be accountable for their racism" (58). Moraga claims that the generic and linguistic *mestizaje* of her account, evident in the combination of languages and "of poetry and essays," represents a necessary "compromise" — in terms of clarity and impact — to acknowledge both audiences (vi). Generic and stylistic mixing also reveal an awareness of language function and textual construction and their manipulations. The blurring of textual categories takes into account Moraga's intended audiences — Anglo-American feminists who fail to interrogate their racialized privilege; and Chicana daughters, those from the first generation of Chicanas to gain university educations — who are sophisticated, knowing readers. The stylistic and generic characteristics of Moraga's book evince a writerly aesthetic aimed at satisfying or challenging the presumptions and interests of her dual audience. And both aesthetic and audience exclude the mother.

While Moraga describes her book as an "emotional/political chronology" that is temporally and discursively unteleological (i), she does have a goal in mind: the construction of a maternally authenticated "Chicana lesbian" category. Linguistic conflict has a pivotal role to play in this process. Moraga responds to her so-called Calibanic dilemma not by making her own use of the invader's curse but by seeking to reculturate herself in Spanish, the mother's language that she wants to inhabit: "I want the language, feel my tongue rise to the occasion of feeling at home, in common. I know this language in my bones . . . and then it escapes me . . . 'You don't belong. ¡Quítate!' [Get out!]" (141). To this end, Moraga erects clear boundaries around a "masculine" English and a "feminine" Spanish, a linguistic parallel to the racial dichotomies in which she operates.[7] English is figured as an imposed linguistic closet that inhibits Moraga from expressing lesbian desire: "the language was not cutting it. ¿Entiendes?" (141). Here the erotic dimensions of the rival languages are emphasized by the Spanish question "¿Entiendes?," that apart from meaning "do you understand?" is also an idiom for "are you queer?" The Spanish word constructs the sexual as an epistemological problem of "knowing, rather than being" (Smith and Bergman 12). But the question in Moraga's hands implies that it is not English but her mother's language which is the appropriate vehicle of lesbian desire, the medium in which Moraga's "true" lesbian self can come out and be. This is the message of her book's final poem and statement:

la lengua que necesito	[the tongue I need
para hablar	to speak
es la misma que uso	is the same I use
para acariciar	to caress
tú sabes.	you know.
you know the feel of woman	
lost en su boca	. . . in the mouth
amordazada	gagged
it has always been like this.	
profundo y sencillo	profound and simple
lo que nunca	that which never
pasó	crosses
por sus labios	their/your lips]
but was	
utterly	
utterly	

heard. (149)

With this conclusion the conjunction of "lesbian" and "Chicana" is achieved. An emphatic, authoritative coming to voice in Spanish of lesbian desire is proclaimed, although the effect is muted somewhat by the English words of the last lines. Yet as her testimonial's culmination, even this rhetoric does not guarantee the identity security Moraga seeks. Only a few pages beforehand, Moraga recounts a ritual public coming-out at a conference, a venue that epitomizes the worldly gulf between mother and daughter: "La boca [the mouth] spreads its legs open to talk, open to attack. 'I am a lesbian. And I am a Chicana,' I say to the men and women at the conference. I watch their faces twist up on me. 'These are two inseparable facts of my life. I can't write or talk about one without the other" (142). It is this notion of the lesbian and the Chicana as facts—immutable, authentic, epistemologically transparent, and defiant—that her coming out as a Chicana lesbian in this instance renders insecure. Moraga's identity claims in this scene appear to be delimited and discursively contained by what Butler calls "the conceit of autonomy implied by self-naming" (*Bodies That Matter* 228). "Chicana," "*mestiza*," "mother," "female," and "lesbian," function as secure markers; they mean what Moraga says. But her meanings pass over the contaminated and contingent relations they have with each other, and with the categories of "Anglo," "white," "father," "male," and "heterosexual." To construct her rhetorical bridge between cultures, Moraga defines both Anglo and Chicana as culturally, sexually, racially, and linguistically pure, as either fit or unfit for the uncontaminated identity that she now claims.

Transcultural unthinkability

Loving in the War Years articulates a drive towards the certainty of what its author asserts is a secured Chicana lesbian identity, one rhetorically disencumbered of Anglo contaminants. Yet, the boundaries of Moraga's desired self-definition remain fluid and contested, for as Carlos Muñoz Jr. has pointed out, Chicanos are "the most racially mixed nonwhite people in U.S. society" and "difficult to define in traditional race . . . terms" (8). In a racialized sense, Chicano *mestizaje* thus poses the epistemological problem of recognizing bodily borders in the face of the proliferation of racialized signifiers so often apparent in one family. Those signifiers are responsible for the paradox of a posited racial distinctiveness that not only eludes definition, but undermines the conceptual and ontological coherence of categories like race and ethnicity. The bodily limits Moraga enforces in order to claim a purified Chicananess that somehow resolves her racialized predicament are paralleled by similar border patrols of her sexual and linguistic guises. She responds to her stated ambition of "refusing the split" between Anglo and Chicano by taking the one-way bridge back into the reassuringly secure zone of a Chicananess defined in antagonistic, antithetical relation to the Anglo, but safely beyond him.

Moraga's particular embodiment of Chicana lesbianness thus always threatens to show up as nonsensical the lines she draws between and around white and brown, and Chicano and Anglo. Evident in *Loving in the War Years*, then, is a compulsion identified by Judith Butler: a desire to regard such categories as gender, race, sexuality, and even language, as "univocal signifiers," the ontological preconditons for "a model of truth and falsity which not only contradicts its own performative fluidity, but serves a social policy of . . . regulation and control" ("Performative Acts" 282). As Moraga fashions of and for herself a Chicana lesbian self, her identity manoeuvres never escape from the hegemonic processes that strive to maintain identity categories as natural and immutable, in short, as unthinkable in transcultural terms. Indeed, as a document of a Manichean schema of mutual exclusivities, *Loving in the War Years* not only reveals an ambivalent relation to prescriptive discourses but, in places, confirms them.

Paul Allatson

NOTES

[1] This is a revised version of the essay that appeared in *Antípodas* 11-12 (1999/2000): 103-21. My thanks to Diana Palaversich, Roslyn Jolly, and Roderick Marsh for their comments and inputs. *Mil gracias, también, a* Susana Chávez-Silverman for our ongoing discussions on many of the issues canvassed here.

[2] The genealogy and divergent applications of transcultural discourse, a Latin American analytical mode increasingly used to plot Latino cultures in the United States, are by now well-known in Anglophone criticism. The mode originates with the Cuban Fernando Ortiz's *Contrapunteo Cubana del tabaco y azúcar (Cuban Counterpoint)*, from 1940. Speaking of the transformations of African and European elements in Cuba, Ortiz noted the inadequacy of the English-language terms "acculturation" and "assimilation" when used to describe cross-cultural processes. For Ortiz, the concepts implied European ascendancy in "the process of

transition from one culture to another" and assumed a metropolitan imposition of culture on passively receptive peripheries or subordinate sectors, without the metropolis itself being affected by contact-zone involvement (*Cuban Counterpoint* 102-3). As an alternative, Ortiz proposed three simultaneous processes. To the notion of cultural acquisition (acculturation), he added partial cultural destruction, uprooting, and loss (deculturation), and the productions of "new cultural phenomena" (neoculturation) (102-3). In this essay, I retain this tripartite schema and add to it the notion of "reculturation," or the wilful embrace of or return to a cultural practice or identification previously denied or precluded. For excellent overviews of transculturation in its Latin American guises after Ortiz, and its slow moves into Anglophone criticism in the United States, see Spitta, and Taylor.

³ Moraga is not the only proponent of a queer Aztlán. That possibility is explored by Luis Alfaro in his manifesto-like "Orphan of Aztlán," the final segment of his prose and poetry sequence, "Cuerpo Politizado." A less celebratory take on Aztlán from a male perspective is provided by Gil Cuadros's story "My Aztlan: White Place" in his collection *City of God*. For analyses of these queer revisions of Aztlán, see my "'*Siempre feliz en mi falda'*: Luis Alfaro's Simulative Challenge" and "AIDS and the Resignification of 'Chicano Queer' in the Work of Gil Cuadros."

⁴ La Adelita is the name of a heroine of the Mexican Revolution popularized in Mexican folklore and corridos, or ballads. Her name symbolizes all *soldaderas* or *guerilleras* who, according to Tey Diana Rebolledo, "followed their men into war and at times fought beside them." La Adelita has provided a model and symbolic focus for many Mexican and Chicana writers (57). See also Cantú.

⁵ Lancaster's notion of a macho economy of the body derives from his studies of sexual cultures in Nicaragua; however, it also has ramifications outside the context with which he is concerned.

⁶ Malinche was Hernán Cortés's maligned native translator and consort, a figure who has been reclaimed by many Mexican and Chicana writers and reimagined as a model of New World transcultural subjectivity. The most widely cited descriptions of Malinche's disparaged symbolic function — evident in her synonym *la Chingada* — are found in chapter four of Octavio Paz's *El laberinto de la soledad* (1950), his canonical exploration of (male) Mexican national identity. Paz characterized Mexican identity as a masculine unease attributable to the notion that *mestizo* identity makes all Mexicans the illegitimate children of the raped indigenous mother and the dominant European father. In Paz's lexicon, the notion of *mestizo* illegitimacy underwrites Malinche/*Chingada* discourse in which women are potentially disparaged as traitors while the Mexican man is defined as the "*hijo de la chingada*, . . . the offspring of violation, abduction or deceit." (87-88). As centred on Malinche, the abject scripts of *mestizaje* impact on the ways rival signifying systems battle over the racialized female body. For Chicanos who inherit this discourse of gendered negativity and heterosexualized cultural generation, the transcultural clash is exacerbated by their place in a nation with its own history of patriarchal imperialism. Norma Alarcón, for example, sees the invocation of Malinche as a mnemonic of conquest centred on a Chicano "family quarrel" over gender power (182). For Alvina Quintana, such gender battles replay "the unresolved conflicts" stemming from colonization by Spain and the U.S.A. (16). For other elaborations see, for example: Segura and Pesquera; Ordóñez; Quintana; Rebolledo; Herrera-Sobek; and Pratt.

⁷ It is interesting to note that in his autobiography, *Hunger of Memory*, Richard Rodriguez also genders Spanish and English languages in this way, although his ideological motivations are opposed to Moraga's. As Martin Danahay notes, the conservative and closeted Rodriguez struggles to "resist . . . his 'effeminate yearning' for the intimate sounds of Spanish" (298). Moraga, on the other hand, struggles to avow an ethnicized lesbian desire by relearning "the intimate sounds of Spanish."

WORKS CITED

Alarcón, Norma. "Chicana's Feminist Literature: A Re-Vision Through Malintzin/Or Malintzin: Putting Flesh Back on the Object." *This Bridge Called My Back: Writings By Radical Women of Color*. Es. Cherríe Moraga and Gloria Anzaldúa. 2nd ed. New York: Kitchen Table/Women of Color, 1983. 182-90.

Alfaro, Luis. "Cuerpo politizado." *Uncontrollable Bodies: Testimonies of Identity and Culture* . Ed. Rodney Sappington and Tyler Stallings. Seattle: Bay Press, 1994. 217-41.

Allatson, Paul. "AIDS and the Resignification of Chicano Queer in the Work of Gil Cuadros." *Journal of Homosexuality* (forthcoming 2001).

------ , "'*Siempre feliz en mi falda'* : Luis Alfaro's Simulative Challenge." *GLQ* 5 (1999): 199-230.

Arteaga, Alfred. *Chicano Poetics: Heterotexts and Hybridities* . Cambridge: Cambridge UP, 1997.

Beverley, John. *Subalternity and Representation: Arguments in Cultural Theory*. Durham: Duke UP, 2000.

Butler, Judith. *Bodies That Matter*. New York and London: Routledge, 1993.

------ , "Performative Acts and Gender Constitution: An Essay in Phenomenology and Feminist Theory." *Performing Feminisms: Feminist Critical Theory and Theatre* . Ed. Sue-Ellen Case. Baltimore: John Hopkins UP, 1990. 270-83.

Cantú, Norma. "Women, Then and Now: An Analysis of the Adelita Im ge Versus the Chicana as Political Writer and Philosopher." *Chicana Voices: Intersections of Class, Race and Gender.* Ed. Teresa Córdova, et al. Austin: NACS, 1990. 8-10.

Chávez-Silverman, Susana. "Chicanas in Love: Sandra Cisneros Talking Back and Alicia Gaspar de Alba 'Giving Back the Wor(l)d.'" *Chasqui* 27.1 (1998): 33-46.

Chow, Rey. *Writing Diaspora: Tactics of Intervention in Contemporary Cultural Studies* . Bloomington: Indiana UP, 1993.

Cixous, Heléne. "The Laugh of the Medusa." Trans. Keith Cohen and Paula Cohen. *SIGNS* 1 (1976): 875-93.

Cuadros, Gil. *City of God*. San Francisco: City Lights, 1994.

Danahay, Martin. "Richard Rodriguez's Poetics of Manhood." *Fictions of Masculinity: Crossing Cultures, Crossing Sexualities.* Ed. Peter F. Murphy. New York: New York UP, 1994. 290-302.

Fanon, Frantz. *Black Skin/White Masks*. Trans. Charles Lam Markmann. London: Paladin, 1970.

Fuss, Diana. *Essentially Speaking: Feminism, Nature and Difference*. New York: Routledge, 1989.

Garber, Marjorie. *Vested Interests: Cross-Dressing and Cultural Anxiety*. London: Penguin, 1992.

Gilmore, Leigh. *Autobiographics: A Feminist Theory of Women's Self-Representation*. Ithaca: Cornell UP, 1994.

Herrera-Sobek, María. "The Politics of Rape: Sexual Transgression in Chicana Fiction." *Chicana Creativity and Criticism: Charting New Frontiers in American Literature*. Ed. María Herrera-Sobek and Helena María Viramontes. Houston: Arte Público, 1988. 171-81.

Lancaster, Roger N. "'That We Should All Turn Queer?': Homosexual Stigma in the Making of Manhood and the Breaking of a Revolution in Nicaragua." *Conceiving Sexuality: Approaches to Sex Research in a Post-Modern World*. Ed. Richard G. Parker and John H. Gagnaan. New York: Routledge, 1995. 135-56.

Moraga, Cherríe. *The Last Generation: Prose and Poetry*. Boston: South End, 1993.

------ , *Loving in the War Years: Lo que nunca pasó por sus labios*. Boston: South End, 1983.

Mullen, Harryette. "Optic White: Blackness and the Production of Whiteness." *Diacritics* 24:2.3 (1994): 71-89.

Muñoz Jr., Carlos. *Youth, Identity, Power: The Chicano Movement*. London and New York: Verso, 1989.

Negrón-Muntaner, Frances. "Cherríe Moraga." *Latin American Writers on Gay and Lesbian Themes: A Bio-Critical Sourcebook*. Ed. David William Foster. Westport: Greenwood, 1994. 254-62.

Ordóñez, Elizabeth. "Sexual Politics and the Theme of Sexuality in Chicana Poetry." *Women in Hispanic Literature: Icons and Fallen Idols*. Ed. Beth Miller. Berkeley: U of California P, 1983. 316-39.

Ortiz, Fernando. *Contrapunteo Cubano del tabaco y azúcar*. La Habana: J. Montero, 1940.

------ , *Cuban Counterpoint: Tobacco and Sugar*. 1940. Trans. Harriet de Onís. Introd. Bronislaw Malinowski and Fernando Coronil. Durham: Duke UP, 1995.

Paz, Octavio. *El laberinto de la soledad. Postdata. Vuelta a El laberinto de la soledad*. 1950. 3a ed. México, D.F.: Fondo de Cultura Económica, 1999.

Pratt, Mary Louise. "'Yo Soy La Malinche': Chicana Writers and the Poetics of Ethno-nationalism." *Callalloo* 16 (1993): 859-73.

Quintana, Alvina E. *Home Girls: Chicana Literary Voices*. Philadelphia: Temple UP, 1996.

Rebolledo, Tey Diana. *Women Singing in the Snow: A Cultural Analysis of Chicana Literature*. Tucson: U of Arizona P, 1995.

Rodriguez, Richard. *Hunger of Memory: The Education of Richard Rodriguez , An Autobiography*. New York: Bantam, 1983.

Segura, Denise A., and Beatriz M. Pesquera. "Beyond Indifference and Antipathy: The Chicana Movement and Chicana Feminist Discourse." *Aztlán* 19.2 (1988-1990): 69-92.

Smith, Paul Julian, and Emile L. Bergman, eds. "Introduction." *¿Entiendes? Queer Readings, Hispanic Writings*. Durham and London: Duke UP, 1995. 1-14.

Smith, Valerie. "Reading the Intersections of Race and Gender in Narratives of Passing," *Diacritics* 24:2-3 (1994): 43-57.

Spitta, Silvia. *Between Two Waters: Narratives of Transculturation in Latin America*. Houston: Rice UP, 1995.

Taylor, Diana. "Transculturating Transculturation." *Performing Arts Journal* 13.2 (1991): 90-104.

Yarbro-Bejarano, Yvonne. "De-constructing the Lesbian Body: Cherríe Moraga's *Loving in the War Years*." *The Lesbian and Gay Studies Reader*. Ed. Henry Abelove, Michèle Ana Barale and David M. Halperin. New York: Routledge, 1993. 595-603.

14.
REVISITING THE THIRD SPACE:
READING DANZY SENNA'S *CAUCASIA*[1]

I must be the bridge to nowhere
But my true self
And then I will be useful
--Kate Rushin

I would meet these young mixed-blood people, and I'd always look at them
and feel like we knew each other. We recognized something similar, but there was no story
underneath, no way to really access it. I wanted a space
where we could be everything or all of who we are.
--Rebecca Walker

we need each other critically
--Essex Hemphill

Introduction

In her introduction to *Black British Feminism: A Reader*, Heidi Mirza addresses the current fashion amongst scholars to inhabit the realm of marginality, constructed as "the third space." "But what is this 'third space,'" Mirza challenges, "the place of 'hybridity' and 'translation' which privileges those who claim to be oppressed?" (20). Valorizing the specificity of a Black British feminist location and politics, Mirza disputes the logic of black and white male critics' appropriation of black feminist epistemologies. She writes, "[these critics articulate] a new 'imperialism of oppression' as they enter the (counter-hegemonic) space of the truly dispossessed and seek, through a perverse legitimacy of their 'displacement' or search for 'new knowledge,' to know it better than we know it ourselves" (20).

For its illumination of postcolonial mimicry, Freud's skewed conception of mixed-race subjects, "who taken all around resemble white men but who betray their coloured descent by some striking feature," appears in Homi Bhabha's discussion of hybridity in *The Location of Culture*. Descriptions such as this curiously situate white maleness at the normative center and define mixed subjects only in (superficially) imitative relation to this center. Elaborating on Homi Bhabha's argument, Annamarie Jagose posits that "any prioritization of the *mestiza* must not be on account of her alleged ability to secure a space beyond the border's adjudication of cultural difference but on account of her foregrounding of the ambivalence which enables even as it destabilizes the colonial relationship" (224). In both Jagose and Bhabha's terms, the mixed-race disruption of the colonized/colonizer relationship only serves to reinscribe its duality. Without question, both critics successfully articulate the highly operative power imbalance between colonizer and colonized. However, given strict parameters of difference such as these in which mixed-race people are mere mimics of white men or troubling racial signifiers, the location of the so-called "third space," as it is theorized here, obscures the material conditions of white supremacy, specifically the degree that segregation precludes the very possibility of a "third space." ² This location further denies the reality that mixed-race people of African descent are members of the black community.   In this essay, I re-visit "the third space" by examining a relationship between two women who "inhabit" it, the mixed-race sisters of Danzy Senna's *Caucasia* (1998). In this analysis of their relationship, I argue that the differences between two mixed-race women, and the possibilities they inspire, provide an alternative model for defining difference, one that must be operative in the lives of all people in order for real change to occur.

A Passing Fancy?

For generations, since Lydia Maria Child's short story "The Quadroons" first appeared in 1841, the anxieties of miscegenation, the injustices of slavery, and the parameters of American identity have all fallen squarely on literary depictions of the so-called "tragic mulatto." ³ As critical attention to this tradition has steadily increased over the last three decades, scholars have unearthed an American preoccupation with the sensation of miscegenation that has sustained an uninterrupted dialectic of mixed-race characterization between African American and Euro-American authors since the mid-nineteenth century. From William Dean Howells and Frank Webb's passing narratives to William Faulkner and Ralph Ellison's existential men, from Thomas Dixon's mongrels to Charles Chesnutt's defiant relations, from Harriet Beecher Stowe's calculating concubines to Frances Harper's race women, the literature of racial mixing tells a story that is at once universal and yet quite particular.[4]

As critic Adrienne Johnson Gosselin affirms, the mixed figure embodies a tradition that is "characterized by betrayal and race-denial, haunted by racial impurity, and ... bears the stigma of relations unsanctionable in the United States" (47). In that this figure cannot conform to the guise of blackness, she or he is often (mis)read as white. Because of the strict legislation of the color line, the mixed-race failure to stay put threatens to be mistaken for a version of passing: when persons of mixed heritage do not "act black," the only alternative is to "act white."

Early depictions of women of mixed ancestry in nineteenth-century fiction have prompted debate among African American critics since Houston Baker and Barbara Christian argued that "mulatta" (read nearly white) characters were invented to appeal to white readers, a thesis supported by Alice Walker in 1983.[5] Although Frances Smith Foster insisted on a black readership, the mixed heroine's appearance made a lasting impression on both black *and* white readers. In 1985, Foster added "color and contour" to these figures by asserting "not only is [the tragic mulatta heroine] pious and pure, ... she is also beautiful and more refined than most white women" to the degree that she "is the epitome of True Womanhood" (34). This insistence on the whiteness of racially-mixed beauty returns in Ann DuCille's study *The Coupling Convention* ("the white face of the mulatto" 8) and leads critic Deborah McDowell to cite Barbara Christian as she argues, "The image of the Lady combined and conflated physical appearance with character traits. Immortalized particularly in the Southern antebellum novel, the image required 'physical beauty [that is, fair skin] ... fragility, refinement and helplessness.'" (38).[6]

While nineteenth-century ideal standards of white femininity certainly bear relevance to these characterizations, the critical investment in reading attractive mixed heroines as "white" both renders invisible mixed women's subjectivity and wrongly accepts beauty as possessed *only by whites*. Further, disagreement amongst critics as to the racial (in)authenticity of the mixed woman leads Deborah McDowell to uncritically ponder, "Does the mulatta figure serve or subvert dominant ideologies of race and gender?" (54). Lines of inquiry such as this contribute to confusion over the mulatta's racial allegiances: is she complicitous with white supremacist acts or evidence of their limits? Framed in this way, the mulatta figure sits on the fence of the color line, awaiting the condemning scrutiny of her skeptical critics.

Consider one person's response to Valerie Smith's public presentation of films and novels with the passing theme: "[the audience member] suggested that the project was inherently retrograde, since it focused on the conditions of African Americans light-skinned enough to pass as white. Her comment presupposed that to examine constructions of mixed-race characters replicates the problematic of black self-loathing that may well have contributed to the overrepresentation of such figures in black narratives" (56-57). Responding to Smith's encounter, Gosselin states, "it is a reaction I have encountered frequently in my black literature courses, where often any representation of mixed-race characters is considered inauthentic in terms of African-American culture. ... Rather than dismiss such narratives as 'non-representational' (whether written or visual), cultural criticism may do well to interrogate the arbitrary categories such texts are meant to represent" (64). In the vein of Hazel Carby's reconsideration of these figures as "mediating devices," both Smith and Gosselin insist that the conditions of these figures "are productive sites for considering how the intersectionality of race, class, and gender ideologies are constituted and denied" (Smith 57). [7]

Significantly, these later assessments converge with a strengthening political movement in the U.S. that advocates for the legal recognition of racially-mixed people, a movement that attained increased visibility during its campaign for a "multiracial" box on the 2000 Census. [8] Even as early as 1992, Maria Root declared that "the emergence of a racially mixed population is transforming the 'face' of the United States" (3) in her groundbreaking anthology *Racially Mixed People in America*. Though the history of populations of mixed descent dates back to the founding of this country, the last decade has seen unprecedented political activism and literary production on behalf of the unique experiences and voices of these communities. In 1994, Carol Camper's collection, *Miscegenation Blues*, addressed "an increasing urgency in the lives of many women to end isolation and to understand racial multiplicity within our own bodies, families and cultures" (xv). That same year, Root's second anthology, *The Multiracial Experience*, outlined a "bill of rights for racially mixed people."

Since the reversal of state laws against interracial marriage in the U.S. in 1967 (Root 1994, xv), the first generation of legally-sanctioned mixed-race people has come of age and the literature of this growing population, like all emerging communities, requires its own critical voice. As this discussion of Danzy Senna's novel reveals, in that women of mixed ancestry are uniquely situated in relation to race, gender and sexuality, literary productions by these women require a theoretical language that adequately interprets and engages simultaneously these multiple yet interactive sites of identity. Furthermore, as I argue in my conclusion, while it may outline the specifics of an emerging community, this critical approach bears relevance beyond this "category."

Mixed Race and the Difference it Makes

In *Essentially Speaking: Feminism, Nature and Difference*, published in 1989, Diana Fuss succinctly and fairly accurately articulates the two competing positions of essentialism and social constructionism: "For the essentialist, the body occupies a pure, pre-social, pre-discursive space. The body is 'real,' accessible, and transparent; it is always there and directly interpretable through the senses. For the constructionist, the body is never simply there, rather it is composed of a network of effects continually subject to sociopolitical determination" (5). In the discussion that ensues, Fuss considers at length the limitations and political implications of both theoretical stances as she surveys the work of French feminists, African American (male) post-structuralist critics, and lesbian and gay theorists. In her chapter on "Post-Structuralist Afro-American Literary Theory," for instance, Fuss acknowledges the black feminist resistance to "theory" in favor of "more essentialist arguments," which arise out of "political necessity" (95).

Although Fuss's work appeared over ten years ago, the problem of essentialism vs. constructionism still haunts many critical circles. This is particularly the case in scholarship pertaining to marginalized communities, which wishes to resist essentialism while defending a specific subject position. In such formulations, difference is conceived of as two-dimensional--self vs. other, sameness vs. difference--and lacking in originality. Either scripted by society, biologically rooted, or discursively upheld, difference as such forecloses the range of individual expression and/or the impact of individual non-conformity to these competing--and certainly politically urgent--definitions of identity. Furthermore, these positions require that identity itself be one of two: male vs. female, black vs. white, heterosexual vs. homosexual. This binaristic tendency was evident in the discussion of the third space of my introduction. Again, theories of difference rely on the either/or model. Or, in the case of mixed-race people, *neither/nor*. As Audre Lorde argues, "Much of Western European history conditions us to see human differences in simplistic opposition to each other: dominant/subordinate, good/bad, up/down, superior/inferior" (114).[9] Given the theoretical limitations described above, I argue that a critical perspective on the lived experience and literary representation of women of mixed heritage must challenge theories of difference which insist on the inferiority of the subordinate party.

A national bestseller, Danzy Senna's *Caucasia* is the first work of fiction that concerns the lives of contemporary women of mixed heritage. [10] Published in 1998, *Caucasia* is a *Bildungsroman* concerning the two mixed-race daughters of Deck Lee, a Harvard-educated African American professor at Boston University, and Sandy Lee, a Cambridge-bred WASP whose ancestry reaches back to Cotton Mather. After their parents divorce over political differences-- her mother's activism vs. her father's intellectualism--and her mother's involvement in a underground liberation movement forces her to flee the F.B.I., Birdie and Cole are separated for six years. Since she can pass for white, Birdie accompanies her mother on an interstate run from the law. Meanwhile, her sister Cole and their father venture to Brazil--a naïve attempt to escape the race wars of mid-1970s Boston--with his new African American girlfriend, a mother-substitute with whom the brown-skinned Cole can more easily identify. The novel opens with Birdie and Cole's harmonious childhood universe and ends with their reconciliation. Through its examination of Birdie and Cole's unique intimacy, Senna's novel shatters the dualistic terms of sameness and difference.

The novel opens,

> Before I ever saw myself, I saw my sister. When I was still too small for mirrors, I saw her as the reflection that proved my own existence. Back then, I was content to see only Cole, three years older than me, and imagine that her face--cinnamon-skinned, curly-haired, serious--was my own. (5)

As the above passage illustrates, Cole's "reflection" confirms Birdie's existence. In later scenes in the novel, when Birdie's racial ambiguity condemns her to painful encounters with other children and adults, her early desire to possess her sister's features--her "cinnamon-skin" and "curly hair"--becomes apparent. While her pale skin and straight hair facilitate her social mobility from African American to white, her failure to satisfy accepted racial categorization and conform to any given community induce her alienation. Birdie's ability to slip in and out of the color line situates her in a unique position in which it is *only her mixed-race sister* who can recognize her as distinctively different. Early on, Birdie learns to define herself solely in relationship to Cole, her first and only mirror. Cole thus represents in part the abatement of Birdie's longing for recognition. In this way, Birdie's self-definition hinges on Cole's and the identification that occurs between the two sisters introduces a "third space" of experience.

In the attic of their South End home, the sisters create a safe haven where "the outside world was as far away as Timbuktu--some place that could never touch us" (6-7). As their parents shout "muted obscenities" (7) from below, Cole and Birdie talk in a language of their own invention: "We were trying to block [our parents' voices] out with talk of Elemeno. Cole was explaining to me that it wasn't just a language, but a place and a people as well" (7). For Cole and Birdie, the childhood universe of Elemeno shelters them from their race-obsessed parents and the outside world. "The Elemenos," explained Cole, "could turn not just from black to white, but from brown to yellow to purple to green, and back again." They were "a constantly shifting people, constantly changing their form, color, pattern, in a quest for invisibility. [T]heir changing routine was a serious matter--less a game of make-believe than a fight for the survival of their species. ... their power lay precisely in their ability to disappear into any surrounding." (7). In Cole's vision, the Elemenos possess the capacity to escape the legislation of identity even as they enter and exit its territories. Cole's reasoning is curiously reminiscent of the post-structuralist tendency to destabilize categories of subjectivity. And, like the post-structuralist programme, its valuation of invisibility "evacuat[es] historical experience from the construction of raced and gendered bodies" (Smith 1994, 51). As Birdie pointedly asks, "What was the point of surviving if you had to disappear?" (8). Here, Birdie challenges the notion that people of mixed heritage must retreat into the familiar terrains of invisibility. Instead, she intimates that "the Elemenos" have a place of their own.

To elaborate on the vision that Senna presents here, I contend that Birdie and Cole's relationship introduces a new way of thinking about difference. Unlike the theoretical formulations I discussed above, whose difference relies on a normative white maleness, I propose a revisionist conception of difference that foregrounds the *difference(s)* between two mixed-race women.

To position a mixed-race woman in relation to *another* mixed-race woman, as illustrated in the above passages, emphasizes the limitations of binaristic theories of difference which rely on negation and subordination (self/other, white/black, male/female, etc.). In these formulations, what is deemed normative is white, heterosexual and male. Since Birdie and Cole's *difference from each other* undoes our traditional notions of difference in which a normative standard oppresses its corresponding deviant, difference here is no longer tyrannically hierarchical, nor is it oppositional. [11]   Instead, the identification that occurs between Birdie and Cole captures an instance of difference that is *non*-oppositional. Because Birdie and Cole fail to uphold any normative standard precisely as a result of their outsider status, I define the relationship between them as *difference from difference*. Difference and identity exist here not by means of negation, but possibility.

The Erotics of Sisterhood

As I mentioned in the introduction, Lydia Maria Child is widely recognized as an early progenitor of the tragic mulatta tradition. Thus, in "The Quadroons," the relationship between Rosalie, the quadroon, and her white master Edward, is constructed as a failed romance. William Wells Brown's novel, *Clotel, or The President's Daughter* (1853), the first novel by an African-American, cleverly revises Child's tragic plot by integrating the quadroon's plight with the ugly details of the institution of slavery, a system which blatantly turns people into property. Instead of Child's sacrificed quadroon(s), Brown's Clotel endures the loss of her child, is sold to Mr. French, and later re-sold to Mr. Cooper. Although Child's abolitionist version of the sacrificed mulatto figure may elicit sympathy, it inevitably sustains white hegemony and black dependence. As Jerry Bryant argues, "the [slave] victim always remains an object of sympathy, dependent on help from others, not an autonomous subject capable of choice and action" (22). Conversely, Brown surpasses this limited characterization through his exploitation of the "intimate" connection with slavery that impels Clotel to a greater feeling of defiance. [12]

Like Child's Rosalie, Clotel's experience as a slave is similarly mediated by her gender. As Brown writes, "Every married woman in the far South looks upon her husband as unfaithful, and regards every quadroon servant as a rival" (150). The victim of Mrs. French's jealousy, Clotel is "ordered to cut off her long hair" only "a few days" after her arrival (150). In his descriptions of the hostile jealousy Clotel endures from Mrs. French as well as from the other slave women, Brown dramatizes the degree that women of mixed ancestry fall within the intersecting economic functions of chattel slavery and sexual commerce. In one of the slave women's terms, "'[Clotel] tinks she white, when she come here wid dat long har of hers'" (150). According to this reasoning, Clotel's racial/slave status is elevated through her striking and ambiguous physical appearance such that her (attractive) features threaten the racial distinctions between slave and free. However, the women's preoccupation with Clotel's hair reveals the extent that Clotel's "exceptional" looks subject her to the intertwining economic manipulations of chattel slavery and compulsory heterosexuality in which black women were the "concubines, mistresses, and sexual slaves of white males" (King 297). As the text conveys, "Mr. French found no difficulty in getting a purchaser for the quadroon woman, for such are usually the most marketable kind of property" (151). That Clotel later benefits from her short hair when she passes as a white man and escapes evidences the oppressive marketability of her uniquely racialized gender. "Wit dat long har of hers," she may appear to be separate from her darker sisters. Yet her physical beauty merely exacts a higher price on the slave auction block.

In *Caucasia*, Senna revises Clotel's experience in a late-twentieth-century context. When their parents enroll Birdie and Cole into an Afrocentric school, the schoolgirls corner Birdie in the girls' bathroom and threaten to cut off her hair: "Maria grabbed the scissors from Cathy. 'You think Ali's gonna like you when you don't got no hair?'" (47). Like the episode above in *Clotel*, Birdie's "'long, stringy hair'" (46) provokes her classmates' antagonism. However, in this case, instead of competing over a master's seeming benevolence, the girls' behavior is rooted in competition for a boy. When she reaches early adolescence, Birdie later internalizes the patriarchal meaning of girlhood in which young women's bodies are valued only for male pleasure: "I did feel different--more conscious of my body as a toy" (65).

Unlike, in the case of Clotel, her literary precursor, Birdie's humiliation in the girls' bathroom is alleviated by her sister's intervention:

> Word spread around the school quickly. Cole was my protector. Nobody messed with me, but they didn't talk to me, either. I often found myself alone, picking at my scabs with a fervor, as if trying to find another body buried inside. I often pondered whether it was better to be harassed or ignored. My insomnia grew worse. Cole slept soundly beside me ... (49)

Birdie's description of her relationship with Cole signifies the multiple dimensions of their intimacy. As her "protector," Cole's defense of her sister typifies the complex meaning of their allegiance. For Birdie, sisterhood means unconditional loyalty, devotion and recognition in the face of a violent, polarized world. Birdie's desire to "find another body inside" exhibits the full extent that her ostracization occurs as a result of the ambiguous body she cannot escape. Again, Cole's ability to fit into the black community makes her a perfect ally for Birdie, but Cole's protective presence cannot completely undo Birdie's isolation.

Years later, when Birdie decides to abandon her mother to look fo r her sister, she thinks to herself, "It wasn't Boston I was looking for. It was my sister, whispering stories to me to help me fall asleep, holding my hand, telling me in Elemeno that everything was going to be all right" (317). As Nel says of Sula in Toni Morrison's often-quoted novel, "All that time, all that time, I thought I was missing Jude.' And the loss pressed down on her chest and came up into her throat. 'We was girls together,' she said, as though explaining something" (174). In her reading of *Sula,* Margaret Schramm persuasively argues that "a central theme is the quest for the perfect mother, one whose love is unconditional and whose devotion to her children is selfless" (167). Deprived of this relationship with their mothers, both Nel and Sula "unconsciously expect continuous, selfless love...from each other as surrogate mothers" (167). Since her mother fails to offer Birdie the recognition she craves, Birdie seeks out affirmation and seemingly unconditional acceptance from her mixed-race sister. For both Nel and Birdie, separation means the loss of shared experience, belonging, and identification.

Only fourteen, Birdie escapes her mother's secret domicile in New Hampshire, takes a bus to Boston, secures six hundred dollars from her white grandmother in Cambridge, and travels to California alone in search of Cole. It is in the search for her sister that Birdie finally refuses to live a lie by her mother's side: "There was a long silence while my mother and I just stared at each other, taking in each other's hair and skin and bones. It seemed at that moment that we had never really looked at each other like that, like strangers" (335). The text leaves unclear whether Sandy is in true danger of incarceration and, at different moments, attributes her paranoia to both madness and guilt for her criminal involvement in the liberation movement.   However, what remains integral to Birdie's rebellion is her decision to no longer cater to her mother's desire to "disappear" (389).   Consequently, Sandy's plan for her daughter to pass as white and Jewish aggravates Birdie's longing for Cole. As Birdie suggests early on, disappearing is not the solution.   The universe of *Caucasia* insists on the recognition of mixed-race women.

When Birdie tricks her maternal grandmother into giving her airfare to find Cole, her grandmother condemns her, "It was doomed from the start. Tragedy in the making.   Your mother should have stuck to her world." Responding not only to her grandmother but to the logic that defines women of mixed ancestry as tragic, Birdie "snaps" in response, "'You and all your ancestors are the tragedies.   Not me.   You walk around pretending to be so liberal and civilized in this big old house, but you're just as bad as the rest of them.   This whole world--it's based on lies'" (365).   Birdie's early experience with passing teaches her that nothing could be more poorly defined than the boundaries of whiteness.   Countering her grandmother's ignorance, Birdie refutes the mythologies of race that divide her own family as her mixed-race act of resistance reveals the intersection between confronting a racist society and defying one's own blood relations. (Incidentally, Birdie's act is not limited to mixed-race women.   It also exemplifies the type of interfamilial anti-racist work *all* daughters of narrow-minded white grandmothers and grandfathers can do.)

After arriving in Oakland, Birdie tracks her sister down through her father.   Ever the unrelenting intellectual, he admits that work on his seven-hundred-page book, *The Petrified Monkey: Race, Blood, and the Origins of Hypocrisy*, made it impossible for him to pursue the "project" (389) of locating his ex-wife and daughter.   Birdie listens to her father's lecture with contempt.

"'If race is so make-believe," she counters, "'why did I go with Mum? You gave me to Mum 'cause I looked white. You don't think that's real? Those are the facts'" (393). In her challenge to her father's argumentation, that "race is a complete illusion ... not only a construct but a scientific error" (391), Birdie demands that his theoretical concerns take into consideration his "flesh and blood" (393). Birdie's objection confirms that race is not simply a construct, nor is it essential. Instead, it is written all over the bodies of her and her sister, their shared experiences and their unique--and respective--ways of knowing.

Shortly after Birdie contradicts her father's life's work, he escorts her to her sister's home in Berkeley. Cole's roommates inform Birdie that her sister is in a café with a friend down the street. Finally, Birdie reencounters her sister:

> And as her eyes moved over my face, I felt a slight heat, like a match held
> close to the flesh, but not touching. ... And we just watched each other
> then, watched for that minute when the whole restaurant seemed to grow
> quiet, grow still, the bodies around us melting into one another, into a
> blanket that surrounded us, and then I began to float toward the back of
> the café, like an apparition, a memory of myself, toward my sister, who
> rose to meet me. (401-402)

In this passage, we witness the fulfillment of longing that has led Birdie to courageously rebel against her white mother, white grandmother, and African American father. In the presence of Cole, Birdie returns to the safe, erotic world of their childhood as their environment is suggestively transformed into a "blanket." "Like a match," Cole's gaze burns "a slight heat" on Birdie's face. Summoning the "fire imagery" (McDowell 1993, 622) of Nella Larsen's *Passing* (1929), Senna's text illuminates the degree that the erotic occurs when subjects are most visible to each other. "When I speak of the erotic," writes Audre Lorde, "I speak of it as an assertion of the lifeforce of women; of the creative energy empowered, the knowledge and use of which we are now reclaiming in our language, our history, our dancing, our loving, our work, our lives" (55). Writing in response to Larsen, Senna invents a world in which the survival of one mixed-race woman does not ultimately mean the other's fatality. Birdie's reunion with Cole thus facilitates the recuperation of the "memory of [her]self" -- that is, the girl who felt safe, secure, and loved before she was torn away from her one and only mirror.

In her psychoanalytic discussion of Nella Larsen's *Quicksand*, Barbara Johnson argues that Helga Crane's "narcissistic deficit" could be attributed to Crane's absent black father and neglectful white mother and stepfather. She writes, "Helga thus has no early relations with black people, except the image of her father as both desirable and unreliable, and she has increasingly negative relations with the white people who are her only family" (257). This reasoning implies that an appropriate mirror for a biracial girl child would be either a white mother or a black father. Johnson is not alone in this reasoning. Claudia Tate's reading of the same novel similarly argues that the plot is driven by Helga's search for her lost (black) father. However, what both Helga Crane and Birdie share in common is the absence of a loving *black mother*, the most appropriate mirror for a black/biracial baby girl. For this reason, Cole functions as a mother-substitute who can restore Birdie's faith, wholeness, and sense of belonging.

As the events leading up to Birdie and Cole's reunion reveal, *Caucasia* portrays the powerful outcomes of what I term *passionate recognition*. For to recognize means to admit the validity of, that is, to confirm another's legitimacy; to recall knowledge of, that is, to validate the memory of a shared experience; to perceive clearly; to admit as being one entitled to be heard; to acknowledge with a show of approval or appreciation; to acknowledge the independence of; and, to acknowledge acquaintance with, that is, to recognize an existing relationship. In all cases, recognition is motivated by desire. Birdie's longing for passionate recognition drives her to resist racial categories in which she cannot be recognized, whether as a result of her phenotypical "ambiguity" or because of her mixed-race heritage. In her desire to reunite with Cole, she must first resist and refute (her mother's) logic of passing for white, (her grandmother's) white supremacist longing for racial purity, *as well as* (her father's) social constructionist reasoning that race is merely an illusion.

Yet as the novel conveys, racial difference may have dubious origins, but it continues to bear profound consequences. But even more significantly, Birdie and Cole's relationship documents the *productive* value of difference. For what Birdie achieves in order to attain the passionate recognition she shares with Cole models what it would take for any one of us to know ourselves and each other outside of the protocols of race, class, gender, sexuality and/or nationality. For the romance of revolutions, which normally demand our unquestioning allegiance, require ideal types and an ideal future, while the work of passionate recognition, in which we demand the best of ourselves, is a realized present. As Lorde writes, "we sharpen self-definition by exposing the self in work and struggle together with those whom we define as different from ourselves, although sharing the same goals" (123). As a practical tool for immediate change, the joy of passionate recognition is attained through risk, memory, respect, yearning, patience, trust, and surrender.

Yet how many of us are capable of doing the work that passionate recognition entails? How many of us are willing and able to see beneath the superficiality of stereotypes? To see with passionate eyes? Imagine what we would see if we risked the naked intimacy of passionate recognition with our presumed allies as well as our assumed adversaries, completely uninhibited by the scripted relationships prescribed by nationalism, white supremacy, compulsory heterosexuality and patriarchy. Imagine if difference were a site of possibility rather than a mechanism of domination that controls who and what we may become. Even Birdie realizes that she and Cole are two different people, that even a "mulatto nation" may not be the answer. After their reunion, Birdie admits, "We were sisters, but we were as separate in our experiences as two sisters could be" (409).

The work of passionate recognition may begin with identi fication but it is characterized by struggle and discovery. Through passionate acts of recognition we can become citizens of the world, valuing ourselves as much as we value others, dedicated to the liberation of all people and the boundlessness of our own potential. We are only limited by those encounters in which we fail to see ourselves and each other.

Conclusion: What Literature Can Do

In preparation for this essay, I invited students on the last day of class in a graduate seminar to take out a piece of paper and answer my question, "What do you see?" as I stood in front of the classroom and wrote "Figure 1" next to me on the chalkboard. As I encouraged them to respond honestly, I promised them I didn't have the correct answers. I had no precise expectations, but their responses surpassed what I could have imagined. Despite three months of shared discussion and debate, for the most part, all of the students, both black and white, saw the same thing: "wavy hair," "dark ringlet curls," "skin like chocolate milk," "skin not fully white/light," "big smile," "nice outfit," and "courage." But the other mixed-race woman in the class wrote, "Where do you fit? 'What are you?' 'Where's your family from?' 'What's your racial background?' 'Is you black or white?' 'Half and Half' 'Half breed' 'High Yellow' ... I remember noticing you last semester, long before I met you. I thought you were beautiful. And about the second or third time I saw you, it hit me that all that made me uncomfortable about myself in childhood, I valued in your appearance." [13]

As Gloria Anzaldúa writes in her essay "La concientia de la mestiza," "though it is a source of intense pain, [the energy of *mestiza* consciousness] comes from a continual creative motion that keeps breaking down the unitary aspect of each new paradigm" (379). In the midst of perceptions whose fixations on my gender and race markers threatened to define me as a mere hodgepodge of striking features, my one classmate's identificatory response broadened the meaning of our identities. To the extent that my classmate "saw" me, she made it possible for me to exist in much larger terms, terms that pronounced how invisible I was to the others. Further, as everyone neglected to mention my lesbian identity, the intimacy of her answer captured the integral relationship between her desire for me and her childhood memories. In her recognition of me, she created a place for queer mixed-race women and our interlocking histories.

When I introduced myself to Danzy Senna the night she read from *Caucasia* in Boston's Waterstone's bookstore back in 1998, she told me I looked familiar to her. I knew we had never met before, but I remember feeling the same way. As we quickly offered summaries of hometowns and alma maters, it was as if we were each looking for that long lost sister, that shared history, and a temporary reprieve from our lives of uniqueness.

In this reading of Senna's novel, I submit that it is the work of mixed-race women writers to retell history as we know it and, from this, to reinvent the world. As Alice Walker writes, "It is, in the end, the saving of lives that we writers are about. Whether we are 'minority' or 'majority.' It is simply in our power to do this. We do it because we care. ... We care because we know this: *The life we save is our own*" (14).

Michele Hunter

NOTES

[1] This paper was presented at the Collegium for African American Research's "Crossroutes: The Meanings of 'Race'for the Twenty-First Century" conference, held in Sardinia, Italy, March 21-25, 2001. I am grateful to the organizers for this rewarding opportunity. I must also thank the members of my "Feminist Theory" course for their generous and reflective participation in my impromptu classroom experiment, especially Valerie Ruffin and Katherine Skinner, as well as the students in my "Introduction to Women's Studies" courses who regularly remind me of the necessity for passionate recognition. This article also benefitted from Neil Brooks and Teresa Hubel's editorial comments, conversations with Dr. Dorcas Bowles, and the loving support of Jacqueline Francis.

[2] In her discussion of mixed-race and racial discourse, Jayne O. Ifekwunigwe's reasoning resonates with Homi Bhabha's. She writes, "By signaling the *process* of opening up hybrid spaces and looking at the sociocultural dynamics -- as performances -- of "race," gender, ethnicity, nation, class, sexuality and generation and their relationship to the mechanisms of power, my conceptualization of *métissage* is similar to Homi Bhabha's conception of a 'third space'" (20). While I agree with the project of "opening up" so-called "hybrid spaces," what theories of performativity fail to engage are the historical limits of subjectivity, the intertextual and multi-dimensional range of art and literature, the complex nature of desire, and the value of feminist epistemologies. See my article, "'Doing' Judith: Race, Mixed Race and Performativity" (Ed. Mary Brewer, *Exclusions in Feminist Thought*, Brighton/Portland: Sussex Academic Press, 2001).

[3] Jean Fagan Yellin, in her study *Women & Sisters*, identifies this story as the initiator of this tradition: "[Child is] known for inventing the character of the Tragic Mulatto--a slave woman of mixed race who wants to conform to patriarchal definitions of true womanhood but is prevented from doing so by the white patriarchy" (53). In Yellin's reasoning, a mistaken desire for assimilation marks this character: "The pathos of the Tragic Mulatto rests in the contradiction between her sincere efforts to adhere to the patriarchal definition of true womanhood and the patriarchy's insistence that she violate this norm" (72). For Yellin, mixed-race women are deemed pathological precisely as a result of their simultaneous inferiority to and proximity to a "true womanhood." It is analyses like this one which wrongly locate the pathology of racism and sexual commerce onto its "victims."

Because of the functional diversity of mixed characters and their historical specificity, Child's position as initiator of one tradition is similarly debatable. For instance, Barbara Christian claims Cora Munro (from Cooper's *The Last of the Mohicans*, 1826) to have foreshadowed "the many octoroons who appear in the literature of the nineteenth century, for she meets with a tragic end" (16). In his study on interracial literature, Werner Sollors traces these characterizations to the other side of the Atlantic. As a means of anticipating William Wells Brown and the specifically American literary tradition that Senna's novel engages and transforms, I have chosen Child as a more suitable candidate.

[4] Consider James Kinney's assessment: "as a theme, miscegenation has often been used to symbolize conceptual structures such as racial clash or disharmony, black and white value systems, human divisions or human ability to overcome obstacles, good and evil, and alienation and the search for identity" (28).

5 Ann DuCille, *The Coupling Convention* (New York/Oxford: Oxford UP, 1993) 7. Alice Walker, *In Search of Our Mother's Gardens* (New York: Harcourt Brace Janovich, 1983) 301.
6 McDowell supports her conclusion by citing both Christian and Walker: "'The closest black women could come to such an ideal, at least physically,' Christian continues, 'would...have to be the mulatta, quadroon, or octoroon.' Iola fulfills this physical requirement. 'My! but she's putty,' says the slave through whose eyes we first see her. 'Beautiful long hair comes way down her back; putty blue eyes, and jis ez white ez anybody in dis place' (p. 38). This ideal dominates novels by black women in the nineteenth century, due, as Alice Walker argues reasonably, to a predominantly white readership 'who could identify human feeling, humanness, only if it came in a white or near-white body.' She concludes, 'Fairness' was and is the standard of Euro-American femininity'" (39).
7 For instance, in her essay "(Un)Natural Boundaries: Mixed Race, Gender, and Sexuality," Karen Maeda Allman argues that "the sex/gender system is profoundly and interdependently racialized and racializing; race is also thoroughly endendered and engendering; and compulsory heterosexuality depends upon rigidity in gender roles and is reinforced by the promotion of racial purity" (280).
8 In his book *Spurious Issues*, Rainier Spencer maintains that "Because racial categorization is an impossible myth that we must move away from ... the assertion of multiracial identity (which necessarily requires acceptance of biological racial classification) is therefore every bit as untenable and inconsistent as the monoracial myth on which it is founded" (6). I agree with Spencer's claim that "all racial classification is problematic" (6) and that adding yet another category is not the solution to ending racial discrimination. However, Spencer's study and its arguments against mixed-race subjectivity rely too heavily on scientific and governmental definitions of race and thereby ignore the role of *culture*, artistic expression, and/or other modes of individual and collective resistance to white supremacy, all of which significantly impact the meaning of race, perhaps even more than the institutions Spencer analyzes. To put it differently, race is not simply a "top-down" signifier.
9 In her essay "Age, Race, Class and Sex: Women Redefining Difference," Lorde further states: "Institutionalized rejection of difference is an absolute necessity in a profit economy which needs outsiders as surplus people. As members of such an economy, we have *all* been programmed to respond to the human differences between us with fear and loathing and to handle that difference in one of three ways: ignore it, and if that is not possible, copy it if we think it is dominant, or destroy it if we think it is subordinate. But we have no patterns for relating across our human differences as equals. As a result, those differences have been misnamed and misused in the service of separation and confusion" (115).
10 To my knowledge, there is no criticism available to date concerning this novel other than its book reviews.
11 As Diana Fuss writes, "the signifier 'Other,' in its applications if not always its theorizations, tends to disguise how there may be other Others--subjects who do not quite fit into the rigid boundary definitions of (dis)similitude, or who indeed may be left out of the Self/Other binary altogether" ("Interior Colonies," 22).
12 Brown writes, "The infusion of Anglo-Saxon with African blood has created an insurrectionary feeling among the slaves of America hitherto unknown. Aware of their blood connection with their owners, these mulattoes labor under the sense of their personal and social injuries; and tolerate, if they do not encourage in themselves, low and vindictive passions" (212). According to the Carol Publishing edition, these lines are "adapted" from John R. Beard's *The Life of Toussaint Ouverture*, published in 1853. Where Child's plot ends in tragedy in "The Quadroons," Brown relies on the historical record of slave insurrection to authenticate

Clotel's rebellious impulses. Brown's (and Beard's) attribution of slave insurrection to "the infusion of Anglo-Saxon blood" guarantees the inevitability of the mulatto's revenge and sets an early precedent for Birdie's later battles.
[13] There was one important exception. The African American woman in the class wrote, "Reminds me of my sister."

WORKS CITED

Allman, Karen. "(Un)Natural Boundaries: Mixed Race, Gender, and Sexuality" Ed. Maria Root. *The Multiracial Experience: Racial Borders as the New Frontier*. Thousand Oaks/London/New Delhi: Sage Publications, 1996.

Anzaldúa, Gloria. "La conciencia de la mestiza: Towards a New Consciousness." *Making Face, Making Soul* Ed. Anzaldúa. San Francisco: Aunt Lute Books, 1990. 377-89.

Bhabha, Homi. *The Location of Culture*. New York: Routledge, 1994.

Bryant, Jerry H. *Victims and Heroes: Racial Violence in the African American Novel*. Boston: U of Massachusetts P, 1997.

Camper, Carol, ed. *Miscegenation Blues: Voices of Mixed Race Women*. Toronto: SisterVision, 1994.

Christian, Barbara. *Black Women Novelists: The Development of a Tradition, 1892-1976*. Westport: Greenwood Press, 1980.

DuCille, Ann. *The Coupling Convention: Sex, Text, and Tradition in Black Women's Fiction*. New York/Oxford: Oxford UP, 1993.

Foster, Frances Smith. "Adding Color and Contour to Early American Self-Portraitures: Autobiographical Writings of Afro-American Women." *Conjuring: Black Women, Fiction, and Literary Tradition*. Eds., Marjorie Pryse and Hortense Spillers. Bloomington: Indiana UP, 1985.

Fuss, Diana. *Essentially Speaking: Women, Nature and Difference*. New York: Routledge, 1989.

_____. "Interior Colonies: Frantz Fanon and the Politics of Identification." *Diacritics*. 24(2-3). Summer-Fall 1994. 20-42.

Gosselin, Adrienne Johnson. "Racial Etiquette and the (White) Plot of Passing: (Re)Inscribing 'Place' in John Stahl's *Imitation of Life*." *Canadian Review of American Studies/Revue Canadienne d'études américaines*. 28.3 (1998): 47-67.

Jagose, Annamarie. "Slash and Suture: Post/Colonialism in *Borderlands/La Frontera: The New Mestiza*." *Feminism and the Politics of Difference*. Eds. Sneja Gunew and Anna Yeatman.

Boulder/San Francisco: Westview, 1993: 212-27.

Johnson, Barbara. "The Quicksands of the Self: Nella Larsen and Heinz Kohut." Eds. Elizabeth Abel, Barbara Christian, and Helene Moglen. *Female Subjects in Black and White: Race, Psychoanalysis and Feminism*. Berkeley/Los Angeles/London: U of California P, 1997: 252-265.

Ifekwunigwe, Jayne O. *Scattered Belongings: Cultural Paradoxes of "Race," Nation and Gender*. New York: Routledge, 1999.

King, Deborah. "Multiple Jeopardy, Multiple Consciousness: The Context of a Black Feminist Ideology." (1988). *Words of Fire: An Anthology of African-American Feminist Thought*. Ed. Beverly Guy-Sheftall. New York: New Press, 1995: 294-317.

Kinney, James. *Amalgamation! Race, Sex, and Rhetoric in the Nineteenth-Century American Novel*. Westport: Greenwood Press, 1985.

Lorde, Audre. *Sister/Outsider*. Freedom, CA: The Crossing Press, 1984.

McDowell, Deborah. "'It's Not Safe. Not Safe at All": Sexuality in Nella Larsen's *Passing*." Eds. Abelove, Barale, Halperin. *The Lesbian and Gay Studies Reader*. New York/London: Routledge, 1993: 616-625.

_____. *"The Changing Same": Black Women's Literature, Criticism, and Theory*. Bloomington/Indianapolis: Indiana UP, 1995.

Mirza, Heidi Safia. *Black British Feminism: A Reader*. London/New York: Routledge, 1997.

Morrison, Toni. *Sula*. New York: Knopf, 1973.

Root, Maria P.P. "Mixed-Race Women." Ed. Naomi Zack. *Race/Sex: Their Sameness, Difference, and Interplay*. New York/London: Routledge, 1997: 157-172.

_____. *The Multiracial Experience: Racial Borders as the New Frontier*. Thousand Oaks/London/NewDelhi: Sage Publications, 1996.

_____. *Racially Mixed People in America*. Newbury Park/London/Dehli: Sage Publications, 1992.

Senna, Danzy. *Caucasia*. New York: Riverhead Books, 1998.

Smith, Valerie. "Reading the Intersection of Race and Gender in Narratives of Passing." *Diacritics*. 24.2-3 (Summer-Fall 1994): 43-57.

Spencer, Rainier. *Spurious Issues: Race and Multiracial Identity Politics in the United States*. Boulder: Westview Press, 1999.

Walker, Alice. *In Search of Our Mother's Gardens: Womanist Prose by Alice Walker*. New York: Harcourt Brace Janovich, 1983.

Yellin, Jean Fagan. *Women & Sisters: The Anti-Slavery Feminists in American Culture*. New Haven: Yale UP, 1989.

Notes on the authors

Peter Clandfield teaches 20th-century Literature and Film at Queen's University and at Royal Military College of Canada in Kingston, Ontario. He has contributed an essay on African American detectives in "Homicide: Life on the Street" to the recent collection *Closely Watched Brains*. Currently he is working on projects about the use of landmark urban locations in British and Canadian novels and fiction films.

Neluka Silva is a Senior Lecturer at the Department of English, University of Colombo, Sri Lanka. She completed her PhD research on Nationalism and Gender in Contemporary South Asian Literature. She is currently editing two books which deal with issues of hybridity and identity in Sri Lanka respectively. Her research also deals with South Asian theatre and teledrama. She has been an actress and director in the theatre in Sri Lanka for the last 15 years or so.

Teresa Zackodnik is an Assistant Professor at the University of Alberta, specializing in African American literature and literary theory, and Asian American fiction. Articles have appeared in *Writing Ethnicity* (ECW P, 1996), *Essays on Canadian Writing, MELUS, Ariel, Nineteenth-Century Feminisms, Nineteenth-Century Prose*. Her current project, a book on 19th-century African American feminist culture titled *"Press, Platform, Pulpit": African American Women's Political Culture in the Era of Reform*, examines black women's oratory and political culture.

Myriam Perregaux is currently a Lecturer in the English Department of the University of Geneva. She is also working on a Ph.D. at the School of English, Trinity College, Dublin. She has a B.A/M.A. in English literature from the University of Geneva and a M. Phil. in Women's Studies from Trinity College. She is interested in questions related to identity, space, power and representation, especially in the field of emergent literatures.

Bella Adams works as a part-time Lecturer in English at the Universities of Sunderland and Northumbria, UK. Her research interests include the aesthetic, deconstruction, feminist theory, post-colonial theory and American literature. She is currently writing a book on Amy Tan as part of the Contemporary World Writer Series (Manchester UP and St. Martin's Press). A number of articles on Amy Tan are also forthcoming.

Jennifer Sparrow is an Assistant Professor at Medgar Evers College, City University of New York. Her dissertation examines appropriations of *The Tempest* in the works of colonial and postcolonial Caribbean writers. She is a contributing editor to the Caribbean section of *Who's Who in Contemporary Women Writers* (forthcoming, Routledge, 2001). In addition, she has published articles and presented conference papers on Jean Rhys, Phyllis Shand Alfrey, Maryse Condé, Edwidge Danticat, Mayotte Capécia, and Michelle Cliff. Her publications include an essay entitled "Capécia, Condé, and the Antillean Woman's Identity Quest," for *MaComére*, the Journal of the Association of Caribbean Women Writers and Scholars, and "Caliban Orders History: George Lamming and *The Tempest*," in *Wadabagei: A Journal of the Caribbean and its Diaspora* . Jennifer Sparrow has recently given papers on Caribbean Literature at "The Second International Conference on Caribbean Literature," Paget, Bermuda (1999) and at "New Modernisms," Philadelphia, Pennsylvania (2000).

Jennifer Gibbs is a Fellow in the University of Utah's Ph.D. in Creative Writing Program and holds and M.F.A. in Creative Writing from Bowling Green State University. Her fiction, essays, and reviews have appeared in various literary magazines, most recently *The Chattahoochee Review* .

Elizabeth DeLoughrey is an Assistant Professor of English at Cornell University. This article reflects some of the issues addressed in her forthcoming book *Archipelagraphy: Anglophone Pacific and Caribbean Literatures*. She has previously published in *Ariel, Thamyris, SPAN*, and the *Journal of Caribbean Literature* as well as in the collection *Constructing Indigeneity*.

Rita Keresztesi Treat is Assistant Professor of English at the University of Oklahoma. "Writing Culture and Performing Race in Mourning Dove's *Cogewea, The Half-Blood* (1927)" is part of her future book-length project on American ethnic modernism between the World Wars. Another article, "Romancing the Borderlands: Josephina Niggli's *Mexican Village* (1945)," will be published in the forthcoming volume, *Romancing History/Historicizing Romance*, edited by Susan Strehle and Mary Paniccia Carden. Her translation of an early Hungarian-language essay by George Lukács, "Aesthetic Culture," was published in *The Yale Journal of Criticism* 11 (Fall 1998): 365-379.

Kathryn Nicol is a postgraduate student in the Department of English Literature at the University of Edinburgh. Her research interests include contemporary women's writing, writing on discourses of difference, and feminist theory. She is currently researching a thesis on the novels of Toni Morrison and Kathy Acker.

Yvette Tan was born in Singapore and obtained her Bachelor of Arts (Honours in History) at the University of Western Australia. She is presently a Ph.D. student at the University of Adelaide (Department of English and Cultural Studies). This paper is her first official publication.

Margaret D. Stetz, Associate Professor of English and Women's Studies at Georgetown University, is author of *British Women's Comic Fiction, 1890-1990: Not Drowning, But Laughing* (2001), as well as co-author, with Mark Samuels Lasner, of *England in the 1880s* (1989); *England in the 1890s* (1990); and *The Yellow Book: A Centenary Exhibition* (1994). With Bonnie B. C. Oh, she is also co-editor of *Legacies of the Comfort Women of WWII* (2001).

Paul Allatson is Lecturer in Spanish Studies at the University of Technology, Sydney, and has a PhD in Latino Studies from the University of New South Wales. He has published articles on Latino, Latin American, and Spanish Golden Age fiction and performance texts, Latino queer identities, postcolonial theory, and Australian transcultural art. With Laura Gutiérrez (Uni. of Iowa) he is currently writing *A Glossary of Latino Cultural and Literary Studies* intended as a resource for students and teachers of Latino Studies. His other current research project is on representations of Cuban exile in U.S. popular culture and the changing relations between Cuban and other Latino sectors from 1898 to 2000.

Michele Hunter is currently a Ph.D. candidate at the Institute for Women's Studies at Emory University. She is working on a dissertation examining the presentation of race in the early novel. Her coming out stories are included in *does your mama know? An Anthology of Coming Out Stories* (Ed. Lisa Moore. Decatur, Georgia: Red Bone Press, 1997).

Teresa Hubel is an Associate Professor in the English Department at Huron University College. She has written a number of articles on various subjects: on Indian literature in English, British colonial literature, the operations of class in the university and in literary texts, and, most recently, on the historical conflict between the temple dancers of South India and the Indian feminist movement. Her book, *Whose India: The Independence Struggle in British and Indian Fiction and History*, was published by Duke University Press in 1996. She is currently engaged in a long-term research project about the representation of the white and Anglo-Indian working classes in colonial India.

Neil Brooks is an Associate Professor of English at Huron University College specializing in twentieth century fiction, American Literature, and African American literature. He has published articles on several novelists including James Weldon Johnson, Walter White, Julian Barnes, Thomas Pynchon, Ford Madox Ford, and Rex Stout. He is currently working on a manuscript exploring the passing novels of the Harlem Renaissance.

En Torno al Teatro Breve

Bajo la dirección de Margot Versteeg

Amsterdam/Atlanta, GA 2001. 136 pp. (Foro hispánico 19)
ISBN: 90-420-1384-2   EUR 27,-/US-$ 25.-

Editions Rodopi B.V.
USA/Canada: One Rockefeller Plaza, Ste. 1420, New York, NY 10020,
Tel. (212) 265-6360,
Call toll-free (U.S. only) 1-800-225-3998, Fax (212) 265-6402
All other countries: Tijnmuiden 7, 1046 AK Amsterdam, The Netherlands.
Tel. ++ 31 (0)20 611 48 21, Fax ++ 31 (0)20 447 29 79
Orders-queries@rodopi.nl   www.rodopi.nl

JAMES JOYCE AND THE FABRICATION OF AN IRISH IDENTITY

Edited by Michael Patrick Gillespie

Amsterdam/Atlanta, GA 2001. VII,193 pp.
(European Joyce Studies 11)
ISBN: 90-420-1426-1   Bound EUR 46,-/US-$ 43.-
ISBN: 90-420-1416-4   Paper   EUR 18,-/US-$ 17.-

Contents: Biographical Note. Michael Patrick GILLESPIE: James Joyce and the Fabrication of an Irish Identity: An Introduction. Vincent J. CHENG: "Terrible Queer Creatures": Joyce, Cosmopolitanism, and the Inauthentic Irishman. Garry LEONARD: Holding on to the Here and the Now: Juxtaposition and Identity in Modernity and in Joyce. Maria PRAMAGGIORE: Unmastered Subjects: Identity as Fabrication in Joseph Strick's *A Portrait of an Artist as a Young Man* and *Ulysses*. Colleen JAURRETCHE: Poetry, Prayer and Identity in *Finnegans Wake*. John RICKARD: "A quaking sod": Hybridity, Identity and Wandering Irishness. Margot BACKUS: Sexual Figures and Historical Repression in "The Dead". Kevin DETTMAR: Vocation, Vacation, Perversion: Stephen Dedalus and Homosexual Panic. Joan JASTREBSKI: Pig Dialectics: Women's Bodies as Performed Dialectical Images in the Circe Episode of *Ulysses*. Lauren ONKEY: Teaching Joyce's Multiple Identities. Contributors.

Editions Rodopi B.V.
USA/Canada: One Rockefeller Plaza, Ste. 1420, New York, NY 10020,
Tel. (212) 265-6360, *Call toll-free* (U.S.only) 1-800-225-3998,
Fax (212) 265-6402
All Other Countries: Tijnmuiden 7, 1046 AK Amsterdam, The Netherlands.
Tel. ++ 31 (0)20 6114821, Fax ++ 31 (0)20 4472979
orders-queries@rodopi.nl   **www.rodopi.nl**

Time, Narrative & the Fixed Image/ Temps, Narration & Image Fixe

Edited by/sous la direction de Mireille Ribière et Jan Baetens

Amsterdam/Atlanta, GA 2001. 226 + 40 pp. ill.
(Faux Titre 208)
ISBN: 90-420-1366-4   EUR 57,-/US-$ 53.-

This volume focuses on the relationship between time, narrative and the fixed image. As such, it highlights renewed interest in the temporality of the fixed image, probably one of the most important trends in the formal and semiotic analysis of visual media in the past decade.

The various essays discuss paintings, the illustrated covers of books, comics or graphic novels, photo-stories, postcards, television and video art, as well as aesthetic practices that defy categorization such as Chris Marker's masterpiece *La Jetée*. The range of works and practices examined is reflected in the different theoretical approaches and methods used, with an emphasis on semiology and narratology, and, to a lesser extent, aesthetics and psychoanalysis. The interest of this book, however, does not stem exclusively from the range and scope of the artefacts examined, or the methodological issues that are addressed; its fundamental importance rests in the contributors' readiness to question the differentiation between fixed and moving images which all too often provides a convenient, if not altogether convincing, starting point for image analysis. .

The originality and value of the contribution that <I>Time, Narrative and the Fixed Image/Temps, Narration et image fixe</I> makes to the body of theoretical writing on visual media lies in this challenging and comprehensive approach.

Editions Rodopi B.V.

USA/Canada: One Rockefeller Plaza, Ste. 1420, New York, NY 10020, Tel. (212) 265-6360,
Call toll-free (U.S. only) 1-800-225-3998, Fax (212) 265-6402
All other countries: Tijnmuiden 7, 1046 AK Amsterdam, The Netherlands.
Tel. ++ 31 (0)20 611 48 21, Fax ++ 31 (0)20 447 29 79
Orders-queries@rodopi.nl   www.rodopi.nl

LEO H. HOEK

Titres, toiles et critique d'art
Déterminants institutionnels du discours
sur l'art au dix-neuvième siècle en France

Amsterdam/Atlanta, GA 2001. 389 pp. (Faux Titre 210)

ISBN: 90-420-1386-9 **EUR 82,-/US-\$ 77.-**

Dans *Titres, toiles et critique d'art*, Leo H. Hoek interroge deux types de discours — les titres picturaux et la critique d'art — sur les fondements institutionnels de leur fonctionnement discursif et social. Les diverses formes de manifestation des titres picturaux et les jugements de l'art par un journaliste débutant comme Emile Zola, servent de points de départ à un examen approfondi de la fonction institutionnelle du discours sur l'art au dix-neuvième siècle français. L'interaction entre les 'règles de l'art' et les changements institutionnels dans le 'champ artistique' (Pierre Bourdieu) permet à l'auteur de mettre en lumière le rôle social des titres picturaux et de la critique d'art. Il s'avère que la poétique des titres picturaux et l'évaluation de l'œuvre d'art sont toutes les deux motivées beaucoup plus par les déterminants institutionnels que constituent les rapports de force entre les positions dans le champ artistique, que par les qualités présumées des œuvres commentées. Cette exploration interdisciplinaire du rôle ambigu et fascinant qu'ont joué ces deux types de commentaire sur l'art, se situe à l'entrecroisement de plusieurs disciplines concourantes comme l'histoire de l'art, l'histoire littéraire et la sociologie institutionnelle et donc au coeur même de l'étude des rapports entre le texte et l'image.

Editions Rodopi B.V.
USA/Canada: One Rockefeller Plaza, Ste. 1420, New York, NY 10020,
Tel. (212) 265-6360, *Call toll-free* (U.S.only) 1-800-225-3998,
Fax (212) 265-6402
All Other Countries: Tijnmuiden 7, 1046 AK Amsterdam, The Netherlands.
Tel. ++ 31 (0)20 6114821, Fax ++ 31 (0)20 4472979
orders-queries@rodopi.nl **www.rodopi.nl**

Theodor Fontane and the European Context

Literature, Culture and Society in Prussia and Europe
Proceedings of the Interdisciplinary Symposium at the
Institute of Germanic Studies, University of London in March
1999.
Edited by Patricia Howe and Helen Chambers
Amsterdam/Atlanta, GA 2001. 270 pp. (Internationale
Forschungen zur Allgemeinen und Vergleichenden Literatur-
wissenschaft 53)
ISBN: 90-420-1236-6   EUR 50,-/US-$ 47.-

On the centenary of Fontane's death and at the turn of the
century these essays take a new look at this supreme
chronicler of Prussia and of the Germany that emerges after
1871. Written by scholars from different countries and
disciplines, they focus on novels and theatre reviews from the
perspectives of philosophy, sociology, comparative literature
and translation theory, and in the contexts of topography and
painting. Connections and crosscurrents emerge to reveal new
aspects of Fontane's poetics and to produce contrasting but
complementary readings of his novels. He appears in the
company of predecessors and contemporaries, such as Scott,
Thackeray, Saar, Ibsen, Turgenev, but also in that of writers he
has rarely, if ever, been seen beside, such as E.T.A. Hoffmann,
Stendhal, Trollope, Henry James and Edith Wharton, Beckett
and Faulkner. The historical novel and the social position of
women are each a recurring focus of interest. Fontane
emerges as receptive to other voices, as a precursor of
developments in modern narrative, and confirmed as the
novelist who brings the nineteenth-century German novel
closest to the broad traditions of European realism.

 Editions Rodopi B.V.
USA/Canada: One Rockefeller Plaza, Ste. 1420, New York, NY
10020,
Tel. (212) 265-6360, Call toll-free (U.S. only) 1-800-225-
3998, Fax (212) 265-6402
All other countries: Tijnmuiden 7, 1046 AK Amsterdam, The
Netherlands.
Tel. ++ 31 (0)20 611 48 21, Fax ++ 31 (0)20 447 29 79
Orders-queries@rodopi.nl   www.rodopi.nl

FRENCH 'CLASSICAL' THEATRE TODAY
Teaching, Research, Performance

Ed. by Philip Tomlinson

Amsterdam/Atlanta, GA 2001. 307 pp. (Faux Titre 205)
ISBN ; 90-420-1355-9   € 55,-/US-$ 51.-

Arising from the activities of the Centre for Seventeenth-Century
French Theatre, this volume proposes a selection of eighteen
essays by internationally renowned scholars aimed at all those
who value and work with the theatre of seventeenth-century
France, whether in teaching, research or performance. Frequently
seeking out the interfaces of these areas, the essays cover
historiography (including that of opera), the theory and practice
of textual editing, visualizing – in terms of both theatre architec-
ture and the significance of playtext illustration - , approaches to
study and research (including the most recent applications of
computer technology), and performance studies which relate the
classical canon to contemporary French and other cultures.
Always suggesting new directions, challenging the epistemological bases of the very concept of French classical theatre, the
essays provide a snapshot of scholarship in the field at the dawn
of a new millennium, and offer an ideal opportunity to reassess
its past whilst looking to its future.

Editions Rodopi B.V.
USA/Canada: One Rockefeller Plaza, Ste. 1420, New York, NY 10020,
Tel. (212) 265-6360, *Call toll-free* (U.S.only) 1-800-225-3998,
Fax (212) 265-6402
All Other Countries: Tijnmuiden 7, 1046 AK Amsterdam, The Netherlands.
Tel. ++ 31 (0)20 6114821, Fax ++ 31 (0)20 4472979
orders-queries@rodopi.nl   **www.rodopi.nl**

Travellers in Time and Space
Reisende durch Zeit und Raum.
The German Historical Novel. Der deutschsprachige historische Roman.

Ed. by/Hrsg. von Osman Durrani and Julian Preece.
Amsterdam/Atlanta, GA 2001. IX,473 pp. (Amsterdamer Beiträge zur neueren Germanistik 51)
ISBN: 90-420-1405-9   Bound EUR 91,-/US-$ 85.-
ISBN: 90-420-1395-8   Paper EUR 34,-/US-$ 32.-

Inhalt: Osman DURRANI: Introduction. Günter MÜHLBERGER and Kurt HABITZEL: The German Historical Novel from 1780 to 1945: Utilising the Innsbruck Database. Florian KROBB: "Zeitgemäß an der Hand der Geschichte": Berthold Auerbach und der deutsch-jüdische historische Roman des 19. Jahrhunderts. Jefferson S. CHASE: Half-Faded Pictures: Die Judenbuche as Historical Fiction. James JORDAN: "Die Geschichte ist die Geschichte ihrer zahlreichen Interpretationen". Ota Filip's Wallenstein und Lukretia. Daniel STEUER: Thomas Bernhards Auslöschung. Ein Zerfall. Zum Verhältnis zwischen Geschichtsschreibung, Autobiographie und Roman. Christa HEINE TEXEIRA: Lion Feuchtwanger : Der falsche Nero, Zeitgenössische Kritik im Gewand des historischen Romans: Erwägungen zur Entstehung und Rezeption. Bettina HEY'L: Victor Meyer-Eckhardts Erzähltexte über die Französische Revolution 1924 bis 1951: Zu Problemen der Gattungsgeschichte des historischen Romans im zwanzigsten Jahrhundert. J.J. LONG: Compensation for History? Dieter Kühn's Beethoven und der Schwarze Geiger. Herbert UERLINGS: Die Erneuerung des historischen Romans durch interkulturelles Erzählen. Zur Entwicklung der Gattung bei Alfred Döblin, Uwe Timm, Hans Christoph Buch und anderen. Helen BRIDGE: Biographical Fiction by GDR Women Writers: Reassessing the Cultural Heritage. Paul O'DOHERTY: Zionism bad, Zionists ... good? Two GDR Historical Novels as Journalism: Arnold Zweig's Traum ist teuer and Rudolf Hirsch's Patria Israel. Fabian LAMPART: Zeitaporie und Geschichtstropen in Achim von Arnims Die Kronenwächter. Helen HUGHES: The Material World: A Comparison between Adalbert Stifter's Historical Novel Witiko and Robert Bresson's Film Lancelot du Lac. Stefan NEUHAUS: Zeitkritik im historischen Gewand? Fünf Thesen zum Gattungsbegriff des Historischen Romans am Beispiel von Theodor Fontanes Vor dem Sturm. Robert HALSALL: The Individual and the Epoch: Hermann Broch's Die Schlafwandler as a Historical Novel. Fritz WEFELMEYER: Geschichte als Verinnerlichung. Hermann Brochs Der Tod des Vergil. Theresia KLUGSBERGER: Wissen und Leidenschaft. Maria Janitschek: Esclarmonde und Marie von Najmayer: Der Stern von Navarra. Historische Romane zweier österreichischer Schriftstellerinnen der Jahrhundertwende. Christina UJMA: Zwischen Rebellion und Resignation: Frauen, Juden und Künstler in den historischen Romanen Fanny Lewalds. Simon WARD: Werner Bergengruen's Am Himmel wie auf Erden : The Historical Novel and 'Inner Emigration'. Franziska MEYER: "Unsere Zeit braucht solche Männer": Georg Forster im historischen Roman der DDR. Meg TAIT: Stefan Heym's Schwarzenberg: Actually Existing Utopia? Astrid HERHOFFER: Geschichte gegen den Strich: Auf der Suche nach der eigenen Vergangenheit in Christa Wolfs Kassandra und Peter Weiss' Ästhetik des Widerstands. Ian FOSTER: Joseph Roth's Radetzkymarsch as a Historical Novel. Agnès CARDINAL: Ina Seidel. From Das Wunschkind to Lennacker: Strategies of Dissimulation. Caroline BLAND: Prussian, Rhinelander or German? Regional and National Identities in the Historical Novels of Clara Viebig. Kurt HABITZEL: Der historische Roman der DDR und die Zensur. Silke HASSLER: Das Märchen vom letzten Gedanken. Zu Edgar Hilsenraths historischem Roman aus dem Kaukasus. Maike OERGEL: 'Wie es wirklich wurde': The Modern Need for Historical Fiction, or the Inevitability of the Historical Novel. Carl TIGHE: Pax Germanica in the future-historical. List of Contributors.

Rodopi

Editions Rodopi B.V. Amsterdam, New York, NY
Orders-queries@rodopi.nl   www.rodopi.nl

'Les Tentations de saint Antoine' and Flaubert's Fiction
A Creative Dynamic

Mary Neiland

Amsterdam/Atlanta, GA 2001. 201 pp. (Faux Titre 204)
ISBN: 90-420-1345-1   EUR 37,-/US-$ 34.-

This book reveals the extensive and dynamic interplay between *Les Tentations de saint Antoine* and the rest of Flaubert's fiction. Mary Neiland combines two critical approaches, genetic and intertextual criticism, in order to trace the development of selected topoï and figures across the three versions of *La Tentation* and on through Flaubert's other major works. Each chapter is devoted to one of these centres of interest, namely, the banquet scene, the cityscape, the crowd, the seductive female and the Devil. Detailed study of these five areas exposes a remarkable intimacy between writings that appear at a far remove from each other. The networks of recurring images located demonstrate for the first time the obsessive nature of Flaubert's writing practice; the pursuit of these networks across his fictional writings exposes his developing technique; and *La Tentation* is revealed as both a privileged moment of expression and as a place of auto-reflection.
This volume will be of interest to students and specialists of Flaubert as well as to those interested in genetic and intertextual criticism.

Editions Rodopi B.V.
USA/Canada: One Rockefeller Plaza, Ste. 1420, New York, NY 10020,
Tel. (212) 265-6360,
Call toll-free (U.S. only) 1-800-225-3998, Fax (212) 265-6402
All other countries: Tijnmuiden 7, 1046 AK Amsterdam, The Netherlands.
Tel. ++ 31 (0)20 611 48 21, Fax ++ 31 (0)20 447 29 79
Orders-queries@rodopi.nl   www.rodopi.nl

Conrad Between the Lines
Documents in a Life

Ed. by Gene M. Moore, Allan H. Simmons, and J.H. Stape.
Amsterdam/Atlanta, GA 2000. VI,251 pp. (The Conradian)
ISBN: 90-420-1555-1   EUR 46,-/US-$ 42.50-

This volume makes available a variety of texts by Joseph Conrad's friends and contemporaries, ranging from a sailing memoir by his oldest English friend to a dramatic adaptation of his novel Victory, and from his secretary's notebook to his last will and testament. Often mentioned or cited by scholars, these texts are here published in full for the first time. They also reveal Conrad speaking "between the lines" in various voices, and raise theoretical questions about the social nature of authorship and the construction of authorial canons.

Contents:
Foreword. G.F.W. HOPE: Friend of Conrad (Ed. by Gene M. Moore) The "Knopf Document": Transcriptions and Commentary (Ed. by J.H. Stape). Basil MACDONALD HASTINGS: "Victory". (Ed. by Gene M. Moore and Allan H. Simmons). Wilfred PARTINGTON: Joseph Conrad Behind the Scenes (Ed. by Gene M. Moore). Richard CURLE: The History of Mr. Conrad's Books (Ed. by Allan H. Simmons). L.M. HALLOWES: Note Book of Joseph Conrad (Ed. by Allan H. Simmons and J.H. Stape). Conrad's Last Will and Testament (Ed. by Hans van Marle)

 Editions Rodopi B.V.
USA/Canada: One Rockefeller Plaza, Ste. 1420, New York, NY 10020,
Tel. (212) 265-6360, Call toll-free (U.S. only) 1-800-225-3998, Fax (212) 265-6402
All other countries: Tijnmuiden 7, 1046 AK Amsterdam, The Netherlands.
Tel. ++ 31 (0)20 611 48 21, Fax ++ 31 (0)20 447 29 79
Orders-queries@rodopi.nl   www.rodopi.nl

Schuld Und Sühne?

Kriegserlebnis und Kriegsdeutung in deutschen Medien der Nachkriegszeit (1945-1961) Internationale Konferenz vom 01 - 04.09.1999 in Berlin.

Hrsg. von Ursula Heukenkamp

Amsterdam/Atlanta, GA 2001. 403 pp.
(Amsterdamer Beiträge zur neueren Germanistik 50.1)
ISBN: 90-420-1425-3   Bound EUR 75,-/US $70.-
ISBN: 90-420-1415-6   Paper EUR 27,-/US $26.-

Inhalt
Vorbemerkung

Rodopi

Editions Rodopi B.V.
USA/Canada: One Rockefeller Plaza, Ste. 1420, New York, NY 10020,
Tel. (212)265-6360, Toll-free (U.S. only) 1-800-225-3998, Fax (212) 265-6402
All other countries: Tijnmuiden 7, 1046 AK Amsterdam, The Netherlands.
Tel. ++ 31 (0)20 611 48 21, Fax ++ 31 (0)20 447 29 79

Orders-queries@rodopi.nl   **www.rodopi.nl**

Schuld Und Sühne?

Kriegserlebnis und Kriegsdeutung in deutschen Medien der Nachkriegszeit (1945-1961) Internationale Konferenz vom 01 - 04.09.1999 in Berlin.

Hrsg. von Ursula Heukenkamp

Amsterdam/Atlanta, GA 2001. 405-827 pp.
(Amsterdamer Beiträge zur neueren Germanistik 50.2)
ISBN: 90-420-1445-8   Bound EUR 80,-/US $74.-
ISBN: 90-420-1435-0   Paper EUR 30,-/US $28.-
Bde 1-2 ISBN: 90-420-1445-5

Inhalt
Vorbemerkung
Band II: KRITIK DER ERINNERUNG

Rodopi

Editions Rodopi B.V.
USA/Canada: One Rockefeller Plaza, Ste. 1420, New York, NY 10020,
Tel. (212)265-6360, Toll-free (U.S. only) 1-800-225-3998, Fax (212) 265-6402
All other countries: Tijnmuiden 7, 1046 AK Amsterdam, The Netherlands.
Tel. ++ 31 (0)20 611 48 21, Fax ++ 31 (0)20 447 29 79

Orders-queries@rodopi.nl   **www.rodopi.nl**

Essays on the Song Cycle and on Defining the Field

Essays on the Song Cycle and on Defining the Field. Proceedings of the Second International Conference on Word and Music Studies at Ann Arbor, MI, 1999.

Edited by Walter Bernhart and Werner Wolf in collaboration with David Mosley Amsterdam/Atlanta, GA 2001. XII,253 pp. (Word and Music Studies 3)

ISBN: 90-420-1575-6   EUR 57.-/US-$ 53.-
ISBN: 90-420-1565-9   EUR 23.-/US-$ 21.-

This volume assembles twelve interdisciplinary essays that were originally presented at the Second International Conference on Word and Music Studies at Ann Arbor, MI, in 1999, a conference organized by the International Association for Word and Music Studies (WMA).

The contributions to this volume focus on two centres of interest. The first deals with general issues of literature and music relations from culturalist, historical, reception-aesthetic and cognitive points of view. It covers issues such as conceptual problems in devising transdisciplinary histories of both arts, cultural functions of opera as a means of reflecting postcolonial national identity, the problem of verbalizing musical experience in nineteenth-century aesthetics and of understanding reception processes triggered by musicalized fiction.

The second centre of interest deals with a specific genre of vocal music as an obvious area of word and music interaction, namely the song cycle. As a musico-literary genre, the song cycle not only permits explorations of relations between text and music in individual songs but also raises the question if, and to what extent words and/or music contribute to creating a larger unity beyond the limits of single songs. Elucidating both of these issues with stimulating diversity the essays in this section highlight classic nineteenth- and twentieth-century song cycles by Franz Schubert, Robert Schumann, Hugo Wolf, Richard Strauss and Benjamin Britten and also include the discussion of a modern successor of the song cycle, the concept album as part of today's popular culture.

Editions Rodopi B.V.

USA/Canada: One Rockefeller Plaza, Ste. 1420, New York, NY 10020,

Tel. (212) 265-6360, Call toll-free (U.S. only) 1-800-225-3998, Fax (212) 265-6402

All other countries: Tijnmuiden 7, 1046 AK Amsterdam, The Netherlands.

Tel. ++ 31 (0)20 611 48 21, Fax ++ 31 (0)20 447 29 79

Orders-queries@rodopi.nl   **www.rodopi.nl**

Jean Ricardou
De *Tel Quel* au nouveau roman textuel

Michel Sirvent

Amsterdam/Atlanta, GA 2000. 154 pp.
(Collection Monographique Rodopi en Littérature Française Contemporaine 36)
ISBN: 90-420-1591-8   EUR 25,-/US-$ 23.50

Editions Rodopi B.V.
USA/Canada: One Rockefeller Plaza, Ste. 1420, New York, NY 10020, Tel. (212) 265-6360,
Call toll-free (U.S. only) 1-800-225-3998, Fax (212) 265-6402
All other countries: Tijnmuiden 7, 1046 AK Amsterdam, The Netherlands.
Tel. ++ 31 (0)20 611 48 21, Fax ++ 31 (0)20 447 29 79
Orders-queries@rodopi.nl   **www.rodopi.nl**

SUSAN PETIT

Franҫoise Mallet-Joris

Amsterdam/Atlanta, GA 2001. 158 pp.
(Collection Monographique Rodopi en Littérature Française
Contemporaine 37)
ISBN: 90-420-1216-1   € 25,-/US-$ 23.-

From the 1950's, with *Le Rempart des béguines, La Chambre rouge, Cordélia, Les Mensonges* and *L'Empire céleste*, down into the 1990's, with *Adriana Sposa, Divine, Les Larmes, La Maison dont le chien est fou* and *Sept démons dans la ville*, the work of Françoise Mallet-Joris has exercised a very special fascination over a very large readership. The content of her work, ever developing yet faithful to residual, either lived or observed, studied experience, is wide-ranging and unflinching – family relationships, the individual psyche, belief systems that move from quasi-nihilism to the mystical, sexuality, feminine consciousness, creativity, larger social frameworks, etc. – and she can move with ease from portrayal of the hypercontemporary to the researched – and finely imagined – historical reconstruction. Susan Petit, whose lively and elegantly written study addresses all these, and other, factors, argues modestly but wisely that "the works of Mallet-Joris provide stimulating, thought-provoking and coherent ways of apprehending ourselves and our human situation". One need ask no more of an author who, though perhaps personally drawn to certain perspectives, maintains an admirable openness and multiplicity of interrogation of existence.

Editions Rodopi B.V.
USA/Canada: One Rockefeller Plaza, Ste. 1420, New York, NY 10020,
Tel. (212) 265-6360, *Call toll-free* (U.S.only) 1-800-225-3998,
Fax (212) 265-6402
All Other Countries: Tijnmuiden 7, 1046 AK Amsterdam, The Netherlands.
Tel. ++ 31 (0)20 6114821, Fax ++ 31 (0)20 4472979
orders-queries@rodopi.nl   **www.rodopi.nl**